TOOLKIT FOR INTERMEDIATE ACCOUNTING
ELEVENTH CANADIAN EDITION

CONCEPTUAL FRAMEWORK FOR FINANCIAL REPORTING

Information underlying financial statements should be prepared based on concepts and principles in this framework. This framework also provides a useful summary of concepts and principles for analysis of financial reporting and accounting issues.

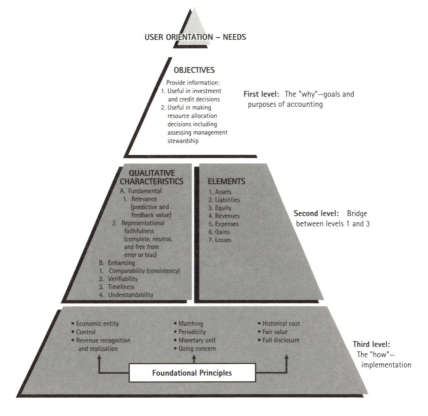

TOOLKIT FOR INTERMEDIATE ACCOUNTING
ELEVENTH CANADIAN EDITION

GAAP HIERARCHY

The GAAP hierarchy identifies the sources that should be consulted in applying GAAP, beginning with the most authoritative (or primary) sources.

Under ASPE, the primary sources of GAAP are as follows:

- *CICA Handbook*–Sections 1400 to 3870, including appendices; and
- accounting guidelines, including appendices.

Other sources under ASPE include:

- background information and basis for conclusion documents issued by the AcSB;
- pronouncements by accounting standard-setting bodies in other jurisdictions;
- approved drafts of primary sources of GAAP where no primary sources apply (such as exposure drafts);
- research studies;
- accounting textbooks, journals, studies, and articles;
- other sources, including industry practice.

Under IFRS, GAAP incorporates:

- IFRS;
- IAS;
- interpretations (IFRIC or the former Standards Interpretation Committee [SIC]).

Other sources under IFRS include:

- pronouncements of other standard-setting bodies,
- other accounting literature, and
- accepted industry practices.

ASSET VALUATION

Below is a chart summarizing asset categories and valuation models. Note that in general, an asset is written down to a lower value if its carrying value exceeds the future benefits that the asset can bring to the entity. Note also that management intent (i.e., whether management intends to collect, sell, or use the asset to generate revenues, etc.) can give further insight into determination of a valuation model.

	ASPE Valuation Model (and Reference)	IFRS Valuation Model (and Reference)	Management Intent
CASH	Cost/transaction value (not specifically addressed in HB)	Cost/transaction value (not specifically addressed in IFRS)	N/A
INVESTMENTS (NO SIGNIFICANT INFLUENCE)	Cost/amortized cost or FV-NI (HB 3856)	Amortized cost or FV-NI (FV-OCI can be elected for equity investments not held for trading purposes) (IFRS 9, IAS 39)	Under IFRS, if a debt investment is managed on a contractual yield basis where the entity's business model requires that the entity hold the investment to maturity, the amortized cost model applies.
RECEIVABLES	Lower of cost/amortized cost and net realizable value (HB 3856)	Lower of cost/amortized cost and net realizable value (IFRS 9, IAS 39)	To collect
INVENTORY	Lower of cost and net realizable value (HB 3031)	Lower of cost and net realizable value (IAS 2)	To sell
INVESTMENTS (SIGNIFICANT INFLUENCE)	Equity method or cost method (if shares are quoted in an active market, cannot use cost method; may use FV-NI) (HB 3051)	Equity method (IAS 28)	To exercise significant influence over the operating, investing, and financing activities of the investee
PROPERTY, PLANT, AND EQUIPMENT (INVESTMENT PROPERTY)	Cost model (HB 3061)	Cost model or revaluation model. (All investment property is accounted for under either the cost model or fair value model). (IAS 16 and 40)	To hold for use in generating revenues
PROPERTY, PLANT, AND EQUIPMENT (HELD FOR SALE)	Lower of carrying value and fair value less costs to sell (HB 3475)	Lower of carrying value and fair value less costs to sell (IFRS 5)	To sell
INTANGIBLE ASSETS	Cost model (HB 3064)	Cost model or revaluation model (revaluation model can only be applied if asset has an active market fair value) (IAS 38)	To hold for use in generating revenues

TOOLKIT FOR INTERMEDIATE ACCOUNTING
ELEVENTH CANADIAN EDITION

DEFINITIONS

Definitions of elements of financial statements are central to qualitative analysis of financial reporting issues. Ideally, these concepts/criteria and definitions should be committed to memory. ASPE definitions of the elements are found in HB 1000 and HB 3400. IFRS definitions are found in IFRS Introductory Materials.

	Definition	Recognition (general rule)	Measurement (general rule)
ASSETS	• Represent some economic benefit to the entity, • The entity has control over that benefit, and • The benefit results from a past transaction or event.	• Meets definition, and • Measurable.	• See Asset Valuation
LIABILITIES	• Represent a present duty or responsibility, • The duty or responsibility obligates the entity, leaving it little or no discretion to avoid it, and • The duty or responsibility results from a past transaction or event.	• Meets definition, and • Measurable.	• At transaction cost or present value of future cash flows
EQUITY	• Residual interest in net assets (ownership interests).	• Meets definition, and • Measurable.	• At transaction cost or fair value of proceeds/shares
REVENUES	• Increases in economic resources, that result from an entity's ordinary activities.	• Earnings approach: recognize revenues when risks and rewards pass and services are rendered, the vendor has no continuing involvement, costs and revenues can be measured reliably, and collection is probable. • IFRS 15 Approach: Step 1: Identify the contract with Customers; Step 2: Identify the separate performance obligations (POs) in the contract; Step 3: Determine the transaction price; Step 4: Allocate the transaction price to the separate POs; Step 5: Recognize revenue when each PO is satisfied.	• At transaction cost or (if the sale is non-monetary, has commercial substance, and is reciprocal) at fair value of product/ service given up, or what is acquired, if more reliably measurable
EXPENSES	• Decreases in economic resources that result from an entity's ordinary activities.	• Meets definition, and • Measurable.	• At transaction cost or best estimate
GAINS	• Increases in equity (net assets) from peripheral or incidental transactions.	• Meets definition, and • Measurable.	• At transaction cost
LOSSES	• Decreases in equity (net assets) from peripheral or incidental transactions.	• Meets definition, and • Measurable.	• At transaction cost or best estimate
OTHER COMPREHENSIVE INCOME	• Defined under IFRS as: revenues, expenses, gains, and losses that are recognized in comprehensive income, but excluded from net income. • Not used in ASPE.	• Meets definition, and • Measurable.	• At transaction cost or best estimate

TOOLKIT FOR INTERMEDIATE ACCOUNTING
ELEVENTH CANADIAN EDITION

SUMMARY OF ACCOUNTING METHODS

This chart summarizes commonly accepted accounting methods that should be mastered. Brief descriptions and examples of each method are included in the study guide. For each method, also remember to consider the incremental impact on net income and key ratios.

Revenue Recognition

- Percentage-of-completion method
- Zero-profit method (not mentioned under ASPE)
- Completed-contract method (not mentioned under IFRS)

Estimating Uncollectible Accounts Receivable

- Percentage-of-receivables approach
- Mix between percentage-of-sales approach and percentage-of-receivables approach

Inventory Cost Formulas

- FIFO
- Weighted average cost
- Specific identification

Inventory Estimation Methods

- Gross profit method
- Retail method

Depreciation of Property, Plant, and Equipment

- Straight-line method
- Diminishing balance method
- Unit of production (or activity) method

TOOLKIT FOR INTERMEDIATE ACCOUNTING
ELEVENTH CANADIAN EDITION

SUMMARY OF KEY RATIOS

When doing ratio analysis, apply key ratios relevant to the company and its environment, keeping in mind that certain ratios are more important than others in certain situations.

RATIO	FORMULA	WHAT IT MEASURES
I. Liquidity		
1. Current ratio	$\dfrac{\text{Current assets}}{\text{Current liabilities}}$	Short-term debt-paying ability
2. Quick or acid-test ratio	$\dfrac{\text{Cash, marketable securities, and receivables (net)}}{\text{Current liabilities}}$	Immediate short-term liquidity
3. Current cash debt coverage ratio	$\dfrac{\text{Net cash provided by operating activities}}{\text{Average current liabilities}}$	Company's ability to pay off its current liabilities in a specific year from its operations
II. Activity		
4. Receivables turnover	$\dfrac{\text{Net sales}}{\text{Average trade receivables}}$	Liquidity of receivables
5. Inventory turnover	$\dfrac{\text{Cost of goods sold}}{\text{Average inventory}}$	Liquidity of inventory
6. Asset turnover	$\dfrac{\text{Net sales}}{\text{Average total assets}}$	How efficiently assets are used to generate sales
III. Profitability		
7. Profit margin on sales	$\dfrac{\text{Net income}}{\text{Net sales}}$	Net income generated by each dollar of sales
8. Rate of return on assets	$\dfrac{\text{Net income}}{\text{Average total assets}}$	Overall profitability of assets
9. Rate of return on common share equity	$\dfrac{\text{Net income minus preferred dividends}}{\text{Average common shareholders' equity}}$	Profitability of owners' investment
10. Earnings per share	$\dfrac{\text{Net income minus preferred dividends}}{\text{Weighted average shares outstanding}}$	Net income earned on each common share
11. Price earnings ratio	$\dfrac{\text{Market price of shares}}{\text{Earnings per share}}$	Ratio of the market price per share to earnings per share
12. Payout ratio	$\dfrac{\text{Cash dividends}}{\text{Net income}}$	Percentage of earnings distributed as cash dividends
IV. Coverage		
13. Debt to total assets	$\dfrac{\text{Total debt}}{\text{Total assets}}$	Percentage of total assets provided by creditors
14. Times interest earned	$\dfrac{\text{Income before interest charges and taxes}}{\text{Interest charges}}$	Ability to meet interest payments as they come due
15. Cash debt coverage ratio	$\dfrac{\text{Net cash provided by operating activities}}{\text{Average total liabilities}}$	Company's ability to repay its total liabilities in a specific year from its operations
16. Book value per share	$\dfrac{\text{Common shareholders' equity}}{\text{Number of common shares outstanding at SFP date}}$	Amount each share would receive if the company were liquidated at the amounts reported on the statement of financial position

TOOLKIT FOR INTERMEDIATE ACCOUNTING
ELEVENTH CANADIAN EDITION

AN OVERVIEW FRAMEWORK FOR CASE ANALYSIS

(See also the Case Primer on the Student Website for more detail and tips.)

1. *Analysis of environment and company*

Consider:

(a) Stakeholders—What is at stake and what information is needed by users?

(b) Role—What is your role (controller, financial analyst, etc.)?

(c) Business environment—What economic and business environment is the company operating in (recession, market expansion, etc.)?

(d) Company—What does the company do? How does it earn revenues? What types of costs does it incur? What are its business risks? What is the company's financial history, especially in the recent past? Are the company's key ratios within acceptable industry norms? Do the company's key ratios show trends of improvement or decline?

(e) Constraints—What are the constraints in analysis of this case (GAAP, time, cost, etc.)?

(f) Overall conclusion based on above?

2. *Issue identification—for complex issues, consider legalities, economic substance, and/or management intent*

3. *Issue analysis*

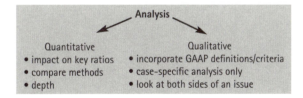

4. *Recommendation/conclusion—tie back to role and environment*

TOOLKIT FOR INTERMEDIATE ACCOUNTING
ELEVENTH CANADIAN EDITION

STUDY STEPS

This framework of study steps provides a well-rounded approach to studying accounting material and analyzing new issues in accounting.

1. *Understand the transaction/arrangement from a business perspective (issue identification).*

- Draw a diagram showing parties involved and details of the transaction (for example, legalities).
- On a very basic level, determine what is *given up* and what is *received by* the entity.
- Prepare a rough journal entry. You may not be able to prepare a journal entry with numbers at this stage, but it is useful to consider which accounts would be debited and credited. Preparing a rough journal entry at this stage will often draw your attention to an issue.
- Try to determine the economic substance of the transaction. Consider management intent and/or if the entity's business risks changed after the transaction (and if so, how).

Note: The above analysis is essential when identifying and analyzing complex transactions where the issue is not evident.

2. *Understand how the transaction fits into the financial reporting model and conceptual framework (analysis).*

- List "recognition," "measurement," and "presentation/disclosure" down the left-hand side of the page and fill in relevant principles, concepts, definitions, and criteria beside each category. Refer to the charts and illustrations in this study guide for complete lists of principles, concepts, definitions, and criteria.
- Try to identify any problems and/or issues that might be encountered in accounting for the transaction and financial statement disclosure. These are usually the result of the nature of the transaction. You may have already identified these as part of Step 1.
- Try to identify where professional judgement will be required.

Note: This process also helps establish a framework for case analysis for more complex transactions.

3. *Become proficient with any required calculations (skills).*

- For many of the more complex calculations, accountants have developed worksheets that are invaluable in doing the calculations. These must be mastered, with a solid understanding of the mechanics behind each work sheet.
- In order to master calculations, you should do as many exercises and problems as you can. There are many exercises and problems with answers and explanations included in this study guide. There are also numerous exercises and problems in the text and on the student website.
- When doing an exercise or problem, attempt it first without referring to the answer in order to help identify your weaknesses. Afterwards, check your work against the answer. There is no point in doing exercises and problems if you are not checking your answers.

ELEVENTH CANADIAN EDITION

STUDY GUIDE TO ACCOMPANY

Intermediate Accounting

VOLUME 1: CHAPTERS 1 – 12

Donald E. Kieso, PhD, CPA
KPMG Peat Marwick Emeritus Professor of Accounting
Northern Illinois University
DeKalb, Illinois

Jerry J. Weygandt, PhD, CPA
Arthur Andersen Alumni Professor of Accounting
University of Wisconsin
Madison, Wisconsin

Terry D. Warfield, PhD
Associate Professor
University of Wisconsin
Madison, Wisconsin

Nicola M. Young, MBA, FCPA, FCA
Saint Mary's University
Halifax, Nova Scotia

Irene M. Wiecek, FCPA, FCA
University of Toronto
Toronto, Ontario

Bruce J. McConomy, PhD, CPA, CA
Wilfrid Laurier University
Waterloo, Ontario

Study Guide prepared by
Bruce Wright, MBA, CPA, CA
Loyalist College
Belleville, Ontario

WILEY

Library and Archives Canada Cataloguing in Publication

Wright, Bruce, 1964-, author
    Study guide to accompany Intermediate accounting, eleventh Canadian edition / study guide prepared by Bruce Wright.

Supplement to: Intermediate accounting.
ISBN 978-1-119-27439-1 (v. 1 : paperback)

    1. Accounting—Problems, exercises, etc. I. Title. II. Title: Intermediate accounting, eleventh Canadian edition.

HF5636.K54 2016 Suppl.   657'.044076   C2016-902138-6

Production Credits
Executive Editors: Emily McGee and Zoë Craig
Senior Marketing Manager: Anita Osborne
Editorial Manager: Karen Staudinger
Developmental Editor: Daleara Jamasji Hirjikaka
Media Specialist, Content Management & Technology: Meaghan MacDonald
Cover and Interior Design: Joanna Vieira
Production Editing: Belle Wong
Typesetting: Thomson Digital
Printing and Binding: ePAC

Printed and bound in the United States of America
1 2 3 4 5 EP 19 18 17 16

John Wiley & Sons Canada, Ltd.
Suite 300, 90 Eglinton Ave East
Toronto, Ontario, Canada, M4P 2Y3

Visit our website at: www.wiley.ca

Contents

PREFACE
To the Student   v
How to Study Accounting   vi

CHAPTER 1
The Canadian Financial Reporting Environment   1

CHAPTER 2
Conceptual Framework Underlying Financial Reporting   13

CHAPTER 3
The Accounting Information System and Measurement Issues   37

CHAPTER 4
Reporting Financial Performance   89

CHAPTER 5
Financial Position and Cash Flows   121

CHAPTER 6
Revenue Recognition   165

CHAPTER 7
Cash and Receivables   187

CHAPTER 8
Inventory   229

CHAPTER 9
Investments   279

CHAPTER 10
Property, Plant, and Equipment: Accounting Model Basics   309

CHAPTER 11
Depreciation, Impairment, and Disposition   351

CHAPTER 12
Intangible Assets and Goodwill   379

Preface

To the Student

The purpose of this study guide is to help you to improve your success rate in solving accounting homework assignments and in answering accounting exam questions. For each chapter we include the following:

OVERVIEW	To briefly introduce the chapter topics and their importance.
STUDY STEPS	To discuss the business transactions or issues pertinent to the chapter topics, including an analysis of key recognition, measurement, and disclosure issues.
TIPS	To alert you to common pitfalls and misconceptions and remind you of important terminology, concepts, and relationships that are relevant to answering specific questions or solving certain problems.
EXERCISES	To provide you with a selection of problems representative of homework assignments that an intermediate accounting student may encounter.
MULTIPLE CHOICE	To provide you with a selection of multiple-choice questions that are representative of common exam questions covering topics in the chapter.
PURPOSES	To identify the essence of each question or exercise and link it to the text material.
SOLUTIONS	To show you the appropriate solution for each exercise and multiple-choice question presented.
EXPLANATIONS	To give you the details of how selected solutions were derived and explain why things are done as shown.
APPROACHES	To coach you on the particular model, computational format, or other strategy to be used to solve particular problems. To teach you how to analyze and solve multiple-choice questions.

This book will provide you with the opportunity to solve accounting problems in addition to the ones assigned by your instructor without having to rely on your teacher for solutions. Many of the exercises and questions contained herein are very similar to material in your intermediate accounting textbook; the difference is, the ones in this book are accompanied with detailed, clearly laid-out solutions.

The use of the multiple-choice questions in this volume and the related suggestions on how to approach them can easily increase your ability (and confidence in your ability) to deal with exam questions of this variety.

HOW TO STUDY ACCOUNTING

The successful study of accounting requires a different approach than most other subjects. In addition to reading a chapter, applying the material through completion of exercises or problems is necessary in developing a true and lasting understanding of the concepts introduced in the text chapter. The study of accounting principles is a combination of theory and practice; theory describes what to do and why, and practice is the application of guidelines to actual situations. We use illustrations to demonstrate how theory works and we use theory to explain why something is done in practice. Therefore, it is impossible to separate the two in the study of accounting.

Learning accounting is a cumulative process. It is difficult to master Chapter 4 until you are thoroughly familiar with chapters 1–3, and so on. Therefore, it is imperative that you keep up with class assignments. And, because accounting is a technical subject, you must pay particular attention to terminology.

Accounting is the language of business. It is an exciting subject that provides a challenge for most business majors. Your ultimate success in life may well depend on your ability to grasp financial data. The effort you expend now will provide rewards for years to come.

We encourage you to follow the four steps for study outlined below to give yourself the best possible chance for a successful learning experience and to make the most efficient use of your time. These steps provide a system of study for each chapter in your text.

Step 1

- Scan the learning objectives at the beginning of each chapter.
- Scan the chapter (or chapter section).
- Glance over the questions at the end of the chapter.

This first step will give you an overview of the material to be mastered.

Step 2

- Read the assigned pages slowly.
- Study carefully, and mark for later attention any sections requiring review.

- Pay particular attention to examples and illustrations.
- Try to formulate tentative answers to end-of-chapter questions.

During this phase, you will be filling in the chapter "outline" you formed in Step 1. Most of the details will fall into place during this phase of your study. The remaining steps are necessary, however, for a keen understanding of the subject.

Step 3

- Carefully read the **Overview**, **Study Steps**, and **Tips** sections of this study guide.
- Do the **Exercises** and **Cases** in this study guide that pertain to the same topics as your homework assignments.
- Review the relevant **Illustrations** in this study guide.
- Do the **Multiple-Choice Questions** in the study guide that pertain to the same topics as your homework assignments.
- Refer back to the text chapter sections that you marked for review, if any. It is likely that any confusion or questions will have been cleared up through your work in the study guide. If a section remains unclear, carefully reread it and rework relevant pages of the study guide.
- Repeat this process for each assigned topic area.

Step 4

- Write out formal answers to homework assignments in the text. This step is crucial because you can determine whether you can independently apply the material you have been studying to new situations. You may find it necessary to go back to the text and/or the study guide to restudy certain sections. This is common and a good indicator that the study assignments are working for you.

Here is some additional guidance to help you get the most out of this study guide:

The **Study Steps** and **Tips**, along with the **Illustrations**, will aid your understanding and retention of the material. Exercises provide examples of application of the text material. These should be very valuable in giving you guidance in completing homework assignments that are often similar in nature and content.

The **Approach** stated for an exercise or question is likely the most valuable feature of this study guide because it provides guidance on how to think through the situation at hand. This thought process can then be used in similar situations. It is impossible to illustrate every situation you may encounter. You can, however, handle new situations by simply applying what you know and making modifications where appropriate. Many students make the mistake of attempting to memorize their way through an accounting book. That, too, is an impossible feat. **Do not rely on memorization**. If this material is going to be useful to you, you must think about what you are reading and always be thinking of why things are as they are.

If you know the reasoning for a particular accounting treatment, it will be much easier to remember that treatment and reconstruct it even weeks after your initial study of it.

Explanations are provided for exercises and questions. These are very detailed so that you will thoroughly understand what is being done and why. These details will serve you well when you complete your homework assignments.

Always make an honest effort to solve the exercises and answer the questions contained in this study guide **before** you look at the solutions. Answering the questions on your own will maximize the benefits you can expect from this book.

The **Multiple-Choice Questions** are self-tests to give you immediate feedback on how well you understand the material. Study the **Approaches** suggested for answering these questions in the study guide. Practise the approaches when answering the multiple-choice questions in the text. Apply them when taking examinations. By doing so, you will learn to calmly, methodically, and successfully process examination questions. This will very likely improve your exam scores.

When you work through an **Exercise** or **Case** in the study guide or in the text, always read the instructions **before** you read all of the given data. This allows you to determine what is being asked of you and what you are to accomplish, before you read the given data. As you tread through the data, you can begin to process it because you can determine its significance and relevance. If you read the data before the instructions, you will likely waste time having to reread the data after you find out what you are to do with it. Also, more importantly, reading the data before the instructions will likely cause you to begin anticipating what will be asked of you, which will often cause you to do analysis other than what is required of you.

Good luck and best wishes for a positive learning experience!

Chapter 1

The Canadian Financial Reporting Environment

OVERVIEW

Accounting is the language of business. Accountants identify, measure, and communicate financial information about economic entities to interested persons. To be useful, financial statements must be clearly understandable and comparable, so that users may compare the performance of one business with the performance of the same business in a prior period, or with the performance of another similar business. Therefore, all general purpose financial statements should be prepared in accordance with generally accepted accounting principles (GAAP). In Canada, the financial statements of private companies should be prepared in accordance with Accounting Standards for Private Enterprises (ASPE) as set out by the AcSB (Canadian Accounting Standards Board), unless they opt to use international GAAP (called International Financial Reporting Standards, or IFRS). ASPE was effective for Canadian private companies for periods beginning on or after January 1, 2011. Financial statements of public companies should be prepared in accordance with IFRS. IFRS is set out by the IASB (International Accounting Standards Board). IFRS was effective for Canadian public companies for periods beginning on or after January 1, 2011.

STUDY STEPS

Understanding the Financial Reporting Environment

It is important to recognize preparer, standard setter, and user perspectives in understanding the financial reporting environment. A company's management prepares financial statements, in accordance with GAAP set by accounting standard-setting bodies, primarily to assist users in making efficient resource (or capital) allocation decisions. Investors need information about the past performance of a company in order to determine whether they should invest in the company. Financial statements should provide information about whether the company is profitable, whether it has paid dividends in the past, and whether it can stay solvent.

It is not necessary to memorize lists of potential users and what their information needs are. However, an understanding of key stakeholders and their respective functions is critical in understanding the financial reporting environment.

For the most efficient and effective flow of capital, there should be information symmetry, meaning that all stakeholders should have equal access to all relevant information. However, perfect information symmetry does not exist in the markets, resulting in an inefficient capital marketplace. The two most common types of information asymmetry problems are adverse selection and moral hazard. Moral hazard is a concept that notes that people will often shirk their responsibilities if they think that no one is watching. If biased managers prepare financial information by overstating assets and/or revenues, or understating liabilities and/or expenses (resulting in aggressive accounting), the financial information they prepare will be less useful to financial statement users, resulting in a less efficient and less effective flow of capital in the capital marketplace.

GAAP, the GAAP Hierarchy, and Professional Judgement

Generally accepted accounting principles (GAAP) provide guidance to accountants in meeting the financial reporting objective of providing financial information that is useful to users and that is decision-relevant. GAAP acts as guidelines to ensure that certain reporting standards are met. For private companies, pension plans, and not-for-profit entities, GAAP is codified in the *CICA Handbook* (produced by the Canadian Institute of Chartered Accountants). For public companies, GAAP is codified in IFRS and IAS (International Accounting Standards). IAS were issued by the IASC (International Accounting Standards Committee), IASB's predecessor, between 1973 and 2001. In general, the term "IFRS" is understood to comprise both IFRS and IAS.

Since no specific rule can be phrased to suit every situation, the guidelines in IFRS and ASPE are quite often general in nature and usually provide a basic principle. For instance, in determining when revenue should be recognized, the traditional earnings approach suggests that revenue should be recognized when performance is substantially complete and collection is reasonably assured. This general guideline is applied in numerous situations and often requires professional judgement in application. A basic principle is preferable to having a rule such as "all revenue must be recognized when goods are shipped." While such a rule would be easy to follow and very clear, it might result in inappropriate accounting. (For example, what if goods are shipped on consignment?) An alternative to the earnings approach to revenue recognition is emerging, called the contract-based approach, which addresses some of the subjectivity in applying the earnings approach. Both approaches are discussed further in Chapter 6.

Therefore, although GAAP provides guidance, it is often of a general nature, requiring interpretation, which in turn requires professional judgement in application. The GAAP guidelines in IFRS and ASPE do not fit every situation, and there may be situations that the guidelines do not specifically cover. The GAAP hierarchy identifies, in order of authority, sources that should be consulted in applying GAAP, beginning with the most authoritative (or primary) sources.

For private companies, pension plans, and not-for-profit entities, the primary sources of GAAP are as follows:

- *CICA Handbook* Sections 1400–3870, including Appendices; and
- Accounting guidelines, including Appendices.

Other sources include:

- Background information and basis for conclusion documents issued by the AcSB
- AcSB implementation guidance
- Pronouncements by accounting standard-setting bodies in other jurisdictions
- Approved drafts of primary sources of GAAP
- Research studies
- Accounting textbooks, journals, studies, and articles
- Other sources including industry practice

For public entities, the primary sources of GAAP are as follows:

- IFRS
- IAS
- IFRIC (International Financial Reporting Interpretation Committee) interpretations

Other sources include:

- Pronouncements of other standard-setting bodies
- Other accounting literature
- Accepted industry practices

In general, primary sources must be looked to first. Where primary sources do not deal with the specific issue at hand, the entity should adopt accounting policies that are consistent with primary sources as well as the concepts laid out in the conceptual framework underlying financial reporting (to be discussed in Chapter 2).

Management Bias in Reporting and Ethical Considerations

Another key thing to remember is that financial statements are prepared by people, often the management of the company. Therefore, there are behavioural aspects to financial reporting. People are not perfect and often act in a self-serving manner. For instance, if a manager knows that shareholders will evaluate his performance based on the company's net income, he might be motivated to report net income higher than it really is.

Reporting bias defeats the purpose of financial reporting since, in the case above, the manager's real performance might be obscured and the shareholders may make an incorrect decision based on the information presented. Where financial statements are prepared in accordance with GAAP, this problem may not be as severe, since the manager will have to follow GAAP (and GAAP will constrain his accounting policy choices). Public companies are required to hire an outside, independent auditor to review financial statements for fairness, which alleviates some of the risk. Outside (external) **auditors** add value because they perform an unbiased, independent review of financial statements to ensure that the information is presented fairly in accordance with GAAP.

TIPS ON CHAPTER TOPICS

- Potential **management bias** may play a key role in the development and choice of accounting policies chosen by management. This should always be kept in mind when analyzing a set of financial statements. Management bias may take the form of overstating assets or revenues, or understating liabilities or expenses.

- Consider the motivations of those who are involved in preparing financial statements. They might not always be pure.

- Because most business owners (shareholders of corporations) are not involved with the operation of the business, the **stewardship function** (measuring and reporting data to absentee owners) is an important function of accounting. This situation greatly increases the need for accounting standards.

- The accounting profession has common standards and procedures called **generally accepted accounting principles** (often referred to as GAAP). The term "generally accepted" can mean either that an authoritative accounting rule-making body has established a principle of reporting in a given area or that over time a given practice has been accepted as appropriate because of its universal application.

- The terms **principles** and **standards** are used interchangeably in practice and throughout this book.

- Accounting is a constantly changing and evolving profession, as seen by Canada's shift to IFRS for public companies. By adopting international

GAAP that nearly 100 other countries have converged to, Canadian public companies are better able to stay competitive globally.

● A private company in Canada may choose to adopt IFRS, even if most of its business is done within Canada. For example, if a private company competes against foreign companies or other Canadian public companies for sales contracts or financing, it may be better able to compete if it adopts the same financial reporting standards as its competitors.

● Standard setting is a political process and therefore GAAP itself is sometimes a compromise. This means that a treatment prescribed in the *CICA Handbook*, for example, may not necessarily agree with the conceptual framework underlying the GAAP therein.

● There are over 150 different sets of GAAP around the world. Countries or groups of countries each have their own GAAP to meet their unique needs, objectives, and conditions (just as Canada has its own GAAP for private enterprises, ASPE). The GAAP of one country may or may not be the same for the same situation in another country. Harmonization in favour of an international GAAP is a main focus of many accounting standard setters to eliminate barriers and improve comparability.

● Although the **International Accounting Standards Board** (IASB) is quickly becoming the dominant accounting standard-setting body in the world, full global adoption of international GAAP and IFRS is still far away. For example, many countries (including Canada) are maintaining their separate national GAAP for private companies, but requiring that public companies follow IFRS.

● The United States has not migrated to IFRS, and whether it will remains to be seen.

● The primary focus of this textbook concerns the development of two types of financial information, which are governed by GAAP: (1) the basic financial statements and (2) the related note disclosures.

● The **basic financial statements** are: (1) the statement of financial position (or the balance sheet under ASPE), (2) the statement of income/comprehensive income (or the income statement under ASPE), (3) the statement of cash flows, and (4) the statement of changes in equity (or statement of retained earnings under ASPE). In addition, note disclosures and other supporting schedules are an integral part of the financial statements.

● The **accrual basis of accounting** is used in preparing the basic financial statements. The accrual basis requires (1) reporting revenues in the period in which they are earned (which may not be the same period in which the related cash is received), and (2) reporting expenses in the period in which they are incurred (which may not be the same period in which the related cash is paid).

● Accounting decisions are not made in a "vacuum." Besides GAAP, many factors influence how a particular transaction is accounted for, including who makes the accounting policy decision, who the end user of the financial information is, and how similar transactions are accounted for in practice.

● Accounting guidelines are not always "black and white." There are many "grey" areas that require **professional judgement**.

● **Auditors** add value because they perform an independent review of financial statements, providing assurance that GAAP has been followed.

CASE 1-1

PURPOSE: This case will review the meaning of generally accepted accounting principles (GAAP) and their significance.

All publicly accountable entities must have their annual financial statements audited by an independent accountant. In accordance with generally accepted auditing standards (which you will study in an auditing class), the auditor expresses an opinion regarding the fairness of the financial statements, which, for a publicly accountable entity, should be in accordance with International Financial Reporting Standards (IFRS).

Instructions

(a) Define generally accepted accounting principles.
(b) List the primary sources of IFRS.

Solution to Case 1-1

(a) The accounting profession refers to common accounting standards and procedures as **generally accepted accounting principles** (GAAP). The word "principles" refers to methods or procedures or standards. The phrase "generally accepted" means having "substantial authoritative support." A method has substantial authoritative support if a rule-making body has approved it or if it has gained acceptance over time because of its universal application in practice.

(b) The primary sources of IFRS (where one should look first for guidance in applying international GAAP) are the following:

- IFRS
- IAS
- IFRIC (International Financial Reporting Interpretation Committee) interpretations

Where these sources do not deal with a particular issue, it is recommended that one look to:

- Pronouncements of other standard-setting bodies (for example, the FASB in the United States)
- Other accounting literature
- Accepted industry practices

ANALYSIS OF MULTIPLE-CHOICE QUESTIONS

Question

1. The process of identifying, measuring, analyzing, and communicating financial information needed by management to plan, evaluate, and control an organization's operations is called:
    a. financial accounting.
    b. managerial accounting.
    c. tax accounting.
    d. auditing.

EXPLANATION: **Financial accounting** is the process that culminates in the preparation of financial reports for the enterprise as a whole for use by parties both internal and external to the enterprise. (Users of these financial reports include investors, creditors, managers, unions, and government agencies.) **Managerial accounting** is the process of identifying, measuring, analyzing, and communicating financial information needed by management to plan, evaluate, and control an organization's operations. (These reports are only for the use of parties internal to the enterprise.) **Tax accounting** usually refers to tax planning, advising on tax matters, and/or preparing tax returns. **Auditing** refers to examination of financial statements by a certified accountant who reviews the information to ensure that management is accounting for economic transactions properly. An auditor attests to the fairness of financial statements and their conformity to generally accepted accounting principles. (Solution = b.)

Question

2. One objective of financial reporting is to provide:
    a. information about the investors in the business entity.
    b. information about the liquidation values of the resources held by the enterprise.
    c. information that is useful in resource allocation decisions.
    d. information that will attract new customers.

EXPLANATION: Before you read the possible answers, think about the overall objective of financial reporting and the key words and concepts within. The overall objective of financial reporting is to provide financial information that is useful to users (primarily capital providers such as investors and lenders) and that is relevant in users' capital (or resource) allocation decisions. Consequently, financial statements should communicate information about:

*   an entity's economic resources and claims to those resources, and
*   changes in those resources and claims. (Solution = c.)

Question

3. The measuring and reporting of data to absentee owners of a corporation is referred to as management's:
   a. fiduciary responsibility.
   b. stewardship function.
   c. accounting standard-setting function.
   d. audit function.

EXPLANATION: Management's responsibility to manage assets with care and trust is its **fiduciary responsibility**. Management does not set accounting standards. Audits are conducted by independent accountants, not management. The **stewardship function** involves measuring and reporting data to absentee owners. (Solution = b.)

Question

4. For public companies in Canada, the most significant source of generally accepted accounting principles is:
   a. provincial securities commissions.
   b. the FASB.
   c. the IASB.
   d. the AcSB.

EXPLANATION: Provincial securities commissions oversee and monitor the capital marketplace, including stock exchanges. The FASB (Financial Accounting Standards Board) is the primary standard-setting organization in the United States (the CICA counterpart in the United States). The AcSB (Canadian Accounting Standards Board) develops and maintains ASPE in Canada. The IASB (International Accounting Standards Board) is the international organization that develops IFRS, which public companies in Canada must conform to. (Solution = c.)

Question

5. Accounting assists in the efficient allocation of scarce resources (or capital) by providing financial information that is:
   i. timely.
   ii. representationally faithful.
   iii. relevant.

   a. i only.
   b. i and ii.

c. i and iii.

d. All of the above.

EXPLANATION: An effective process of capital allocation promotes productivity, encourages innovation, and provides an efficient and liquid market for buying and selling of securities and debt. Think about the role of accounting information in this process. Unreliable and irrelevant information can lead to poor capital allocation. To be useful, information must be relevant to the decision-maker, it must be received in a timely manner, and it must be representationally faithful. (Solution = d.)

Question

6. All of the following organizations influence the development of financial reporting standards in Canada, except the:

a. Canada Revenue Agency (CRA).

b. Accounting Standards Board (AcSB).

c. International Accounting Standards Board (IASB).

d. Financial Accounting Standards Board (FASB).

EXPLANATION: The Canada Revenue Agency (CRA) is responsible for developing rules surrounding and administering federal income tax in Canada. Although the CRA influences accounting practice, it does not influence the development of financial reporting standards as the other organizations do. (Solution = a.)

Question

7. The *CICA Handbook* is divided into four parts, including all of the following, except:

a. EIC Abstracts.

b. Accounting Standards for Private Enterprises.

c. Accounting Standards for Not-for-Profit Organizations.

d. Accounting Standards for Pension Plans.

EXPLANATION: In the past, EIC Abstracts were issued by the Emerging Issues Committee to study and provide rulings for issues not covered or sufficiently dealt with in the *CICA Handbook*. (They were not technically part of the *CICA Handbook*.) In 2009, it was decided that any relevant material from EIC Abstracts to date would be incorporated into their respective *CICA Handbook* sections, and that EIC Abstracts would be withdrawn once Canada moved to IFRS for publicly accountable entities in 2011. The *CICA Handbook* is now divided into four parts: Part I – IFRS (for publicly accountable enterprises), Part II – Accounting Standards for Private Enterprises, Part III – Accounting Standards for Not-for-Profit Organizations, and Part IV – Accounting Standards for Pension Plans. (Solution = a.)

Question

8. Which of the following groups is not part of the governing structure of the IASB?
    a. The IASC Foundation
    b. The IFRS Advisory Council
    c. Securities commissions
    d. The International Financial Reporting Interpretation Committee (IFRIC)

EXPLANATION: The IASC Foundation monitors, reviews the effectiveness of, appoints members to, and funds the IASB. The IFRS Advisory Council is composed of various user groups that provide guidance and feedback to the IASB. The IFRIC studies issues where guidance in IASB is insufficient or non-existent. (Solution = c.)

Question

9. Which of the following steps is not typical in the evolution of a new or revised IFRS?
    a. Discussion Paper is issued.
    b. Topic is identified and placed on the Board's agenda.
    c. Exposure Draft is issued.
    d. Discussions are held with governments for final approval of addition or amendment.

EXPLANATION: Think about the steps involved in the process of producing a new or revised IFRS:
    i.   Through research, topics are identified and placed on the Board's agenda.
    ii. Discussion Paper is produced and issued for comment by the public.
    iii. Exposure Draft is produced and issued for comment by the public.
    iv. Board evaluates comments and changes Exposure Draft, if necessary. The final IFRS is issued, followed by a jurisdictional adoption process.

The IASB does not have to consult with any governments prior to final approval of a new or revised IFRS. (Solution = d.)

Question

10. The essential characteristics of financial accounting involve:
    a. identification and measurement of financial information relating to an economic entity.
    b. identification, measurement, and communication of financial information about an economic entity to interested persons.
    c. identification, measurement, and communication of financial information about an economic entity to management.

   d. identification and communication of financial information about an economic entity to management.

EXPLANATION: Financial accounting involves identification, measurement, and communication of relevant information to all interested decision-makers, whether they are internal or external. (Solution = b.)

Question

11. Under IFRS, a complete set of financial statements includes:

   a. statement of financial position, statement of income/comprehensive income, statement of cash flows, statement of changes in equity, and note disclosures.

   b. statement of financial position, statement of income/comprehensive income, and statement of cash flows.

   c. statement of financial position and statement of income/comprehensive income.

   d. statement of financial position, statement of comprehensive income, and note disclosures.

EXPLANATION: Under IFRS, a complete set of financial statements includes a statement of financial position, statement of income/comprehensive income, statement of cash flows, statement of changes in equity, and note disclosures. (Solution = a.)

Question

12. Under ASPE, a complete set of financial statements includes:

   a. balance sheet, income statement, statement of cash flows, statement of retained earnings, and note disclosures.

   b. balance sheet, income statement, and statement of cash flows.

   c. balance sheet and income statement.

   d. balance sheet, income statement, and note disclosures.

EXPLANATION: Under ASPE, a complete set of financial statements includes a balance sheet, income statement, statement of cash flows, statement of retained earnings, and note disclosures. (Solution = a.)

Question

13. Explain the meaning of **stakeholder** within the context of financial reporting.

   a. A stakeholder is someone who has something at risk in the financial reporting environment.

   b. Stakeholders include only parties external to the company.

   c. Stakeholders include only those parties who own or work for a company.

   d. A stakeholder has no vested interest in the financial reporting environment.

EXPLANATION: Stakeholders are interested parties who have something to gain or lose in the financial reporting environment. For example, an auditor stands to lose her reputation and an investor stands to increase his investment. Therefore, stakeholders are not restricted to those internal to the company. (Solution = a.)

Question

14. Which of the following statements best describes the notion of management bias within the context of financial reporting?

   a. Management bias involves management intentionally misstating financial statements for personal gain.

   b. Management bias results in financial statements that are not neutral and, therefore, not useful.

   c. Management bias is unavoidable.

   d. Management bias involves management intentionally misstating financial statements so that the company can raise funds in capital markets.

EXPLANATION: Recall that the bias of a preparer may affect the quality (and, therefore, usefulness) of the information being prepared. By definition, biased information is not useful. Management bias is avoidable with proper controls in place and transparent financial reporting. (Solution = b.)

Question

15. Explain the significance of professional judgement in applying GAAP.

   a. Professional judgement does not exist in GAAP since it contradicts the concept of comparability.

   b. Professional judgement allows management to contradict IFRS or ASPE.

   c. Professional judgement is rarely used in applying GAAP.

   d. Professional judgement is often required since IFRS and ASPE consist of general principles that need to be interpreted in practice.

EXPLANATION: The use of professional judgement is often necessary and allows flexibility in order to meet the objective of providing financial information that is fair, useful, and decision-relevant. However, if there is a standard in IFRS or ASPE requiring a specific accounting treatment, the IFRS or ASPE standard would take precedence. (Solution = d.)

Chapter 2

Conceptual Framework Underlying Financial Reporting

OVERVIEW

Financial statements are needed for effective decision-making and resource (or capital) allocation. For financial statements to be useful, the following must occur.

1. The financial statements must possess certain essential **qualitative characteristics** (including relevance and representational faithfulness).
2. The **elements** within financial statements should meet generally accepted definitions.
3. Information underlying financial statements should be prepared based on generally accepted **foundational principles**.

These three broad areas, specific concepts within each area, and how they relate are illustrated in the conceptual framework for financial reporting. The conceptual framework is commonly referred to as "first principles," and forms the cornerstone of accounting theory.

STUDY STEPS

Understanding the Importance of a Conceptual Framework

A conceptual framework establishes the following:

- The objective of financial reporting (which is to provide useful information to users)
- The qualitative characteristics that useful information should possess
- The basic elements that should be included in financial statements (including assets and liabilities)
- Which, when, and how financial elements and events should be recognized, measured, and presented/disclosed in the financial statements

Having a conceptual framework that forms a foundation for accounting standards ensures that the resulting standards are generally consistent, coherent, and understandable. A conceptual framework also provides a first principles starting point for dealing with new and emerging accounting issues, and developing future GAAP that is consistent with existing GAAP.

Becoming Proficient in Using the Conceptual Framework in Analysis of Financial Reporting Issues

Review **Illustration 2-1** to help you in this step. However, memorizing the framework is only a means to an end. The end is that you develop sufficient professional judgement to be able to make acceptable accounting decisions within the context of the framework. With no framework, it is very difficult for preparers of financial statements to make sound accounting decisions that are consistent with the overall objective of financial reporting (which is to provide useful information to users).

Using the conceptual framework is the first stage of solid case analysis. Many students are not able to identify key issues in cases because they are not sure what to look for. Keeping the conceptual framework in mind will often highlight key case issues. For example, knowing the definition of a liability according to the conceptual framework, you might be led to question whether a particular transaction results in a liability or not. Liabilities are financial statement elements that represent a present duty or responsibility, where the duty or responsibility obligates the entity, leaving it little or no discretion to avoid it, and where the duty or responsibility results from a past transaction or event. If you know this definition, you may be alerted to an issue in a case where a company has missed recording a liability or has incorrectly recorded a liability. Assets are financial statement elements that represent some economic benefit to the entity, where the entity has control over that benefit, and where the benefits result from a past transaction or event. Similarly, if you know this definition, you may be alerted to a case where a company has missed recording an asset or has incorrectly recorded an asset.

TIPS ON CHAPTER TOPICS

- Although it can sometimes be confusing, accountants often use the terms **assumptions**, **concepts**, **principles**, **conventions**, and **standards** interchangeably. Regardless of the particular term used, they are all a part of GAAP (generally accepted accounting principles).

- In producing financial information, it is not always possible to incorporate all qualitative characteristics, as outlined in the conceptual framework. For example, recording certain assets at their fair value may increase the relevance of financial statements, but compromise verifiability to some extent (if calculation of fair value involves assumptions or use of an entity's own data in a discounted cash flow model, for example). To provide guidance in trading off qualitative characteristics if necessary, the conceptual framework identifies two fundamental qualitative characteristics as essential: **relevance** and **representational faithfulness**.

- Accounting standard setters acknowledge that there are practical limitations and resource constraints to providing financial information. Two concepts, materiality and cost versus benefits, deal with these constraints, providing guidance when it is not clear whether a piece of information should be gathered, recorded, and incorporated into financial statements. **Materiality** refers to how important a piece of information is, or an item's impact on the company's overall financial operations. Materiality is often referred to when discussing relevance, because an item is generally thought to be material if it would make a difference in a user's decision. All material information is relevant and should be included in the financial statements. **Cost versus benefits** weighs the cost of providing the information against the benefits of doing so. These concepts are not included in the conceptual framework itself, but are generally accepted in practice.

- As an example of the **materiality** constraint, consider the cost of an item that will benefit operations for five years. Normally, it would be recorded as an asset and depreciated (expensed) over the related five-year period as dictated by the matching principle. However, if the item is a recycling container that cost $20, the amount is deemed to be immaterial and insignificant and the whole amount is handled with expedience; that is, it is expensed in the period when the container is purchased. This departure from the matching principle is justified by the materiality constraint because expensing the recycling container, instead of recording it as an asset and depreciating it, would not change the financial statements to an extent that would cause a reasonable person to change a decision they are making.

- Foundational principles are concepts that help explain how to achieve the objectives of financial reporting, and produce information with the qualitative characteristics and elements listed in the second level of the conceptual framework. The 10 foundational principles can be grouped into three categories.

  1. In the **recognition/derecognition** category are: economic entity assumption, control, revenue recognition and realization principle, and matching principle.

(continued)

2. In the **measurement** category are: periodicity assumption, monetary unit assumption, going concern assumption, historical cost principle, and fair value principle.

3. In the **presentation and disclosure** category is: full disclosure principle.

● Another way to group the foundational principles is to consider that some of them are assumptions, such as the **economic entity assumption**, the **periodicity assumption**, the **monetary unit assumption**, and the **going concern assumption**. These four assumptions could be considered to form the basis for the other six principles. For example, the historical cost principle would not be appropriate if it were not for the going concern assumption. If an entity is not expected to continue in business, then plant assets would be reported on the statement of financial position at their liquidation value or net realizable value (estimated selling price less estimated cost of disposal) rather than at their historical cost.

● The term **recognition** refers to the process of formally recording or incorporating an item in the accounts and financial statements of an entity. The term **derecognition** refers to the process of formally removing an item from the accounts and financial statements of an entity.

● The **revenue recognition and realization** principle is applied before the matching principle is applied. The **revenue recognition and realization** principle gives guidance in determining what revenues to recognize in a given period. The **matching** principle then gives **guidance** as to what expenses to recognize during the period. According to the **revenue recognition and realization** principle, revenues are recognized according to the earnings approach, under ASPE. The new IFRS 15 approach is a contract-based approach to revenue recognition. The **matching principle** states that expenses should be recognized in the same period in which related revenues are recognized, whenever reasonable and possible.

● There are concerns about applying the **matching principle** unconditionally. It is not considered acceptable to "match" if the resulting cost deferral (intended for expense recognition in a future period(s) when related revenues will be recognized) results in the creation of an "asset" on the statement of financial position that does not meet the definition of an asset. Hence, more emphasis is now put on the **statement of financial position** impact of the entry (rather than the **income statement** impact of the entry).

● The new **contract-based approach** to revenue recognition and realization emphasizes the statement of financial position, and focuses more on contractual rights and performance obligations created by entering into a contract with a customer. Revenues are recognized when performance obligations are satisfied.

● There are three common methods of **expense recognition**: (1) cause and effect (matched against revenue in the period), (2) systematic and rational allocation, and (3) immediate expense recognition. You should be able to explain and give examples for each of these. (See **Case 2-3**.)

● The **economic entity assumption** allows us to identify an economic activity or transaction with an economic entity (such as a corporation), and requires that only the activities or transactions of the economic entity (and the activities or transactions of any other entities that the economic entity has control over) be included in the economic entity's financial statements. For example, a parent company is required to prepare consolidated financial

Illustration 2-1 1 7

statements, which group together the assets, liabilities, and results of operations of all entities that are under the parent company's control into one set of consolidated financial statements.

● Note that current proposed definitions of **asset** and **liability** mirror one another. Under the current proposed definitions, assets or liabilities are defined as follows: they involve present economic resources or obligations (respectively), for which the entity has a present exclusive right/access or enforceable obligation (respectively).

● This material is essential in any analysis of financial reporting issues. You will find that these definitions and principles continually come up in discussions of many different issues.

ILLUSTRATION 2-1

Conceptual Framework for Financial Reporting

At the first level, the **objectives** identify the goals and purposes of financial accounting. At the second level are the **qualitative characteristics** that make financial accounting information useful and the **elements** (assets, liabilities, and so on) or specific terms used in financial statements. At the final, or third, level are the **foundational principles** that help explain which, when, and how financial elements and events should be recognized, measured, and presented/disclosed by the financial reporting system.

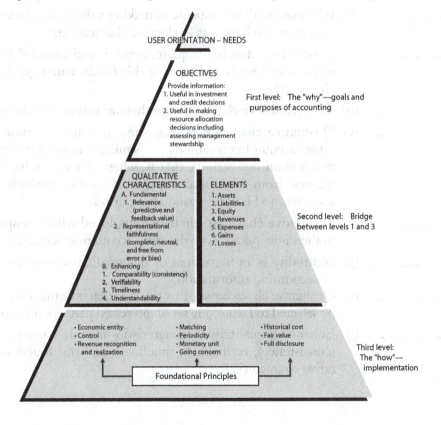

CASE 2-1

PURPOSE: This case is designed to review the qualitative characteristics that make accounting information useful for decision-making purposes.

The qualitative characteristics that make accounting information useful for decision-making purposes are as follows:

- Relevance
- Predictive value
- Feedback value
- Representational faithfulness
- Completeness
- Neutrality

- Free from error or bias
- Comparability (consistency)
- Verifiability
- Timeliness
- Understandability

Instructions

Fill in the blank to identify the appropriate qualitative characteristic(s) being described in each of the statements below. A qualitative characteristic may be used more than once.

_____ (a) Two fundamental qualitative characteristics that make accounting information useful for decision-making purposes.

_____ (b) Information that is capable of making a difference in a decision is said to have this qualitative characteristic.

_____ (c) Information that is complete, neutral, and reasonably free of error or bias is said to have this fundamental qualitative characteristic.

_____ (d) Two qualitative characteristics that are related to relevance.

_____ (e) Qualitative characteristic requiring an entity to apply the same accounting methods to similar events for successive accounting periods; that is, when an entity selects one method from a list of alternative acceptable methods, that same method is used period after period.

_____ (f) Qualitative characteristic being employed when companies in the same industry use the same accounting principles.

_____ (g) Neutrality is an ingredient of this qualitative characteristic of accounting information.

_____ (h) Qualitative characteristic that requires that information cannot be selected to favour one set of interested parties over another.

_____ (i) Enhancing qualitative characteristics include comparability (consistency), verifiability, timeliness, and this fourth qualitative characteristic.

_____ (j) When information provides a basis for forecasting annual earnings for future periods, it is said to have this qualitative characteristic of accounting information.

_____ (k) Qualitative characteristic regarding the quality of information that confirms or corrects users' prior expectations.

_____ (l) Qualitative characteristic requiring that information be available to decision-makers before it loses its ability to influence their decisions.

_____ (m) Qualitative characteristic requiring that financial statements include all information necessary to portray the underlying events and transactions.

_____ (n) Representational faithfulness includes completeness, neutrality, and this third qualitative characteristic (which is necessary in order for financial statements to be reliable).

_____ (o) Qualitative characteristic requiring that a company cannot suppress information just because such disclosure is embarrassing or damaging to the entity.

_____ (p) Qualitative characteristic requiring that the amounts and descriptions in financial statements agree with the elements and substance of economic events that these amounts and descriptions purport to represent.

_____ (q) Qualitative characteristic requiring that independent measurers, using the same measurement methods, obtain similar results.

_____ (r) Qualitative characteristic requiring that the numbers and descriptions in financial statements represent what really existed or happened.

_____ (s) Qualitative characteristic requiring that information be free of personal bias.

_____ (t) Qualitative characteristic requiring a high degree of consensus among individuals on a given measurement.

_____ (u) Qualitative characteristic requiring that financial information be of sufficient quality and clarity so that those who have a reasonable knowledge of business and accounting can use the information.

Solution to Case 2-1

(a) Relevance and representational faithfulness

(b) Relevance

(c) Representational faithfulness

(d) Predictive value and feedback value

(e) Comparability (consistency)

(f) Comparability (consistency)

(g) Representational faithfulness

(h) Neutrality

(i) Understandability

(j) Predictive value

(k) Feedback value

(l) Timeliness   (q) Verifiability

(m) Completeness   (r) Representational faithfulness

(n) Free from error or bias   (s) Neutrality

(o) Neutrality   (t) Verifiability

(p) Representational faithfulness   (u) Understandability

APPROACH: Before beginning to fill in the blanks required, visualize the diagram for the hierarchy of qualitative characteristics (**Illustration 2-1**). Also, take a few minutes to consider the individual characteristics listed and think of the key phrases involved in describing those items. For example:

- **Relevance**: The information is capable of making a difference in a decision.
- **Predictive value**: The information helps users make predictions about the outcome of past, present, and future events.
- **Feedback value**: The information helps to confirm or correct prior expectations.
- **Representational faithfulness**: There is correspondence or agreement between the accounting numbers and descriptions and the resources or events that the numbers and descriptions purport to represent.
- **Completeness**: Financial statements should include all information necessary to portray the underlying events and transactions.
- **Neutrality**: Information is not selected to favour one set of interested parties over another and is to be free from bias toward a predetermined result.
- **Free from error or bias**: Information must be reliable.
- **Comparability (consistency)**: Information is to be measured and reported in a similar manner for different enterprises, and a company is to apply the same methods to similar accountable events from period to period.
- **Verifiability**: This is demonstrated when a high degree of consensus can be secured among independent measurers using the same measurement methods.
- **Timeliness**: Information must be available to decision-makers before it loses its ability to influence their decisions.
- **Understandability**: Information provided by financial reporting should be comprehensible to those who have a reasonable understanding of business and economic activities and are willing to study the information with reasonable diligence.

ILLUSTRATION 2-2

Elements of Financial Statements

Assets: Present economic resources that have some economic benefit to the entity, where the entity has control over that benefit, and where the benefits result from a past transaction or event.

Illustration 2-3 21

Liabilities: Present economic burdens that represent a present duty or responsibility, where the duty or responsibility obligates the entity, leaving it little or no discretion to avoid it, and where the duty or responsibility results from a past transaction or event.

Equity/net assets: Residual interest in an entity that remains after deducting its liabilities from its assets. In a business enterprise, the equity is the ownership interest.

Revenues: Increases in economic resources, either by inflows or other enhancements of an entity's assets or by settlement of its liabilities, resulting from ordinary activities of the entity.

Expenses: Decreases in economic resources, either by outflows or reductions of assets or by incurrence of liabilities, resulting from an entity's ordinary revenue-generating activities.

Gains: Increases in equity (net assets) from peripheral or incidental transactions of an entity and from all other transactions and other events and circumstances affecting the entity during a period, except those that result from revenues or investments by owners.

Losses: Decreases in equity (net assets) from peripheral or incidental transactions of an entity and from all other transactions and other events and circumstances affecting the entity during a period, except those that result from expenses or distributions to owners.

ILLUSTRATION 2-3

Foundational Principles

Economic entity assumption: The assumption that an economic activity can be identified with a particular unit of accountability. The activities of an economic entity can and should be kept separate and distinct from its owners and all other economic entities. The entity concept does not necessarily refer to a legal entity.

Control principle: The principle that other economic entities under a parent entity's control are generally included in the parent's economic entity. Under IFRS, a parent entity has control over an investee economic entity when it has power over the investee; exposure, or rights, to variable returns from its involvement with the investee; and the ability to use its power over the investee to affect the amount of the parent entity's returns.

Revenue recognition and realization principle: The principle that dictates when revenue should be recognized (recorded).

Under the traditional **earnings approach to revenue recognition**, revenues are recognized when (1) **risks and rewards have passed and/or the earnings process is substantially complete**, (2) **the revenue is measurable, and** (3) **the revenue is collectible (realized or realizable)**. Revenues are **realized** when products (goods or services, merchandise, or other assets) are exchanged for cash or claims to cash. Revenues are **realizable** when assets received or held are readily convertible into cash or claims to cash. Assets are readily convertible when they are saleable or interchangeable in an active market at readily determinable prices without significant additional cost. The earnings process is substantially complete when the entity has substantially accomplished what it must do to be entitled to the benefits represented by the revenues. This is an income statement approach that ASPE continues to follow.

Under the new IFRS **contract-based approach to revenue recognition**, there is greater emphasis on the statement of financial position, and the contractual rights and performance obligations created by entering into a contract with a customer. The new standard follows a five-step approach to revenue recognition: (1) **Identify the contract with the customer**, (2) **Identify the performance obligations in the contract**, (3) **Determine the transaction price**, (4) **Allocate the transaction price to each performance obligation**, and (5) **Recognize revenue when each performance obligation is satisfied**.

Matching principle: The principle that dictates that expenses be matched with revenues whenever it is reasonable and practical to do so. (In other words, "Let the expense follow the revenue.") Expenses (efforts) are recognized in the same period as the related revenue (accomplishment) is recognized. Thus, a factory worker's wages are not recognized as an expense when cash is paid, or when the work is performed, or when the product is produced. Instead, the wages are recognized as an expense in the period when they actually make their contribution to the revenue-generating process (in the period the related product is sold). However, the matching principle **may not be** appropriate if the result is a cost deferral (debit) on the statement of financial position that does not meet the **definition of an asset**.

Periodicity assumption: The assumption that the economic life of a business can be divided into artificial time periods. Although some companies choose to subdivide the entity's life into months or quarters, others report financial statements only annually.

Monetary unit assumption: The assumption that only transaction data capable of being expressed in terms of money should be included in the accounting records of the economic entity. All transactions and events can be measured in terms of a common denominator: units of money. A corollary is the added assumption that the unit of measure remains constant from one period to the next. (Some people call the corollary the "stable dollar assumption.")

Going concern assumption: The assumption that the enterprise will continue in operation long enough to carry out its existing objectives and commitments. It assumes the entity will continue in operation long enough to recover the cost of its assets. This assumption serves as a basis for other principles such as the historical cost principle. Because of this assumption, liquidation values of assets are not relevant (in most cases). Management must assess the company's ability to continue as a going concern and take into account all available information, looking out at least 12 months from the statement of financial position date.

Historical cost principle: The principle that an asset should initially be recorded at acquisition cost, measured by the amount of cash (or cash equivalents) that was paid or received or the fair value that was attributed to the transaction when it took place. Acquisition cost of an asset includes all costs necessary to acquire the item and get it in the place and condition ready for its intended use.

Fair value principle: The principle that in certain situations and industries, recording certain assets and liabilities at fair value may be more useful than recording them at historical cost, where fair value is actually an exit price (a price to sell or transfer the asset or liability) as of the measurement date.

Full disclosure principle: The principle that information should be provided when it is important enough to influence the judgement and decisions of an informed user. An entity is to disclose, through the data contained in the financial statements and the information in the notes that accompany the statements, all information necessary to make the statements not misleading. To be recognized in the main body of the financial statements, an item should meet the definition of one of the basic elements, be measurable with sufficient certainty, and be relevant and faithfully representative. The notes to financial statements generally amplify or explain the items presented in the body of the statements. Information in the notes does not have to be quantifiable, nor does the information in the notes need to qualify as elements of the financial statements. Overall, a balance between sufficient detail and sufficient condensation of information should be achieved.

CASE 2-2

PURPOSE: This case will test your comprehension of the essence and significance of the foundational principles, as well as the constraints of financial reporting.

The foundational principles in the conceptual framework are as follows:

(a) Economic entity assumption

(b) Control principle

(c) Revenue recognition and realization principle

(d) Matching principle

(e) Periodicity assumption

(f) Monetary unit assumption

(g) Going concern assumption

(h) Historical cost principle

(i) Fair value principle

(j) Full disclosure principle

The key constraints of financial reporting are as follows:

(k) Materiality constraint   (l) Cost versus benefits constraint

 Before you begin to read and answer the items listed, it would be helpful to briefly think about what you know about each of the foundational principles and constraints of financial reporting. An explanation of each foundational principle appears in **Illustration 2-3**, and an explanation of the materiality and cost versus benefits constraints appears in **Tips on Chapter Topics**.

Instructions

For each of the following statements, identify (by letter) the foundational principle or constraint of financial reporting that is **most directly** related to the given description. Each code letter may be used more than once.

_____ 1. This requires that revenue be recognized in accordance with the earnings approach.

_____ 2. This states that all information necessary to ensure that the financial statements are not misleading should be reported.

_____ 3. This assumption eliminates the need to record assets at liquidation value.

_____ 4. This requires that measurement of the standing and progress of entities be made at regular intervals rather than at the end of the business's life.

_____ 5. This states that if a parent company owns 75% of the voting shares of another (investee) entity, the investee entity is considered part of the parent's economic entity.

_____ 6. This requires that the recorded amount of an asset at acquisition be the amount of cash (or cash equivalents) that was paid or received or the fair value that was ascribed to the transaction when it took place.

_____ 7. This requires that notes to financial statements be prepared to fully explain the items presented in the main body of the financial statements.

_____ 8. This requires that the president of a business not loan his spouse the company's credit card for personal gasoline purchases.

_____ 9. This requires that expenses be recognized in the same period that the related revenues are recognized, provided the statement of financial position is not misstated as a result.

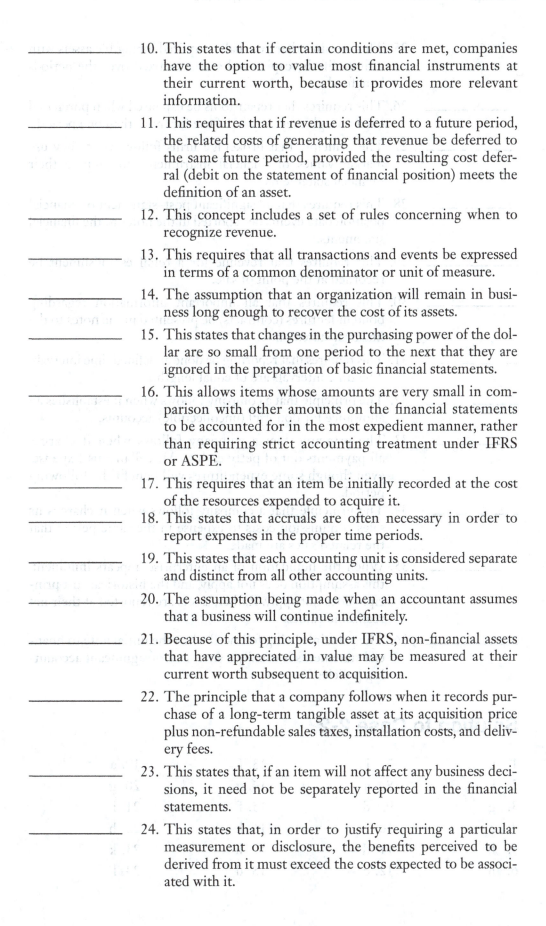

10. This states that if certain conditions are met, companies have the option to value most financial instruments at their current worth, because it provides more relevant information.

11. This requires that if revenue is deferred to a future period, the related costs of generating that revenue be deferred to the same future period, provided the resulting cost deferral (debit on the statement of financial position) meets the definition of an asset.

12. This concept includes a set of rules concerning when to recognize revenue.

13. This requires that all transactions and events be expressed in terms of a common denominator or unit of measure.

14. The assumption that an organization will remain in business long enough to recover the cost of its assets.

15. This states that changes in the purchasing power of the dollar are so small from one period to the next that they are ignored in the preparation of basic financial statements.

16. This allows items whose amounts are very small in comparison with other amounts on the financial statements to be accounted for in the most expedient manner, rather than requiring strict accounting treatment under IFRS or ASPE.

17. This requires that an item be initially recorded at the cost of the resources expended to acquire it.

18. This states that accruals are often necessary in order to report expenses in the proper time periods.

19. This states that each accounting unit is considered separate and distinct from all other accounting units.

20. The assumption being made when an accountant assumes that a business will continue indefinitely.

21. Because of this principle, under IFRS, non-financial assets that have appreciated in value may be measured at their current worth subsequent to acquisition.

22. The principle that a company follows when it records purchase of a long-term tangible asset at its acquisition price plus non-refundable sales taxes, installation costs, and delivery fees.

23. This states that, if an item will not affect any business decisions, it need not be separately reported in the financial statements.

24. This states that, in order to justify requiring a particular measurement or disclosure, the benefits perceived to be derived from it must exceed the costs expected to be associated with it.

_____ 25. This requires that externally acquired intangible assets with a finite life be capitalized and amortized over the periods benefited.

_____ 26. This requires that repair tools be expensed when purchased even though they may be of use for more than one period.

_____ 27. The principle that brokerage firms follow when they use market values of financial instruments to prepare their financial statements.

_____ 28. This requires that all significant post–statement of financial position date events be reported in the notes to the financial statements.

_____ 29. This requires that revenue for a retail establishment be recorded at the point of sale.

_____ 30. This requires that all important information regarding bond indentures (contracts) be presented in the notes to the financial statements.

_____ 31. This requires that reporting be done at defined time intervals. The time intervals are of equal length.

_____ 32. The principle that a company follows when it establishes an allowance for doubtful (uncollectible) accounts.

_____ 33. The principle that a company follows when it charges all payments out of petty cash to Miscellaneous Expense, even though some expenditures will benefit the following period.

_____ 34. The principle that a company follows when it charges its sales commission costs to expense in the same period that the related sales are made.

_____ 35. When the liquidation of an enterprise appears imminent, this assumption does not apply, and the historical cost principle does not apply. Rather, assets are reported at their net realizable values.

_____ 36. The principle being followed when the initial note to financial statements is usually a summary of significant accounting policies.

Solution to Case 2-2

1. c	7. j	13. f	19. a
2. j	8. a	14. g	20. g
3. g	9. d	15. f	21. i
4. e	10. i	16. k	22. h
5. b	11. d	17. h	23. k
6. h	12. c	18. d	24. l

25. d	28. j	31. e	34. d
26. k	29. c	32. d	35. g
27. i	30. j	33. k	36. j

CASE 2-3

PURPOSE: This case is designed to review three methods of matching expenses with revenues as well as examples of each.

There are three common methods of expense recognition: (1) cause and effect, (2) systematic and rational allocation, and (3) immediate recognition.

Instructions

Describe each of the three bases of expense recognition and give a few examples of each for a retail establishment.

Solution to Case 2-3

1. **Cause and effect**: When there is a direct association between the expiration of a cost and a particular revenue transaction, revenue recognition should cause expense recognition; that is, the cost should be expensed in the same time period that the related revenue is recognized.

   Examples: Cost of goods sold, sales commission expense, freight-out.

2. **Systematic and rational allocation**: This method is used when a cost that benefits the revenue-generating process of more than one accounting period cannot be related to particular revenue transactions. A relationship between the cost and revenues is assumed to exist, even though a close cause-and-effect relationship between revenue and the cost cannot be determined. Under this method, the cost is initially accounted for as an asset and then allocated to the periods benefited (as an expense) in a systematic and rational manner. The allocation method used should appear reasonable to an unbiased observer and should be consistently applied from period to period. In applying systematic and rational allocation, however, any debits to the statement of financial position must still meet the definition of an asset. Arbitrary cost deferrals for the sake of "matching" are not considered acceptable.

   Examples: Depreciation of plant assets, amortization of intangibles, amortization of prepaids (such as rent and insurance).

3. **Immediate recognition**: This method is used for costs that fall into at least one of the following categories:

   (a) Their incurrence during the period provides no discernible future benefits.

   (b) They must be incurred each accounting period, and no buildup of expected future benefits occurs.

(c) By their nature, they relate to current revenues even though they cannot be directly associated with any specific revenues.

(d) The amount of cost to be deferred can be measured only in an arbitrary manner or great uncertainty exists regarding the realization of future benefits.

(e) Uncertainty exists regarding whether allocating them to current and future periods will serve any useful purpose.

(f) They are measures of asset costs recorded in prior periods from which no future benefits are now discernible.

Examples: Sales salaries and wages, office salaries and wages, utilities, maintenance and repairs, advertising, accounting and legal costs, research and development expense, writeoff of a worthless patent.

- Costs incurred by a manufacturing company are often classified into two groups: product costs and period costs. **Product costs**, such as material, labour, and manufacturing overhead, attach to the product and are carried into future periods (as a balance in inventory) if the product remains unsold at the end of the current period; therefore, expense recognition of those costs is deferred to the period of sale. This is an acceptable treatment provided that the future benefit (expected revenues) exceeds the amounts deferred. Product costs are expensed in the period of sale in accordance with the cause and effect basis of expense recognition. **Period costs**, such as officers' salaries and other administrative items, are expensed immediately, even though benefits associated with these costs may be realized in the future, because no direct relationship between cost and revenue can be determined for these costs, and it is highly uncertain what, if any, benefits will accrue in the future.

- For a manufacturing company, depreciation of an office building is determined and expensed based on systematic and rational allocation. On the other hand, depreciation of factory machinery is a component of manufacturing overhead; thus, it is an element of product cost. The amount of depreciation that pertains to the products produced during a period is first determined by use of the selected depreciation method. The amount of depreciation that ends up being reflected as an expense on the income statement for the same period depends on the number of products sold (not produced) during the period; it is included as a part of cost of goods sold expense.

ANALYSIS OF MULTIPLE-CHOICE QUESTIONS

Question

1. The objectives of financial reporting include all of the following except to provide information that:

   a. is useful to Canada Revenue Agency (CRA) in allocating the tax burden to the business community.

   b. is useful to those making investment and credit decisions.

   c. is useful in making resource allocation decisions including assessing management stewardship.

   d. identifies the economic resources (assets), the claims to those resources (liabilities), and the changes in those resources and claims.

EXPLANATION: Financial reporting is for the use of investors, potential investors, management, and other interested parties; it is not for the CRA. The information required by the CRA is provided by the reporting entity on tax forms and is referred to as income tax accounting, as opposed to financial reporting. (Solution = a.)

Question

2. According to the conceptual framework for financial reporting, predictive value is an ingredient of:

	Relevance	Representational faithfulness
a.	Yes	Yes
b.	No	Yes
c.	No	No
d.	Yes	No

EXPLANATION: In the conceptual framework, under qualitative characteristics of accounting information, predictive value is linked to relevance, and not representational faithfulness. Therefore, we want to respond "Yes" to the relevance column and "No" to the representational faithfulness column. (Solution = d.)

Question

3. According to the conceptual framework for financial reporting, neutrality is an ingredient of:

	Relevance	Representational faithfulness
a.	Yes	Yes
b.	No	Yes
c.	No	No
d.	Yes	No

EXPLANATION: In the conceptual framework, under qualitative characteristics of accounting information, neutrality is linked to representational faithfulness, and not relevance. Therefore, we want to respond "No" to the relevance column and "Yes" to the representational faithfulness column. (Solution = b.)

Question

4. If the FIFO inventory method was used last period, it should be used for the current and following periods because of:

   a. materiality.   c. timeliness.

   b. verifiability.   d. comparability (consistency).

EXPLANATION: Selection "a" is incorrect because materiality refers to a constraint whereby an item is to be given strict accounting treatment unless it is insignificant. Selection "b" is incorrect because verifiability refers to when a high degree of consensus can be secured among independent measurers using the same measurement methods. Selection "c" is incorrect because timeliness refers to availability of information before that information loses its ability to influence users' decisions. Selection "d" is correct because comparability and consistency are qualitative characteristics of accounting information that state that accounting policies should be applied consistently to similar accountable events from period to period. (Solution = d.)

Question

5. Which of the following transactions does not represent a gain to the organization?
   a. A bookstore selling a computer for a profit
   b. A consulting company selling a block of land it was holding for future expansion
   c. The Ottawa Senators selling season tickets
   d. A lawyer selling a pair of theatre tickets for more than she paid for them

EXPLANATION: A gain is defined as an increase in equity from a peripheral or incidental transaction. Ask yourself whether the revenue earned in each situation would be in the normal course of business for the enterprise or if it is an incidental or peripheral transaction. Bookstores are not in the business of regularly selling computers. Land held for expansion would not represent a normal transaction for a consulting firm and a lawyer does not regularly sell theatre tickets. The Ottawa Senators, however, would sell season tickets in the normal course of business. (Solution = c.)

Question

6. Which of the following does not represent a liability to the organization?
   a. Salaries earned for work performed last week by employees
   b. Money received by Northern Air in advance of a flight to take place next week
   c. Inventory purchased but not paid for
   d. The visit by the owner of a company to a car lot to pick out the car she wants to buy for the company next week

EXPLANATION: A liability is a present duty or responsibility, where the duty or responsibility obligates the entity, leaving it little or no discretion to avoid it, and where the duty or responsibility results from a past transaction or event. Situations "a," "b," and "c" all represent present duties or responsibilities arising from past transactions, while "d" represents a transaction that has not yet taken place, as the owner has not purchased the vehicle yet and certainly can change her mind. Thus the obligation is not enforceable. (Solution = d.)

Question

7. The assumption that an enterprise will remain in business indefinitely and will not liquidate in the near future is called the:
   - a. economic entity assumption.
   - c. monetary unit assumption.
   - b. going concern assumption.
   - d. periodicity assumption.

EXPLANATION: Selection "a" is incorrect because the economic entity assumption states that the activities of an economic entity should be kept separate and distinct from all other economic entities. Selection "c" is incorrect because the monetary unit assumption states that all transactions and events can be measured in terms of a common denominator: units of money. Selection "d" is incorrect because the periodicity assumption states that the economic activities of an enterprise can be divided into equally spaced artificial time periods. Selection "b" is correct because the going concern assumption implies that an enterprise will continue in business and will not liquidate within the foreseeable future. (Solution = b.)

Question

8. Pluto Magazine Company sells space to advertisers. The company requires an advertiser to pay for services one month before publication. Advertising revenue should be recognized when:
   - a. an advertiser places an order.
   - c. the related cash is received.
   - b. a bill is sent to an advertiser.
   - d. the related ad is published.

EXPLANATION: The last sentence of the question asks us the point at which revenue should be recognized. ASPE would follow the earnings approach where revenue is generally recognized when (1) risks and rewards have passed and/or the earnings process is substantially complete, (2) the revenue is measurable, and (3) the revenue is collectible. The new IFRS 15 model would follow the contract-based approach following a five-step approach: (1) identify the contract with the customer, (2) identify the performance obligations in the contract, (3) determine the transaction price, (4) allocate the transaction price to each performance obligation, and (5) recognize revenue as each performance obligation is satisfied. In this case, the timing of the revenue recognition will be the same under both ASPE and IFRS. At the points when an order is placed and a bill is sent to an advertiser, the earnings process is not substantially complete. At the point when the cash is received in advance of the publication, the revenue is realized but not earned. The revenue should be recognized when the related ad is published. (Solution = d.)

Question

9. The historical cost principle provides that:
   - a. items whose costs are insignificant compared with other amounts on the financial statements may be accounted for in the most expedient manner.

b. assets, liabilities, and equities must be expressed in terms of a common denominator.

c. the recorded amount of an acquired item should be the amount of cash (or cash equivalents) that was paid or received or the fair value that was ascribed to the transaction when it took place.

d. the expenses of generating revenue should be recognized in the same period that the related revenue is recognized.

EXPLANATION: Briefly define the historical cost principle before you read the answer selections. See **Illustration 2-3**. Selection "a" describes the materiality constraint. Selection "b" describes the monetary unit assumption. Selection "d" relates to the matching principle. (Solution = c.)

Question

10. If revenue is received in the current period, but it is not earned until a future period, the related expenses of generating the revenue should **not** be recognized until that future period. This guideline is an application of the:

a. revenue recognition and realization principle.

b. full disclosure principle.

c. matching principle.

d. cost versus benefits constraint.

EXPLANATION: The revenue recognition and realization principle discusses when revenues should be recognized. The matching principle states that expenses should be recognized in the same period that the revenue they helped to generate is recognized. Thus, if revenue is deferred, the related expenses should also be deferred. This treatment is required, provided the resulting cost deferral meets the definition of an asset (inventory, for example). (Solution = c.)

Question

11. The process of reporting an item in the financial statements of an enterprise is:

a. recognition.   c. allocation.

b. realization.   d. incorporation.

EXPLANATION: The term "recognition" refers to the process of formally recording or incorporating an item in the accounts and financial statements of an entity. An item that gets recorded in the accounts is eventually reported in the financial statements of the enterprise. Realization is the process of converting non-cash resources and rights into money and is most precisely used in accounting and financial reporting to refer to sales of assets for cash or claims to cash. The term "allocation" refers to the process or result of allocating (assigning costs or systematically spreading costs). The term "incorporation" refers to the process of establishing a business in the corporate form of organization. (Solution = a.)

Question

12. Information cannot be selected to favour one set of stakeholders over another. This guidance comes from the:
    a. materiality constraint.
    b. cost versus benefits constraint.
    c. neutrality qualitative characteristic.
    d. full disclosure principle.

EXPLANATION: See the approach to **Case 2-1**. The neutrality qualitative characteristic states that information cannot be selected to favour one set of stakeholders over another. (Solution = c.)

Question

13. When an entity charges the entire cost of an electric pencil sharpener to expense in the period when it was purchased, even though the appliance has an estimated life of five years, it is applying the:
    a. matching principle.
    b. materiality constraint.
    c. historical cost principle.
    d. cost versus benefits constraint.

EXPLANATION: When an item benefits operations of more than one period, the matching principle often dictates that the cost of the item be allocated (spread) systematically over the periods benefited. However, the materiality constraint dictates that an immaterial item need not be given strict accounting treatment; it can be given expedient treatment. The cost of a pencil sharpener would obviously be small and thus immaterial. Consequently, the materiality constraint is justification for departing from the matching principle in accounting for the cost of the pencil sharpener. (Solution = b.)

Question

14. The value of a conceptual framework is that:
    a. it provides the correct answer for every financial reporting problem.
    b. it reduces the use of professional judgement and therefore management bias.
    c. it does not allow choice.
    d. it provides an established and accepted body of concepts and objectives that may be applied to any situation.

EXPLANATION: A conceptual framework improves consistency of standards, yet still allows professional judgement to be used. It does not provide a correct answer to every problem. (Solution = d.)

Question

15. The main decisions being made by external users of financial statements involve:
    a. resource allocation.
    b. investment and credit decisions.
    c. assessing management stewardship.
    d. all of the above.

EXPLANATION: The objectives of financial reporting recognize that users are making investment, credit, and resource allocation decisions and assessing management stewardship. (Solution = d.)

Question

16. The traits that make information useful are:

    a. comparability and consistency.   c. understandability.
    b. relevance.   d. all of the above.

EXPLANATION: Information must be comparable (consistent), relevant, and understandable to be useful. (Solution = d.)

Question

17. Which of the following best describes the periodicity assumption?
    a. The lifespan of the business is the only relevant period to consider in financial reporting.
    b. It is relevant to divide the lifespan of the business into smaller units so that the company may report to users on a more frequent basis.
    c. Dividing the lifespan of a business into smaller units creates too many allocation problems and, therefore, the periodicity assumption precludes its use.
    d. The only relevant reporting period is the fiscal year.

EXPLANATION: Users need timely information, whether it is daily, monthly, quarterly, or annually. Therefore, it is necessary to divide the lifespan into units (usually monthly, quarterly, and annually) to allow users to analyze the information on a regular basis. (Solution = b.)

Question

18. It is not always possible to incorporate all the concepts or ideas in the conceptual framework since some are in conflict with each other. Identify the conflicting concepts in the following scenario:

    It normally takes three months for the company to finalize its year-end numbers. By the time the auditor has audited the financial statements, it is five months into the next year.

a. Understandability versus timeliness

b. Materiality versus representational faithfulness

c. Representational faithfulness versus timeliness

d. Timeliness versus consistency

EXPLANATION: The longer the company takes to ensure that the numbers are accurate, the more faithfully representative the financial statements will be. The financial statements lose relevance, however, the less timely they are. (Solution = c.)

Question

19. Identify the conflicting concepts in the following ASPE scenario:

Unsure as to whether to book revenues now or when greater certainty exists with respect to collectibility, the company decides to recognize revenues in the period when the goods are delivered.

a. Revenue recognition and realization versus neutrality

b. Revenue recognition and realization versus materiality

c. Matching versus revenue recognition and realization

d. Full disclosure versus revenue recognition and realization

EXPLANATION: The ASPE revenue recognition and realization principle dictates that revenues should be recognized when risks and rewards have passed and/or the earnings process is substantially complete, if the revenue is measurable, and when the revenue is collectible. This principle, along with accrual accounting, would normally require earlier recognition of revenue. However, neutrality dictates that information cannot be selected to favour one set of stakeholders over another. If collection of the revenue cannot be reasonably assured, the option that does not overstate income is the more neutral choice and should be selected. (Solution = a.)

Question

20. Professional corporation and limited liability partnerships (LLP) have evolved

   i. for tax planning.

   ii. for limited liability protection.

   iii. to limit liability of the partners for the negligence of other partners.

   a. i and ii   c. ii and iii

   b. i and iii   d. All of the above

EXPLANATION: Professional accounting firms in Canada are prohibited from incorporating to attain limited liability protection. LLP legislation provides that a partner is not personally liable for any debts, obligations, or liabilities of the firm that arise from any negligent act by another partner. It does not reduce or limit the general liability of the firm. (Solution = b.)

Chapter 3

The Accounting Information System and Measurement Issues

OVERVIEW

This chapter is divided into two parts.

The first part of the chapter discusses the steps involved in the accounting cycle and emphasizes the subject of adjusting entries. Throughout an accounting period, cash receipts and cash disbursements are recorded. At the end of the accounting period, adjusting entries are required so that revenues and expenses are reflected according to the accrual basis of accounting. Adjusting entries are simply entries required to bring account balances up to date. The failure to record proper adjustments (adjusting entries) will cause errors on both the statement of income/comprehensive income and the statement of financial position.

Sometimes measurement is not straightforward. The second part introduces tools and techniques that will help you measure financial statement elements. Measurement calculations often involve time value concepts. Appendix 3B provides a foundation for doing present value calculations.

STUDY STEPS

Understanding the Importance of Debits and Credits and the Accounting Cycle

Do not underestimate the importance of being able to journalize a transaction and prepare financial statements. Many students struggle through intermediate accounting without being able to master it because they do not have fundamental bookkeeping skills.

Debits and credits are fundamental building blocks in understanding financial reporting.

The best approach to this material is to attempt as many problems as possible and to verify answers against the solutions provided. This will reinforce the mechanics involved, the double-entry bookkeeping system, and the importance of balancing. You may be proficient in this area if you have covered this material in detail in a previous course and are very familiar with the mechanics and terminology involved. If you have not taken introductory accounting recently, a review of this material would be beneficial.

The accounting cycle involves capturing data, journalizing and posting it to the general ledger, taking a trial balance, making adjustments to the trial balance, summarizing and classifying accounts for inclusion in financial statements, and closing statement of income/comprehensive income accounts.

Adjustments to the trial balance are usually made at month end, when financial statements are prepared. They involve corrections to accounts (often due to reconciliations with external information or subledgers), accruals, and entries to adjust the value of assets and liabilities to ensure that they are properly valued.

Preparation of financial statements requires grouping of trial balance accounts into account categories. This reduces the amount of information that is presented, since too much detail on the financial statements makes them difficult to interpret. This step requires significant professional judgement. Some companies like to provide more detail and some prefer less. Materiality is another consideration. That is, if an account is considered to be so insignificant that it would not affect decisions made by users, the amount is not shown separately on the financial statements.

Both IFRS and ASPE require the use of accrual accounting since it provides more useful information to users. Under the accrual method, in general, events on or before the financial statement date, which affect the elements defined in the conceptual framework, are recorded. In effect, the accrual method brings the accounts up to date, resulting in more complete and useful financial statements.

Measuring Financial Statement Elements

Measuring the value of a simple transaction, such as the company paying $100 cash for supplies, is straightforward. However, measurement of the initial recognition of some assets and liabilities is not as straightforward and involves the use of estimates. To be consistent with the conceptual framework introduced in Chapter 2, we must consider not only the initial measurement, but also subsequent measurement (for example, at subsequent financial reporting dates).

TIPS ON CHAPTER TOPICS

- This chapter is an extremely important one. An ability to think and work quickly with the concepts in this chapter is necessary in understanding subsequent chapters. Although adjusting entries were probably taught in your introductory accounting course, you are likely to discover new dimensions to the subject in this intermediate accounting course. Pay close attention when studying this chapter!

- When you encounter a transaction, analyze it in terms of its effects on the elements of the basic accounting equation (or balance sheet equation). A correct analysis will maintain balance in the basic accounting equation; however, maintaining balance in the basic accounting equation does not necessarily mean that the analysis is correct. For example, in recording a transaction, if an asset account and a liability account should have been increased, but instead an asset account and a shareholders' equity account are increased, the basic accounting equation may still be in balance but the resulting entry would be incorrect. The **basic accounting** equation is as follows:

ASSETS = LIABILITIES + SHAREHOLDERS' EQUITY

Or

A = L + SE

- Assets are economic resources. Liabilities and shareholders' equity are sources of resources; liabilities are creditor sources, and shareholders' equity is shareholder sources (owner investments and undistributed profits). The basic accounting equation simply states that the total assets (resources) at a point in time equal the total liabilities plus total shareholders' equity (sources of resources) at the same point in time.

- **An understanding of the following terms is important.**

  1. **Event**: A happening of consequence. An event is generally the source or cause of changes in assets, liabilities, and shareholders' equity. Events may be external or internal.

  2. **Transaction**: An external event involving a transfer or exchange between two or more entities.

  3. **Account**: A systematic arrangement that shows the effect of transactions and other events. A separate account is kept for each type of asset, liability, shareholders' equity, revenue, expense, gain, loss, dividend, and other comprehensive income (or loss) account.

  4. **Permanent and temporary accounts**: Permanent (real) accounts are asset, liability, and shareholders' equity accounts; they appear on the

(*continued*)

statement of financial position. Temporary (nominal) accounts are revenue, expense, gain, loss, dividend, and other comprehensive income (or loss) accounts; except for dividends, they appear on the statement of income/comprehensive income. Temporary accounts are periodically closed; permanent accounts are left open.

5. **Ledger**: The book (or electronic database) containing the accounts. Each account usually has a separate page. A general ledger is a collection of all accounts. A subsidiary ledger contains the details of a specific general ledger account.

6. **Journal**: The book of original entry where transactions and other selected events are initially recorded.

7. **Posting**: The process of transferring the essential facts and figures from the book of original entry to the ledger accounts.

8. **Trial balance**: A list of all open accounts in the ledger and their balances. A trial balance may be prepared at any time.

9. **Adjusting entries**: Entries made at the end of an accounting period to bring all accounts up to date on an accrual accounting basis so that correct financial statements can be prepared.

10. **Financial statements**: Statements that reflect the collecting, tabulating, and final summarizing of the accounting data. Financial statements include the statement of financial position (or the balance sheet under ASPE), the statement of income/comprehensive income (or the income statement under ASPE), the statement of cash flows, and the statement of changes in shareholders' equity (or statement of retained earnings under ASPE).

11. **Closing entries**: The formal process by which all temporary accounts are reduced to zero, and net income or net loss is determined and transferred to Retained Earnings, and other comprehensive income (or loss) is determined and transferred to Accumulated Other Comprehensive Income.

● **Transactions** are the economic events of an entity recorded by accountants. Some events (happenings of consequence to an entity) are not measurable in terms of money and do not get recorded in the accounting records. Hiring employees, placing an order for supplies, greeting a customer, and quoting prices for products are examples of activities that do not by themselves constitute transactions.

● **Adjusting entries** are often required so that revenues and expenses are reflected on the accrual basis of accounting (revenues recognized when earned and expenses recognized when incurred) rather than on the cash basis of accounting. Therefore, adjusting entries reflect the accruals and prepayments of revenues and expenses and also estimated expenses. Adjusting entries are simply entries required to bring account balances up to date before financial statements can be prepared. Failure to record proper adjustments will cause errors in both the statement of income/comprehensive income and the statement of financial position.

- **Accruals** result from **cash** flows that occur **after** expense or revenue recognition. That is, cash is paid or received in a future accounting period for an expense incurred or a revenue earned in the current period.

- **Prepayments** result from **cash** flows that occur **before** expense or revenue recognition. That is, cash is paid for expenses that apply to one (or more than one) future accounting period(s), or cash is received for revenue that is earned in one (or more than one) future accounting period(s). The portion of the expense that applies to future periods is deferred by reporting the deferred portion as a prepaid expense (asset) on the statement of financial position. The portion of the revenue that applies to future periods is deferred by reporting the deferred portion as an unearned revenue (liability) on the statement of financial position.

- You should be able to define the following four terms and describe the related adjusting entry for each.

  1. A **prepaid expense** is an expense that has been paid but not incurred (used or consumed) yet. An adjusting entry for a prepaid or deferred expense involves an EXPENSE account (such as rent expense) and an ASSET account (such as prepaid rent).

  2. An **unearned revenue** is a revenue that has been collected but not earned yet. An adjusting entry for an unearned revenue involves a LIABILITY account (such as unearned revenue) and a REVENUE account. For example, if cash is collected for a magazine subscription, the cash account should increase, and an unearned revenue account should also increase. The unearned revenue would become earned when the magazine is mailed to the customer. At that time, the unearned revenue account would decrease and the appropriate revenue account would increase.

  3. An **accrued expense** is an expense that has been incurred (used or consumed) but not yet paid. An adjusting entry for an accrued expense involves an EXPENSE account (such as salaries and wages expense) and a LIABILITY account (such as salaries and wages payable).

  4. An **accrued revenue** is a revenue that has been earned but not collected yet. An adjusting entry for an accrued revenue involves an ASSET account (such as accounts receivable) and a REVENUE account. For example, if a painter has painted a house, but has not received payment yet as at the financial statement date, an accrued revenue should be recorded by increasing accounts receivable and increasing the appropriate revenue account. As a result, revenues reported on the statement of income will reflect amounts that were actually earned in the period (in accordance with the accrual basis of accounting).

- An **unearned revenue** may also be called a **deferred revenue** because recognition of revenue in the statement of income is being deferred to a future period. An unearned (or deferred) revenue is a credit carried on the statement of financial position to be released to the statement of income in a future period when the related revenue is earned.

(continued)

● An adjusting entry for prepaid insurance expense (expense paid, but not incurred yet) involves an expense account and an asset account. The expense account is often called Insurance Expense or Expired Insurance. Possible titles for the asset account include Prepaid Insurance, Deferred Insurance Expense, Prepaid Insurance Expense, Deferred Insurance, and Unexpired Insurance.

● An adjusting entry for unearned rent revenue (revenue collected, but not earned yet) involves a revenue account and a liability account. The revenue account is often called Rent Revenue or Rental Income or Rent Earned. Possible titles for the liability account include Unearned Rent Revenue, Unearned Rent, Deferred Rent Revenue, Rent Revenue Received in Advance, and Rental Income Collected in Advance. The use of Prepaid Rent Revenue as an account title is **not** appropriate because the term "prepaid" usually refers to the payment of cash in advance, not the receipt of cash in advance.

● In an adjusting entry to record accrued salaries and wages expense (expense incurred, but not paid yet), the debit is to an expense account and the credit is to a liability account. The expense account is usually titled Salaries and Wages Expense. Possible names for the liability account include Salaries and Wages Payable, Salaries Payable, Wages Payable, and Accrued Salaries and Wages Payable.

● In an adjusting entry to record accrued interest income (interest income earned, but not received yet), the debit is to an asset account and the credit is to a revenue account. Possible names for the asset account include Interest Receivable and Accrued Interest Receivable. Possible names for the revenue account include Interest Income, Interest Revenue, and Interest Earned.

● In an adjusting entry for an accrual (accrued revenue or accrued expense), the word "accrued" is **not** needed in either account title. If you choose to use the word "accrued" in an account title, it is appropriate to do so **only** in the statement of financial position account title. For example, the entry to record accrued salaries and wages of $1,000 is as follows:

Salaries and Wages Expense	1,000	
Salaries and Wages Payable		1,000

The word "accrued" is not needed in either account title, but it could be used in the liability account title if desired. (The account title would then be Accrued Salaries and Wages Payable.) It would be wrong to insert the word "accrued" in the expense account title. Some people simply call the liability account Accrued Salaries and Wages (rather than Salaries and Wages Payable) but we advise that you include the key word "Payable" and omit the unnecessary word "Accrued."

● When preparing homework assignments, working through the **Study Guide**, and answering exam questions, pay careful attention to whether a prepayment situation relates to a **cash inflow** or **cash outflow** for the entity in question. Be sure you then use the proper related account for recording the cash receipt or disbursement and correct terminology in explaining the scenario. If cash is **received**, the amount will generally be recorded by a credit to either a (earned) revenue account or an unearned revenue account. If cash is **paid**, the amount will generally be recorded by a debit to either an expense account or a prepaid expense account.

● Notice that **none** of the adjusting entries discussed in Chapter 3 involves the **Cash** account. Therefore, if you are instructed to record **adjusting entries**, double-check your work when it is completed. If you have used the Cash account in any adjusting entry, it is very likely in error. (The only time Cash belongs in an adjusting entry is when a bank reconciliation discloses a need to adjust the Cash account—this will be explained in Chapter 7—or when an error has been made that involves the Cash account, in which case a correcting entry is required).

● Notice that each adjusting entry discussed in this chapter involves a statement of financial position account **and** a statement of income account.

● An unadjusted trial balance is referred to as either "unadjusted trial balance" or simply "trial balance." An adjusted trial balance is referred to as either "adjusted trial balance" or the "adjusted trial."

● Closing entries are necessary at the end of an accounting period to prepare the temporary accounts (revenue, expense, gain, loss, dividend, and other comprehensive income or loss accounts) for the recording of transactions in the next accounting period. Closing entries are prepared after the temporary account balances have been used to prepare the current period statement of income/comprehensive income. Only temporary accounts are closed. Permanent accounts are never closed; their balances continue into the next accounting period. **Temporary** accounts are often called **nominal** accounts; **permanent** accounts are often called **real** accounts.

● A temporary revenue or gain account with a credit balance is closed by a debit to that account and a credit to Income Summary. A temporary expense or loss account with a debit balance is closed by a credit to that account and a debit to Income Summary. The Income Summary account is closed to a shareholders' equity account (Retained Earnings for a corporation) and is often called the Revenue and Expense Summary.

● If a separate account is used to record owner withdrawals or owner distributions (such as Dividends for a corporation or Owner's Drawings for a proprietorship or partnership), this account is also closed at the end of the accounting period, but not to the Income Summary account, because it is not a component of the net income calculation. Rather, this account is closed directly to Retained Earnings (for a corporation) or to Owner's Capital (for a proprietorship or partnership).

● Because Other Comprehensive Income (or Loss) accounts are also temporary accounts but not included in the net income calculation, these accounts are closed directly to Accumulated Other Comprehensive Income, which is a component of shareholders' equity. Thus, the shareholders' equity section of the statement of financial position contains the following classifications of permanent accounts, which are carried forward (continued) into the next

(continued)

accounting period: Common Shares (investments by shareholders), Retained Earnings, and Accumulated Other Comprehensive Income.

● A **post-closing trial balance** contains only permanent accounts because the temporary accounts all have a zero balance after the closing process. A post-closing trial balance is prepared to verify the equality of debits and credits after the closing process.

● The ability to capture information completely and accurately is an essential and fundamental skill in accounting.

● When measuring the value of a financial statement element, accountants must ask and answer three questions:

1. Which **model or technique** should be used?

   The selected model will depend on the item being measured. You should be familiar with two common valuation techniques.

   a. **Income models**, which convert future amounts to current amounts.

   b. **Market models,** which use prices and other information generated from market transactions involving identical or similar transactions. Many market models are beyond the scope of this course.

2. Which **inputs** should be used?

   Inputs to various models can include estimates of cash flows, interest rates used to discount the cash flows, and other uncertainties or risks. Inputs and assumptions that are more reliable are better.

3. Does the resulting measurement result in **useful information**?

● If you are unfamiliar with present value calculations, you should review the material in Appendix 3B. Two generally accepted approaches to **discounted cash flows** are the:

1. **traditional approach**, where the discount rate reflects all risks in the cash flows, but the cash flows are assumed to be certain.

2. **expected cash flow approach**, where a risk-free discount rate is used to discount cash flows that have been adjusted for uncertainty.

● According to **IFRS 13**, when measuring fair value an entity must consider:

1. the item being measured—for example, the nature, condition, and location of the asset.

2. how the item would be or could be used by market participants; generally an asset should be valued based on its highest and best use in the market, regardless of how the entity is actually using it.

3. the market that the item would be (or was) bought and sold in; for example, if a company buys and sells shares on the TSX, then the company would use market values as quoted by the TSX.

4. which model, if any, should be used to measure fair value; if no pure market values are available, valuation techniques such as the cost, income, or market models are used. IFRS 13 classifies the quality of inputs used in estimating fair values into three categories depending on their level of subjectivity.

Illustration 3-1   45

ILLUSTRATION 3-1

Double-Entry (Debit and Credit) Accounting System

The debit and credit rules are summarized below:

Asset Accounts			Liability Accounts	
Debit	Credit		Debit	Credit
Increase	Decrease		Decrease	Increase
+	–		–	+

Dividends Account			Shareholders' Equity Accounts	
Debit	Credit		Debit	Credit
Increase	Decrease		Decrease	Increase
+	–		–	+

Expense Accounts			Revenue Accounts	
Debit	Credit		Debit	Credit
Increase	Decrease		Decrease	Increase
+	–		–	+

Normal Balance ↑ (Expense Accounts)

Normal Balance ↑ (Revenue Accounts)

Notice that the accounts above are arranged in such a way that all of the increases ("+" signs) are on the outside and all of the decreases ("–" signs) are on the inside of this diagram.

- An **account** is an individual accounting record of increases and decreases in a specific asset, liability, shareholders' equity, revenue, expense, gain, loss, dividend, or other comprehensive income item. In its simplest form, an account consists of three parts: (1) the title of the account, (2) a left or debit side, and (3) a right or credit side. If these components are aligned to resemble the letter T, the format is referred to as **T-account format**.

- "Credit" does **not** always mean favourable or unfavourable. In accounting, "debit" and "credit" simply mean left and right, respectively. "Debit" is a term that refers to the left side of any account. Thus, the debit side of an account is always the left side. "Credit" is a term that refers to the right side of any account. Thus, the credit side of an account is always the right side of the account. The phrase "to debit an account" means to enter an amount on the debit (left) side of an account. Debit can be abbreviated as "Dr.," and credit can be abbreviated as "Cr."

- A "+" indicates an increase and a "–" indicates a decrease. Therefore, a transaction that causes an increase in an asset is recorded by a debit to the

(continued)

related asset account; a transaction that causes a decrease in an asset is recorded by a credit to the related asset account.

● The normal balance of an account is the side where increases are recorded. Therefore, the normal balance of an asset account is a debit balance; the normal balance of a liability account is a credit balance.

● In the double-entry system of accounting, for each transaction journalized, total debits must equal total credits.

● Each account line that appears on the financial statements corresponds either to an account in the general ledger or to a set of accounts in the general ledger grouped together.

● At this stage in your study of accounting, you should be able to quickly and correctly identify the debit and credit rules for any given account. If you are not comfortable with this process, review and practise using the rules until you improve. If you memorize the rules for an asset account, you can determine the rules for all other types of accounts by knowing which accounts follow the same rules as asset accounts, and which accounts follow opposite rules to asset accounts. Increases in assets are recorded by debits. Because liabilities and shareholders' equity are on the other side of the equation in the basic accounting equation, they must have debit and credit rules opposite to the rules for asset accounts. Therefore, increases in liabilities and shareholders' equity accounts are recorded by credits. Revenues earned increase owners' equity (shareholders' equity for a corporation) so the rule to record increases in revenue is the same as the rule to record increases in an owners' equity account (increases are recorded by credits). Expenses and owners' withdrawals decrease owners' equity, so the rule to record increases in expenses and owners' withdrawals (increases are recorded by debits) is opposite to the rule to record increases in an owners' equity account.

EXERCISE 3-1

PURPOSE: This exercise will test your understanding of the debit and credit rules.

Instructions

For each account listed below, put a check mark (✓) in the appropriate column to indicate if it is increased by an entry on the debit (left) side of the account or by an entry on the credit (right) side of the account. The first one is done for you.

	Debit	Credit
1. Cash	✓	
2. Sales Revenue		
3. Sales Commission Expense		
4. Advertising Expense		

	Debit	**Credit**
5. Salaries and Wages Payable	_____	_____
6. Prepaid Insurance	_____	_____
7. Property Tax Payable	_____	_____
8. Property Tax Expense	_____	_____
9. Dividends	_____	_____
10. Interest Income	_____	_____
11. Salaries and Wages Expense	_____	_____
12. Rent Revenue	_____	_____
13. Unearned Rent Revenue	_____	_____
14. Equipment	_____	_____
15. Notes Payable	_____	_____
16. Building	_____	_____
17. Accounts Payable	_____	_____
18. Supplies	_____	_____
19. Accounts Receivable	_____	_____
20. Common Shares	_____	_____
21. Retained Earnings	_____	_____
22. Mortgage Payable	_____	_____
23. Notes Receivable	_____	_____
24. Notes Payable	_____	_____
25. Supplies Expense	_____	_____
26. Dividend Revenue	_____	_____
27. Unrealized Loss	_____	_____
28. Unrealized Gain—OCI	_____	_____
29. Utilities Expense	_____	_____
30. Accrued Liabilities	_____	_____

In essence, you are being asked to identify the normal balance of each of the accounts listed. The normal balance of an account is the side on which increases are recorded.

Solution to Exercise 3-1

APPROACH: For each account, determine the classification (for example: asset, liability, shareholders' equity, revenue, expense, gain, loss, dividend, or other comprehensive income or loss), and think about the corresponding debit and credit rules for the classification. Refer to **Illustration 3-1** and the related **Tips** for more information about debit and credit rules. In determining the classification of an account, look for key words, if any, in each account title. For example: (1) the words "Revenue" or "Income" are often associated with a revenue account, (2) the words "Expense" or "Incurred" are often associated with an expense account, (3) the words "Receivable" or "Prepaid Expense" refer to types of asset accounts, and (4) the words "Payable" or "Unearned Revenue" refer to types of liability accounts.

	Debit	Credit	Classification
1. Cash	✓		Asset
2. Sales Revenue		✓	Revenue
3. Sales Commission Expense	✓		Expense
4. Advertising Expense	✓		Expense
5. Salaries and Wages Payable		✓	Liability
6. Prepaid Insurance	✓		Asset
7. Property Tax Payable		✓	Liability
8. Property Tax Expense	✓		Expense
9. Dividends	✓		Dividend
10. Interest Income		✓	Revenue
11. Salaries and Wages Expense	✓		Expense
12. Rent Revenue		✓	Revenue
13. Unearned Rent Revenue		✓	Liability
14. Equipment	✓		Asset
15. Notes Payable		✓	Liability
16. Building	✓		Asset
17. Accounts Payable		✓	Liability
18. Supplies	✓		Asset
19. Accounts Receivable	✓		Asset
20. Common Shares		✓	Shareholders' Equity (Contributed Capital)
21. Retained Earnings		✓	Shareholders' Equity (Earned Capital)
22. Mortgage Payable		✓	Liability
23. Notes Receivable	✓		Asset
24. Notes Payable		✓	Liability
25. Supplies Expense	✓		Expense
26. Dividend Revenue		✓	Revenue
27. Unrealized Loss	✓		Loss
28. Unrealized Gain—OCI		✓	Other Comprehensive Income
29. Utilities Expense	✓		Expense
30. Accrued Liabilities		✓	Liability

EXERCISE 3-2

PURPOSE: This exercise will review how to record transactions in the general journal.

Transactions for the Motorboat Repair Shop Inc. for August 2017 are listed below.

1. August 1   Joan and Phillip began the business by each depositing $2,500 of personal funds in the business bank account in exchange for common shares of the newly formed corporation.

2. August 2   Joan rented space for the shop behind a strip mall and paid August rent of $800 out of the business bank account.

3. August 3   The shop purchased supplies for cash, $3,000.

4. August 4   The shop paid *Cupboard News*, a local newspaper, $300 for an ad appearing in the Sunday edition.

5. August 5   The shop repaired a boat for a customer. The customer paid cash of $1,300 for services rendered.

6. August 13   The shop purchased supplies for $900 by paying cash of $200 and charging the rest on account.

7. August 14   The shop repaired a boat for Zonie Kinkennon, a champion skier, for $3,600. Phillip collected $1,000 in cash and put the rest on Zonie's account.

8. August 24   The shop collected cash of $400 from Zonie Kinkennon.

9. August 28   The shop paid $200 to Mini Maid for cleaning services for the month of August.

10. August 31   The board of directors of the corporation declared a total dividend of $400 to its shareholders.

Instructions

(a) For each transaction, explain the impact on the accounts, and translate that impact into debit and credit terms.

(b) Journalize the transactions listed above. Include a brief explanation with each journal entry.

Solution to Exercise 3-2

(a)   1. Increase in Cash.   Debit Cash.
            Increase in Common Shares.   Credit Common Shares.

        2. Increase in Rent Expense.   Debit Rent Expense.
            Decrease in Cash.   Credit Cash.

3.	Increase in Supplies.	Debit Supplies.
	Decrease in Cash.	Credit Cash.
4.	Increase in Advertising Expense.	Debit Advertising Expense.
	Decrease in Cash.	Credit Cash.
5.	Increase in Cash.	Debit Cash.
	Increase in Service Revenue.	Credit Service Revenue.
6.	Increase in Supplies.	Debit Supplies.
	Decrease in Cash.	Credit Cash.
	Increase in Accounts Payable.	Credit Accounts Payable.
7.	Increase in Cash.	Debit Cash.
	Increase in Accounts Receivable.	Debit Accounts Receivable.
	Increase in Service Revenue.	Credit Service Revenue.
8.	Increase in Cash.	Debit Cash.
	Decrease in Accounts Receivable.	Credit Accounts Receivable.
9.	Increase in Office Expense.	Debit Office Expense.
	Decrease in Cash.	Credit Cash.
10.	Increase in Dividends.	Debit Dividends.
	Increase in Dividends Payable.	Credit Dividends Payable.

● In transaction 2, the $800 paid was for a rent expense not incurred yet as at August 2 (the date of the transaction). An alternative way of recording transaction 2 on August 2 would be to increase Prepaid Rent (Debit Prepaid Rent) and decrease Cash (Credit Cash). Recording the entry this way would require an adjusting entry at the end of August to increase Rent Expense (Debit Rent Expense) and decrease Prepaid Rent (Credit Prepaid Rent) for the $800 rent expense incurred/consumed as at the end of the month. Alternative ways of recording prepayments and accruals are reviewed in **Illustration 3-2** and **Illustration 3-3**.

● Referring to transactions 3 and 6, Supplies is an asset account in which supplies purchased may be recorded. An adjusting entry would be required prior to preparation of financial statements, to increase Supplies Expense (Debit Supplies Expense) and decrease Supplies (Credit Supplies) for the amount of supplies consumed as at the financial statement date.

APPROACH: For each transaction, think about the accounts involved, and apply debit and credit rules to translate the impact identified in part (a) into a journal entry. Refer to **Illustration 3-1** to review debit and credit rules for each type of account.

GENERAL JOURNAL

	Date	Account Titles and Explanations	Debit	Credit
(b)				
2017				
1.	Aug. 1	Cash	5,000	
		Common Shares		5,000
		(Issued common shares for cash)		
2.	2	Rent Expense	800	
		Cash		800
		(Paid August rent)		
3.	3	Supplies	3,000	
		Cash		3,000
		(Purchased supplies for cash)		
4.	4	Advertising Expense	300	
		Cash		300
		(Paid *Cupboard News* for advertising)		
5.	5	Cash	1,300	
		Service Revenue		1,300
		(Received cash for service fees earned)		
6.	13	Supplies	900	
		Cash		200
		Accounts Payable		700
		(Purchased supplies for cash and on credit)		
7.	14	Cash	1,000	
		Accounts Receivable	2,600	
		Service Revenue		3,600
		(Performed services for customer for cash and on credit)		
8.	24	Cash	400	
		Accounts Receivable		400
		(Received cash from Zonie Kinkennon on account)		
9.	28	Office Expense	200	
		Cash		200
		(Paid Mini Maid for cleaning services)		
10.	31	Dividends	400	
		Dividends Payable		400
		(Declared dividends to shareholders)		

EXERCISE 3-3

PURPOSE: This exercise will provide you with examples of adjusting entries for the accrual of expenses and revenues.

The following information relates to the Yuppy Clothing Sales Company at the end of 2017. The accounting period is the calendar year. This is the company's first year of operations.

1. Employees are paid every Friday for the five-day workweek ending on that day. Salaries and wages amount to $2,400 per week. The accounting period ends on a Thursday.
2. On October 1, 2017, Yuppy borrowed $8,000 cash by signing a note payable due in one year at 8% interest. Interest is due when the principal is paid.
3. A note for $2,000 was received from a customer in a sales transaction on May 1, 2017. The note matures in one year and bears 12% interest. Interest is due when the principal is due.
4. A portion of Yuppy's parking lot is used by executives of a neighbouring company. A person pays $6 per day for each day's use, and the parking fees are due by the fifth business day following the month of use. The fees for December 2017 amount to $1,260.

Instructions

Using the information given above, prepare the necessary adjusting entries at December 31, 2017.

Solution to Exercise 3-3

1. Salaries and Wages Expense 1,920

    Salaries and Wages Payable 1,920

    ($2,400 ÷ 5 = $480; $480 × 4 = $1,920 accrued salaries and wages)

2. Interest Expense 160

    Interest Payable 160

    ($8,000 × 8% × $\frac{3}{12}$ = $160 accrued interest expense)

3. Interest Receivable 160

    Interest Income 160

    ($2,000 × 12% × $\frac{8}{12}$ = $160 accrued interest revenue)

4. Accounts Receivable 1,260

    Service Revenue 1,260

EXPLANATION: Think about what is to be accomplished by each of the adjustments required in this exercise, and write down the definitions for accrued expense and accrued revenue. An **accrued expense** is an expense that has been incurred but not yet paid in cash or recorded. The "incurred" part results in an increase in Expense (debit) and the "not yet paid" part results in an increase in Payable (credit). An **accrued revenue** is a revenue that has been earned but not yet received in cash or recorded. The "earned" part results in an increase in Revenue (credit) and the "not yet received" part results in an increase in Receivable (debit).

EXERCISE 3-4

PURPOSE: This exercise will provide you with examples of adjusting entries for prepaid expenses (deferred expenses) and unearned revenues (deferred revenues).

The following information relates to the "I AM" Magazine Company at the end of 2017. The accounting period is the calendar year.

1. An insurance premium of $8,000 was paid on April 1, 2017, and was charged to Prepaid Insurance. The premium covers a 24-month period beginning April 1, 2017.
2. The Office Supplies account showed a balance of $3,500 at the beginning of 2017. Office supplies costing $12,000 were purchased during 2017 and debited to the asset account. Office supplies of $2,200 were on hand at December 31, 2017.
3. On July 1, 2017, cash of $48,000 was received from subscribers (customers) for a 36-month subscription period beginning on that date. The receipt was recorded by a debit to Cash and a credit to Unearned Subscription Revenue.
4. At the beginning of 2017, the Unearned Advertising Revenue account had a balance of $75,000. During 2017, collections from advertisers of $800,000 were recorded by credits to Advertising Revenue. At the end of 2017, revenues received but not earned are calculated to be $51,000.

Instructions

Using the information given above, prepare the necessary adjusting entries at December 31, 2017.

Solution to Exercise 3-4

1. Insurance Expense $\qquad$ 3,000
    $\qquad$ Prepaid Insurance $\qquad$ 3,000

    $\left(\$8,000 \times \dfrac{9}{24} = \$3,000 \text{ expired cost}\right)$

2. Supplies Expense   13,300
        Office Supplies   13,300

        ($3,500 + $12,000 − $2,200 = $13,300 supplies
        consumed)

3. Unearned Subscription Revenue   8,000
        Subscription Revenue   8,000

        ($48,000 × $\frac{6}{36}$ = $8,000 earned revenue)

4. Unearned Advertising Revenue   24,000
        Advertising Revenue   24,000

        ($75,000 − $51,000 = $24,000 earned revenue)

EXPLANATION: Think about what is to be accomplished by each of the adjustments required in this exercise, and write down the definitions for prepaid expense and unearned revenue. A **prepaid expense** is an expense that has been paid in cash and recorded as an asset before it is used or consumed. In a case where the prepayment was recorded as an increase in an asset account (such as Prepaid Expense or Supplies), the adjusting entry will record an increase in Expense (debit) and a decrease in the recorded Asset (credit) due to use or consumption of the asset (which was recorded at the time of prepayment). An **unearned revenue** is a revenue that has been received in cash and recorded as a liability before it is earned. In a case where the cash receipt was recorded as an increase in a liability account (such as Unearned Revenue), the adjusting entry will record a decrease in the recorded liability Unearned Revenue (debit) and an increase in Revenue (credit), to reflect the earned revenue portion of the liability recorded in the earlier cash receipt.

It is helpful to sketch a T account for each related asset or liability account. For each account, enter the amounts before adjustment, enter the desired ending balance, and notice how the required adjustment amount can be determined from the facts entered in the T account. For the above transactions, the T accounts would appear as follows:

1.

Prepaid Insurance			Insurance Expense		
24-month Premium	8,000	12/31 Adj. 3,000	12/31 Adj. 3,000		
Desired Ending Balance	5,000		Ending Balance 3,000		

2.

Office Supplies			Supplies Expense		
Beg. Bal.	3,500	12/31 Adj. 13,300	12/31 Adj. 13,300		
Acquisitions	12,000				

Illustration 3-2 5 5

Desired Ending Balance	2,200		Ending Balance	13,300	

3.

Subscription Revenue			Unearned Subscription Revenue		
	12/31 Adj.	8,000	12/31 Adj.	8,000	Cash Receipts	48,000
	Ending Balance	8,000			Desired Ending Balance	40,000

4.

Advertising Revenue			Unearned Advertising Revenue		
	Cash Receipts	800,000			Beg. Bal.	75,000
	12/31 Adj.	24,000	12/31 Adj.	24,000		
	Ending Balance	824,000			Desired Ending Balance	51,000

ILLUSTRATION 3-2

Summary of Adjustments and Related Adjusting Entries

Type of Adjustment	Accounts Affected	Reason for Adjustment	Account Balances before Adjustment	Adjusting Entry
1. Prepaid Expense	Asset and Expense	(a) Prepaid expense initially recorded in asset account has been consumed, or	Asset overstated, Expense understated	Dr. Expense Cr. Asset
		(b) Prepaid expense initially recorded in expense account has not been consumed.	Asset understated, Expense overstated	Dr. Asset Cr. Expense
2. Unearned Revenue	Liability and Revenue	(a) Unearned revenue initially recorded in liability account has been earned, or	Liability overstated, Revenue understated	Dr. Liability Cr. Revenue
		(b) Unearned revenue initially recorded in revenue account has not been earned.	Liability understated, Revenue overstated	Dr. Revenue Cr. Liability

Type of Adjustment	Accounts Affected	Reason for Adjustment	Account Balances before Adjustment	Adjusting Entry
3. Accrued Expense	Expense and Liability	Expense incurred has not been paid or recorded.	Expense understated, Liability understated	Dr. Expense Cr. Liability
4. Accrued Revenues	Asset and Revenue	Revenue earned has not been collected or recorded.	Asset understated, Revenue understated	Dr. Asset Cr. Revenue
5. Estimated Item	Asset and Expense	(a) A previously recorded long-lived asset has now been partially consumed, or	Asset overstated, Expense understated	Dr. Expense Cr. Contra Asset
		(b) An existing asset is not fully realizable.	Asset overstated, Expense understated	Dr. Expense Cr. Contra Asset

EXPLANATION:

1. When expenses are paid for before they are incurred, the payment may be recorded either by a debit to an asset account (prepaid expense) or by a debit to an expense account. At the end of the accounting period, the accounts are adjusted as needed. If the prepayment was initially recorded in a prepaid (asset) account, an adjusting entry transfers the consumed portion to an expense account. On the other hand, if the prepayment was initially recorded using an expense account, an adjusting entry is required only if a portion of the expense remains prepaid or unconsumed at the end of the accounting period (in which case the unconsumed portion is transferred to an asset account). (See **Illustration 3-3** for an example.)

2. When revenues are received before they are earned, the receipt may be recorded either by a credit to a liability account (unearned revenue) or by a credit to a revenue account. At the end of the accounting period, the accounts are adjusted as needed. If the collection was initially recorded as a credit to a liability account (unearned revenue), an adjusting entry transfers the earned portion to a revenue account. On the other hand, if the cash receipt was initially recorded in a revenue account, an adjusting entry is required only if a portion of the revenue remains unearned at the end of the accounting period (in which case the unearned portion is transferred to a liability account). (See **Illustration 3-3** for an example.)

3. Expenses are often incurred before they are paid or recorded. An expense incurred but not yet paid or recorded is called an **accrued expense**. If at the end of an accounting period an accrued expense has not been recorded (for example, if an expense has not been billed by the vendor yet), it must be recorded by way of an adjusting entry. A good example of an accrued expense is one that accrues with the passage of time (such as interest expense).

4. Revenues are often earned before they are collected or recorded. Revenue earned but not received or recorded is called an **accrued revenue**. If at the end of an accounting period an accrued revenue has not been recorded (for example, if revenue has been earned but not billed to the customer yet), it must be

Illustration 3-3 57

recorded by way of an adjusting entry. A good example of an accrued revenue is one that accrues with the passage of time (such as interest revenue).

5. The cost of most long-lived tangible assets is allocated to expense in a systematic and rational manner. The entry to record this allocation of cost due to consumption of the benefits yielded by the asset is a debit to Depreciation Expense and a credit to Accumulated Depreciation. The amortization of intangibles is treated in a similar manner. A reduction in the net realizable value of accounts receivable or inventories is recorded in an adjusting entry by a debit to expense and a credit to a contra asset account.

● Examine each type of adjustment explained above and notice the logic of the resulting entry. For example, an adjustment to recognize supplies used (when the supplies were recorded in an asset account upon purchase) should reduce assets and increase expenses.

● Keep in mind that for accrued items (accrued revenues and accrued expenses), the timing of the related cash flow **follows** the period in which the relevant revenue or expense is recognized. Conversely, with prepayment-type items (unearned revenues and prepaid expenses), the related cash flow **precedes** the period in which the relevant revenue or expense is recognized.

● For example, assume the accounting period is the calendar year. Consider an accrued expense such as accrued salaries and wages at the end of 2017. An adjusting entry will be recorded at the end of 2017, so the expense will be reported on the 2017 statement of income. The related cash payment to employees will take place in the following accounting period (2018, in this case). For another example, consider a prepaid expense such as the prepayment of rent in December 2017 for January 2018 occupancy. The cash payment occurs in December 2017. The expense is incurred and recognized in the following accounting period (January 2018).

ILLUSTRATION 3-3

Alternative Treatments of Prepaid Expenses and Unearned Revenues

When a company writes a cheque to pay for an item that affects expense in at least two different time periods (such as for an insurance premium or a licence or dues), the bookkeeper may record the payment in one of two ways: as a prepaid expense (asset) or as an expense. The first way is used most often in introductory accounting textbooks; the second is used most often in the real world. Regardless of the way the payment is recorded, an appropriate adjusting entry should be made at the end of the accounting period so that correct balances appear on the statement of income and the statement of financial position. In the example below, a $1,200 payment is made on April 1, 2017, for a 12-month insurance premium covering the time between April 1, 2017, and March 31, 2018. (Assume a calendar-year reporting period.) A comparison of the two possible approaches appears below.

Prepayment (Cash Paid) Initially Debited to Asset Account			OR	Prepayment (Cash Paid) Initially Debited to Expense Account		
4/1	Prepaid Insurance	1,200		4/1	Insurance Expense	1,200
	Cash		1,200		Cash		1,200
12/31	Insurance Expense	900		12/31	Prepaid Insurance	300
	Prepaid Insurance		900		Insurance Expense		300

After the entries are posted, the accounts appear as follows:

Prepaid Insurance					Prepaid Insurance		
4/1	1,200	12/31 Adj.	900	12/31 Adj.	300		
12/31 Bal.	300			12/31 Bal.	300		

Insurance Expense					Insurance Expense		
12/31 Adj.	900			4/1	1,200	12/31 Adj.	300
12/31 Bal.	900			12/31 Bal.	900		

Notice that regardless of the path, you end up at the same place—with a balance of $300 in Prepaid Insurance and a balance of $900 in Insurance Expense. The result is consistent with the objective of adjusting entries: to report balances in accordance with the accrual basis of accounting.

Reversing entries are never required, but some companies use them to make recording transactions easier in the next accounting period. Reversing entries are used only for some adjusting entries. For example, the 12/31 adjusting entry illustrated in the left column would **not** be reversed in a reversing entry since doing so would result in re-establishing an asset amount that the adjusting entry recorded as expired. The adjusting entry illustrated in the right column **can be** reversed since a reversing entry would record $300 of insurance expense in the new accounting period (2018), which is the period we expect the remaining $300 of premium to pertain to.

When a company receives cash from a customer in advance of earning the related revenue, the bookkeeper may record the receipt in one of two ways: as an unearned revenue (liability) or as an earned revenue. The first way is used most often in introductory accounting textbooks; the second is used most often in the real world. Regardless of the way the receipt is recorded, an appropriate adjusting entry should be made at the end of the accounting period so that correct balances appear on the statement of income and the statement of financial position. In the example below, $1,200 is received on May 1, 2017, for a 12-month magazine subscription covering the time between May 1, 2017, and April 30, 2018. (Assume a calendar-year reporting period.) A comparison of the two possible approaches appears below:

Unearned Revenue (Cash Received) Initially Credited to Liability Account		OR	Unearned Revenue (Cash Received) Initially Credited to Revenue Account	
5/1　Cash	1,200		5/1　Cash	1,200
Unearned Subscription Revenue	1,200		Subscription Revenue	1,200
12/31　Unearned Subscription Revenue	800		12/31　Subscription Revenue	400
Subscription Revenue	800		Unearned Subscription Revenue	400

After posting the entries, the accounts appear as follows:

Unearned Subscription Revenue			Unearned Subscription Revenue	
12/31 Adj.　800	5/1　1,200			12/31 Adj.　400
	12/31 Bal.　400			12/31 Bal.　400

Subscription Revenue			Subscription Revenue	
	12/31 Adj.　800		12/31 Adj.　400	5/1　1,200
	12/31 Bal.　800			12/31 Bal.　800

Notice that the balances in the accounts are the same regardless of the approach used—Unearned Subscription Revenue has a balance of $400, and Subscription Revenue has a balance of $800 at December 31, 2017.

A reversing entry would not be used with the approach illustrated in the left column; however, a reversing entry can be used with the approach illustrated in the right column.

EXERCISE 3-5

PURPOSE: This exercise will provide you with examples of adjusting entries for:

1. prepaid expenses when cash payments are recorded in an asset (permanent) account.
2. prepaid expenses when cash payments are recorded in an expense (temporary) account.

3. unearned revenues when cash receipts are recorded in a liability (permanent) account.

4. unearned revenues when cash receipts are recorded in a revenue (temporary) account.

Thus, this exercise reviews the alternative treatments of prepaid expenses and unearned revenues discussed in **Illustration 3-3**.

Each situation described below is **independent** of the others.

1. Office supplies are recorded in an asset account when acquired. There was $400 of office supplies on hand at the beginning of the period. Cash purchases of office supplies during the period amounted to $900. A count of office supplies at the end of the period shows $320 of office supplies on hand.

2. Office supplies are recorded in an expense account when acquired. There was $400 of office supplies on hand at the beginning of the period. Cash purchases of office supplies during the period amounted to $900. A count of office supplies at the end of the period shows $320 of office supplies on hand. No reversing entries are used.

3. Receipts from customers for magazine subscriptions are recorded as a liability when cash is collected in advance of magazine delivery. The beginning balance in the liability account was $6,700. During the period, $54,000 was received for subscriptions. At the end of the period, it was determined that the balance of the Unearned Subscription Revenue account should be $8,000.

4. Receipts from customers for magazine subscriptions are recorded as revenue when cash is collected in advance of magazine delivery. The beginning balance in the liability account was $6,700. During the period, $54,000 was received for subscriptions. At the end of the period, it was determined that the balance of the Unearned Subscription Revenue account should be $8,000. No reversing entries are used.

Instructions

For each of the **independent** situations above:

(a) Prepare the appropriate adjusting entry in general journal form.

(b) Indicate the amount of revenue or expense that will appear on the statement of income for the period.

(c) Indicate the balance of the applicable asset or liability account at the end of the period.

(d) Indicate the amount of cash received or paid during the period.

(e) Indicate the change in the applicable asset or liability account from the beginning of the period to the end of the period.

It would be helpful to draw T accounts for each situation. Enter the facts given for each account. Solve for the adjusting entry amount that would be necessary to "reconcile" the facts given.

Solution to Exercise 3-5

1. (a) Office Supplies Expense   980
           Office Supplies   980
   (b) Office Supplies Expense $980
   (c) Office Supplies $320
   (d) Cash paid $900
   (e) Decrease in Office Supplies $80

APPROACH:

Office Supplies			ENTRY NEEDED TO COMPLETE ACCOUNTS	Office Supplies Expense	
Beg. Bal.	400				
Acquisitions	900	(980) ← →		(980)	
Desired Ending Balance	320			Ending Balance	980

2. (a) Office Supplies Expense   80
           Office Supplies   80
   (b) Office Supplies Expense $980
   (c) Office Supplies $320
   (d) Cash paid $900
   (e) Decrease in Office Supplies $80

APPROACH:

Office Supplies			ENTRY NEEDED TO COMPLETE ACCOUNTS	Office Supplies Expense	
Beg. Bal.	400	(80) ← →		Acquisitions	900
Desired Ending Balance	320				(80)
				Ending Balance	980

Compare situation (1) with situation (2). Notice the facts are the same **except** for the account debited for acquisitions of office supplies. The adjusting entries are different, but the facts and financial statement effects of both situations are the same.

3. (a) Unearned Subscription Revenue   52,700
           Subscription Revenue   52,700

    (b) Subscription Revenue $52,700
    (c) Unearned Subscription Revenue $8,000
    (d) Cash received $54,000
    (e) Increase in Unearned Subscription Revenue $1,300

APPROACH:

Subscription Revenue		ENTRY NEEDED TO COMPLETE ACCOUNTS	Unearned Subscription Revenue		
	(52,700) ←	→ (52,700)	Beg. Bal.	6,700
			Receipts	54,000
Ending Balance	52,700		Desired Ending Bal.	8,000

4. (a) Subscription Revenue   1,300
           Unearned Subscription Revenue   1,300

    (b) Subscription Revenue $52,700
    (c) Unearned Subscription Revenue $8,000
    (d) Cash received $54,000
    (e) Increase in Unearned Subscription Revenue $1,300

APPROACH:

Unearned Subscription Revenue		ENTRY NEEDED TO COMPLETE ACCOUNTS	Subscription Revenue		
Beg. Bal.	6,700	(1,300) ← → (1,300)	Receipts	54,000
Desired Ending Bal.	8,000		Ending Balance	52,700

2. Assuming reversing entries **are** used.

    (a) Office Supplies   320
           Office Supplies Expense   320

    (b) Office Supplies Expense $980
    (c) Office Supplies $320
    (d) Cash paid $900
    (e) Decrease in Office Supplies $80

APPROACH:

Office Supplies Expense				Office Supplies	

<table>
<tr><td colspan="2">Office Supplies Expense</td><td></td><td></td><td colspan="2">Office Supplies</td></tr>
<tr><td>Reversing</td><td>400</td><td rowspan="2">ENTRY
NEEDED TO
COMPLETE
ACCOUNTS</td><td rowspan="2">(320)</td><td>Beg. Bal.</td><td>400</td></tr>
<tr><td>Acquisitions</td><td>900</td><td>(320)</td><td>Reversing</td><td>400</td></tr>
</table>

Office Supplies Expense
Reversing 400
Acquisitions 900 | (320)
Ending Bal. 980

ENTRY NEEDED TO COMPLETE ACCOUNTS

Office Supplies
Beg. Bal. 400 | (320) | Reversing 400
Desired Ending Bal. 320

4. Assuming reversing entries **are** used.

(a) Subscription Revenue 8,000
        Unearned Subscription Revenue 8,000

(b) Subscription Revenue $52,700

(c) Unearned Subscription Revenue $8,000

(d) Cash received $54,000

(e) Increase in Unearned Subscription Revenue $1,300

APPROACH:

Unearned Subscription Revenue
Reversing 6,700 | Beg. Bal. 6,700
                   (8,000)
                 Desired Ending Bal. 8,000

ENTRY NEEDED TO COMPLETE ACCOUNTS

Subscription Revenue
(8,000) | Reversing 6,700
          Receipts 54,000
Ending Balance 52,700

EXERCISE 3-6

PURPOSE: This exercise will illustrate the preparation of adjusting entries from an unadjusted trial balance and additional data.

The following list of accounts and their balances represents the unadjusted trial balance of Tami Corp. at December 31, 2017.

	Dr.	Cr.
Cash	$ 15,000	
Accounts receivable	122,500	
Allowance for doubtful accounts		$ 1,875
Inventory	162,500	
Prepaid insurance	7,350	
Prepaid rent	33,000	
Investment in Lamb Corp. bonds	45,000	
Land	25,000	

	Dr.	Cr.
Equipment	260,000	
Accumulated depreciation		45,000
Accounts payable		23,275
Bonds payable (net of $3,750 discount)		121,250
Common shares		250,000
Retained earnings (January 1, 2017)		201,650
Sales revenue		533,275
Rent revenue		25,500
Cost of goods sold	410,250	
Freight-out	22,500	
Salaries and wages expense	87,500	
Interest expense	9,000	
Miscellaneous expense	2,225	
	$1,201,825	$1,201,825

Additional information:

1. On March 31, 2017, Tami rented a warehouse for $2,750 per month, paid $33,000 in advance, and debited Prepaid Rent to record the payment.

2. On September 1, 2017, Tami received $25,500 rent from its lessee for a 12-month lease on a parking lot, beginning on that date. The receipt was recorded by a credit to Rent Revenue.

3. Tami estimates that 1% of the credit sales made during 2017 will result in accounts receivable that will ultimately become uncollectible. All sales are made on credit (on account).

4. Prepaid Insurance contains the $7,350 premium cost of a policy that is for a two-year term and was taken out on May 1, 2017.

5. On April 1, 2017, Tami issued 125, $1,000, 8% bonds, maturing on April 1, 2027, at 97% of par value. Interest payment dates are April 1 and October 1. The straight-line method is used to amortize any bond premium or discount. Amortization is recorded only at year end.

6. The regular rate of depreciation is 10% of acquisition cost per year. Acquisitions and retirements during a year are depreciated at half this rate. Assets costing $16,000 were retired during the year. On December 31, 2016, the balance of Plant and Equipment was $230,000.

7. On September 1, 2017, Tami purchased 45, $1,000, 10% Lamb Corp. bonds, at par. The bonds mature on August 31, 2019. Interest is to be received every August 31 and February 28.

Instructions

Prepare the year-end adjusting entries in general journal form using the information above. (Round amounts to the nearest dollar.)

Solution to Exercise 3-6

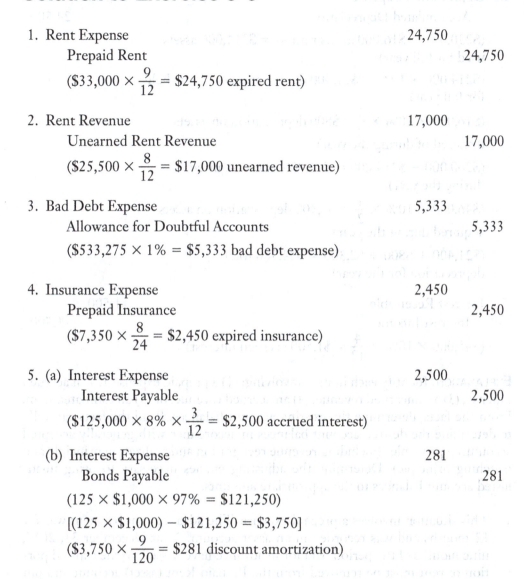

1. Rent Expense   24,750

    Prepaid Rent   24,750

$(\$33,000 \times \frac{9}{12} = \$24,750 \text{ expired rent})$

2. Rent Revenue   17,000

    Unearned Rent Revenue   17,000

$(\$25,500 \times \frac{8}{12} = \$17,000 \text{ unearned revenue})$

3. Bad Debt Expense   5,333

    Allowance for Doubtful Accounts   5,333

$(\$533,275 \times 1\% = \$5,333 \text{ bad debt expense})$

4. Insurance Expense   2,450

    Prepaid Insurance   2,450

$(\$7,350 \times \frac{8}{24} = \$2,450 \text{ expired insurance})$

5. (a) Interest Expense   2,500

        Interest Payable   2,500

$(\$125,000 \times 8\% \times \frac{3}{12} = \$2,500 \text{ accrued interest})$

  (b) Interest Expense   281

        Bonds Payable   281

$(125 \times \$1,000 \times 97\% = \$121,250)$

$[(125 \times \$1,000) - \$121,250 = \$3,750]$

$(\$3,750 \times \frac{9}{120} = \$281 \text{ discount amortization})$

- If the estimate for uncollectible accounts receivable is based on a percentage of net sales, the bad debt expense amount is a percentage of net sales, and any existing balance in the Allowance for Doubtful Accounts (Allowance) account will **not** affect the amount of the adjusting entry. If the estimate for uncollectible accounts receivable is based on an aging of accounts receivable or a percentage of accounts receivable existing at the statement of financial position date, the estimate for uncollectible accounts receivable is the desired ending balance for the Allowance account (meaning any existing balance in the Allowance account **will** affect the amount of the adjusting entry). This topic will be more thoroughly reviewed in Chapter 7.

- An interest rate is an annual rate unless otherwise indicated. For preparing an adjusting entry involving interest, calculate interest assuming the rate given is for a whole year, unless it is evident that this is not the case.

6. Depreciation Expense   24,500
       Accumulated Depreciation   24,500

    ($230,000 − $16,000 assets retired = $214,000 assets
    used for full year)

    ($214,000 × 10% = $21,400 depreciation on assets held
    for full year)

    ($16,000 × 10% × $\frac{1}{2}$= $800 depreciation on assets
    disposed of during the year)

    ($260,000 − $214,000 = $46,000 assets acquired
    during the year)

    ($46,000 × 10% × $\frac{1}{2}$ = $2,300 depreciation on assets
    acquired during the year)

    ($21,400 + $800 + $2,300 = $24,500 total
    depreciation for the year)

7. Interest Receivable   1,500
       Interest Income   1,500

    ($45,000 × 10% × $\frac{4}{12}$ = $1,500 accrued interest)

EXPLANATION: Identify each item as involving: (1) a prepaid expense, (2) an accrued expense, (3) an unearned revenue, (4) an accrued revenue, or (5) an estimated item. From the facts, determine the existing account balances. Read the facts carefully to determine the desired account balances in accordance with generally accepted accounting principles (including revenue recognition and realization principle and matching principle). Determine the adjusting entries necessary to bring unadjusted account balances to the appropriate amounts.

1. This situation involves a prepaid expense. The advance rent payment was for 12 months and was recorded in an asset account. As at December 31, 2017, nine months of the period paid for in advance have passed, so the expired portion of rent must be removed from the Prepaid Rent (asset) account and put into the Rent Expense account.

2. This situation involves unearned revenue. On September 1, 2017, cash was received and recorded as follows:

    Cash   25,500
       Rent Revenue   25,500

    At December 31, 2017, before adjustment, there is no Unearned Rent Revenue account on the trial balance; however, we need a balance of $17,000 ($25,500 × $\frac{8}{12}$) in Unearned Rent Revenue as at the statement of financial position date. Therefore, in an adjusting entry, Unearned Rent Revenue is credited for $17,000 and Rent Revenue is debited for the same amount. The debit to Rent Revenue in this exercise reduces the balance in the earned revenue account to the amount actually earned during 2017 ($8,500).

3. This situation involves an estimated expense. The bad debt expense for the year is estimated to be 1% of credit sales and all sales are on account. Thus, an expense of $5,333 (1% of $533,275 sales) is recorded and an Accounts Receivable contra account (Allowance for Doubtful Accounts) is credited for proper valuation of net Accounts Receivable. The $1,875 opening balance in the Allowance for Doubtful Accounts account does not affect the adjusting entry amount in this example, because the bad debt estimate is calculated based on a percentage of sales.

4. This item involves a prepaid expense. Before adjustment, the total cost of the insurance premium is in the Prepaid Insurance account. The expired portion of insurance cost must be taken out of Prepaid Insurance (with a credit to the account) and put into Insurance Expense (with a debit to the account).

5. This situation involves an accrued expense and amortization of a related bond discount. Interest must be accrued because the last interest payment date was October 1, meaning three months of interest (earned in October, November, and December) have not been recorded yet. The discount (3% of the par value) is to be amortized on a straight-line basis from the date of issuance (April 1, 2017) to the date of maturity (April 1, 2027), which is a 10-year period.

6. Of the $260,000 ending balance in Equipment, $230,000 represents items held during the whole year. There were retirements of $16,000 during the year so we can calculate that acquisitions amounted to $46,000. The company policy requires that acquisitions and retirements be depreciated for only one half of a year in years of acquisition and retirement; that is, at a 5% rate. Depreciating assets at 10% of acquisition cost per year is equivalent to depreciating assets over a 10-year period using the straight-line method.

7. This situation involves an accrued revenue. Interest must be accrued for the period since the last interest payment date, which was four months ago. The 10% stated interest rate is expressed on an annual basis.

EXERCISE 3-7

PURPOSE: This exercise will review the preparation of closing entries.

The adjusted trial balance for Apex Corporation at December 31, 2017, appears as follows:

APEX CORPORATION
Adjusted Trial Balance
December 31, 2017

	Debit	Credit
Cash	$2,000	
Accounts receivable	2,200	
Supplies	2,100	
Accounts payable		$ 700
Accrued liabilities		80

	Debit	Credit
Common shares		3,000
Retained earnings (January 1, 2017)		1,300
Dividends	600	
Service revenue		4,900
Rent expense	800	
Advertising expense	300	
Office expense	200	
Utilities expense	80	
Unrealized gain or loss—OCI	1,700	
	$9,980	$9,980

Instructions

(a) Prepare the appropriate closing entries at December 31, 2017.

(b) Explain why closing entries are necessary.

Solution to Exercise 3-7

(a)

Service Revenue	4,900	
Income Summary		4,900

     (To close the revenue account to Income Summary)

Income Summary	1,380	
Rent Expense		800
Advertising Expense		300
Office Expense		200
Utilities Expense		80

     (To close expense accounts to Income Summary)

Income Summary	3,520	
Retained Earnings		3,520

     (To close Income Summary to Retained Earnings)

     ($4,900 total revenues − $1,380 total expenses = $3,520 credit balance in Income Summary before closing)

Accumulated Other Comprehensive Income	1,700	
Unrealized Gain or Loss—OCI		1,700

     (To close Unrealized Gain or Loss—Other Comprehensive Income to Accumulated Other Comprehensive Income)

Retained Earnings	600	
Dividends		600

     (To close Dividends to Retained Earnings)

(b) Closing entries are necessary because they prepare the temporary (nominal) accounts for the recording of transactions in the next accounting period. Closing entries produce a zero balance in each of the temporary accounts so that in the next accounting period, they can be used to accumulate data only pertaining to that period. Because of closing entries, the revenues of 2017 are not mixed with the revenues of the prior period (2016). Closing entries are also necessary in order to update the Retained Earnings and Accumulated Other Comprehensive Income accounts. Closing entries formally recognize in the ledger the transfer of net income (or loss) and dividends declared to Retained Earnings, and the transfer of other comprehensive income (or loss) to Accumulated Other Comprehensive Income.

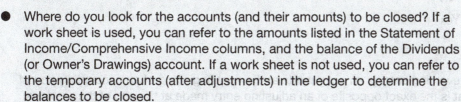

● The Income Summary account is used only in the closing process. Before it is closed, the balance in this account must equal the net income or net loss figure for the period.

● Where do you look for the accounts (and their amounts) to be closed? If a work sheet is used, you can refer to the amounts listed in the Statement of Income/Comprehensive Income columns, and the balance of the Dividends (or Owner's Drawings) account. If a work sheet is not used, you can refer to the temporary accounts (after adjustments) in the ledger to determine the balances to be closed.

EXERCISE 3-8

PURPOSE: This exercise will provide practice in determining which adjusting entries may be reversed.

Instructions

The following entries are adjusting entries prepared by the Bent Tree Company at December 31, 2017 (end of the accounting period). The company has a policy of using reversing entries when appropriate. For each adjusting entry below, indicate if reversing it at the beginning of 2018 would be appropriate. Indicate your answer by circling "yes" or "no."

Yes No (a) Prepaid Advertising   4,500
              Advertising Expense   4,500
Yes No (b) Interest Expense   800
              Bonds Payable   800
Yes No (c) Interest Receivable   690
              Interest Income   690
Yes No (d) Unearned Rent Revenue   900
              Rental Revenue   900

Yes	No	(e) Insurance Expense	1,600	
		Prepaid Insurance		1,600
Yes	No	(f) Salaries and Wages Expense	1,100	
		Salaries and Wages Payable		1,100

Solution to Exercise 3-8

(a) Yes

(b) No

(c) Yes

(d) No

(e) No

(f) Yes

A reversing entry is an entry made at the very beginning of an accounting period that is the exact opposite of an adjusting entry made at the end of the previous accounting period. The recording of reversing entries is an **optional** step in the accounting cycle. The **purpose** of a reversing entry is to simplify the recording of transactions in the next accounting period. The use of reversing entries does not change the amounts reported in financial statements.

EXPLANATION: Write down what the related reversing entry would look like and then (1) think about the effects the reversing entry would have on the account balances in the next accounting period, and (2) think about whether those effects are appropriate or not. It is appropriate to reverse an adjusting entry involving a prepaid expense or unearned revenue **only if** the adjusting entry increases (rather than decreases) a statement of financial position account. It is **always** appropriate to reverse an adjusting entry involving an accrual. It is **never** appropriate to reverse an adjusting entry for depreciation or accrual of bad debts.

(a) An adjusting entry for a prepaid expense can be reversed if the adjusting entry increases an asset or liability account. This adjusting entry increases Prepaid Advertising (an asset account).

(b) Never reverse an adjustment for amortization of a discount or premium.

(c) An accrual-type adjustment can always be reversed.

(d) Reversal of this entry would put back into the Unearned Rent Revenue account the amount that the adjusting entry indicated has been earned.

(e) An adjusting entry for a prepaid expense can be reversed only if it increases a statement of financial position account. This adjustment decreases an asset account (Prepaid Insurance).

Illustration 3-4   71

(f) An accrual-type adjustment can always be reversed. You can tell the adjusting entry is for an accrued expense because the debit is to an expense account and the credit is to a payable account.

EXERCISE 3-9

PURPOSE: This exercise will give you practice in identifying adjusting entries that may be reversed.

Instructions

Refer to **Exercise 3-6** and the **Solution to Exercise 3-6**. Indicate the adjusting entries that can be reversed.

Solution to Exercise 3-9

EXPLANATION: Review the adjusting entries in the Solution to **Exercise 3-6** and apply the guidelines discussed in **Exercise 3-8** for determining whether a reversing entry would be appropriate. Accrual-type adjusting entries can always be reversed. Therefore, items 5a and 7 can be reversed. Estimated items, such as depreciation of plant assets and recording of bad debts, should never be reversed. As well, amortization of discounts and premiums on receivables and payables should never be reversed. Therefore, items 3, 6, and 5b should **not** be reversed. Adjusting entries involving deferrals can be reversed **only if** the original cash entry involved a temporary account (revenue or expense account) rather than a prepaid or unearned account (a permanent account), and the adjustment **increases** a pre-paid expense or unearned revenue account. Therefore, item 2 **can be** reversed but items 1 and 4 should **not** be reversed.

ILLUSTRATION 3-4

Reversing Entries for Accrued Expenses Illustrated and Comparison of System Using Reversing Entries with System Where No Reversing Entries Are Used

An entity can choose to use or not use reversing entries. The advantage of using reversing entries is that the reversing entry (reversal) of an adjustment for accrued expense (or accrued revenue) facilitates the recording of the subsequent payment (or receipt) of cash. In the next accounting period, the payment (or receipt) can then be recorded to a temporary account rather than a permanent account.

When an entity chooses **not** to use a reversing entry for an accrued expense (or accrued revenue) at the end of year 1 and the entity wishes to record the subsequent payment (or receipt) of cash in year 2 to a temporary account rather than a permanent account, the adjustment process at the end of year 2 can accommodate the situation.

Assume the following data apply to GuardDog Corp.

1. The company began operations in 2017.
2. During 2017, interest of $80,000 was paid.
3. At the end of 2017, accrued interest on a note payable amounted to $5,500.
4. During 2018, interest of $50,000 was paid.
5. At the end of 2018, accrued interest amounted to $8,200.
6. During 2019, interest of $65,000 was paid.
7. At the end of 2019, accrued interest amounted to $3,000.

There are three paths the information could take through the accounting records. Regardless of the path taken, the true amount of expense incurred should be reported on the statement of income each year, and the amount incurred but not paid should be reported on the statement of financial position at the end of each period. Examine each path below.

	Reversing entries	Payment entries recorded to
PATH A	Yes	temporary account
PATH B	No	permanent and temporary account
PATH C	No	temporary account

The effects that the above paths have on the accounts are illustrated on the following pages. The description of the flow of data through the accounting records is organized into the following sections:

I. The journal entries in 2017–2019.

II. The postings of journal entries to T accounts in 2017–2019.

III. The account balances resulting at the end of 2017–2019.

I. The journal entries in 2017–2019:

		PATH A			PATH B			PATH C		
		Reversing entries are **made**. Payment entries are charged to a **temporary** account (Interest Expense).			Reversing entries are **not** made. Payment entries are allocated to a **permanent account** (Interest Payable) and to a **temporary** account (Interest Expense).			Reversing entries are **not** made. Payment entries are charged to a **temporary** account (Interest Expense).		
Date	EVENT	Account	Debit	Credit	Account	Debit	Credit	Account	Debit	Credit
During 2017	(1) Paid $80,000 interest	Interest Expense / Cash	80,000	80,000	Interest Expense / Cash	80,000	80,000	Interest Expense / Cash	80,000	80,000
12/31/17	(2) Adjusting entry—$5,500 accrued interest	Interest Expense / Interest Payable	5,500	5,500	Interest Expense / Interest Payable	5,500	5,500	Interest Expense / Interest Payable	5,500	5,500
12/31/17	(3) Closing entry	Income Summary / Interest Expense	85,500	85,500	Income Summary / Interest Expense	85,500	85,500	Income Summary / Interest Expense	85,500	85,500
1/1/18	(4) Reversing entry	Interest Payable / Interest Expense	5,500	5,500	NONE			NONE		
During 2018	(5) Paid $50,000 interest	Interest Expense / Cash	50,000	50,000	Interest Payable / Interest Expense / Cash	5,500 / 44,500	50,000	Interest Expense / Cash	50,000	50,000
12/31/18	(6) Adjusting entry—$8,200 accrued interest	Interest Expense / Interest Payable	8,200	8,200	Interest Expense / Interest Payable	8,200	8,200	Interest Expense / Interest Payable	2,700	2,700
12/31/18	(7) Closing entry	Income Summary / Interest Expense	52,700	52,700	Income Summary / Interest Expense	52,700	52,700	Income Summary / Interest Expense	52,700	52,700
1/1/19	(8) Reversing entry	Interest Payable / Interest Expense	8,200	8,200	NONE			NONE		
During 2019	(9) Paid $65,000 interest	Interest Expense / Cash	65,000	65,000	Interest Payable / Interest Expense / Cash	8,200 / 56,800	65,000	Interest Expense / Cash	65,000	65,000
12/31/19	(10) Adjusting entry—$3,000 accrued interest	Interest Expense / Interest Payable	3,000	3,000	Interest Expense / Interest Payable	3,000	3,000	Interest Expense / Interest Payable	5,200	5,200
12/31/19	(11) Closing entry	Income Summary / Interest Expense	59,800	59,800	Income Summary / Interest Expense	59,800	59,800	Income Summary / Interest Expense	59,800	59,800

II. The postings of journal entries to T accounts in 2017–2019:

	PATH A	PATH B	PATH C
	Reversing entries **are** made.	Reversing entries are **not** made.	Reversing entries are **not** made.
	Payment entries are charged to **temporary** account (Interest Expense).	Payment entries are allocated to a **permanent** account (Interest Payable) **and** to a **temporary** account (Interest Expense).	Payment entries are charged to a **temporary** account (Interest Expense).

	PATH A Interest Expense	PATH A Interest Payable	PATH B Interest Expense	PATH B Interest Payable	PATH C Interest Expense	PATH C Interest Payable
(1) During 2017	80,000		80,000		80,000	
(2) 12/31/17 Adj.	5,500	5,500	5,500	5,500	5,500	5,500
Balances 12/31/17	85,500	5,500	85,500	5,500	85,500	5,500
(3) 12/31/17 Closing	85,500		85,500		85,500	
(4) 1/1/18 Reversing	5,500	5,500				
(5) During 2018	50,000		44,500	5,500	50,000	
(6) 12/31/18 Adj.	8,200	8,200	8,200	8,200	2,700	2,700
Balances 12/31/18	52,700	8,200	52,700	8,200	52,700	8,200
(7) 12/31/18 Closing	52,700		52,700		52,700	
(8) 1/1/19 Reversing	8,200	8,200				
(9) During 2019	65,000		56,800	8,200	65,000	
(10) 12/31/19 Adj.	3,000	3,000	3,000	3,000	5,200	5,200
Balances 12/31/19	59,800	3,000	59,800	3,000	59,800	3,000
(11) 12/31/19 Closing	59,800		59,800		59,800	

III. The account balances resulting at the end of 2017–2019:

AMOUNT OF ITEM	PATH A	PATH B	PATH C
Interest Expense on Statement of Income for year ended Dec. 31, 2017	$85,500	$85,500	$85,500
Interest Payable on Statement of Financial Position at December 31, 2017	$5,500	$5,500	$5,500
Interest Paid on Statement of Cash Flows for year ended Dec. 31, 2017	$80,000	$80,000	$80,000
Interest Expense on Statement of Income for year ended Dec. 31, 2018	$52,700	$52,700	$52,700
Interest Payable on Statement of Financial Position at Dec. 31, 2018	$8,200	$8,200	$8,200
Interest Paid on Statement of Cash Flows for year ended Dec. 31, 2018	$50,000	$50,000	$50,000
Interest Expense on Statement of Income for year ended Dec. 31, 2019	$59,800	$59,800	$59,800
Interest Payable on Statement of Financial Position at Dec. 31, 2019	$3,000	$3,000	$3,000
Interest Paid on Statement of Cash Flows for year ended Dec. 31, 2019	$65,000	$65,000	$65,000

EXERCISE 3-10

PURPOSE: This exercise will give you practice in calculating discounted cash flows using both the traditional and expected cash flow approaches. It will also help you evaluate which approach is most appropriate in a given set of circumstances.

General Inc. owns 20% of the common shares of Bronson Ltd. The other 80% are owned by the Bronson family. General acquired the shares 11 years ago through a financing transaction. Each year, General has received a dividend from Bronson. Bronson has been in business for 75 years and continues to have strong operations and cash flows. General must determine the fair value of this investment at its year end. Since there is no market on which the shares are traded, General must use a discounted cash flow model to determine fair value.

General management intends to hold the shares for six more years, at which time they will sell the shares to the Bronson family under an existing agreement for $800,000. There is no uncertainty in this amount. Management expects to receive dividends of $50,000 for each of the six years, although there is a 20% chance that dividends could be $30,000 each year. The risk-free rate is 4% and the risk-adjusted rate is 7%.

Instructions

(a) Calculate the fair value of the investment in Bronson using the traditional approach.

(b) Calculate the fair value of the investment in Bronson using the expected cash flow approach.

(c) In this case, which discounted cash flow model is best and why?

Solution to Exercise 3-10

(a) Annual expected cash   = $50,000 × 4.76654   = $238,327

    Sale proceeds   = $800,000 × 0.66634   = $533,072

    Fair value of investment   = $238,327 + $533,072   = $771,399

(b) Probability weighted annual cash flow is

    ($50,000 × 80%) + ($30,000 × 20%)   = $46,000

    Annual expected cash   = $46,000 × 5.24214   = $241,138

    Sale proceeds   = $800,000 × 0.79031   = $632,248

    Fair value of investment   = $241,138 + $632,248   = $873,386

(c) The expected cash flow approach is best since the cash flows are uncertain.

EXPLANATION:

(a) Under the traditional approach, cash flows are discounted using the risk-adjusted rate, so we use 7%.

Using a financial calculator:

I	7%
N	6
PMT	$(50,000)
FV	$(800,000)
Type	0

PV = $771,401

(b) Under the expected cash flow approach, uncertain cash flows are discounted using the risk-free rate, so we use 4%.

Using a financial calculator:

I	4%
N	6
PMT	$(46,000)
FV	$(800,000)
Type	0

PV = $873,390

EXERCISE 3-11

PURPOSE: This exercise will give you practice in determining the fair value of an asset under IFRS 13.

Embury Company owns specialized equipment that was purchased as part of the acquisition of Rowan Inc. The equipment has a book value of $1,700,000, but according to IFRS, it is assessed for impairment on an annual basis. To perform this impairment test, Embury must estimate the fair value of the equipment. It has developed the following cash flow estimates related to the equipment based on internal information. Each cash flow estimate reflects Embury's estimate of annual cash flows over the next eight years. The equipment is assumed to have no residual value after the eight years. (Assume the cash flows occur at the end of each year.)

Year	Cash Flow Estimate
1–3	$200,000
4–6	280,000
7–8	430,000

Embury determines, using their own assumptions, that the appropriate discount rate for this estimation is 7%.

Instructions

(a) There are three levels of inputs under IFRS 13. What types of inputs are used by Embury?

(b) To the nearest dollar, what is the estimated fair value of the equipment?

Solution to Exercise 3-11

(a) Embury used unobservable internal company data in the valuation of their IFRS 13 valuation of specialized equipment. Unobservable inputs such as these are considered Level 3 inputs, which are the most subjective of all three in the hierarchy. As such, this would require greater disclosures to give financial statement users more information about the related uncertainty.

(b) Present value

Cash flow 1–3	=	$200,000 × 2.62432	=	$ 524,864
Cash flow 4–6	=	$280,000 × 2.62432 × 0.81630	=	$ 599,825
Cash flow 7–8	=	$430,000 × 1.80802 × 0.66634	=	$ 518,045
Fair value of equipment				$1,642,734

EXPLANATION:

(a) Cash flows are discounted using the rate of 7%. The present value of the cash flow for years 1 to 3 is the present value of an annuity received for three periods. The present value of the cash flow for years 4 to 5 is the present value of an annuity received for three periods, and this lump is then discounted back three more years. The present value of the cash flow for years 7 to 8 is the present value of an annuity received for two periods, and this lump is then discounted back six more years. The discount rate used for all parts is 7%.

Using a financial calculator:

	Year 1–3	Year 4–6	Year 7–8
I	7%	7%	7%
N	3	3	2
PMT	$(200,000)	$(280,000)	$(430,000)
PV to beginning of annuity	$ 524,863	$ 734,808	$ 777,448
I		7%	7%
N		3	6
PMT			
FV		$ 734,808	$ 777,448
PV	$ 524,863	$ 599,823	$ 518,046

Total PV = $1,642,732

EXERCISE 3-12

PURPOSE: This exercise will give you practice using present value concepts to calculate the value of a bond liability at the time the bond is issued (selling price).

SmartCycle Inc. manufactures cycling equipment. Recently, the company's president has requested construction of a new plant to meet the increasing demand for the company's bikes. After a careful evaluation of the request, the board of directors has decided to raise funds for the plant by issuing $3 million of 9% term corporate bonds on March 1, 2017, due on March 1, 2027, with interest payable each March 1 and September 1. At the time of issuance, the market rate for similar financial instruments is 8%.

Instructions

As SmartCycle's controller, determine the selling price of the bonds:

(a) using a time diagram and PV tables.
(b) using a financial calculator.
(c) using spreadsheet software (MS-Excel).

Solution to Exercise 3-12

(a) Time diagram and PV tables

Time diagram: SmartCycle Inc.

PV = ?   I = 8% ÷ 2 = 4%
PV-OA = ?

<table>
<tr><td></td><td></td><td></td><td></td><td></td><td></td><td>Principal
$3,000,000
Interest</td></tr>
<tr><td>$135,000</td><td>$135,000</td><td>$135,000</td><td>$135,000</td><td>$135,000</td><td>$135,000</td></tr>
<tr><td>0</td><td>1</td><td>2</td><td>3 ...... 18</td><td>19</td><td>20</td></tr>
</table>

n = 20

Formula for the interest payments:

$$
\begin{aligned}
\text{PV-OA} &= R(\text{PVF-OA}n,i) \\
&= \$135,000 \ (\text{PVF-OA}20,4\%) \\
&= \$135,000 \ (13.59033) \\
&= \$1,834,695
\end{aligned}
$$

Formula for the principal:

$$
\begin{aligned}
\text{PV} &= FV(\text{PVF}n,i) \\
&= \$3,000,000 \ (\text{PVF}20,4\%) \\
&= \$3,000,000 \ (0.45639) \\
&= \$1,369,170
\end{aligned}
$$

The selling price of the bonds is $1,834,695 + $1,369,170 = $3,203,865

(b) Using a financial calculator:

PV	?	Yields $ 3,203,854.90
I	4%	
N	20	
PMT	$ (135,000)	
FV	$(3,000,000)	
Type	0	

(c) Using spreadsheet software (MS-Excel)

$$
\begin{aligned}
\text{Formula:} &= \text{PV(rate,nper,pmt,fv,type)} \\
&= \text{PV(4\%,20,-135000,-3000000,0)} \\
&= \$3,203,854.90
\end{aligned}
$$

ANALYSIS OF MULTIPLE-CHOICE QUESTIONS

Question

1. Which of the following is a temporary account?
    a. Prepaid Insurance
    c. Insurance Expense
    b. Unearned Revenue
    d. Interest Receivable

EXPLANATION: Before looking at the answer selections, think about the meaning of the term "temporary account." A temporary account is an account that is closed at the end of an accounting period (for example, revenue and expense accounts). A permanent account is never closed (for example, asset and liability accounts). Prepaid Insurance and Interest Receivable are asset accounts. Unearned Revenue is a liability account. Insurance Expense is a temporary account. (Solution = c.)

Question

2. Which of the following errors will cause an imbalance in the trial balance?
    a. Omission of a transaction in the journal
    b. Posting an entire journal entry twice to the ledger
    c. Posting a credit of $720 to Accounts Payable as a credit of $720 to Accounts Receivable
    d. Listing the balance of an account with a debit balance in the credit column of the trial balance

EXPLANATION: Analyze each error (answer selection) and look for the selection that will cause an imbalance (selection "d"). Selections "a," "b," and "c" do not cause an imbalance in the trial balance. (Solution = d.)

Question

3. Which of the following statements is associated with the accrual basis of accounting?
    a. The timing of cash receipts and disbursements is emphasized.
    b. A minimum amount of record keeping is required.
    c. This method is used less frequently by businesses than the cash method of accounting.
    d. Revenues are recognized in the period they are earned, regardless of the time period when the cash is received.

EXPLANATION: Write down the key words and phrases in the definition of accrual accounting. Compare each answer selection with your definition and choose the one that best matches. Using the **accrual basis of accounting**, events that change a company's financial statements are recorded in the periods in which the events occur. Thus, revenues are recognized in the period in which they are earned, and expenses are recognized in the period in which they are incurred, regardless of when the related cash is received or paid. Answer selections "a" and "b" refer to the cash basis of accounting. (Solution = d.)

Question

4. An accrued expense is an expense that:
    a. has been incurred but has not been paid.
    b. has been paid but has not been incurred.
    c. has been incurred for which payment is to be made in instalments.
    d. will never be paid.

EXPLANATION: Write down a definition for **accrued expense**. Compare each answer selection with your definition and choose the best match. Expenses may be paid for in the same period in which they are incurred, or they may be paid for in the period before or after the period in which they are incurred. An **accrued expense** refers to an expense that has been incurred but has not yet been paid. It will be paid for in a period subsequent to the period in which it was incurred. (Solution = a.)

Question

5. In reviewing some adjusting entries, you observe an entry that contains a debit to Prepaid Insurance and a credit to Insurance Expense. The purpose of this journal entry is to record a(n):
    a. accrued expense.　　　　　c. expired cost.
    b. prepaid expense.　　　　　d. prepaid revenue.

EXPLANATION: Write down the entry so you can see what the entry does. Notice the entry records a prepaid expense (an asset). Then examine each answer selection one at a time. A debit to Prepaid Insurance records an increase in a prepaid expense. A prepaid expense is an expense that has been paid but has not been incurred. An accrued expense is an expense that has been incurred but not yet paid. An expired cost is an expense or a loss. "Prepaid revenue" is a bad term for "unearned revenue" (or deferred revenue). (Solution = b.)

Question

6. An adjusting entry to record an accrued expense involves a debit to a(n):
    a. expense account and a credit to a prepaid account.
    b. expense account and a credit to Cash.
    c. expense account and a credit to a liability account.
    d. liability account and a credit to an expense account.

EXPLANATION: Write down a definition for **accrued expense** and the types of accounts involved in an adjusting entry to accrue an expense. Find the answer selection that describes your entry.

Dr.   Expense
        Cr.   Liability

Notice the logic of the entry. An **accrued expense** is an expense that has been incurred but not yet paid. Thus, you record the incurrence of the expense by increasing an expense account and you record the "not yet paid" aspect by increasing a liability account. (Solution = c.)

Question

7. The failure to record an adjusting entry to accrue an expense will result in an:
    a.   understatement of expenses and an understatement of liabilities.
    b.   understatement of expenses and an overstatement of liabilities.
    c.   understatement of expenses and an overstatement of assets.
    d.   overstatement of expenses and an understatement of assets.

EXPLANATION: Write down the adjusting entry to record an accrued expense. Analyze the effects of the entry. This will help you to determine the effects of failure to record that entry.

Dr.   Expense   xx
        Cr.   Liability   xx

This entry increases expenses and liabilities. Therefore, failure to make this entry would result in an understatement of expenses and an understatement of liabilities. (Solution = a.)

Question

8. Which of the following properly describes a prepayment for which an adjusting entry will typically have to be made at a future date?
    a.   Cash is received after revenue is earned.
    b.   Cash is received before revenue is earned.
    c.   Cash is paid after an expense is incurred.
    d.   Cash is paid in the same time period that an expense is incurred.

EXPLANATION: Think about the nature of prepayments and the timing of revenue or expense recognition relative to cash flow. **Prepayments** result from cash flows that occur **before** expense or revenue recognition. That is, cash is paid for expenses before they are used or consumed or cash is received for revenues before they are earned. The portion of an expense to be used or consumed in a future period is deferred by reporting a prepaid expense (asset). The portion of a revenue to be earned in a future period is deferred by reporting unearned revenue (liability) on the statement of financial position.

Accruals result from cash flows that occur **after** expense or revenue recognition. That is, cash is to be paid or received in a future period for an expense incurred or a revenue earned in the current period. Items "a" and "c" above are accrual situations. Item "d" is neither an accrual nor a deferral situation. (Solution = b.)

Question

9. An adjusting entry to allocate a previously recorded asset to expense involves a debit to an:

    a. asset account and a credit to Cash.

    b. expense account and a credit to Cash.

    c. expense account and a credit to an asset account.

    d. asset account and a credit to an expense account.

EXPLANATION: Write down the sketch of an adjusting entry to transfer an asset to expense. Compare each answer selection with your entry and choose the one that matches.

> Dr.   Expense
>   Cr.   Asset   (Solution = c.)

Question

10. Which of the following adjusting entries will cause an increase in revenues and a decrease in liabilities?

    a. Entry to record an accrued expense

    b. Entry to record an accrued revenue

    c. Entry to record the consumed portion of an expense paid in advance and initially recorded as an asset

    d. Entry to record a portion of revenue received in a prior period (initially recorded as unearned revenue) as earned in the current period

EXPLANATION: For each answer selection, write down the sketch of the adjusting entry described and the effects of each half of the entry. Compare the stem of the question with your analyses to determine the correct answer.

The entry to record an accrued expense is:

> Dr.   Expense
>   Cr.   Liability

The effects of the entry are to increase expenses and to increase liabilities. The entry to record an accrued revenue is:

> Dr.   Asset
>   Cr.   Revenue

The effects of the entry are to increase assets and to increase revenues.

The entry to record the consumed portion of a prepaid expense initially recorded as an asset is:

Dr.	Expense	
	Cr.	Asset

The effects of the entry are to increase expenses and to decrease assets.

The entry to record the earned portion of unearned revenue initially recorded as a liability is:

Dr.	Liability	
	Cr.	Revenue

The effects of the entry are to decrease liabilities and to increase revenues. (Solution = d.)

Question

11. The Office Supplies account had a balance at the beginning of year 3 of $1,600. Payments for acquisitions of office supplies during year 3 amounted to $10,000 and were recorded by a debit to the asset account. A physical count at the end of year 3 revealed that office supplies costing $1,900 were on hand. The required adjusting entry at the end of year 3 will include a debit to:

   a.   Office Supplies Expense for $300.
   b.   Office Supplies for $300.
   c.   Office Supplies Expense for $9,700.
   d.   Office Supplies for $1,900.

   EXPLANATION: Draw T accounts. Enter the data given and solve for the adjusting entry. Compare each alternative answer with the adjusting entry you have sketched in the accounts. (Solution = c.)

Question

12. The Office Supplies account had a balance at the beginning of year 3 of $1,600. Payments for acquisitions of office supplies during year 3 amounted to $10,000 and were recorded as a debit to the expense account. A physical count

at the end of year 3 revealed that office supplies costing $1,900 were on hand. Reversing entries are used by this company. The required adjusting entry at the end of year 3 will include a debit to:

a. Office Supplies Expense for $300.

b. Office Supplies for $300.

c. Office Supplies Expense for $9,700.

d. Office Supplies for $1,900.

EXPLANATION: Draw T accounts. Enter the data given and solve for the adjusting entry. Compare each alternative answer with the adjusting entry you have sketched in the accounts. (Solution = d.)

Office Supplies Expense			ENTRY NEEDED TO COMPLETE ACCOUNTS	Office Supplies		
Reversing	1,600			Beg. Bal.	1,600	
Acquisitions	10,000	(1,900) ← →			(1,900)	Reversing 1,600
				Desired		
Ending Bal.	9,700			Ending Bal.	1,900	

Question

13. The Office Supplies account had a balance at the beginning of year 3 of $1,600. Payments for purchases of office supplies during year 3 amounted to $10,000 and were recorded by a debit to an expense account. A physical count at the end of year 3 revealed that office supplies costing $1,900 were on hand. Reversing entries are **not used** by this company. The required adjusting entry at the end of year 3 will include a debit to:

a. Office Supplies Expense for $300.

b. Office Supplies for $300.

c. Office Supplies Expense for $9,700.

d. Office Supplies for $1,900.

e. none of the above.

EXPLANATION: Draw T accounts. Enter the data given and solve for the adjusting entry. Compare each alternative answer with the adjusting entry you have sketched in the accounts. (Solution = b.)

Office Supplies Expense			ENTRY NEEDED TO COMPLETE ACCOUNTS	Office Supplies		
				Beg. Bal.	1,600	
Acquisitions	10,000	(300) ← →			(300)	
				Desired		
Ending Bal.	9,700			Ending Bal.	1,900	

Question

14. The purpose of recording closing entries is to:
    a. reduce the number of temporary accounts.
    b. enable the accountant to prepare financial statements at the end of an accounting period.
    c. prepare temporary accounts for the recording of the next period's revenues, expenses, gains, losses, dividends, and other comprehensive income (or loss).
    d. establish new balances in some asset and liability accounts.

EXPLANATION: Cover up the answer selections while you read the question. Attempt to complete the statement started by the question. Think about when closing entries are made and what they do. Then go through the selections using a process of elimination. Closing entries clear out the balances of temporary accounts so that the accounts are ready to accumulate data in the next accounting period. Selection "c" is correct. Selection "a" is incorrect; closing entries do not change the number of accounts. Selection "b" is incorrect; financial statements are prepared before closing entries are made. If closing entries were posted before financial statements were prepared, the statement of income/comprehensive income would include nothing but zero amounts. Selection "d" is incorrect; closing entries will affect only temporary accounts and shareholders' equity. (Solution = c.)

Question

15. John Chu Limited just purchased a car that will be used by its salesperson. In order to capture this event, the company should record the transaction in the following manner:
    a. Prepare a journal entry and generate a journal and unadjusted trial balance.
    b. Prepare the journal entry and post to a ledger or database.
    c. Prepare the journal entry but do not post to a ledger until month end.
    d. Prepare the journal entry and prepare financial statements.

EXPLANATION: A journal entry must be prepared to capture the transaction. The journal entry must then be posted either to a ledger or database. The company would not generate a trial balance or financial statement until the end of a reporting period. (Solution = b.)

Question

16. Which of the following is true regarding the traditional discounted cash flow approach?
    a. The discount rate is adjusted to accommodate the riskiness of the cash flows.
    b. The cash flows have been adjusted to accommodate their riskiness.

c. This model is best used where cash flows are fairly uncertain.

d. Both a and c are correct.

EXPLANATION: The traditional approach is used when future cash flows are fairly certain (often under contract). The cash flows are then discounted using an adjusted rate that will reflect the riskiness of these cash flows. (Solution = a.)

Question

17. Your client, Fence Company, has a few minor lawsuits outstanding. Your main contact, Sharon Glass, has heard that, though their amount is unknown, these lawsuits must be recorded on the financial statements. Which discounted cash flow approach would you recommend in determining the amount to record on Fence Company's financial statements?

a. Net realizable value approach

b. Traditional approach

c. Expected cash flow approach

d. No discounting is required

EXPLANATION: The traditional approach is best used when cash flows are fairly certain. Since the amount and timing of Fence Company's lawsuits are relatively uncertain, the expected cash flow approach is recommended. (Solution = c.)

Question

18. Speculation Company purchased 2,000 shares of Private Inc., a startup company, during 2017. The value of this investment was based on an internally developed model. Based on the IFRS 13 guideline, at which level in the fair value hierarchy will these investments fall?

a. Level 1

b. Level 2

c. Level 3

d. It is not possible to determine from the information provided

EXPLANATION: **Level 1** inputs provide the most reliable fair values and are based on quoted prices in an active market for the exact same item. **Level 2** inputs consider the evaluation of similar assets and liabilities in active markets, or other observable inputs. **Level 3** inputs provide the least reliable information since much judgement is needed based on the best information available. The valuation of the investment purchased by Speculation includes management judgements about how the markets would value the asset. (Solution = c.)

Chapter 4

Reporting Financial Performance

OVERVIEW

An income statement (often called the "statement of income/earnings" or "statement of comprehensive income") reports on the results of operations of an entity for a specific time period. It is important to classify revenues, expenses, gains, and losses properly on the income statement. In this chapter, we discuss the income statement classifications, as well as the content of the statement of changes in equity (required under IFRS) and the statement of retained earnings (required under ASPE). We also discuss related disclosure issues such as irregular items and earnings per share. Charges and credits that affect income determination must be properly reflected in the financial statements. Errors in the determination of income cause errors on the income statement, statement of changes in equity, and statement of financial position. The concepts of "comprehensive income" and "other comprehensive income" are also discussed.

STUDY STEPS

Understanding the Importance of the Income Statement in Financial Decision-Making

Income statements tell a story about a company's performance within specific time periods. In financial analysis, preliminary review of financial statements usually includes a brief review of the income statement to see if revenues and profits are increasing or decreasing and at what rate. Earnings per share is also noted. If these are decreasing, users should note that company management might be motivated to try to artificially increase them, perhaps by recognizing revenues more aggressively or by deferring expenses. Users should also consider the effects of financial reporting issues in their analysis.

Even before looking at the trends noted above, it is important to determine what the main (and ancillary) business of the company is. Where does it make its money and how? What are its major expenses? This will also give some insight into financial reporting issues that may be material. An example of a common, material financial reporting issue is related to identifying the earnings process of the company, and determining at what point it is complete.

A quick study of the revenue recognition and realization process will also give some insight into the company; that is, are earnings managed? Do the financial statements have predictive value?

Required Disclosures

How information is presented on the income statement is often a matter of professional judgement. Be sensitive to what is required to be disclosed, and what is considered additional information under IFRS and ASPE.

Both IFRS and ASPE require certain minimum disclosures such as revenues, income tax, income from continuing operations, and income from discontinued operations net of tax. However, IFRS and ASPE each have additional required disclosures. For example, ASPE requires disclosure of government assistance, compensation costs, and others. Companies reporting under IFRS are required to show each component of other comprehensive income, net of tax. In general, companies using IFRS are larger companies that may give less detail in their disclosures.

Overall, a modified all-inclusive approach to income measurement is the current standard, which requires that most items be included in income. There are few exceptions that would be recorded as adjustments directly to retained earnings, rather than included in income. (One example of an exception is errors in the income measurement of prior years.) Under IFRS, the concept of comprehensive income is closer to an all-inclusive approach to income measurement, which requires that certain gains and losses be included in other comprehensive income (which appears below income from continuing operations). Remember that the required disclosures under IFRS and ASPE may also appear in the notes to financial statements.

Understanding Components of the Income Statement and Its Predictive Value to Users

Since recurring income or net income from continuing operations is a key number, care should be taken to ensure that items grouped with discontinued operations or other comprehensive income do indeed belong there. For example, there may be a bias on the part of the preparer to classify an impairment loss from assets held for sale as a loss from assets held for sale under discontinued operations, when that loss does not fully meet the criteria for classification as held for sale under discontinued operations.

TIPS ON CHAPTER TOPICS

- The **income statement** or **statement of income/comprehensive income** is often referred to as the "statement of operations" or the "operating statement" because it reports the results of operations for a specific period of time. Other names given to it include the "earnings statement," "statement of earnings," and "profit and loss statement" (or "P&L statement").

- IFRS requires expenses to be presented based on either their **nature** or **function**. Grouping expenses according to their nature focuses on the type of each expense (for example, personnel expenses and depreciation), whereas grouping expenses according to their function focuses on the business activity that each expense relates to (for example, selling costs and administrative costs).

- The concept of comprehensive income is an added dimension to the statement of comprehensive income. Specifically, comprehensive income includes both net income and other comprehensive income. **Other comprehensive income** (OCI) includes items such as unrealized gains or losses on certain investments classified as fair value through other comprehensive income; unrealized gains or losses on revaluation of property, plant, and equipment under the IFRS revaluation model; certain foreign exchange gains or losses; and other gains or losses as defined by IFRS.

- The income statement is often referred to as a link between prior period and current period statements of financial position because it explains a major reason for the change in shareholders' equity (specifically, the results of operations for the period). Beginning shareholders' equity (net assets) can be reconciled with ending shareholders' equity as follows:

	Shareholders' equity at the beginning of the period
+	Common shares issued
−	Dividends
+/−	Results of operations for the period (net income or net loss)
+/−	Other comprehensive income (loss) for the period
=	Shareholders' equity at the end of the period

(continued)

- Dividends and results of operations for the period (net income or net loss) are closed to Retained Earnings (a shareholders' equity account). Other comprehensive income (loss) for the period is closed to **Accumulated Other Comprehensive Income** (AOCI) (also a shareholders' equity account). Thus, AOCI represents the cumulative effect of **other comprehensive income** (OCI) recognized in previous years and the current year.

- A full statement of comprehensive income including other comprehensive income is not required if other comprehensive income is zero. If other comprehensive income is zero, an income statement will meet disclosure requirements.

- The income statement is used by investors and creditors to (1) evaluate the enterprise's past performance in the specified time period, (2) provide a basis for predicting future performance, and (3) help assess the risk or uncertainty of achieving future cash flows.

- The income statement is limited in its usefulness by the accounting policy choices, estimates, and assumptions, which are inherent in the numbers.

- The higher the quality of information in the income statement, the more useful it is to users. **High quality of earnings** refers to the quality of information content and presentation used to determine and disclose earnings. Companies with higher-quality earnings calculate income based on unbiased numbers (content) and provide understandable disclosures (presentation). Higher-quality earnings is considered related to higher sustainability of earnings, which has higher predictive and feedback value to users.

- The income tax consequences of all items appearing above the line "Income from continuing operations before income tax" are summarized in the line "Income tax" (shown before net income). Revenues cause an increase in income tax and expenses cause a decrease in income tax. The income tax consequences of items appearing below the "Income from continuing operations" line are reported within each individual item (hence, these items are reported "net of tax"). This procedure of allocating income tax within a period is referred to as **intraperiod tax allocation**.

- Under ASPE, assets (and related liabilities) that meet the definition of held for sale are presented separately as held for sale on the balance sheet, and retain their original classification as current or non-current assets (or liabilities). Under IFRS, assets held for sale are generally classified as current assets.

- If the assets (and related liabilities) held for sale meet the definition of a discontinued operation (that is, if they are components of an enterprise that have been disposed of or are classified as held for sale), the results of the discontinued operation net of tax (for both current and prior periods) and the related loss on disposal of the discontinued operation would be shown separately on the income statement, below income from continuing operations.

- A gain from operation of a discontinued operation is reported "net of tax" by deducting the tax effect from the related gain. For example, if the tax rate is 30%, a gain from operation of a discontinued operation of $400,000 will be reported at $280,000 net of tax. Likewise, a loss from operation of a discontinued operation of $400,000 will be reported at $280,000 net of tax. The gain situation increases net income, whereas the loss situation reduces net income.

- Corrections of errors in the reporting of prior period revenues and expenses are accounted for in the current period. A prior period adjustment is reported as a net of tax adjustment (debit or credit, whichever is applicable) to the opening balance of Retained Earnings. The prior period adjustment appears on the current period statement of retained earnings or statement of changes in equity.

● Net income minus preferred share dividend requirements (that is, income applicable to common shareholders) is divided by weighted average number of common shares outstanding, to arrive at earnings per share (EPS). This is a key ratio in financial analysis. Under IFRS, EPS must be disclosed on the face of the income statement. In addition, a company that reports a discontinued operation must report EPS for income before discontinued operations as well as EPS for discontinued operations, either on the face of the income statement or in the notes to the financial statements.

● In the EPS calculation, preferred dividends are deducted from net income if preferred dividends were declared. However, if the preferred shares are cumulative, the preferred dividend for the current period is deducted from net income, whether or not a preferred dividend was declared. Dividends declared on common shares have no effect on the EPS calculation.

● EPS is not mentioned under ASPE since many private enterprises have closely held shareholdings by definition.

● Another key ratio is the **price earnings** ratio. This is calculated by dividing the market price per share by the EPS. This ratio is an indicator of how much investors are willing to pay for every dollar of earnings.

EXERCISE 4-1

PURPOSE: This exercise reviews the basic accounting formula (Assets = Liabilities + Owners' Equity) and the connection between the income statement and the balance sheet.

The following data were extracted from the records of Dora Loesing's Cookies, a sole proprietorship:

	Dr.	Cr.
Total assets, beginning of the period	$100,000	
Total liabilities, beginning of the period		$36,000
Owner withdrawals during the period	30,000	
Total assets, end of the period	108,000	
Total liabilities, end of the period		38,000
Owner's contributions during the period		10,000

Instructions

Calculate the amount of net income (or loss) for the period. Show your calculations.

Solution to Exercise 4-1

Beginning owner's equity	$ 64,000[a]
Additional owner contributions	10,000
Owner withdrawals during the period	(30,000)
Subtotal	44,000
Net income (loss) for the period	X
Ending owner's equity	$ 70,000[b]
Solving for X, net income =	$ 26,000

[a]A = L + OE
$100,000 = $36,000 + Beginning owner's equity
Beginning owner's equity = $64,000

[b]A = L + OE
$108,000 = $38,000 + Ending owner's equity
Ending owner's equity = $70,000

APPROACH: The question asks you to solve for net income; however, no information is given regarding revenues and expenses for the period. Only balance sheet data and transactions affecting owner's equity are given. Net income (or net loss) for a period is one reason for a change in the balance of owner's equity. Write down the items that reconcile beginning owner's equity with ending owner's equity, enter the amounts known, calculate beginning and ending owner's equity balances using the basic accounting equation, then solve for the amount of net income. Recall that assets − liabilities = net assets; that is, assets − liabilities = owners' equity at any point in time.

- The basic accounting equation (A = L + OE) is applied at a specific point in time. When you have facts for the equation components at two different points in time for the same entity (such as amounts as at the beginning of a year and amounts as at the end of a year), you can modify the basic accounting equation to reflect that total changes in assets = total changes in liabilities + total changes in owners' equity. Using the symbol Δ to designate change, the following equation also holds true:

$$\Delta A = \Delta L + \Delta E$$

  Reasons for changes in owners' equity include:

  1. additional owner investments,
  2. owner withdrawals, and
  3. results of operations (net income or net loss).

- Net income (or net loss) accounts for the change in owners' equity for a specific period of time, other than from capital transactions. Capital transactions are transactions that involve owners acting in their capacity as owners of the entity.

Illustration 4-1 95

ILLUSTRATION 4-1

Elements of the Income Statement

Revenues: Increases in economic resources either by inflows or enhancements of an entity's assets or settlements of an entity's liabilities resulting from its ordinary activities.

Expenses: Decreases in economic resources, either by outflows or reductions of an entity's assets or incurrence of liabilities resulting from an entity's ordinary revenue-generating activities.

Gains: Increases in equity (net assets) from peripheral or incidental transactions of an entity and from all other transactions and other events and circumstances affecting the entity during a period, except those that result from revenues or investments by owners.

Losses: Decreases in equity (net assets) from peripheral or incidental transactions of an entity and from all other transactions and other events and circumstances affecting the entity during a period, except those that result from expenses or distributions to owners.

Other Comprehensive Income: Gains or losses that are recognized in comprehensive income but excluded from net income.

Revenues take many forms, such as sales revenue, service revenue, dividend revenue, and rent revenue. Expenses also take many forms, such as cost of goods sold, rent, salaries and wages, depreciation, interest, and tax.

Revenues and gains are similar (they both increase net income), and expenses and losses are similar (they both decrease net income). However, these terms are dissimilar in that they convey significantly different information about an enterprise's performance. Revenues and expenses result from an entity's ongoing major or central operations and ordinary activities (for example, from activities such as producing or delivering goods, and rendering services). In contrast, gains and losses result from incidental or peripheral transactions with other entities, and from other events and circumstances affecting the entity. Gains and losses often arise from the sale of investments; disposal of plant assets; settlement of liabilities for an amount other than their book value; and asset impairment, casualty, or theft. Other comprehensive income (OCI) includes items such as unrealized gains or losses on certain investments classified as fair value through other comprehensive income; unrealized gains or losses on revaluation of property, plant, and equipment under the IFRS revaluation model; certain foreign exchange gains or losses; and other gains or losses as defined by IFRS.

Revenues and expenses are commonly displayed as **gross** inflows or outflows, while gains and losses are usually displayed as **net** inflows or outflows. For example, assume a company buys an inventory item for $6,000, sells it for $10,000, and pays a sales representative a $1,000 commission. Assume the same company sells a $15,000 book value (carrying value) plant asset for $20,000, and pays an outside agency $2,100 for finding the buyer. The various flows associated with the first transaction (which is considered part of the company's major operations or ordinary activities) will be reported gross on its income statement, and the various elements of the second transaction (which is considered a peripheral transaction) will be reported net on its income statement. Assuming these were the only two transactions completed during the period and ignoring income tax, the income statement would show the following:

Sales revenue	$10,000
Cost of goods sold	6,000
Gross profit	4,000
Sales commission expense	1,000
Income from operations	3,000
Gain on sale of plant asset	2,900[a]
Net income	$ 5,900

[a]$20,000 proceeds − $15,000 book value − $2,100 finders fee = $2,900 gain on sale.

- Net income results from revenue, expense, gain, and loss transactions. These transactions are summarized on the income statement.

- A single-step income statement has only two groupings (Revenues and Expenses). It eliminates classification problems and is often used for simplicity. A multiple-step income statement (as above), however, separates operating transactions and non-operating transactions and matches costs and expenses with related revenues.

EXERCISE 4-2

PURPOSE: This exercise will help you to determine the types of business activities that would be considered normal (part of ordinary activities) and the types of business activities that would be considered unusual.

Instructions

Determine whether each activity would be considered a normal revenue, expense, gain, or loss, or an unusual gain or loss. Mark an (x) in the appropriate column:

	Normal	Unusual
(a) Losses due to expropriation of assets in a foreign country		
(b) Revenues from the Ottawa Senators selling pop and hot dogs		

	Normal	**Unusual**
(c) Loss due to hurricane at Jamaican subsidiary		
(d) Loss due to hurricane at Calgary subsidiary		
(e) Loss of inventory at a warehouse due to flood in Halifax		
(f) The Toronto Maple Leafs selling hockey jerseys		
(g) Loss due to power outage caused by severe ice storm in Ottawa		
(h) Gain from winning a lawsuit against a major competitor		
(i) Loss due to a strike at a subsidiary		
(j) Gain of $2 million from winning a lottery jackpot from a ticket purchased with company funds		

Solution to Exercise 4-2

APPROACH: Review what is meant by the term "unusual gains and losses." Unusual gains and losses are items that by their nature are not typical of the entity's everyday business activities, or do not occur frequently. What is considered unusual will differ between entities in different industries.

(a) Expropriation of assets is not typical of an everyday business activity and would be considered unusual.

(b) The Ottawa Senators are a hockey team, although vending sales would be part of the normal operations of the organization.

(c) Losses due to a hurricane in Jamaica would be considered fairly normal and frequent in the Caribbean environment. If the losses were severe, they may be considered unusual in nature, but management was fully aware of the regular occurrence of hurricanes in the Caribbean when they established a subsidiary there.

(d) A hurricane in Calgary, however, is not a frequent occurrence. The related loss would be considered unusual in nature.

(e) The loss due to a flood would be considered unusual depending on the regularity of flooding in the area. If the warehouse was built on the flood plains of the Mississippi, it would be considered a normal occurrence, but if flooding is not a regular occurrence in Halifax, it would be considered unusual.

(f) The Toronto Maple Leafs are a hockey team, although merchandise revenues from selling hockey jerseys would be part of the normal operations of the organization.

(g) Ice storms do occur in Ottawa. The severity of the storm and materiality of the losses would determine whether the losses would be considered unusual.

(h) A gain from a lawsuit would be considered an unusual item. It is a result of normal business operations, but financial statement users would want to know that this is not a normal earnings stream for the company, and if material, the gain would be disclosed separately in the income statement.

(i) A strike is considered a normal occurrence in a business setting. The severity and materiality of losses occurring from the strike would determine whether the losses would be considered unusual.

(j) Gain from a lottery winning would be considered an unusual item, and separately disclosed on the income statement so that financial statement users would know that this is not a normal earnings stream for the company.

Although unusual gains and losses are by definition not typical of normal business operations, they are generally included in income from continuing operations. If they are not material in amount, they are combined with other items in the income statement. If they are material, they are disclosed separately, likely in the non-operating section under other gains or losses, but still included in income from continuing operations. Treating a gain or loss as unusual simply means that it should be separately disclosed if material, in order to achieve greater financial statement transparency and predictive value.

ILLUSTRATION 4-2

Sections of a Multiple-Step Income Statement

1. **Operating Section**: A report of the revenues and expenses of the company's principal operations. (This section may or may not be presented on a departmental basis.)

    (a) **Sales or Revenue Section**: A subsection presenting sales, discounts, allowances, returns, and other related information. Its purpose is to arrive at the net amount of sales revenue.

    (b) **Cost of Goods Sold Section**: A subsection that shows the cost of goods that were sold to produce the sales.

    (c) **Selling Expenses**: A subsection that lists expenses resulting from the company's efforts to make sales.

    (d) **Administrative or General Expenses**: A subsection reporting expenses of general administration.

2. **Non-operating Section**: A report of revenues and expenses resulting from the company's secondary or auxiliary activities. In addition, special gains and losses that are infrequent and/or unusual are normally reported in this section. Generally these items break down into two main subsections:

    (a) **Other Revenues and Gains**: A list of the revenues earned or gains incurred from non-operating transactions, generally net of related expenses.

    (b) **Other Expenses and Losses**: A list of the expenses or losses incurred from non-operating transactions, generally net of any related income.

3. **Income Tax**: A short section reporting federal and provincial income tax levied on income from continuing operations.

4. **Discontinued Operations**: Material gains or losses resulting from the disposal of a part of the business (net of tax).

5. **Other Comprehensive Income**: Other gains or losses that are not required by primary sources of GAAP to be included in net income. This section includes gains or losses that are recognized in comprehensive income but excluded from net income (net of tax).

6. **Earnings Per Share**

EXERCISE 4-3

PURPOSE: This exercise will allow you to contrast the multiple-step format and the single-step format of the income statement.

The accountant for Bubble Bath Products, Inc. (a private company) has compiled the following information from the company's records as a basis for an income statement for the year ended December 31, 2017. (There was no change during the year in the 12,000 common shares outstanding.)

Net sales revenue	$970,000
Depreciation of plant assets (60% selling, 40% administrative)	70,000
Dividends	14,400
Rent revenue	30,000
Interest on notes payable	17,000
Market appreciation on land held as an investment	44,000
Purchases	421,000
Freight-in	37,000
Inventory, January 1, 2017	82,000
Inventory, December 31, 2017	81,000
Purchase returns and allowances	11,000
Salaries and wages expense—sales	95,000
Supplies expense—sales	11,400
Income tax	45,000
Salaries and wages expense—administrative	135,900
Administrative expenses	46,700
Advertising expense	20,000
Delivery expense	6,000

Instructions

(a) Prepare a multiple-step income statement.

(b) Prepare a single-step income statement.

Solution to Exercise 4-3

(a)

BUBBLE BATH PRODUCTS, INC.
Income Statement
For the Year Ended December 31, 2017

Sales Revenue			
Net sales revenue			$970,000
Cost of Goods Sold			
Inventory, Jan. 1		$ 82,000	
Purchases	$421,000		
Less purchase returns and allowances	11,000		
Net purchases	410,000		
Freight-in	37,000	447,000	
Total cost of goods available for sale		529,000	
Less inventory, Dec. 31		81,000	
Cost of goods sold			448,000
Gross profit			522,000
Operating Expenses			
Selling expenses			
Salaries and wages	95,000		
Advertising	20,000		
Supplies	11,400		
Depreciation (60% × $70,000)	42,000		
Delivery expense	6,000	174,400	
Administrative expenses			
Salaries and wages	135,900		
Depreciation (40% × $70,000)	28,000		
Administrative expenses	46,700	210,600	385,000
Income from operations			137,000
Other Revenues and Gains			
Rent revenue			30,000
			167,000

Other Expenses and Losses

Interest expense	17,000
Income before income tax	150,000
Income tax	45,000
Net income	$105,000
Earnings per share ($105,000 ÷ 12,000)	$8.75

Dividends declared do not appear on the income statement. They are a distribution of corporate income—**not** a determinant of net income. For private companies, increases in the market value of plant assets are generally not recognized in the accounts until they are realized through the sale of the plant assets. Hence, the market appreciation on the land held as an investment does not appear on the income statement. However, had this asset been an equity investment quoted in an active market, the (unrealized holding) gain would be recognized in net income. (This is discussed further in Chapter 9.)

(b)

BUBBLE BATH PRODUCTS, INC.
Income Statement
For the Year Ended December 31, 2017

Revenues

Net sales	$ 970,000	
Rent revenue	30,000	
Total revenue		1,000,000
Expenses		
Cost of goods sold	448,000	
Selling expenses	174,400	
Administrative expenses	210,600	
Interest expense	17,000	
Total expenses		850,000
Income before income tax		150,000
Income tax		45,000
Net income		$ 105,000
Earnings per share		$ 8.75

● In the single-step income statement, just two groupings exist: revenues and expenses. Expenses are deducted from revenues to arrive at net income or loss. The expression "single-step" is derived from the single subtraction necessary to arrive at net income. Frequently, however, income tax is still reported separately to indicate its direct relationship to income before income tax.

● In the multiple-step income statement, there are three major subtotals presented before arriving at net income. They are: net sales revenue, gross profit, and income from operations. These subtotals emphasize the following:

  1. Expenses are classified by function, such as merchandising or manufacturing (cost of goods sold), selling, and administrative. (Note that for companies under IFRS, classification of expenses by nature is also permitted.)

  2. Operating and subordinate or non-operating activities of the company are separated.

  The "other revenues and gains" and "other expenses and losses" sections include (1) investing and financing revenues and expenses such as interest income, dividend revenue (from dividends received), and interest expense; and (2) the results of non-operating items such as gain on sale of plant assets and investments.

● The nature of an entity's typical operations is critical in determining whether the results of a transaction should be classified as an operating or a non-operating revenue, gain, expense, or loss. For example, consider rental activities. A business specializing in equipment rentals will classify rent revenue as an operating revenue. A retail establishment that occasionally rents its temporarily idle assets to others, however, will classify rent revenue as a non-operating (other) revenue. As a second example, consider the sale of an investment. An investment dealer will report the revenue from a sale as an operating revenue. A retail entity that occasionally sells an investment, however, will report the difference between the proceeds from the sale and the investment's carrying value as a non-operating gain or loss.

● There is no specific order in which the individual selling expenses and administrative expenses are to be listed on the multiple-step income statement. Very often, they appear in order of decreasing amount.

● Many users prefer the multiple-step income statement format because it discloses the amount of income from operations and highlights the difference between regular or operating and irregular or non-operating activities. Irregular revenues, expenses, gains, and losses may not be expected to continue at the same level in future periods.

● Within the income statement, net income from continuing operations (versus income from discontinued operations) is more important to many users since it provides the best indicator of future income.

EXERCISE 4-4

PURPOSE: This exercise will give you practice in identifying components of net income and the order of items appearing on a single-step income statement and on a statement of retained earnings.

Presented below is the adjusted trial balance of Hip Corporation at December 31, 2017. The account titles and balances are **not** in the customary order.

HIP CORPORATION
Adjusted Trial Balance
December 31, 2017

	Debits	Credits
Sales revenue		$958,500
Notes receivable	$ 80,000	
Fair value–net income investments	88,500	
Accounts payable		51,000
Accumulated depreciation—equipment		31,500
Sales discounts	10,500	
Sales returns and allowances	17,500	
Purchase discounts		8,000
Cash	190,000	
Accounts receivable	95,000	
Rent revenue		14,000
Retained earnings		240,000
Salaries and wages payable		22,000
Notes payable		75,000
Common shares, $15 par		300,000
Income tax expense	68,000	
Dividends	70,000	
Allowance for doubtful accounts		6,500
Supplies	11,000	
Freight-in	16,000	
Selling expenses	212,000	
Administrative expenses	114,000	
Land	65,000	
Equipment	130,000	
Inventory	79,000	
Building	104,000	
Purchases	500,000	
Dividend revenue		10,000
Loss on sale of investment	13,000	
Interest income		9,000
Interest expense	12,500	
Bonds payable		100,000
Gain on sale of land		24,500
Accumulated depreciation—building		26,000
Totals	$ 1,876,000	$ 1,876,000

The company uses the periodic inventory system. A physical count of inventory on December 31 resulted in an inventory amount of $100,000.

Instructions

(a) Prepare an income statement for the year ended December 31, 2017, using the single-step format. Assume that 20,000 common shares were outstanding the entire year.

(b) Prepare a statement of retained earnings for the year ended December 31, 2017. Assume that the only changes in retained earnings during the current year were from net income and dividends.

Solution to Exercise 4-4

(a)

HIP CORPORATION
Income Statement
For the Year Ended December 31, 2017

Revenues		
Net sales revenue[a]		$930,500
Gain on sale of land		24,500
Rent revenue		14,000
Dividend revenue		10,000
Interest income		9,000
Total revenues		988,000
Expenses		
Cost of goods sold[b]		487,000
Selling expenses		212,000
Administrative expenses		114,000
Loss on sale of investment		13,000
Interest expense		12,500
Total expenses		838,500
Income before income tax		149,500
Income tax		68,000
Net income		$ 81,500
Earnings per common share ($81,500 ÷ 20,000)		$ 4.08

[a]Net sales revenue:		
Sales revenue		$958,500
Less: Sales discounts	$ 10,500	
Sales returns and allowances	17,500	28,000
Net sales revenue		$930,500

^bCost of goods sold:

Inventory, Jan. 1		$ 79,000
Purchases	$500,000	
Less purchase discounts	8,000	
Net purchases		492,000
Add freight-in		16,000
Cost of goods available for sale		587,000
Less inventory, Dec. 31		100,000
Cost of goods sold		$487,000

The solution presented here reports income tax separately as the last item before net income to indicate its direct relationship to income before income tax. In the single-step format, it is acceptable to list income tax with expenses and omit the subtotal "income before income tax."

(b)

HIP CORPORATION
Statement of Retained Earnings
For the Year Ended December 31, 2017

Balance, January 1	$240,000
Add: Net income	81,500
	321,500
Less: Dividends	70,000
Balance, December 31	$251,500

APPROACH:

1. Go through the adjusted trial balance and lightly cross through any account title that does not pertain to the calculation of net income. With the exception of the balance of Inventory (which is used to calculate cost of goods sold when a periodic inventory system is in use), statement of financial position account balances are not used in determining net income.

2. Calculate subtotals for items such as (a) net sales revenue, (b) cost of goods sold, (c) selling expenses, and (d) administrative expenses. Show your calculations for these subtotals. (In this particular exercise, selling expenses and administrative expenses are already summarized.)

3. Identify revenue and gain items.

4. Identify expense and loss items.

5. Identify income tax for the period.

6. Identify any discontinued operations.

7. Calculate net income.

8. Calculate earnings per share.

9. Identify the retained earnings balance at the beginning of the period.

10. Include any prior period adjustments on the statement of retained earnings. (None are identified in this exercise.)

11. Add net income for the period.

12. Deduct dividends.

13. Arrive at the retained earnings balance at the end of the period.

The account balances in the adjusted trial balance that are **not** used for the solution requested are as follows: Notes Receivable, Fair Value–Net Income Investments, Accounts Payable, Accumulated Depreciation—Equipment, Cash, Accounts Receivable, Salaries and Wages Payable, Notes Payable, Common Shares, Allowance for Doubtful Accounts, Supplies, Land, Equipment, Building, Bonds Payable, and Accumulated Depreciation—Building.

EXERCISE 4-5

PURPOSE: This exercise is designed to give you practice in preparing a statement of income and comprehensive income and a statement of changes in equity.

Presented below is information related to Smith Corp., for the year 2017.

Net sales revenue	$ 692,000
Cost of goods sold	400,000
Selling expenses	32,000
Administrative expenses	24,000
Dividend revenue	10,000
Interest income	7,000
Interest expense	15,000
Writeoff of goodwill due to impairment	25,000
Uninsured loss due to flood (unusual and infrequent)	60,000
Loss from operation of discontinued division (net of tax)	45,000
Loss on disposal of discontinued division (net of tax)	35,000
Unrealized gains on investments designated as gains/losses through other comprehensive income, net of tax	15,000
Depreciation expense omitted in 2015	35,000
Dividends	42,000
Common shares at December 31, 2016	400,000
Retained earnings at December 31, 2016	1,700,000
Accumulated other comprehensive income at December 31, 2016	100,000
Tax rate of 30% on all items	

Instructions

(a) Prepare a statement of income and comprehensive income (multiple-step format) for 2017. Assume that 50,000 common shares were outstanding during 2017, and that no common shares were issued during the year.

(b) Prepare a statement of changes in equity for 2017.

Solution to Exercise 4-5

(a)

SMITH CORP.
Statement of Income and Comprehensive Income
For the Year Ended December 31, 2017

Net sales revenue		$692,000
Cost of goods sold		400,000
Gross profit		292,000
Operating expenses		
Selling expenses	$32,000	
Administrative expenses	24,000	56,000
Income from operations		236,000
Other revenues and gains		
Dividend revenue	10,000	
Interest income	7,000	17,000
		253,000
Other expenses and losses		
Interest expense	15,000	
Impairment loss—goodwill	25,000	
Loss from flood	60,000	100,000
Income before income tax		153,000
Income tax		45,900
Income from continuing operations		107,100
Discontinued operations		
Loss from operation of discontinued division (net of tax)	45,000	
Loss on disposal of discontinued division (net of tax)	35,000	80,000
Net income		27,100
Other comprehensive income		
Unrealized gains on FV-OCI investments, net of tax		15,000
Comprehensive income		$42,100
Per common share:		
Income from continuing operations ($107,100 ÷ 50,000)		$2.14
Loss from discontinued operations (net of tax) ($80,000 ÷ 50,000)		(1.60)
Net income ($27,100 ÷ 50,000)		$0.54

Investments designated as gains/losses through other comprehensive income are termed "FV-OCI investments." Unrealized gains or losses due to increases or decreases in fair value of these investments are recognized in other comprehensive income. (This is discussed further in Chapter 9.)

(b)

SMITH CORP.
Statement of Changes in Equity
For the Year Ended December 31, 2017

	Total	Common Shares	Retained Earnings	Accumulated Other Comprehensive Income
Beginning balance	$2,200,000	$400,000	$1,700,000	$100,000
Correction of prior period error (net of tax)[a]	(24,500)		(24,500)	
Beginning balance, adjusted	2,175,500	400,000	1,675,500	100,000
Dividends	(42,000)		(42,000)	
Net income	27,100		27,100	
Other comprehensive income	15,000			15,000
Comprehensive income				
Ending balance, Dec. 31, 2017	$2,175,600	$400,000	$1,660,600	$115,000

[a]Depreciation expense omitted in 2015 (35,000)
Less: tax savings (30%) 10,500
Net correction to retained earnings (24,500)

If Smith Corp. had a change in accounting policy in 2017, it would not be reflected in the above statement of changes in equity, because this type of change is generally recognized through retrospective restatement. Retrospective restatement involves restating the financial statements for all prior periods presented for comparative purposes (except when full retrospective restatement is not practicable). Only if all comparative years were not disclosed would a cumulative amount be calculated and adjusted through beginning retained earnings.

ILLUSTRATION 4-3

Treatment of Irregular Items

1. **Discontinued Operations**: The results of operations (income or loss) of a component of a business that has been or will be disposed of are reported in a separate income statement category called "discontinued operations." This category appears **after** continuing operations but **before** other comprehensive income. It is reported net of the related income tax effect.

2. **Unusual Gains and Losses**: A gain or loss that arises from an event that is unusual or infrequent should be reported in the income statement as part of "income from continuing operations." If the amount is material, it should be separately disclosed. If the amount is immaterial, it may be combined with other items on the income statement. In a multiple-step income statement, unusual gains and losses are normally classified in the "other revenues and gains" or "other expenses and losses" section, although a separate unusual items section may be displayed. Unusual gains and losses are **not** to be reported net of tax. Rather, the tax consequences of these items are combined with the tax effects of all other components of income from continuing operations in the "income tax" line.

3. **Changes in Accounting Policy**: A change in accounting policy occurs when a company changes from one generally accepted accounting method to another generally accepted accounting method. The initial adoption of an accounting policy is not considered a change in accounting policy. Because such a change significantly reduces comparability and consistency of successive financial statements, a **voluntary** change in accounting policy is allowed only if the newly adopted accounting policy results in the financial statements presenting reliable and more **relevant** information about the effects of the transactions, events, or conditions on the entity's financial position, financial performance, or cash flows. The reason for the change must also be disclosed in the notes to the financial statements. A change in accounting policy is generally recognized through retrospective restatement. The financial statements for all prior periods that are presented for comparative purposes should be restated, except when full retrospective restatement is not practicable. If the effect cannot be determined, or if all comparative years are not disclosed, a cumulative amount would be calculated and adjusted through opening retained earnings. (This is discussed further in Chapter 21.)

4. **Changes in Accounting Estimates (Normal Recurring Corrections and Adjustments)**: A change from one good-faith estimate to another good-faith estimate because of new information or experience constitutes a change in accounting estimate. A change in accounting estimate affects only the related revenue or expense reported in the period of change if the change affects only that period. A change in accounting estimate affects the related revenue or expense in the period of change (called the "current period") and future periods if the change affects both. Examples are a change in estimate of uncollectible accounts receivable (bad debts expense), and a change in estimated service life of a plant (fixed) asset (depreciation expense). A change in accounting estimate is not considered a correction of an error (a prior period adjustment); therefore, it is **not** applied retroactively. However, the impact of the change in accounting estimate on net income should be disclosed. (This is discussed further in Chapter 21.)

EXERCISE 4-6

PURPOSE: This exercise will test your knowledge of income statement elements and their arrangement into major sections on the statement of income and comprehensive income.

Instructions

The following list represents captions that would appear on a statement of income and comprehensive income (multiple-step format). Unscramble the list and prepare a skeleton statement of income and comprehensive income using the captions given. (If you do not wish to write out each caption below you may still test your knowledge by listing the appropriate letters in the correct order.)

(a) Cost of goods sold

(b) Sales revenue

(c) Income tax

(d) Discontinued operations

(e) Other revenues and gains

(f) Income from continuing operations

(g) Loss on disposal of discontinued component of business (net of tax)

(h) Net income

(i) Income from continuing operations before income tax

(j) Loss from operations of discontinued component of business (net of tax)

(k) Income from operations

(l) Other comprehensive income

(m) Gross profit

(n) Other expenses and losses

(o) Comprehensive income

Solution to Exercise 4-6

COMPANY NAME
Statement of Income and Comprehensive Income
For the Year Ended December 31, 20XX

(b) Sales revenue

(a) Cost of goods sold

(m) Gross profit

(k) Income from operations

(e) Other revenues and gains

(n) Other expenses and losses

(i) Income from continuing operations before income tax

(c) Income tax

(f) Income from continuing operations

(d) Discontinued operations

(j) Loss from operations of discontinued component of business (net of tax)

(g) Loss on disposal of discontinued component of business (net of tax)

(h) Net income

(l) Other comprehensive income

(o) Comprehensive income

> The **current operating performance approach** to income reporting would call for all irregular gains and losses and corrections of revenues and expenses of prior periods to be taken directly into the Retained Earnings account, rather than reported in the current period's income statement. The **all-inclusive approach** to income reporting would call for all of these items to be reported in the current period's income statement. Current standards require a **modified all-inclusive approach** to income reporting. This means that with minor exceptions, most items are reported on the statement of income and comprehensive income. (Exceptions include errors in the income measurement of prior years and changes in accounting policies that are applied retrospectively.)

EXERCISE 4-7

PURPOSE: This exercise will enable you to practise identifying the proper classification for items on a statement of income and comprehensive income. It will also give you an example of how the tax effects of various items are reflected on the statement of income and comprehensive income.

Margaret Moylan Corporation had the following transactions and events in 2017. The corporation is subject to a 30% tax rate on all items. All amounts are material. The corporation's primary business activity is the sale of energy products.

1. The corporation experienced an uninsured flood loss in the amount of $60,000 during the year. A flood is unusual and infrequent in the region where the corporation resides.

2. At the beginning of 2015, the corporation purchased an office machine for $108,000 (residual value of $18,000) with a useful life of six years. The bookkeeper used straight-line depreciation for 2015 and 2016, but failed to deduct the residual value in calculating the depreciable base. The same depreciation calculations were used for tax purposes.

3. Sale of securities held as a part of Moylan's investment portfolio resulted in a loss of $62,200 (pretax). The securities in the investment portfolio are classified as gains/losses through net income.

4. When its president died, the corporation realized $100,000 from an insurance policy. The cash surrender value of this policy had been carried on the books as an investment in the amount of $34,000. (The gain is non-taxable.)

5. The corporation disposed of a component of the business at a loss of $140,000 before tax. Assume that this transaction meets the criteria for being classified as discontinued operations. There were no results of operations for this division during 2017.

6. The corporation had an unrealized gain of $40,000 on other gains or losses through other comprehensive income securities acquired during the year. The securities are classified as gains/losses through other comprehensive income.

Instructions

Describe how each of the items above will be reported in a multiple-step statement of income and comprehensive income for 2017. Indicate the amount that will be reported and the section of the statement of income and comprehensive income in which the amount will appear.

Solution to Exercise 4-7

1. A loss of $60,000 will be reported separately in the other expenses and losses section of income from continuing operations.

2. Depreciation expense of $15,000 [($108,000 − $18,000) ÷ 6 years] will appear in the administrative expenses (operating expenses) section of the 2017 statement of income and comprehensive income. The correction of prior periods' depreciation (a prior period adjustment) will not appear on the statement of income and comprehensive income. Rather, a credit of $4,200 (net of tax) will appear on the statement of changes in equity for 2017 as an adjustment to the beginning balance of retained earnings.

   Calculations:

   $108,000 ÷ 6 = $18,000 depreciation taken in 2015.

   $108,000 ÷ 6 = $18,000 depreciation taken in 2016.

   ($108,000 − $18,000) ÷ 6 = $15,000 correct annual depreciation.

   $15,000 × 2 = $30,000 correct depreciation for 2015 and 2016.

   ($18,000 + $18,000) − $30,000 = $6,000 overstated expense in prior years.

   $6,000 − 30% ($6,000) = $4,200 addition to retained earnings (net of tax).

3. A loss of $62,200 will be reported in the other expenses and losses section of the statement of income and comprehensive income. The amount will **not** be reported net of tax.

4. A gain of $66,000 ($100,000 − $34,000) will appear in the other revenues and gains section of the statement of income and comprehensive income. The amount will **not** be reported net of tax. (In this case, the amount has no tax effect anyway.) A good caption for this item is "Gain from proceeds of life insurance policy."

5. A loss of $98,000 ($140,000 − 30% of $140,000) will appear as a "loss on disposal of assets of discontinued component" in the discontinued operations section of the statement of income and comprehensive income.

6. The unrealized gain of $28,000 ($40,000 − 30% of $40,000) will be shown in Other Comprehensive Income (reported separately from net income). The amount will also be "tracked" in Accumulated Other Comprehensive Income, an equity account.

- Discontinued operations include **components** of an enterprise that have been disposed of (by sale, abandonment, or spinoff) or are classified as **held for sale**.

- To be considered discontinued, the operations have been, or will be, disposed of and the entity will not have any continuing involvement.

- A **component of an entity** has operations, cash flows, and financial elements that are clearly distinguishable from the rest of the entity. IFRS and ASPE generally allow only major lines of business or geographical areas to be included in a component. It may be difficult at times to distinguish **disposal of an asset** from **disposal of a component.** The key distinction is whether the asset or component generates its own operations and cash flows, and has its own financial elements. If a discontinued business is a separate component, it would qualify for separate presentation as a discontinued operation on the statement of income and comprehensive income.

- If not yet disposed of, the assets of a component can be classified as held for sale and qualify for separate presentation as a discontinued operation on the statement of income and comprehensive income when all of the following criteria are met:

  - There is an authorized plan to sell.

  - The asset is available for immediate sale in its current state.

  - There is an active program to find a buyer.

  - Sale is probable within one year.

  - The asset is reasonably priced and actively marketed.

  - Changes to the plan are unlikely.

- Assets **held for sale** (whether part of discontinued operations or not) are remeasured to the lower of carrying value and fair value less cost to sell. Under ASPE, assets held for sale are presented separately on the balance sheet as held for sale (if material), and retain their original classification as assets that are current or non-current. Under IFRS, assets held for sale are generally classified as current assets, and presented separately on the statement of financial position as held for sale.

ANALYSIS OF MULTIPLE-CHOICE QUESTIONS

Question

1. In a multiple-step income statement, the excess of gross profit over operating expenses is called:
   a. net margin.
   c. net profit.
   b. income from operations.
   d. earnings.

EXPLANATION: Visualize a multiple-step income statement. Net sales revenue less cost of goods sold yields gross profit (sometimes called "gross margin"). Gross profit less operating expenses equals income from operations. From there, other revenues and gains are added, other expenses and losses are deducted, and income tax is deducted to arrive at net income. Another popular term for net income is "earnings." Net profit would likely refer to net income. "Net margin" is not a term applied to the income statement. (Solution = b.)

Question

2. The following expense and loss items were among those incurred by Springer Company during 2017:

Rent for office space	$700,000
Loss on sale of office furniture	65,000
Interest	112,000
Accounting and legal fees	145,000
Freight-out	68,000

One half of the rented premises is occupied by the sales department. What is the amount that should be classified as general and administrative expenses in Springer's income statement for 2017?

   a. $765,000   c. $740,000
   b. $910,000   d. $495,000

EXPLANATION: For each item listed, identify where it is reported. Then sum the items that you identify as general and administrative (G&A) expenses.

Rent for office space:	One half selling; one half G&A
Loss on sale of equipment:	Other expenses and losses
Interest:	Other expenses and losses
Accounting and legal fees:	G&A expenses
Freight-out:	Selling expenses

One half of office space (0.5 × $700,000)	$350,000
Accounting and legal fees	145,000
General and administrative expenses	$495,000

(Solution = d.)

Question

3. Which of the following is **not** a selling expense?
   a. Advertising expense   c. Freight-out
   b. Salaries and wages expense—   d. Store supplies consumed
       office

EXPLANATION: Determine the classification of each account. Items "a," "c," and "d" are selling expenses because they are associated with the sales function. Salaries and wages expense—office is related to normal operations, but it is not related to the sales function of the business. Therefore, it is not classified as a selling expense. (Solution = b.)

Question

4. The accountant for Orion Sales Company is preparing the income statement for 2017 and the statement of financial position at December 31, 2017. The January 1, 2017 inventory balance will appear:

   a. only as an asset on the statement of financial position.

   b. only in the cost of goods sold section of the income statement.

   c. as a deduction in the cost of goods sold section of the income statement and as a current asset on the statement of financial position.

   d. as an addition in the cost of goods sold section of the income statement and as a current asset on the statement of financial position.

EXPLANATION: The January 1, 2017 inventory amount is the beginning inventory figure. Beginning inventory is a component of the cost of goods available for sale for the period, which is a component of cost of goods sold. (Solution = b.)

Question

5. The following amounts relate to the current year for Rita Company:

Beginning inventory	$ 24,000
Ending inventory	33,000
Purchases	190,000
Purchase returns	11,800
Freight-out	7,000

The amount of cost of goods sold for the period is:

   a. $174,000.   c. $162,200.

   b. $181,000.   d. $169,200.

EXPLANATION: Write down the calculation model for cost of goods sold. Enter the amounts given and solve for the unknown.

$	24,000		Beginning Inventory
+	190,000	+	Purchases
–	11,800	–	Purchase Returns and Allowances
		–	Purchase Discounts
		+	Freight-in
	202,200	=	Cost of Goods Available for Sale
–	33,000	–	Ending Inventory
$	169,200	=	Cost of Goods Sold

(Solution = d.)

Freight-out is classified as a selling expense, not a component of cost of goods sold. "Freight-out" is often called "transportation-out." "Transportation-in" is another name for "freight-in."

Question

6. A material loss should be presented separately, as a component of income from continuing operations, when it is:

   a. unusual in nature or infrequent in occurrence.

   b. an unrealized loss on investments designated as gains/losses through other comprehensive income.

   c. an extraordinary loss.

   d. a cumulative effect of a change in accounting policy.

EXPLANATION: A material loss that is (1) unusual in nature or (2) infrequent in occurrence should be treated as an unusual loss, disclosed separately in other expenses and losses, and therefore included in income from continuing operations. An unrealized holding loss on investments designated as gains/losses through other comprehensive income would be included in other comprehensive income. Under IFRS, classifying items as extraordinary is not allowed, and under ASPE, there is no guidance on this topic. (Solution = a.)

Question

7. During the year ended December 31, 2017, Delta Corporation incurred the following material, infrequent losses:

   • A factory was shut down during a major strike by employees; costs were $135,000.

   • A loss of $67,000 was incurred on the abandonment of computer equipment used in the business.

   • A loss of $78,000 was incurred as a result of flood damage to a warehouse.

   What would be the total amount of unusual loss to be reported separately in Delta's 2017 income statement?

   a. $135,000   c. $213,000

   b. $78,000   d. $280,000

EXPLANATION: Review the criteria for treatment as an unusual gain or loss. Unusual gains and losses are items that by their nature are not typical of everyday business or do not occur frequently. In the question at hand, the first two items on the list are considered normal occurrences in a business setting and would not be considered unusual. Therefore, the only possible unusual loss is the loss from flood damage. A flood would be considered unusual in some locations but not others. The question facts indicate that a flood is considered infrequent for Delta. (Solution = b.)

Question

8. When a piece of office equipment is sold at a gain of $700,000 less related tax of $280,000, and the gain is not considered unusual or infrequent, the income statement for the period would show these effects as:
   a. an unusual item net of applicable income tax, $420,000.
   b. a prior period adjustment net of applicable income tax, $420,000.
   c. a gain net of applicable income tax, $420,000.
   d. a gain of $700,000 and an increase in income tax expense of $280,000 (that is, not net).

EXPLANATION: A gain or loss on disposal of property, plant, and equipment is **not** unusual. Therefore, the gain would be classified with "other revenues and gains" in income from continuing operations. The related tax effect would be reflected in the "income tax expense" figure. The only items reported net of tax are discontinued operations, other comprehensive income items, changes in accounting policy, and prior period adjustments. The tax effects of all other transactions are summarized in the amount captioned "income tax expense" on the income statement. (Solution = d.)

Question

9. A correction of an error in prior periods' income will be reported:

	On the income statement	Net of tax
a.	Yes	Yes
b.	No	No
c.	Yes	No
d.	No	Yes

EXPLANATION: Write down what you know about accounting for a correction of an error in prior periods' income. A correction of an error is a prior period adjustment. It is reported net of tax as an adjustment to the beginning retained earnings balance on the statement of retained earnings in the period the error is corrected. (Solution = d.)

Question

10. KBR Company had the following errors occur in its financial statements:

	2016	2017
Ending inventory	$11,000 understated	$17,000 overstated
Depreciation expense	$22,000 overstated	$13,000 overstated

Assuming that none of the errors were detected or corrected, by what amount will retained earnings at December 31, 2017, be misstated?

a. $18,000 understated

b. $20,000 overstated

c. $30,000 understated

d. $13,000 understated

e. None of the above

EXPLANATION: Explain the effects of each error separately and then combine your results. The $11,000 understatement of ending inventory for 2016 causes an $11,000 understatement of net income for 2016 and an $11,000 overstatement of net income for 2017 (because the ending inventory for 2016 is the beginning inventory for 2017); this nets to zero impact on the retained earnings balance at December 31, 2017. The $22,000 overstatement of depreciation expense in 2016 causes an understatement of net income for 2016 and a corresponding $22,000 understatement of retained earnings at December 31, 2016, and at December 31, 2017. The $17,000 overstatement of ending inventory for 2017 causes an overstatement of net income for 2017 and a $17,000 overstatement of retained earnings at December 31, 2017. A $13,000 overstatement of depreciation expense for 2017 causes a $13,000 understatement of net income for 2017 and a $13,000 understatement of retained earnings at December 31, 2017. The net effect on retained earnings at December 31, 2017, is, therefore, a $22,000 understatement plus a $17,000 overstatement plus a $13,000 understatement, which equals an $18,000 understatement. (Solution = a.)

Question

11. When a component of a business has been discontinued during the year, that component's operating losses of the current year should be included in the:

    a. income statement as part of the income (loss) from operations of the discontinued component.

    b. income statement as part of the gain (loss) on disposal of the discontinued component.

    c. income statement as part of the income (loss) from continuing operations.

    d. statement of retained earnings as a direct decrease in retained earnings.

EXPLANATION: There are two possible lines in the "discontinued operations" section of the income statement: (1) income (loss) from operations of discontinued component, and (2) gain or loss on disposal of discontinued component. The results of operations of the discontinued component for the year would be reported in the first line. (Solution = a.)

Estimated future losses are not included in the loss from operations since they would be implicitly reflected in the fair value estimate of the assets held for sale or sold. (The second line of the discontinued operations presentation.)

Question

12. Which of the following statements is most true regarding the income statement?
    a. The income statement is accurate and very reliable as it is based on accrual accounting and is prepared by knowledgeable people (management).
    b. Care must be taken when reviewing a company's income statement since it may be subject to bias.
    c. All income statements have the same information value as they have standard presentations and must adhere to the disclosures required by IFRS and ASPE.
    d. The income statement is of little value when the statement of cash flows is also prepared for the company.

EXPLANATION: The income statement, while providing good information for predicting future cash flows and assessing management stewardship, has many limitations, including the fact that the information may be biased. (Solution = b.)

Question

13. Revenues and gains are reported separately on the income statement for which of the following reasons?
    a. More information and detail is always better than less.
    b. Users need to know how much a company is earning from its main or ordinary operations.
    c. Gains (and losses) are generally unusual items and are, therefore, required to be disclosed separately.
    d. This practice adheres to the materiality concept.

EXPLANATION: Gains are often non-recurring and, by definition, do not arise from ordinary activities of the business. Gains are not always unusual. Furthermore, more information is not always better than less. Although users appreciate a certain amount of detail, there comes a point when too much detail may obscure more important information. (Solution = b.)

Question

14. The following is a list of income statement components. Which of these items is not required to be disclosed according to IFRS and ASPE?
    a. Income or loss before discontinued operations
    b. Results of discontinued operations
    c. Net income or loss for the period
    d. Cost of goods sold

EXPLANATION: Cost of goods sold is desirable in terms of disclosure; however, it is not required under IFRS or ASPE. (Solution = d.) Note that if the expenses are classified according to function under IFRS, then Cost of Sales is shown (IAS 1.103).

Question

15. Under IFRS, basic and diluted EPS are required to be presented as follows:
    a. on the face of the statement of income and comprehensive income.
    b. in the notes to the financial statements.
    c. on the statement of cash flows.
    d. either in the notes to the financial statements or on the statement of income and comprehensive income.

EXPLANATION: Under IFRS, basic and diluted EPS must be shown on the face of the income statement. (Solution = a.)

Question

16. Which of the following income statement captions would be found on an income statement classified by nature of expense?
    a. Depreciation and amortization expense
    b. Administrative costs
    c. Selling costs
    d. Distribution costs

EXPLANATION: Classification of expenses by function requires that expenses be classified according to business activity functions (such as "b," "c," and "d" above). Classification of expenses by nature focuses on classification by type of expense. (Solution = a.)

Chapter 5

Financial Position and Cash Flows

OVERVIEW

A statement of financial position reports on an entity's financial position at a point in time. A statement of cash flows reports the sources of cash receipts and uses of cash payments during the period. In this chapter, we discuss classification of items on the statement of financial position and the statement of cash flows, along with related disclosure issues. It is extremely important that items be properly classified on financial statements. Errors in classifying items on financial statements will result in incorrect ratio analysis, which can lead to misinterpretation of the information conveyed. This can affect decisions that are being made based on the financial statements.

STUDY STEPS

Understanding the Usefulness and Limitations of the Statement of Financial Position and Statement of Cash Flows

The Statement of Financial Position

The statement of financial position gives information about a company's liquidity, solvency, and financial flexibility, among other things. Liquidity is an indication of the company's ability (or inability) to meet upcoming current liabilities, and to continue operating. Solvency is an indication of a company's overall ability to pay its debts and related interest obligations, and also refers to how much debt has been used to finance the company's asset acquisitions (relative to equity financing). Liquidity and solvency affect a company's overall financial flexibility, or ability (or inability) to adapt financially to changing situations. For instance, a highly leveraged company (one with significant debt) with fixed debt repayment commitments is not as financially flexible, and may be more exposed to risk of business failure in hard times since it must come up with the debt repayments or, in the worst-case scenario, go bankrupt. When making their investment decisions, creditors often rely on the statement of financial position to assess a company's liquidity and ability to service debt.

Key statement of financial position ratios are the **current ratio** (which provides a measure of liquidity) and **debt to equity** (or total assets) ratio (which provides a measure of solvency). For example, a company with a relatively high debt to equity ratio would require more assets to meet fixed debt obligations and would be considered less solvent and riskier than a company with a low debt to equity ratio.

Some major limitations of the statement of financial position are the following.

1. Many assets and liabilities are stated at their historical cost (which, for certain assets, may be less relevant than current fair value).
2. Judgements and estimates are used in determining many of the items reported on the statement of financial position.
3. The statement of financial position necessarily leaves out many items that are relevant to the business, but cannot be recorded objectively.

Importance of note disclosures to supplement the numbers   The information on the face of the statement of financial position does not tell the whole story and, therefore, must be supplemented by note disclosures. For instance, a statement of financial position might show long-term debt of $10 million. While this is useful for users to know, it is insufficient information because it does not answer such questions as: When is it due? What is the interest rate? Is it secured by assets of the company? This information is normally shown in the notes to the financial statements. Note disclosures can include additional information about balances on the statement of financial position, and additional information about items, contracts, or events that are not included on the statement of financial position, such as contingencies, commitments, subsequent events, and others. Notes also give essential disclosures, including information about estimates in the statement of financial position, how assets are valued, and items that are not in the statement of financial position due to inability to measure. Where possible, notes to the financial statements should be referred to on the face of the statement of financial position in order to direct users' attention to them.

Notes are an integral part of the financial statements and the disclosure process. Financial statements should never be read without also reading the accompanying notes.

The classified statement of financial position　Most statements of financial position are classified between current and non-current assets and liabilities. A time frame of one year (or the operating cycle of the company, whichever is longer) is used to distinguish between current and non-current. This classification allows users to assess the liquidity of the company.

Assets are generally listed in order of liquidity, with cash being first. In specialized industries, this might not always be the case.

The Statement of Cash Flows

This statement summarizes how a company gets its cash (sources) and what it spends its cash on (uses). It classifies these sources and uses of cash between operating, investing, and financing activities.

One of the more important numbers on the statement of cash flows is net cash used or provided by operating activities (a company's primary revenue-producing activities). This is an important number because in the long run, a company that cannot generate net positive cash flow from its primary business activities will most likely not survive for long! A company with significant net positive cash flow from operating activities is a healthy company because it relies less on external sources of financing in order to continue operating, and because the excess cash can be used for expansion, paying down debt, or paying dividends. Net cash used or provided by operating activities is calculated by converting information on the statement of income/comprehensive income and statement of financial position from accrual basis to cash basis.

Investing activities and financing activities are classified separately on the statement of cash flows, below operating activities. Investing activities include acquisitions and disposals of long-term assets and other investments that are not included in cash equivalents. Financing activities include activities that change the size and composition of a company's debt and equity structure, and related transactions (such as payment of dividends).

Classification of cash flow activity on the statement of cash flows provides useful information to users. For example, if a company is relying on the sale of long-term assets and issuance of debt or shares to fund a significant cash shortfall from its operations, this would be seen on the company's statement of cash flows as net cash used by operating activities, and net cash provided by investing and financing activities. The statement of cash flows can also be used to assess a company's earnings quality. For example, if a company's net income is much higher than its net cash provided by operations, the company may have poor earnings quality that may require further analysis.

Ratio Analysis

There are several common ratios identified in the illustrations in this chapter that you should familiarize yourself with. When determining how to account for a transaction, always consider the impact of the alternatives on key ratios. Note that certain industries focus more on certain ratios due to the nature of the industry. For example, the retail industry considers gross profit to be a key indicator of performance due to the importance of pricing, controlling inventory, and sourcing. The real estate industry might focus more on the debt to equity (or total assets) ratio, as it is a capital-intensive industry. Companies in the real estate industry often require significant financing to acquire and develop properties, and the risk that these companies may not be able to repay their debt may be significant.

It is important to identify the key ratios most relevant to the specific company being analyzed, and to benchmark calculated ratios against industry average ratios, prior years' ratios for the same company, or prior years' ratios for similar companies of similar size. There are many different ratios, and sometimes different ways of calculating each ratio. It is not important to memorize every ratio formula, although knowing how to calculate a few basic ratios will likely prove useful in doing preliminary financial statement analysis.

When looking at ratios calculated by analysts and companies, ensure that you understand how those ratios have been calculated. It is useful to note that a company's management may be motivated to manipulate ratios. For example, by incorrectly classifying a liability as non-current when it should be classified as current, a company would falsely increase its calculated current ratio, perhaps to remain within a required current ratio–based debt covenant.

TIPS ON CHAPTER TOPICS

- Financial statement items are classified based on similar grouping characteristics and are separated within each classification based on differing characteristics. Assets that differ in type, general liquidity characteristics, or expected function should be reported separately. Liabilities that differ in type, general liquidity characteristics, or implications for the enterprise's financial flexibility should be reported separately.

- Memorize the definition of current assets. **Current assets** are cash and other assets that are expected to be converted into cash, sold, or consumed within the year or operating cycle that immediately follows the statement of financial position date, whichever is longer. Think about how various examples of current assets meet this definition. Accounts receivable are current assets because they will be converted to cash shortly after the statement of financial position date. Inventory is a current asset because it will be sold within the year that follows the statement of financial position date. Prepaid insurance is a current asset because it will be consumed (used up) within the next year.

- An **operating cycle** is the average time between paying cash for inputs and receiving cash from the sale of outputs to customers. That is, for an entity that sells products, the operating cycle is the time from paying cash to buy (raw material or finished goods) inventory to selling the inventory and receiving cash (either from a cash sale or the collection of an account receivable originating from a credit sale). Thus, the length of an entity's operating cycle depends on the nature of its business. Unless otherwise indicated, assume that the operating cycle for an entity is less than a year, and apply the one-year test as the cut-off between current and non-current.

- Memorize the definition of current liabilities. **Current liabilities** are obligations that are due within one year from the date of the statement of financial position or within the operating cycle, whichever is longer.

- Note that a significant difference between ASPE and IFRS exists with respect to **classification of current debt under current liabilities**. Under **ASPE**, if a company has refinanced a current debt after the statement of financial position date but before the financial statements are issued, the current debt may be classified with non-current liabilities as at the statement of financial position date. However, under **IFRS**, the statement of financial position should show the conditions existing at the statement of financial position date. Under IFRS, unless at the statement of financial position date there is an existing agreement in place to refinance the debt for at least 12 months, and the decision is solely at the company's discretion, the current debt must be classified with current liabilities at the statement of financial position date (even if the current debt is refinanced before the financial statements are issued). This difference can significantly impact financial statement ratios that are calculated using total current liabilities (such as the current ratio).

- In a classified statement of financial position, any asset that is not classified as a current asset is a non-current asset. There are four non-current asset classifications: non-current investments; property, plant, and equipment; intangible assets; and other assets.

- A fund consists of restricted cash or non-cash assets such as shares and bonds of other companies. Funds are reported in the non-current investment classification. Other non-current investment classifications include investments in non-consolidated subsidiaries or affiliated companies, investments in securities (such as bonds, common shares, or long-term notes), and investments in tangible fixed assets such as land held for speculation.

- In a classified statement of financial position, liabilities are classified as either current or non-current liabilities. The non-current liabilities are usually titled "long-term liabilities" or "long-term debt."

- Current assets are often listed in order of liquidity (nearness to cash), with the most liquid ones (nearest to cash) being listed first. Current liabilities are not listed in any prescribed order; however, notes payable (short-term) is usually listed first, followed by accounts payable, with the remainder of current liabilities often listed in order of descending amount. IFRS financial statements may show assets and liabilities listed in order of reverse liquidity; however,

(continued)

both ASPE and IFRS require proper classification of assets and liabilities between current and non-current.

- Interest is usually due annually or more frequently (semi-annually or monthly, for example). Therefore, interest accrued on long-term debt is generally classified as a current liability. Likewise, interest receivable earned from accrual of interest on long-term receivables is generally classified as a current asset.

- **Short-term** is synonymous with **current**, and **long-term** is synonymous with **non-current**. Therefore, "short-term debt" can be used to refer to current liabilities. Asset classifications are typically titled "current" and "non-current," whereas liability classifications are typically titled "current" and "long-term." All non-current assets (assets in classifications other than "current assets") are resources that are **not** expected to be converted into cash or fully consumed in operations within one year or the operating cycle, whichever is longer.

- If an account title starts with "Allowance for . . .," it is generally a contra statement of financial position asset account.

- A **contra account** is a valuation account whose normal balance (debit or credit) is opposite of the normal balance of the account to which the contra account relates. For example, allowance for doubtful accounts has a normal credit balance, which is opposite to the normal debit balance of the accounts receivable account, which the allowance for doubtful accounts account is contra to. A **valuation account** is an account whose balance is needed to properly value the account to which it relates. An **adjunct account** is a valuation account whose normal balance is the same as the normal balance of the account to which it relates.

- A **contingency** is an existing situation in which there is uncertainty about whether a gain or loss will occur, and that will finally be resolved when one or more future events occurs or fails to occur. Under IFRS, the term **provisions** is similar in concept to contingent losses, as IFRS defines a provision as "any liability of uncertain timing or amount." Therefore under IFRS, if an account title starts with "Provision for . . .," it is likely a statement of financial position liability account. Under ASPE and U.S. GAAP, if an account title starts with "Provision for . . .," it may also be an expense account on the statement of income.

- The balance of liabilities and the balance of shareholders' equity at a point in time simply serve as scorecards of the total amounts of unspecified assets, which have come about from creditor sources (liabilities) and owner sources (shareholders' equity). Thus, you **cannot** determine the amount of cash (or any other specific asset) held by an entity by looking at total shareholders' equity or liabilities, or any account balance within. You must look at the listing of individual assets on the statement of financial position to determine the amount of cash held as at that date.

- A **reserve** is an appropriation of retained earnings. An appropriation of retained earnings refers to a portion of retained earnings that for one reason or another is restricted and cannot be used as a basis for declaration of dividends.

- In answering questions regarding classification of items on a statement of financial position, assume an individual item is material unless it is apparent otherwise.

Illustration 5-1   1 2 7

● Transactions that do not have a cash impact in the financial statement period do not affect the **statement of cash flows**. For example, a current period transaction resulting in a tract of land being purchased in exchange for a long-term note payable with principal and interest due in one year would not affect the statement of cash flows. The transaction would be reflected in statement of financial position accounts, and the notes to the financial statements would disclose details of the transaction.

● **Classification of interest and dividends** on the statement of cash flows may differ under ASPE and IFRS. Under ASPE, interest received and paid, and dividends received, are operating activities, whereas dividends paid is a financing activity. Under IFRS, interest and dividends received may each be classified as either operating or investing activities, and interest and dividends paid may each be classified as either operating or financing activities, provided that they are separately disclosed and consistently classified from period to period.

ILLUSTRATION 5-1

Statement of Financial Position Classifications

Current assets: Includes cash, short-term investments, accounts receivable, inventory, prepaid expenses, and other assets, which are expected to be realizable within the next year or operating cycle, whichever is longer.

Short-term investments: Includes investments in debt and equity securities, which management intends to convert to cash within the next year or operating cycle, whichever is longer. Short-term investments are presented separately and valued at cost/amortized cost or fair value.

Non-current investments: Includes long-term receivables, restricted funds (cash or cash equivalents allocated for acquisition of or additions to non-current assets), non-current investments in debt or equity of other companies (strategic investments), and tangible assets held as investments (such as land held for investment speculation).

Property, plant, and equipment: Includes long-lived tangible assets (land, building, equipment, and machinery) that are currently being used in operations to generate income. Assets in this category are often referred to as "plant assets" or "fixed assets." They are not held for resale.

Intangible assets: Includes assets that lack physical substance, such as patents, copyrights, franchises, trademarks, or trade names that give the holder exclusive right of use for a specified period of time. Their value to a company is generally derived from rights or privileges granted by a governmental or other authority.

Other assets: Includes assets that by common practice are not classified elsewhere.

Current liabilities: Includes obligations that are due within a year from the statement of financial position date or within the operating cycle, whichever is longer.

Long-term liabilities: Includes obligations that are not reasonably expected to be liquidated within the normal operating cycle but instead are payable at some later date.

Capital shares: The exchange value of shares issued.

Contributed surplus: Includes premiums on shares issued, capital donations from owners, and other.

Retained earnings: Excess of net incomes over net losses and dividend distributions since inception of the business. If a portion of retained earnings is appropriated, it is considered an appropriation (or restriction) of retained earnings, which cannot be used as a basis for declaration of dividends. Retained earnings is sometimes referred to as "earned surplus."

Accumulated other comprehensive income: Includes unrealized gains/losses on certain investments, gains/losses on certain hedging transactions, and gains/losses on revalued property, plant, and equipment under IFRS.

EXERCISE 5-1

PURPOSE: This exercise lists examples of statement of financial position accounts and will help you practise determining where they are classified.

Instructions

Indicate which statement of financial position classification is the most appropriate for reporting each account listed below by selecting the abbreviation of the corresponding classification.

CA	Current Assets	OA	Other Assets
STI	Short-Term Investments	CL	Current Liabilities
INV	Non-Current Investments	LTL	Long-Term Liabilities
PPE	Property, Plant, and Equipment	CS	Capital Shares
GW	Goodwill	CON	Contributed Surplus
ITG	Intangible Assets	RE	Retained Earnings

If the account is a contra account, indicate this by putting the abbreviation in parentheses. If the exact classification depends on facts that are not given, indicate this with the abbreviation **DEP** ("depends on") and list the possible classifications. If the account is reported on the statement of income/comprehensive income rather than the statement of financial position, indicate this with the abbreviation **SI/CI**. Assume all items are material.

Classification	Account	Classification	Account
_____	1. Accounts Payable	_____	27. Bond Sinking Fund
_____	2. Accounts Receivable	_____	28. Buildings
_____	3. Accrued Interest Receivable on Long-Term Investments	_____	29. Cash
_____	4. Accrued Interest Payable	_____	30. Cash Surrender Value of Life Insurance
_____	5. Accrued Taxes Payable	_____	31. Certificate of Deposit
_____	6. Accumulated Depreciation— Buildings	_____	32. Common Shares
_____	7. Accumulated Depreciation— Machinery	_____	33. Construction in Process (entity's new plant under construction)
_____	8. Administrative Expenses	_____	34. Creditors' Accounts with Debit Balances
_____	9. Advances by Customers	_____	35. Current Maturities of Bonds Payable (to be paid from Bond Sinking Fund)
_____	10. Advances to Affiliates		
_____	11. Advances to Vendors	_____	36. Current Maturities of Bonds Payable (to be paid from general cash account)
_____	12. Advertising Expense		
_____	13. Allowance for Bad Debts	_____	37. Current Portion of Long-Term Debt
_____	14. Allowance for Depreciation		
_____	15. Allowance for Doubtful Accounts	_____	38. Current Portion of Mortgage Payable
_____	16. Allowance for Excess of Cost over Net Realizable Value of Inventory	_____	39. Customers' Accounts with Credit Balances
_____	17. Allowance for Purchase Discounts	_____	40. Customers' Deposits
_____	18. Allowance for Sales Discounts	_____	41. Deferred Office Supplies
_____	19. Allowance for Uncollectible Accounts	_____	42. Deferred Property Tax Expense
_____	20. Allowance to Reduce Inventory to Net Realizable Value	_____	43. Deferred Rent Revenue
		_____	44. Deferred Service Revenue
_____	21. Appropriation for Bond Sinking Fund	_____	45. Deferred Subscription Revenue
_____	22. Appropriation for Contingencies	_____	46. Deposits on Equipment Purchases
_____	23. Appropriation for Future Plant Expansion	_____	47. Depreciation of Equipment
_____	24. Bank Overdraft	_____	48. Discount on Bonds Payable
_____	25. Bond Interest Payable	_____	49. Discount on Notes Payable
_____	26. Bond Interest Receivable	_____	50. Discount on Notes Receivable
		_____	51. Dishonoured Notes Receivable

Classification	Account	Classification	Account
_____	52. Dividends Payable	_____	82. Mineral Resources
_____	53. Dividend Payable in Common Shares	_____	83. Mortgage Payable
		_____	84. Notes Payable
_____	54. Earned Rent Revenue	_____	85. Notes Payable to Banks
_____	55. Estimated Liability for Income Tax	_____	86. Notes Receivable
_____	56. Estimated Premium Claims Outstanding	_____	87. Notes Receivable from Officers
_____	57. Factory Supplies	_____	88. Office Supplies
_____	58. Finished Goods Inventory	_____	89. Office Supplies Expense
_____	59. Furniture and Fixtures	_____	90. Office Supplies Prepaid
_____	60. Gain on Sale of Equipment	_____	91. Office Supplies Used
_____	61. Goodwill	_____	92. Patents
_____	62. Income Tax Payable	_____	93. Pension Obligation
_____	63. Income Tax Withheld (from employees)	_____	94. Petty Cash Fund
		_____	95. Plant and Equipment
_____	64. Income Taxes Receivable	_____	96. Preferred Share Redemption Fund
_____	65. Interest Income	_____	97. Premium on Bonds Payable
_____	66. Interest Payable	_____	98. Premium on Common Shares
_____	67. Interest Receivable		
_____	68. Investment in Canada Savings Bonds	_____	99. Prepaid Advertising
		_____	100. Prepaid Insurance
_____	69. Investment in Microsoft Shares	_____	101. Prepaid Insurance Expense
		_____	102. Prepaid Office Supplies
_____	70. Investment in BlackBerry Shares	_____	103. Prepaid Property Tax
		_____	104. Prepaid Royalty Payments
_____	71. Investment in Unconsolidated Subsidiary	_____	105. Provision for Bad Debts
		_____	106. Provision for Income Tax
_____	72. Land	_____	107. Rent Revenue
_____	73. Land Held for Future Plant Site	_____	108. Salaries and Wages Payable
		_____	109. Sales Discounts and Allowances
_____	74. Land Used for Parking Lot		
_____	75. Leasehold Costs	_____	110. Selling Expense Control
_____	76. Leasehold Improvements	_____	111. Share Dividends Distributable
_____	77. Loss on Sale of Investments		
_____	78. Machinery and Equipment	_____	112. Share Dividends Payable
_____	79. Machinery and Equipment Sitting Idle	_____	113. Store Supplies
		_____	114. Store Supplies Used
_____	80. Marketable Securities	_____	115. Tools and Dies (5-year life)
_____	81. Merchandise Inventory		

Classification	Account	Classification	Account
_____	116. Tools and Dies (6-month life)	_____	120. Unearned Royalties
_____	117. Unamortized Bond Issue Costs	_____	121. Unearned Subscription Revenue
_____	118. Unamortized Discount on Bonds Payable	_____	122. Unexpired Insurance
_____	119. Unearned Rent Revenue	_____	123. Vouchers Payable
		_____	124. Warranty Liability
		_____	125. Work in Process

Solution to Exercise 5-1

Solution	Explanation and/or Comment
CL	1. These are trade payables usually due within 30 or 60 days.
CA	2. These are trade receivables usually due within 30 or 60 days.
CA	3. Interest receivable is usually due annually or more frequently.
CL	4. A better title is simply Interest Payable (item 66).
CL	5. A better title is simply Taxes Payable.
(PPE)	6. This is a contra account. It is another title for item 14; however, the account name in item 6 is used more frequently as each property, plant, and equipment account usually has its own accumulated depreciation contra account.
(PPE)	7. This is a contra account. It is another title for item 14; however, the account name in item 7 is used more frequently as each property, plant, and equipment account usually has its own accumulated depreciation contra account.
SI/CI	8. This is an operating expense.
DEP: CL or LTL	9. These advances refer to revenue amounts received in advance from customers and are liabilities until the related goods are provided or services are performed.
DEP: CA or INV or OA	10. These advances are loans.
DEP: CA or INV or OA	11. These advances can be prepayments or loans.
SI/CI	12. This is a selling expense.
(CA)	13. This is another title for Allowance for Doubtful Accounts (item 15).
(PPE)	14. This is another title for Accumulated Depreciation (items 6 and 7).

Solution	Explanation and/or Comment
(CA)	15. This is a contra account to Accounts Receivable.
(CA)	16. This is a contra account to Inventory; it is another title for item 20.
(CL)	17. This account reflects amounts included in Accounts Payable that will not be paid because of purchase discounts to be taken.
(CA)	18. This account reflects amounts included in Accounts Receivable that will not be collected because of sales discounts to be allowed.
(CA)	19. This is another title for Allowance for Doubtful Accounts (item 15).
(CA)	20. This account arises because of the lower of cost and net realizable value rule for inventory. It is a contra account to Inventory.
RE	21. This is a restriction on a portion of retained earnings.
RE	22. This is a restriction on a portion of retained earnings.
RE	23. This is a restriction on a portion of retained earnings.
CL	24. When this item exists, it is usually listed as the first item under current liabilities.
CL	25. Bond interest from a bond payable is usually payable annually or more frequently.
CA	26. Bond interest from a bond investment is usually receivable annually or more frequently.
INV	27. A bond sinking fund is an accumulation of funds set aside to help repay a bond issue. It can consist of restricted cash or securities, and is usually listed immediately below current assets with non-current investments.
PPE	28. This is included in Property, Plant, and Equipment.
CA	29. This is unrestricted cash.
DEP: INV or OA	30. The assumption is that the entity will continue the insurance coverage rather than take the cash surrender value of the life insurance policy.
DEP: CA or INV	31. Some Certificates of Deposit are for 90 days, 80 days, 30 months, or 60 months.
CS	32. This reflects the exchange value of common shares that have been issued.
PPE	33. This is one of two exceptions to the general guidelines for items to be included in the PPE classification.

Solution	Explanation and/or Comment
CA	34. A creditor has been overpaid or items purchased on account have been returned for credit after payment of account has been made.
LTL	35. Because assets from the Bond Sinking Fund (which is assumed to be classified under non-current investments) will be used to retire the current maturities of bonds payable, this item may be grouped with LTL.
CL	36. "Current maturities" refers to the portion that is coming due within a year of the statement of financial position date, and as indicated, cash (a current asset) will be used to settle the debt.
CL	37. Some accountants list this item first in the list of current liabilities; others list it last.
CL	38. "Current portion" refers to the portion that is coming due within a year of the statement of financial position date.
CL	39. This arises when customers overpay or return goods after full payment is made.
DEP: CL or LTL	40. A deposit may be an advance payment for goods and services or a security deposit.
CA	41. This is another title for items 88, 90, and 102.
CA	42. This is another title for item 103, Prepaid Property Tax.
DEP: CL or LTL	43. This is another title for item 119, Unearned Rent Revenue.
DEP: CL or LTL	44. A service contract may cover one or more years; revenue has been collected but not earned.
DEP: CL or LTL	45. Some subscriptions are for one year; others are for two or more years. This is another title for item 121, Unearned Subscription Revenue.
PPE	46. This is the second of two exceptions to the general guidelines for items to be included in the PPE classification.
SI/CI	47. This refers to depreciation expense for the current period.
(LTL)	48. This is another title for item 118. In the rare instance that the bonds payable are classified as current, the discount would be current also. Note that current standards also use the net method of accounting for bonds payable (under which the initial bond payable is recorded at present value, rather than recording the maturity value of the bond in a bond payable account along with a [contra] discount on bond payable account that together net to present value).

Solution	Explanation and/or Comment
DEP: (CL) or (LTL)	49. A discount on note payable occurs when the effective (market) interest rate exceeds the stated interest rate on a note payable. Note that current standards also use the net method of accounting for notes payable.
DEP: (CA) or (INV)	50. A discount on note receivable results when the note receivable is issued below par. Note that current standards also use the net method of accounting for notes receivable.
CA	51. A dishonoured note receivable is one that has reached its maturity date and remains uncollected.
CL	52. A dividend is usually paid approximately three to four weeks after it is declared.
CS	53. This is a bad title for Share Dividend Distributable. This is the same as items 111 and 112.
SI/CI	54. This is another title for Rent Revenue.
CL	55. This is another title for Income Tax Payable.
DEP: CL or LTL	56. Premiums in this context are liabilities.
CA	57. This item is similar to a prepaid expense; these supplies will be part of factory overhead (hence, work in process inventory) when used.
CA	58. This is one of three inventory accounts for a manufacturer.
PPE	59. This is included in Property, Plant, and Equipment.
SI/CI	60. This is in the Other Revenues and Gains section of the statement of income/comprehensive income.
GW	61. Goodwill is an indefinite life asset generally shown (above and) separately from intangible assets on the statement of financial position.
CL	62. This is usually payable annually or more frequently.
CL	63. This is usually payable monthly.
CA	64. This is usually receivable annually or more frequently.
SI/CI	65. This is usually included in the Other Revenues and Gains section of the statement of income/ comprehensive income.
CL	66. This is another title for item 4 (item 66 is the preferred title).
CA	67. This is usually receivable annually or more frequently.

Solution	Explanation and/or Comment
DEP: STI or INV	68. If management intends to convert the Canada Savings Bonds to cash in the short term, the investment should be classified as STI; otherwise, it should be classified as INV.
DEP: INV or STI	69. If management intends to convert the shares to cash in the short term, the investment should be classified as STI; otherwise, it should be classified as INV.
DEP: STI or INV	70. If management intends to convert the shares to cash in the short term, the investment should be classified as STI; otherwise, it should be classified as INV.
INV	71. The fact that the investee is a subsidiary means that this is a strategic investment and that management intends to hold this investment in the long term.
PPE	72. This is included in Property under Property, Plant, and Equipment.
INV	73. This land is not being used in current operations and would usually be classified as a non-current investment.
PPE	74. This is included in Property under Property, Plant, and Equipment.
ITG	75. These are costs incurred in obtaining a lease.
PPE	76. Some textbooks suggest classifying Leasehold Improvements with intangible assets. Most companies report them as PPE.
SI/CI	77. Classified under Other Expenses and Losses on the statement of income/comprehensive income.
PPE	78. This is included in Equipment under Property, Plant, and Equipment.
OA	79. Classified separately from Equipment being used in operations to generate income.
DEP: CA or INV	80. This is a title often used to refer to short-term investments; it can also refer to securities (debt and/or equity of other entities) held for long-term purposes.
CA	81. This is another title for Inventory held by a retailer.
PPE	82. Natural resources are classified with PPE.
LTL	83. The portion of this balance due within the next year should be reclassified and reported as a current liability.

Solution	Explanation and/or Comment
DEP: CL or LTL	84. This depends on time to maturity as at the statement of financial position date.
DEP: CL or LTL	85. This depends on time to maturity as at the statement of financial position date.
DEP: CA or INV	86. This depends on time to maturity as at the statement of financial position date.
DEP: CA or INV	87. Officers of a company are considered related parties; separate disclosure must be made of related party transactions.
CA	88. This is another title for items 41, 90, and 102.
SI/CI	89. This is another title for item 91, and an operating expense.
CA	90. This is another title for items 41, 88, and 102.
SI/CI	91. This is another title for item 89, and an operating expense.
ITG	92. This is an Intangible Asset.
LTL	93. This is payable upon employees' retirement.
CA	94. This is usually used up annually or more frequently.
PPE	95. This is included in Property, Plant, and Equipment.
INV	96. This would require rate disclosures.
LTL	97. This is an adjunct-type valuation account. If the related bonds payable are classified as a current liability, this valuation account will also be classified as a current liability. Note that current standards also use the net method of accounting for bonds payable (under which the initial bond payable is recorded at present value, rather than recording the maturity value of the bond in a bond payable account along with an [adjunct] premium on bond payable account that together net to present value).
CON	98. This is an adjunct-type valuation account.
CA	99. This is a prepaid expense.
CA	100. This is another title for items 101 and 122.
CA	101. This is another title for items 100 and 122.
CA	102. This is another title for items 41, 88, and 90.
CA	103. This is another title for item 42.
CA	104. This is a prepaid expense.
SI/CI	105. This is another title for Uncollectible Accounts Expense or Bad Debt Expense.
SI/CI	106. This is another title for Income Tax Expense.

Solution	Explanation and/or Comment
SI/CI	107. This may be classified with Other Revenues and Gains on the statement of income/comprehensive income.
CL	108. This is another title for Accrued Salaries and Wages or Accrued Salaries and Wages Payable. Salaries and Wages Payable is the preferred title.
(SI/CI)	109. This is a contra sales revenue item.
SI/CI	110. A control account is an account in the general ledger for which the detailed transactions appear in a subsidiary ledger.
CS	111. This is another title for items 53 and 112. The title in item 111 is the preferred title.
CS	112. This is another title for items 53 and 111. This is a misleading title because the word "payable" suggests a cash liability, which a share dividend is not.
CA	113. This answer assumes the supplies are on hand (that they have not been used).
SI/CI	114. This item refers to store supplies expense.
PPE	115. This is considered Equipment under Property, Plant, and Equipment.
SI/CI	116. The service life is so short that the benefits yielded will not extend beyond one year. Therefore, the expenditure is not capitalized.
(LTL)	117. This is usually called Bond Issue Costs. According to current standards, costs such as these should not be recognized as an asset because they do not meet the definition and recognition criteria for an asset. The related bonds are usually long-term liabilities, and issue costs would probably be deducted from the related liability, rather than shown in a contra long-term liability account.
(LTL)	118. This is another title for item 48.
DEP: CL or LTL	119. This is another title for item 43.
DEP: CL or LTL	120. Revenue has been received, but not earned; hence, an obligation exists to provide a good, service, or refund in the future.
DEP: CL or LTL	121. This is another title for item 45.
CA	122. This is another title for items 100 and 101, Prepaid Insurance.
CL	123. This is another title for Accounts Payable when a voucher system is being used.
DEP: CL or LTL	124. Some warranties are for more than one year.
CA	125. This is an inventory account for a manufacturer.

APPROACH: For each statement of financial position classification, write down a definition or description of what is to be reported in that classification. Refer to those notes as you go down the list of items to be classified. Your notes should contain the guidelines summarized in **Illustration 5-1**.

EXERCISE 5-2

PURPOSE: This exercise will enable you to practise identifying errors and other deficiencies in a statement of financial position.

Jennings Company has decided to expand its operations. The bookkeeper recently completed the company's statement of financial position presented below to submit to the bank in order to obtain additional funds for expansion.

JENNINGS COMPANY
Statement of Financial Position
For the Year Ended 2017

Current assets	
Cash (net of bank overdraft of $15,000)	$175,000
Accounts receivable (net)	390,000
Inventory, at lower of FIFO cost and net realizable value	413,000
Marketable securities—at cost (fair value $115,000)	110,000
Property, plant, and equipment	
Building (net)	588,000
Office equipment (net)	197,000
Land held for future use	92,000
Intangible assets	
Franchise	90,000
Cash surrender value of life insurance	80,000
Prepaid insurance	6,000
Current liabilities	
Salaries and wages payable	21,000
Accounts payable	96,000
Note payable, due June 30, 2019	100,000
Pension obligation	92,000
Taxes payable	40,000
Note payable, due October 1, 2018	35,000
Discount on bonds payable	47,000
Long-term liabilities	
Bonds payable, 8%, due May 1, 2021	400,000

Shareholders' equity

Common shares, authorized 500,000 shares, issued 305,000 shares   305,000

Contributed surplus   279,000

Retained earnings   ?

Instructions

Prepare a revised statement of financial position in good form. Correct any errors and weaknesses you find in the presentation above. Assume that accumulated depreciation balances for the building and office equipment are $152,000 and $88,000, respectively. The marketable securities are classified as non-current and fair value through other comprehensive income (ignore related income tax considerations). The allowance for doubtful accounts account has a balance of $20,000. The pension obligation is considered to be a long-term liability.

Solution to Exercise 5-2

JENNINGS COMPANY
Statement of Financial Position
December 31, 2017
Assets

Current Assets

Cash		$190,000
Accounts receivable	$410,000	
Less allowance for doubtful accounts	20,000	390,000
Inventory, at lower of FIFO cost and net realizable value		413,000
Prepaid insurance		6,000
Total current assets		999,000

Non-Current Investments

Investments, at fair value with gains and losses in other comprehensive income	115,000	
Land held for future use	92,000	
Cash surrender value of life insurance	80,000	
Total non-current investments		287,000

Property, Plant, and Equipment

Building	$740,000	
Less accumulated depreciation—building	152,000	588,000
Office equipment	285,000	
Less accumulated depreciation—office equipment	88,000	197,000
Total property, plant, and equipment		785,000

Intangible Assets

Franchise ... 90,000

Total assets ... $2,161,000

Liabilities and Shareholders' Equity

Current Liabilities

Bank overdraft	$ 15,000	
Note payable, due October 1, 2018	35,000	
Accounts payable	96,000	
Taxes payable	40,000	
Salaries and wages payable	21,000	
Total current liabilities		$207,000

Long-Term Liabilities

Note payable, due June 30, 2019	100,000	
8% bonds payable, due May 1, 2021	353,000	
Pension obligation	92,000	
Total long-term liabilities		545,000
Total liabilities		752,000

Shareholders' Equity

Paid-in capital

Common shares, 500,000 authorized shares, 305,000 shares issued and outstanding	$305,000	
Contributed surplus	279,000	584,000
Retained earnings		820,000
Accumulated other comprehensive income		5,000
Total shareholders' equity		1,409,000
Total liabilities and shareholders' equity		$2,161,000

EXPLANATION:

1. In general, a bank overdraft in one bank account should not be reflected as an offset to positive cash items (such as a positive cash balance in another bank account). A bank overdraft should be reported as a current liability. The one exception to this rule is if the company has a positive balance bank account at the same bank at which its overdraft bank account is held, and the company has a right of offset; in this situation, the overdraft can be reflected as an offset against that positive balance bank account.

2. Marketable securities classified as fair value through other comprehensive income are reported on the statement of financial position at fair value, with unrealized gains/losses recorded in other comprehensive income, net of tax (in this case, with an increase to Deferred Tax Liability, although in this exercise, we are asked to ignore the tax effects). At the end of each period, other comprehensive income is accumulated in a shareholders' equity account

called Accumulated Other Comprehensive Income. This topic will be more fully explained in Chapter 9.

3. Land held for future use is not classified with property, plant, and equipment because the land is not currently being used in operations.

4. Cash surrender value of life insurance is an intangible item in a legal sense (because it lacks physical substance), but it is classified as a non-current investment for accounting purposes.

5. Prepaid expenses such as prepaid insurance represent prepayments that relate to benefits that are expected to be consumed within the year following the statement of financial position date. Hence, they are current assets.

6. Pension obligation is generally not expected to come due within the next year, and is considered a long-term liability.

7. Discount on Bonds Payable is a contra-type valuation account. Current standards use the net method of accounting for bonds payable, which requires that Bonds Payable be shown net of its related discount or premium.

8. Bonds payable are assumed to be long-term liabilities unless they meet the definition of a current liability.

9. For this exercise, retained earnings can be calculated by determining the amount needed to cause total liabilities and shareholders' equity to equal total assets.

EXERCISE 5-3

PURPOSE: This exercise will enable you to practise identifying errors and other deficiencies in a statement of financial position.

Presented here is a statement of financial position for Gabby Corporation.

GABBY CORPORATION
Statement of Financial Position
December 31, 2017

Current assets	$520,000	Current liabilities	$365,000
Investments	700,000	Long-term liabilities	920,000
Property, plant, and equipment	2,185,000	Shareholders' equity	2,690,000
Intangible assets	570,000		
	$3,975,000		$3,975,000

The following information is available:

1. The current asset section includes: cash $120,000; accounts receivable $190,000, less $10,000 for allowance for doubtful accounts; inventory $230,000; and unearned revenue $10,000 (credit balance). Inventory is stated at replacement cost; original cost based on FIFO is $200,000.

2. The investments section includes the cash surrender value of a life insurance contract $60,000; non-current investments in common shares $230,000; bond sinking fund $220,000; organization costs $70,000; and land upon which a new plant is being constructed $120,000. Investments in common shares are all classified as fair value through other comprehensive income and have fair values equal to their cost.

3. Property, plant, and equipment include buildings $1.6 million, less accumulated depreciation $375,000; equipment $400,000, less accumulated depreciation $240,000; land $500,000; and land held for future use $300,000.

4. Intangible assets include a franchise $140,000; goodwill $80,000; discount on bonds payable $30,000; and construction in process $320,000. (A new plant is under construction and will be ready for use in Gabby's operations within nine months.)

5. Current liabilities include accounts payable $80,000; notes payable—short-term $110,000; notes payable—long-term $150,000; and salaries and wages payable $25,000. They do not include any amount for loss contingencies. The company's lawyer states that it is probable the company will have to pay $60,000 in 2018 due to litigation pending as at the statement of financial position date.

6. Long-term liabilities are composed of 10% bonds payable $800,000 (due June 1, 2025), and pension liability $120,000.

7. Shareholders' equity includes preferred shares, 200,000 shares authorized with 70,000 shares issued for $450,000; and common shares, $2 par value, 300,000 shares authorized with 100,000 shares issued at an average price of $10. In addition, the corporation has retained earnings of $1,240,000.

Instructions

Prepare a corrected statement of financial position in good form.

Solution to Exercise 5-3

GABBY CORPORATION
Statement of Financial Position
December 31, 2017
Assets

Current Assets		
Cash		$ 120,000
Accounts receivable	$ 190,000	
Less allowance for doubtful accounts	10,000	180,000
Inventory, at lower of FIFO cost and net realizable value		200,000
Total current assets		500,000

Non-Current Investments

Investments, at fair value with gains and losses in other comprehensive income	230,000	
Bond sinking fund	220,000	
Cash surrender value of life insurance	60,000	
Land held for future use	300,000	
Total non-current investments		810,000

Property, Plant, and Equipment

Land		620,000	
Building	$1,600,000		
Less accumulated depreciation— building	375,000	1,225,000	
Construction in process		320,000	
Equipment	400,000		
Less accumulated depreciation— equipment	240,000	160,000	
Total property, plant, and equipment			2,325,000

Goodwill	80,000

Intangible Assets

Franchise	140,000
Total assets	$3,855,000

Liabilities and Shareholders' Equity

Current Liabilities

Notes payable	$ 110,000	
Accounts payable	80,000	
Estimated litigation liability	60,000	
Salaries and wages payable	25,000	
Unearned revenue	10,000	
Total current liabilities		$ 285,000

Long-Term Liabilities

Notes payable	150,000	
10% bonds payable, due June 1, 2025	770,000	
Pension liability	120,000	
Total long-term liabilities		1,040,000
Total liabilities		1,325,000

Shareholders' Equity

Paid-in capital

Preferred shares; 200,000 shares authorized, 70,000 shares issued and outstanding .... $ 450,000

Common shares, $2 par value; 300,000 shares authorized, 100,000 shares issued and outstanding 200,000

Contributed surplus 800,000*   1,450,000

Retained earnings 1,080,000**

Total shareholders' equity 2,530,000

Total liabilities and shareholders' equity $3,855,000

*100,000 shares × ($10 − $2) = $800,000.

**The corrected balance for the Retained Earnings account can be calculated as follows:

Retained Earnings, before corrections	$1,240,000
Overstatement of inventory	(30,000)
Organization costs expense	(70,000)
Understatement of litigation liability	(60,000)
Corrected Retained Earnings balance	$1,080,000

The statement of financial position errors affected some statement of income accounts (which were closed to Retained Earnings).

- According to current standards, organization costs of $70,000 should not be capitalized and included with assets, because they do not meet the definition and recognition criteria of an asset.

- The $620,000 amount reported for land is composed of land $500,000; plus land upon which a new plant is being constructed $120,000.

- Current standards use the net method of accounting for bonds payable, which requires that Bonds Payable be shown net of its related discount or premium.

Illustration 5-2 145

ILLUSTRATION 5-2

Operating, Investing, and Financing Activities on the Statement of Cash Flows

Operating activities: Operating activities represent the enterprise's principal revenue-producing activities and all other activities not related to investing and financing. Cash flows from operating activities are generally the cash effects of transactions and other events that enter into the determination of net income.

Investing activities: Investing activities represent the acquisitions and disposals of long-term assets and other investments not included in cash equivalents, including (1) making and collecting loans; (2) acquiring and disposing of debt and equity instruments of other entities; and (3) acquiring and disposing of property, plant, and equipment and other productive assets.

Financing activities: Financing activities represent activities that result in changes in the size and composition of the enterprise's equity capital and borrowings, including (1) obtaining resources from owners and providing them with a return on and a return of their investment; (2) borrowing money and repaying the amounts borrowed, or otherwise settling the obligation; and (3) obtaining and paying for other resources obtained from creditors.

Examples

Operating activities:
  Cash inflows:
    From sale of goods or services (including cash sales and collections on account).
    From other transactions, such as amounts received to settle lawsuits and refunds from suppliers.

  Cash outflows:
    To suppliers for inventory and other goods and services (including cash purchases and payments on account).
    To employees for services.
    To government for taxes.
    To others for items such as payments to settle lawsuits, refunds to customers, and contributions to charities.

Investing activities:
  Cash inflows:
    From sale of property, plant, and equipment.
    From sale of debt or equity securities of other entities.
    From collection of principal on loans to other entities.

Cash outflows:
To purchase property, plant, and equipment.[a]
To purchase debt or equity securities of other entities.
To make loans to other entities.

Financing activities:
Cash inflows:
From sale of equity securities (company's own shares).
From issuance of debt instruments (bonds and notes).

Cash outflows:
To reacquire capital shares.
To pay debt (both short-term and long-term) other than accounts payable.

[a]Generally, only advance payments, the down payment, and other amounts paid in the current period regarding acquisition of property, plant, and equipment and other productive assets will affect investing activities on the statement of cash flows. For example, vendor financing of assets (such as a capital lease) may not have a large cash impact in the period of acquisition, if any, and therefore may not affect the statement of cash flows significantly in that period—although full details of the transaction would be note-disclosed.

- The statement of cash flows summarizes all of the transactions during a period that have an impact on the cash balance. The activity format is used whereby cash inflows and cash outflows are summarized in three categories: operating, investing, and financing.

- The difference between net income and net cash provided by operating activities can be substantial.

- Under ASPE, interest received and paid, and dividends received (that is, interest and dividends included in net income) are operating activities and dividends paid (that is, dividends booked through retained earnings) are financing activities. Under IFRS, interest and dividends received may each be classified as either operating or investing activities, and interest and dividends paid may each be classified as either operating or financing activities, provided that they are separately disclosed and consistently classified from period to period.

- As with the statement of income/comprehensive income, certain information is generally considered to be more important on the statement of financial position and statement of cash flows.

- On the statement of financial position, working capital is important, as is the amount of debt, especially as it relates to the amount of equity. These elements help determine the company's liquidity, solvency, and financial flexibility.

- On the statement of cash flows, net cash provided by/used by operating activities is the most important number since it shows whether a company is generating net positive cash or net negative cash from its core operating activities. In the long term, companies cannot continue to operate if they are not generating net positive cash from their core activities.

EXERCISE 5-4

PURPOSE: This exercise enables you to practise identifying investing and financing activities.

Instructions

Place the appropriate code in the blanks to identify each of the following transactions as giving rise to an:

Code

II	inflow of cash due to an investing activity, or
IO	outflow of cash due to an investing activity, or
FI	inflow of cash due to a financing activity, or
FO	outflow of cash due to a financing activity.

_____   (a) Sell common shares to new shareholders.

_____   (b) Purchase treasury shares.

_____   (c) Borrow money from bank by issuance of short-term note.

_____   (d) Repay money borrowed from bank.

_____   (e) Purchase bonds as an investment.

_____   (f) Sell investment in real estate.

_____   (g) Loan money to an affiliate.

_____   (h) Collect on loan to affiliate.

_____   (i) Buy equipment.

_____   (j) Sell a plant asset.

_____   (k) Pay cash dividends to shareholders.

Solution to Exercise 5-4

(a)	FI	(f)	II
(b)	FO	(g)	IO
(c)	FI	(h)	II
(d)	FO	(i)	IO
(e)	IO	(j)	II

(k) ASPE: FO; IFRS: Outflow of cash due to an operating activity, or FO (depending on classification of payment of dividends in previous years).

APPROACH:

1. For each item, identify whether there is an inflow of cash (debit to Cash) or an outflow of cash (credit to Cash).

2. Write down the definitions for investing activities and financing activities (see below). Analyze each transaction to see if it fits one of these definitions.

   (a) **Investing activities**—include (1) making and collecting loans to other entities; (2) acquiring and disposing of investments in debt and equity securities of other entities; and (3) acquiring and disposing of property, plant, and equipment and other productive assets.

   (b) **Financing activities**—include (1) obtaining capital from owners and providing them with a return on and a return of their investment; (2) borrowing money from creditors and repaying the amounts borrowed; and (3) obtaining and paying for other resources obtained from creditors.

3. Assume purchases and sales of items are for cash, unless otherwise indicated.

- The journal entry to record a transaction that is an investing activity that results in a cash flow will involve: (1) Cash and (2) an asset account (other than Cash and asset accounts related to operating activities), such as Investments (short-term or long-term), Land, Buildings, Equipment, Patent, and Franchise.

- The journal entry to record a transaction that is a financing activity that results in a cash flow will involve: (1) Cash and (2) a liability account or a shareholders' equity account (other than liability accounts related to operating activities), such as Bonds Payable, Notes Payable, Dividends Payable, Common Shares, Contributed Surplus, and Treasury Shares.

EXERCISE 5-5

PURPOSE: This exercise will enable you to practise reconciling net income with net cash provided by operating activities.

The following data relate to J. Wentworth Co. for 2017.

Net income	$77,500
Increase in accounts receivable	8,000
Decrease in prepaid expenses	4,700
Increase in accounts payable	2,800
Decrease in taxes payable	1,100
Gain on sale of investments	1,700
Depreciation expense	3,500
Loss on sale of equipment	600

Instructions

Calculate the net cash provided by operating activities for 2017.

Solution to Exercise 5-5

Net income	$77,500
Adjustments to reconcile net income to net cash provided by operating activities:	
Depreciation expense	3,500
Increase in accounts receivable	(8,000)
Decrease in prepaid expenses	4,700
Increase in accounts payable	2,800
Decrease in taxes payable	(1,100)
Gain on sale of investments	(1,700)
Loss on sale of equipment	600
Net cash provided by operating activities	$78,300

EXPLANATION:

1. Net income is a summary of all revenues earned, all expenses incurred, and all gains and losses recognized in a period. Most revenues earned during the year result in a cash inflow during the same period but there may be some cash and/ or revenue flows that do not correspond. Most expenses incurred during the year result in a cash outflow during the same period but there may be some cash and/or expense flows that do not correspond. To adjust for these differences, decreases and increases in current assets related to operating activities are added back to and subtracted from net income (respectively), and increases and decreases in current liabilities related to operating activities are added back to and subtracted from net income (respectively).

2. Depreciation expense is a non-cash charge (debit) against income. It must be added to net income to arrive at the amount of net cash provided by operating activities.

3. An increase in accounts receivable indicates that revenues earned exceeded cash collected from customers, and net income exceeds net cash provided by operating activities. This requires a subtraction from net income to arrive at net cash provided by operating activities.

4. A decrease in prepaid expenses indicates that prepaid expenses incurred exceeded cash paid for prepaid expenses, and net income is less than net cash provided by operating activities. This requires an addback to net income to arrive at net cash provided by operating activities.

5. An increase in accounts payable indicates that expenses incurred exceeded cash paid for accounts payable, and net income is less than net cash provided by operating activities. This requires an addback to net income to arrive at net cash provided by operating activities.

6. A decrease in taxes payable indicates that tax expense incurred was less than cash paid for taxes, and net income is greater than net cash provided by operating activities. This requires a subtraction from net income to arrive at net cash provided by operating activities.

7. When an investment is sold, the entire proceeds are shown as an investing activity on the statement of cash flows. Therefore, the gain included in net income must be deducted from net income to arrive at net cash provided by operating activities. If this deduction is not made, there would be double counting of the gain amount. For example, if an investment with a carrying value of $4,000 is sold for $7,000, the entire $7,000 proceeds is an investing inflow. However, the $7,000 includes the gain of $3,000 and a recovery of the investment's $4,000 carrying value. If the entire $7,000 should be shown as an investing activity, the $3,000 gain should be deducted from net income to arrive at net cash from operating activities.

8. A loss on sale of equipment does not cause a cash outflow so it is added back to net income to arrive at net cash provided by operating activities. The cash proceeds from sale of the equipment would be shown as a cash inflow from an investing activity.

EXERCISE 5-6

PURPOSE: This exercise will give you practice in preparing a statement of cash flows.

The comparative statements of financial position of Baker Corporation at the beginning and end of year 2017 appear below.

BAKER CORPORATION
Statements of Financial Position

	Dec. 31, 2017	Dec. 31, 2016	Increase/Decrease	
ASSETS				
Cash	$10,500	$7,100	Inc.	3,400
Accounts receivable	19,000	10,100	Inc.	8,900
Prepaid expenses	2,400	3,200	Dec.	(800)
Fair value–net income investments	-0-	11,300	Dec.	(11,300)
Equipment	59,000	42,000	Inc.	17,000
Less: Accumulated depreciation	(10,700)	(5,000)	Inc.	(5,700)
Total	$80,200	$68,700	Inc.	11,500
LIABILITIES AND SHAREHOLDERS' EQUITY				
Accounts payable	$ 6,100	$ 4,500	Inc.	1,600
Unearned revenue	1,700	6,700	Dec.	(5,000)
Common shares	15,000	10,000	Inc.	5,000
Retained earnings	57,400	47,500	Inc.	9,900
Total	$80,200	$68,700	Inc.	11,500

During the year 2017, Baker purchased equipment for $17,000 cash, declared and paid cash dividends of $2,500, sold fair value–net income investments for an amount equal to their December 31, 2016, fair value, and reported net income of $12,400.

Instructions

Prepare a statement of cash flows for Baker Corporation for the year ended December 31, 2017.

Solution to Exercise 5-6

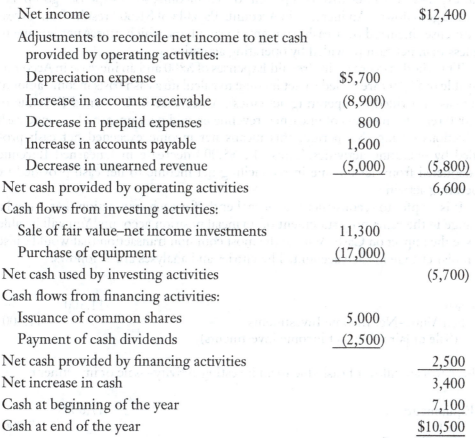

BAKER CORPORATION
Statement of Cash Flows
For the Year Ended December 31, 2017

Cash flows from operating activities:		
Net income		$12,400
Adjustments to reconcile net income to net cash provided by operating activities:		
Depreciation expense	$5,700	
Increase in accounts receivable	(8,900)	
Decrease in prepaid expenses	800	
Increase in accounts payable	1,600	
Decrease in unearned revenue	(5,000)	(5,800)
Net cash provided by operating activities		6,600
Cash flows from investing activities:		
Sale of fair value–net income investments	11,300	
Purchase of equipment	(17,000)	
Net cash used by investing activities		(5,700)
Cash flows from financing activities:		
Issuance of common shares	5,000	
Payment of cash dividends	(2,500)	
Net cash provided by financing activities		2,500
Net increase in cash		3,400
Cash at beginning of the year		7,100
Cash at end of the year		$10,500

EXPLANATION: The net change in cash for the year can be easily determined by calculating the difference between cash at the end of the year ($10,500) and cash at the beginning of the year ($7,100), which yields a net increase of $3,400. The reasons for that net increase of $3,400 can be determined by analyzing all of the transactions that caused changes in all of the statement of financial position accounts other than Cash. The changes in Accounts Receivable, Prepaid Expenses, Accounts Payable, and Unearned Revenues are all due to accruals and prepaids, which help to reconcile the net income figure to the amount of net cash provided by operating activities. The changes in Investments and Equipment are due to transactions that are classified as investing activities. The changes in Accumulated Depreciation are usually due to recording of depreciation expense for the current period, and disposals of plant assets. The changes in non-trade liability accounts (such as Mortgage Payable, Bonds Payable, and Bank Note Payable) and most changes in shareholders' equity accounts are due to transactions that are classified as financing activities.

An increase of $8,900 in Accounts Receivable indicates that sales revenue (on an accrual basis) exceeded cash collections from customers by $8,900, which causes net income to exceed net cash provided by operating activities. So $8,900 is deducted from net income to reconcile net income to a cash basis figure. A decrease of $800 in Prepaid Expenses indicates that prepaid expenses incurred on an accrual basis exceeded cash payments for prepaid expenses by $800, which causes net income to be less than net cash provided by operating activities. (Remember that expenses are a negative component of net income, so as expenses go up, net income goes down.) An increase in Accounts Payable of $1,600 results from excess of expenses incurred over cash payments to suppliers, which causes net income to be less than net cash provided by operating activities.

Thus, both a decrease in Prepaid Expenses of $800 and an increase in Accounts Payable of $1,600 are added to net income to calculate a cash basis income amount (net cash provided by operating activities). A decrease in Unearned Revenue of $5,000 reflects an excess of unearned revenue earned over unearned revenue cash collections during this period; this means net income exceeded net cash provided by operating activities. Thus, the $5,000 decrease in Unearned Revenue is deducted from net income in reconciling net income to net cash provided by operating activities.

It is helpful to reconstruct the journal entry for each transaction that caused a change in the remaining statement of financial position accounts. You will be able to see the impact on Cash. Assume the most common transaction that would cause a similar change in each account. The entries and analyses are as follows:

Cash	11,300	
Fair Value–Net Income Investments		11,300
(Sale of fair value–net income investments)		

There was an inflow of cash due to an investing activity—sale of investments.

Equipment	17,000	
Cash		17,000
(Purchase of equipment)		

There was an outflow of cash due to an investing activity—purchase of property, plant, and equipment.

Depreciation Expense	5,700	
Accumulated Depreciation—Equipment		5,700
(Recording of depreciation for current period)		

Note this is a non-cash item. It is merely allocating the cash cost of the equipment over the equipment's useful life.

Cash	5,000	
Common Shares		5,000
(Sale of common shares)		

There was an inflow of cash due to a financing activity—issuance of common shares (obtaining resources from owners).

Retained Earnings	2,500	
Cash		2,500
(Declaration and payment of cash dividends)		

There was an outflow of cash due to a transaction that the company classifies as a financing activity—payment of dividends (giving owners a return on their investment).

Income Summary	12,400	
Retained Earnings		12,400
(Net income amount is closed to Retained Earnings)		

The balance of the Income Summary account before closing is a summary figure reflecting all revenues and all expenses for the period. Most revenues increase cash and most expenses decrease cash, so we use net income (a summary of all revenues and all expenses) as our starting point in calculating net cash provided by operating activities. The net income figure is then "adjusted" for the following items:

1. revenue transactions that did not bring a cash inflow this period.
2. expense transactions that did not require a cash outflow this period.
3. revenue items of another period that produced a cash inflow this period.
4. expense items of another period that produced a cash outflow this period.

The result is the amount of net cash provided or used by operating activities (a cash basis income figure).

ILLUSTRATION 5-3

A Summary of Financial Ratios

Ratio	Formula for Calculation	Purpose or Use
I. Liquidity		
1. Current ratio	$\dfrac{\text{Current assets}}{\text{Current liabilities}}$	Measures short-term debt-paying ability.
2. Quick or acid-test ratio	$\dfrac{\text{Cash, marketable securities, and receivables (net)}}{\text{Current liabilities}}$	Measures immediate short-term liquidity.
3. Current cash debt coverage ratio	$\dfrac{\text{Net cash provided by operating activities}}{\text{Average current liabilities}}$	Measures the company's ability to pay off its current liabilities in a specific year from its operations.
II. Activity		
4. Receivables turnover	$\dfrac{\text{Net sales}}{\text{Average trade receivables (net)}}$	Measures liquidity of receivables.
5. Inventory turnover	$\dfrac{\text{Cost of goods sold}}{\text{Average inventory}}$	Measures liquidity of inventory.
6. Asset turnover	$\dfrac{\text{Net sales}}{\text{Average total assets}}$	Measures how efficiently assets are used to generate sales.
III. Profitability		
7. Profit margin on sales	$\dfrac{\text{Net income}}{\text{Net sales}}$	Measures net income generated by each dollar of sales.
8. Rate of return on assets	$\dfrac{\text{Net income}}{\text{Average total assets}}$	Measures overall profitability of assets.
9. Rate of return on common share equity	$\dfrac{\text{Net income minus preferred dividends}}{\text{Average common shareholders' equity}}$	Measures profitability of owners' investment.
10. Earnings per share	$\dfrac{\text{Net income minus preferred dividends}}{\text{Weighted average shares outstanding}}$	Measures net income earned on each common share.
11. Price earnings ratio	$\dfrac{\text{Market price of shares}}{\text{Earnings per share}}$	Measures the ratio of the market price per share to earnings per share.
12. Payout ratio	$\dfrac{\text{Cash dividends}}{\text{Net income}}$	Measures percentage of earnings distributed in the form of cash dividends.
IV. Coverage		
13. Debt to total assets	$\dfrac{\text{Total debt}}{\text{Total assets}}$	Measures the percentage of total assets provided by creditors.
14. Times interest earned	$\dfrac{\text{Income before interest charges and taxes}}{\text{Interest charges}}$	Measures ability to meet interest payments as they come due.

15. Cash debt coverage ratio	$\dfrac{\text{Net cash provided by operating activities}}{\text{Average total liabilities}}$	Measures ability to repay total liabilities in a specific year from its operations.
16. Book value per share	$\dfrac{\text{Common shareholders' equity}}{\text{Outstanding shares}}$	Measures the amount each share would receive if the company were liquidated at the amounts reported on the statement of financial position.

Throughout the remainder of the text, ratios are provided to help you understand and interpret the information provided. The above chart is a summary of ratios that will be used throughout the text.

ANALYSIS OF MULTIPLE-CHOICE QUESTIONS

Question

1. The amount of time that is expected to elapse until an asset is realized or otherwise converted into cash is referred to as:

   a. solvency.
   c. liquidity.
   b. financial flexibility.
   d. exchangeability.

EXPLANATION: Liquidity refers to the amount of time that is expected to elapse until an asset is realized or otherwise converted into cash or until a liability has to be paid; liquidity refers to the "nearness to cash" of assets and liabilities. Solvency refers to an enterprise's ability to pay its debts as they mature. Liquidity and solvency affect an entity's financial flexibility, which measures the ability of an enterprise to take effective actions to alter the amounts and timing of cash flows so it can respond to financial adversity and adapt to unexpected needs and opportunities. (Solution = c.)

Question

2. The Lana Johnson Company has the following obligations at December 31, 2017:

Accounts payable	$ 75,000
Taxes payable	65,000
Notes payable issued November 1, 2017, due October 31, 2018	70,000
Bonds payable issued December 1, 2008, due November 30, 2018 (to be paid by use of a sinking fund)	120,000

The amount that should be reported for total current liabilities at December 31, 2017, is:

a. $330,000.

c. $210,000.

b. $140,000.

d. $75,000.

EXPLANATION: Write down the definition (or key phrases therein) of a current liability. (A **current liability** is an obligation that is due within one year from the date of the statement of financial position or within the operating cycle, whichever is longer.) A current liability that will be retired using non-current assets may be classified as a long-term liability as at the statement of financial position date. Analyze each of the obligations listed to see if it meets the criteria for being classified as current.

Accounts payable and taxes payable will both be due shortly after the statement of financial position date and will require cash to liquidate the debts. The notes payable are due within a year of the statement of financial position date and there is no evidence to indicate that non-current assets will be used for settlement; thus, the notes payable are a current liability. The bonds payable are coming due within a year, but they will be retired using a sinking fund (restricted cash or securities currently classified as a non-current investment). Total current liabilities equals $75,000 + $65,000 + $70,000 = $210,000. (Solution = c.)

Question

3. Land held for a future plant site should be classified with:

a. current assets.

c. property, plant, and equipment.

b. non-current investments.

d. intangible assets.

EXPLANATION: Review the descriptions of each asset classification. The land is not being used in operations, so it does not belong in property, plant, and equipment. It is not lacking physical existence, so it cannot be an intangible asset. The land is not expected to be converted to cash or sold or consumed within the next year or operating cycle, so it is not a current asset. The land should be classified with non-current investments. (Solution = b.)

Question

4. Working capital is:

a. current assets less current liabilities.

b. total assets less total liabilities.

c. the same as retained earnings.

d. capital that has been reinvested in the business.

EXPLANATION: The excess of total current assets over total current liabilities is referred to as "working capital." Working capital represents the net amount of a company's relatively liquid resources. It is the "liquid buffer" available to meet the financial demands of the operating cycle. (Solution = a.)

Question

5. Treasury shares are classified as a(n):
    a. current asset.
    b. non-current investment.
    c. other asset.
    d. contra shareholders' equity item.

EXPLANATION: Treasury shares are company shares that the company previously issued, and later redeemed, but did not cancel. The acquisition of treasury shares represents a contraction of owners' equity; thus it is reported as a reduction of shareholders' equity. (Solution = d.)

Question

6. Which of the following is classified as an intangible asset on a statement of financial position?
    a. Long-term receivable
    b. Non-current investment in shares of another enterprise
    c. Licences
    d. Accounts receivable

EXPLANATION: Intangible assets lack physical substance and usually have a high degree of uncertainty concerning their future benefits. Although receivables and investments in shares lack physical existence, they are properly classified elsewhere and are not considered intangible assets. Accounts receivable are classified as current assets; long-term receivables and non-current investments in shares are classified as non-current investments; and licences are classified as intangible assets. (Solution = c.)

Question

7. Which of the following should **not** be found in the non-current investment section of the statement of financial position?
    a. Land held for speculation
    b. Bond sinking fund
    c. Cash surrender value of life insurance
    d. Patent

EXPLANATION: A patent is classified as an intangible asset. Non-current investments, often referred to simply as investments, are normally one of four types:
1. Investments in securities, such as bonds and common shares, which management does not intend to convert to cash in the short term
2. Investments in tangible fixed assets not currently used in operations, such as land held for speculation or a future plant site

3. Investments set aside in special funds such as a sinking fund, pension fund, or plant expansion fund. The cash surrender value of life insurance is included here

4. Investments in non-consolidated subsidiaries or affiliated companies ("strategic" investments) (Solution = d.)

Question

8. Which of the following is a contra account?
   a. Premium on bonds payable   c. Patents
   b. Unearned revenue   d. Accumulated depreciation

EXPLANATION: After reading the question and before reading the answer selections, write down the description of the term "contra account." (A **contra account** is a valuation account whose normal balance is opposite of the balance of the account to which it relates.) Premium on bonds payable is an adjunct type valuation account (its normal balance is the same as the normal balance of the account to which it relates). Unearned Revenue and Patents are not valuation accounts. Accumulated Depreciation is a valuation account for property, plant, and equipment. The normal balance of an Accumulated Depreciation account is a credit and the normal balance of a property, plant, and equipment account is a debit. Hence, Accumulated Depreciation is a contra account. (Solution = d.)

Question

9. Which of the following should be classified as a cash inflow in the investing activities section of a statement of cash flows?
   a. Cash sale of inventory
   b. Sale of delivery equipment at book value
   c. Proceeds on sale of common shares
   d. Issuance of a note payable to a bank

EXPLANATION: Read the question and, before reading the answer selections, write down the items that appear in the definition of investing activities. (**Investing activities** include making and collecting loans to others; acquiring and disposing of shares and bonds of other entities; and acquiring and disposing of property, plant, and equipment and other productive assets.) Think of the items included in that definition that would produce a cash inflow (collecting loans and disposing of investments and property, plant, and equipment). As you analyze each answer selection, consider the type of activity it represents. Cash sale of inventory is an operating activity. Sale of common shares is a financing activity. Issuance of a note payable is a financing activity. Sale of equipment is an investing activity. (Solution = b.)

Question

10. In preparing a statement of cash flows under ASPE, an example of a cash flow from an operating activity is:
    a. payment to employees for services.
    b. payment of dividends to shareholders.
    c. receipt of proceeds from sale of an investment.
    d. receipt of proceeds from sale of common shares to shareholders.

EXPLANATION: Operating activities include the cash effects of transactions related to the company's main revenue-producing activities and all other activities that are not related to investing or financing. Operating activities include collections from customers and payments for inventory, other goods and services, and taxes. Under ASPE, interest received and paid and dividends received are classified as operating activities, and dividends paid are classified as a financing activity. (Under IFRS, interest and dividends received may each be classified as either operating or investing activities, and interest and dividends paid may each be classified as either operating or financing activities, provided that they are separately disclosed and consistently classified from period to period.) Sale of an investment is an investing activity. Sale of common shares is a financing activity. However, payment to employees for services is always considered an operating activity. (Solution = a.)

Question

11. In preparing a statement of cash flows, the sale of property, plant, and equipment at an amount greater than its book value should be classified as a(n):
    a. operating activity.   c. financing activity.
    b. investing activity.   d. extraordinary activity.

EXPLANATION: Think about the nature of each of the three categories in a statement of cash flows and select the one involving disposal of plant assets.
1. **Operating activities**: Operating activities represent the enterprise's principal revenue-producing activities and all other activities not related to investing and financing. Cash flows from operating activities are generally the cash effects of transactions and other events that enter into the determination of net income.
2. **Investing activities**: Investing activities represent the acquisitions and disposal of long-term assets and other investments not included in "cash equivalents," including (a) making and collecting loans; (b) acquiring and disposing of debt and equity instruments of other entities; and (c) acquiring and disposing of property, plant, and equipment and other productive assets.
3. **Financing activities**: Financing activities represent activities that result in changes in the size and composition of the enterprise's equity capital and borrowings, including (a) obtaining resources from owners and providing them with a return on and a return of their investment; (b) borrowing money and

repaying the amounts borrowed, or otherwise settling the obligation; and (c) obtaining and paying for other resources obtained from creditors.

There is **no** category called "extraordinary activity" on a statement of cash flows. The fact that the asset was sold for a price exceeding its book value does not affect the answer because the entire proceeds from the sale should be reported in the investing activities section. In the operating activities section, the amount of gain included in net income is deducted (excluded) from net income to arrive at "net cash provided by operating activities." (Solution = b.)

Question

12. In a statement of cash flows, proceeds from the issuance of common shares should be classified as a cash inflow from:

    a. operating activities.   c. financing activities.

    b. investing activities.   d. lending activities.

EXPLANATION: The issuance of common shares by a corporation is the company's way of obtaining resources from an owner (in other words, it is an owner investment in the business). Financing activities include obtaining resources from owners. There is no category called "lending activities." (Solution = c.)

Question

13. Which of the following would be classified as an investing activity on a statement of cash flows?

    a. Issuance of bonds payable at a premium

    b. Purchase of land to be used in operations

    c. Issuance of common shares at the current market price of $5

    d. Payment of dividends to shareholders

EXPLANATION: Think about the types of items that are included in investing activities. Investing activities include making and collecting loans; acquiring and disposing of investments (both debt and equity); and acquiring and disposing of property, plant, and equipment. Issuance of bonds and issuance of shares (regardless of price) are both financing activities that usually bring an inflow of cash. Payment of dividends may or may not be classified as a financing outflow, depending on whether the financial statements are prepared in accordance with ASPE or IFRS. The purchase of land (regardless of use) is an investing outflow. (Solution = b.)

Question

14. In preparing a statement of cash flows under ASPE, payment of interest to a creditor should be classified as a cash outflow due to:

    a. operating activities.   c. financing activities.

    b. investing activities.   d. borrowing activities.

EXPLANATION: Borrowing money is a financing activity and repaying the principal borrowed is a financing activity. However, under ASPE, paying interest on amounts borrowed is an operating activity. There is no category called "borrowing activities." (Solution = a.)

Question

15. Alley Cat Corporation had net income for 2017 of $4 million. Additional information is as follows:

Depreciation of plant assets	$1,800,000
Amortization of intangibles	$450,000
Increase in accounts receivable	$850,000
Increase in accounts payable	$1,000,000

Alley Cat's net cash provided by operating activities for 2017 was:

a. $2,050,000. c. $6,250,000.

b. $6,4000,000. d. $7,650,000.

EXPLANATION: The depreciation and amortization amounts are items that reduce net income but do not cause a decrease in cash during the current period. The increase in accounts receivable indicates that sales revenue earned for the period exceeded cash collections from customers, and therefore net income exceeded net cash provided by operating activities. The increase in accounts payable indicates that expenses incurred exceeded cash payments for accounts payable expense type items, which caused net income to be less than net cash provided by operating activities. The solution is as follows:

Net income	$4,000,000
Depreciation of plant assets	1,800,000
Amortization of intangibles	450,000
Increase in accounts receivable	(850,000)
Increase in accounts payable	1,000,000
Net cash provided by operating activities	$6,400,000

(Solution = b.)

Question

16. Net cash flow from operating activities for 2017 for Hampton Corporation was $77,000. The following items are reported on the financial statements for 2017 (prepared under ASPE):

Depreciation expense	$7,000
Cash dividends paid on common shares	4,000
Increase in accounts receivable	5,000

Based only on the information above, Hampton's net income for 2017 was:

a. $75,000.

d. $86,000.

b. $71,000.

e. none of the above.

c. $93,000.

EXPLANATION: Write down the format for reconciliation of net income to net cash provided by operating activities. Fill in the information given. Solve for the unknown.

Net income	$ X
Depreciation expense	7,000
Increase in accounts receivable	(5,000)
Net cash provided by operating activities	$77,000

Solving for X, net income = $75,000. Cash dividends paid on common shares has no effect on this calculation because under ASPE, cash dividends paid is not an operating activity; it is classified as a financing activity. (Solution = a.)

Question

17. Free cash flow is:

a. net cash provided by operating activities minus capital expenditures and dividends.

b. net cash provided by operating activities minus retirement of debt and purchases of treasury shares.

c. the amount of cash obtained from donations.

d. the amount of net cash increase during the period.

EXPLANATION: One method of examining a company's financial flexibility is to do a free cash flow analysis. This analysis starts with net cash provided by operating activities and ends with free cash flow, which is calculated as net cash provided by operating activities less capital expenditures and dividends. Free cash flow is the amount of discretionary cash flow a company has for purchasing additional investments, retiring its debt, purchasing treasury shares, or simply adding to its liquidity. This measure is an indication of a company's level of financial flexibility. (Solution = a.)

Question

18. Net cash provided by operating activities divided by average total liabilities equals the:

a. current cash debt coverage ratio.

c. free cash flow.

b. cash debt coverage ratio.

d. current ratio.

EXPLANATION: Visualize the calculation of each ratio or calculation referenced in the answer selections. The current cash debt coverage ratio equals net cash provided by operating activities divided by average current liabilities. The cash debt coverage ratio equals net cash provided by operating activities divided by average total liabilities. Free cash flow is calculated as net cash provided by operating activities less capital expenditures and dividends. The current ratio is current assets divided by current liabilities. (Solution = b.)

Question

19. Activity ratios measure the effectiveness of asset usage. One such ratio is the:
    a. inventory turnover ratio.
    c. quick ratio.
    b. current ratio.
    d. rate of return on assets.

EXPLANATION: Activity ratios include the (1) receivables turnover ratio, (2) inventory turnover ratio, and (3) asset turnover ratio. The current ratio and the quick (or acid-test) ratio are both liquidity ratios. The rate of return on assets ratio is a profitability ratio. (Solution = a.)

Question

20. The current ratio is 3:1 for the Hamstock Company at December 31, 2017. What is the impact on that ratio of a collection of accounts receivable?
    a. Current ratio is increased.
    c. Current ratio is unaffected.
    b. Current ratio is decreased.

EXPLANATION: Reconstruct the journal entry for the transaction. Analyze the effect of the debit portion of the entry on each element of the ratio and then analyze the effect of the credit portion of the entry on each element of the ratio. The entry to record collection of accounts receivable involves a debit to Cash and a credit to Accounts Receivable. There is no change in the total amount of current assets. There is no change in the total amount of current liabilities. Thus, there is no change in the current ratio, which equals current assets divided by current liabilities. (Solution = c.)

Question

21. Although the statement of financial position provides useful information to users, it has significant limitations, including:
    a. valuation, use of estimates, and lack of completeness.
    b. valuation and lack of completeness.
    c. lack of completeness.
    d. use of estimates.

EXPLANATION: The statement of financial position has many limitations, the main ones being predominant use of the historical cost model, the fact that accrual accounting requires use of estimates (such as for bad debts), and the fact that due to inability to measure certain items such as certain contingencies, many items are not reported on the statement of financial position. (Solution = a.)

Question

22. Chan Limited offers a five-year warranty with the products it sells. The warranty includes an obligation to fix the product under warranty should the product break. The "stand ready" obligation to provide coverage over the warranty period is:

    a. a cost of doing business and should be expensed as incurred.

    b. unconditional.

    c. conditional.

    d. not disclosed in financial statements.

EXPLANATION: Historically, warranty costs have been accrued as costs/obligations when related revenues are recognized. In general, warranty costs are not expensed as incurred; this would be inconsistent with accrual accounting. The "stand ready" obligation to provide coverage over the warranty period is unconditional, as Chan Limited has an unconditional obligation to provide coverage over the five-year warranty period. This unconditional obligation is recognized as a liability in the same period as the related sale, as long as it meets the definition of a liability. Warranties as they relate to revenue recognition are discussed further in Chapter 6. Contingencies are discussed further in Chapter 13. (Solution = b.)

Chapter 6

Revenue Recognition

OVERVIEW

Revenue recognition that is faithfully representative requires a sound understanding
of the nature of sales transactions from a business perspective. Especially in unique,
atypical, and complex business transactions, analyzing the related economics and
legalities is important in order to highlight potential areas of risk that may affect
revenue recognition policy. The two widely accepted approaches to recognizing
revenues are (1) the asset-liability (contract-based) approach, and (2) the earnings
approach. The new IFRS 15 *Revenues from Contracts with Customers* adopts the
asset-liability approach. The IASB has determined that this brings more discipline
to the measurement of revenue. ASPE continues to follow the earnings approach,
which recognizes and measures revenue based on whether it has been earned.
This chapter also highlights revenue recognition issues that can arise from situations such as right of return, repurchase agreements, consignments, warranties, and
others. The mechanics of revenue recognition for long-term contracts is discussed
in the chapter appendix 6A.

STUDY STEPS

Understanding Revenue Recognition from a Business Perspective

Revenues are increases in a company's economic resources that result from its ordinary operations. Therefore, to determine the timing and amount of revenue recognition, it is critical to understand how an entity earns its money. Are goods, services, or both transferred in normal revenue transactions? Does the entity include warranties or services to the customer to be delivered after the point of sale, perhaps in order to be more competitive within its industry? How and when does the customer pay the entity? In earning revenues, are there any constructive obligations that signal that the entity acknowledges a potential economic burden, which may not even be stated in a law or contract? The business perspective of sales transactions should be analyzed in order to highlight revenue recognition issues and achieve fair and faithfully representative disclosure of revenues.

- When analyzing accounting issues such as revenue recognition, it is important to consider the **economics** of these transactions. For example, is the company economically better off? Does the company take on any new risks when it enters into sales transactions?

- Consider the **legalities** and obligations surrounding a company's sales transactions. Are there contractual or constructive obligations that need to be analyzed in order to determine when revenue has been earned?

- The **asset-liability** approach requires the use of a five-step process for revenue recognition. Revenue is then recognized when the performance obligation is satisfied.

- ASPE uses the **earnings approach**, which begins with an analysis of the entity's earnings process.

ILLUSTRATION 6-1

The Asset-Liability Approach to Revenue Recognition

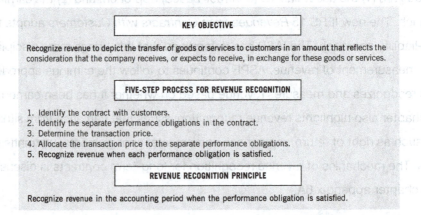

KEY OBJECTIVE

Recognize revenue to depict the transfer of goods or services to customers in an amount that reflects the consideration that the company receives, or expects to receive, in exchange for these goods or services.

FIVE-STEP PROCESS FOR REVENUE RECOGNITION

1. Identify the contract with customers.
2. Identify the separate performance obligations in the contract.
3. Determine the transaction price.
4. Allocate the transaction price to the separate performance obligations.
5. Recognize revenue when each performance obligation is satisfied.

REVENUE RECOGNITION PRINCIPLE

Recognize revenue in the accounting period when the performance obligation is satisfied.

Illustration 6-1   167

1. Identify the contract with customers.

   Contracts with customers are legally enforceable agreements that create rights or obligations. If the remaining rights exceed the remaining performance obligations, the contract is an asset (a contract asset). Conversely, if the remaining performance obligations exceed the remaining rights, the contract is a liability (a contract liability). **Until performance (by one or both parties) occurs, no net asset or net liability occurs.**

2. Identify separate performance obligations.

   A performance obligation exists if the customer can benefit from the good or service on its own or together with other resources. If the contract contains multiple performance obligations, a company must determine whether each product or service is distinct. If each of the goods or services is distinct but is interdependent and interrelated, these goods and services are combined and accounted for as one performance obligation.

3. Determine the transaction price.

   The transaction price is the amount of consideration the company expects to receive from a customer in exchange for transferring goods and/or services. In determining the transaction price, companies must consider (1) variable consideration, (2) time value of money, (3) non-cash consideration, and (4) consideration paid or payable to the customer.

4. Allocate transaction price to separate performance obligations.

   If more than one performance obligation exists in a contract, the transaction price should be allocated based on relative fair values. The best measure of fair value is the stand-alone selling price of the good or service. Estimates of the stand-alone selling price can be based on (1) adjusted market assessment, (2) expected cost plus a margin approach, or (3) a residual approach.

5. Recognize revenue when performance obligation is satisfied.

   A company satisfies its performance obligation when the customer obtains control of the good or service. Control is indicated by the customer's ability to direct the use of and obtain substantially all the remaining benefits from the asset or service and by the customer's ability to prevent others from controlling the asset or service. Companies satisfy performance obligations either at a point in time or over a period of time. According to IFRS 15.35, companies should recognize revenue over a period of time only if (1) the customer receives and consumes benefits as the seller performs, (2) the customer controls the asset as it is created or enhanced, or (3) the company does not have an alternative use for the asset and has a right to payment for its performance.

The Earnings Approach to Revenue Recognition (ASPE)

The earnings approach to revenue recognition recognizes revenues when the following criteria are met:

Performance is achieved, which means the following.

1. **The risks and rewards of ownership are transferred to the customer (for sale of goods) and/or the earnings process is substantially complete.**
2. The vendor has **no continuing involvement in, nor effective control over,** the goods sold.
3. Costs and revenues can be **measured reliably.**
4. **Collectibility** is probable.

Sometimes there is one very important step or act in the earnings process that signals substantial completion or performance, and therefore a sale. This is called a "critical event." For a sale of goods, shipment is often the critical event, as legal title often passes either at the start or end of a shipment.

- The critical event is often evidenced by an outside exchange; for example, delivery of inventory to someone outside the company in exchange for consideration or rights to consideration.

- When there is just one critical event, the earnings process is termed a **discrete earnings process**, and revenue is recognized when that critical event is completed. When the earnings process is continuous, depending on the information available, revenue may be recognized gradually as each major step in the earnings process is completed.

- For goods, a sale occurs when the **risks and rewards of ownership** of the goods are transferred from seller to purchaser and/or when all significant acts in the earnings process are complete.

- The concept of risks and rewards is also central to the definition of an asset. Assets have three essential characteristics: there is some economic benefit to the entity, the entity has some control over that benefit, and the benefits result from a past transaction or event.

TIPS ON CHAPTER TOPICS

- All revenues cause an increase in net assets (shareholders' equity); thus, a revenue item also results in either an increase in assets or a decrease in liabilities. In the conceptual framework, **revenues** are defined as increases in economic resources, either by way of inflows or enhancements of an entity's assets or by settlement of its liabilities, which result from an entity's **ordinary activities**. Revenues normally arise from sale of goods, rendering of services, or use by others of the entity's resources, yielding rent, interest, royalties, or dividends.

- To **recognize** means to record in the accounts. To recognize a revenue means to record an item as revenue in the accounts and thus include the item as revenue in the financial statements. Likewise, to recognize an asset means to record an increase in an asset account. Recognition is "the process of including an item in the financial statements of an entity" (*CICA Handbook*). For an asset or liability, recognition involves recording not only acquisition or incurrence of the item but also later changes in it, including removal from the accounts and therefore financial statements.

- **Revenue** is a **gross** amount (an amount before costs are subtracted), whereas a **gain** is a **net** amount (an amount after costs are subtracted). Gains (as opposed to revenues) commonly result from transactions and other events that do not involve an earnings process. For gain recognition, the emphasis is on being realized or realizable, rather than earned. Gains are commonly recognized at the time of an asset sale or the disposition of a liability, or when fair values of certain assets change. The following example illustrates how revenue is a gross concept and gain is a net concept.

A company sells two assets for $1,000 each. The first asset is an inventory item that cost $600. The second asset is a piece of equipment that cost $900 and has been depreciated $300 thus far. The first item would cause the following to be reflected in the statement of income:

Sales revenue	$1,000
Cost of goods sold	600
Gross profit	400

The second item would cause the following to be reflected in the "Other Revenues and Gains" section of a multiple-step statement of income:

Gain on sale of equipment	$400*

*$900 cost − $300 accumulated depreciation = $600 book value
 $1,000 selling price − $600 book value = $400 gain

In the case of the second item, it is not an item held for sale in the ordinary course of business. The proceeds ($1,000) and the related cost (carrying value of $600) are netted, and only the net amount ($400 gain) appears on the face of the statement of income.

- The term **income** is sometimes used to refer to a gross amount (such as dividend income, rental income, and interest income), which makes its usage synonymous with "revenue" at times. The term "income" is also used to refer to a net amount, such as net income for a period. Thus, if an exam question asks for the calculation of income to be recognized for the current period for a long-term construction contract using the percentage-of-completion method, it may be unclear whether the question is asking for income meaning "revenue" or income meaning "gross profit" (revenue net of related costs). If it is a multiple-choice question, a calculation of both revenue and gross profit may quickly solve the mystery.

- It is useful to consider revenue recognition in terms of "defaults"—specifically, consider when revenue would be recognized in the absence of other information or uncertainties. For example:

  1. Revenue from selling products is usually recognized at the date of sale or the date of delivery to customers.

  2. Revenue from services rendered is usually recognized when services have been performed and are billable.

  3. Interest, rent, and royalty revenue from permitting others to use the entity's assets is usually recognized as time passes or as the assets are used.

(continued)

- For a sale of goods, who has the risks and rewards of ownership is often clearly stated in the sales contract. For example, if the sales contract or invoice reads "Terms of sale: **f.o.b. shipping point**," then legal title transfers to the buyer when the goods leave the seller's shipping dock. If the sales contract or invoice reads "Terms of sale: **f.o.b. destination**," then legal title transfers to the buyer when the goods arrive at the buyer's location.

- Where there is **measurement uncertainty**, accrual accounting prefers that, unless the uncertainty cannot be measured, the revenue be recorded along with a cost or reduction of revenues to account for the related uncertainty.

- Where payment terms extend over a longer period, the amount receivable (and therefore the amount of revenue recorded) should be **discounted to reflect the time value of money**. IFRS states that the **discount rate** should be either (1) the prevailing rate for a similar note receivable or (2) the imputed rate that discounts the cash flows to the current cash selling price of the item or service sold, whichever is more clearly distinguishable. If the current cash selling price of the item or service sold is not known, (1) the prevailing rate for a similar note receivable may be used. If the current cash selling price of the item or service is known, (2) the imputed rate that discounts the cash flows to the current cash selling price of the item or service sold may be used.

- To allocate the overall price of a **bundled sale** to its separate components, ideally, the **relative fair value method** is used (where the purchase price is allocated based on the relative fair values of the components). Alternatively, the **residual value method** can be used (where the fair value of the undelivered item is subtracted from the overall price).

- When customers have **rights of return**, a company should recognize a refund liability and an asset for the cost of estimated inventory returns. If the company is unable to estimate the level of returns with any reliability, it should not report any revenue until the returns become predictive. Under ASPE, sales revenue is generally reported at the full amount with sales returns and allowance being shown as a contra account.

- Some asset transfer transactions include **repurchase agreements**. When a company has an obligation or a right to repurchase the assets from its customer for an amount greater than or equal to its selling price, then the transaction is reported as a financing (borrowing) transaction.

- When a company such as a travel agent (agent) is booking cruises for customers that will ultimately be provided by a cruise line (principal), then a **principal-agent relationship** exists. Amounts collected on behalf of the principal are not revenue of the agent. Instead, revenue for the agent is the amount of commission (net) it receives.

- Service-type (extended) **warranties** are treated as separate performance obligations. Companies should allocate a portion of the transaction price to service-type warranties, when present.

- Goods shipped on consignment are **not** considered sold, as revenue recognition criteria are not met at the time of shipment. The consignor retains ownership and legal title of the goods until the consignee sells the goods to a customer.

- Goods on consignment should be reported as inventory by the consignor, not the consignee.

- For some long-term contracts, such as construction-type contracts, development of military and commercial aircraft, weapons delivery systems, and space exploration hardware, it is more appropriate to recognize revenue over a period of time as each performance obligation is satisfied.

- If at least one of the criteria in IFRS 15.35 is met, and if the company can reasonably estimate its progress towards satisfaction of the performance obligations, then the **percentage-of-completion method** can be used to recognize revenue.

- Progress toward completion can be measured using the **cost-to-cost basis**, or the **units of delivery basis.**

- If a company is unable to estimate its progress toward completion, then the **zero-profit method** is used. Under ASPE, the method to recognize revenues and expenses only at the end of the contract is called the **completed-contract method**.

EXERCISE 6-1

PURPOSE: This exercise will allow you to determine the transaction price when the price is dependent on future events.

Browning Biotech enters into a licensing agreement with Alpha Pharmaceutical for a drug under development. Browning will receive a payment of $15,000 if the drug receives regulatory approval. Based on prior experience with the drug-approval process, Browning determines that it is 90% likely that the drug will gain approval, with a 10% chance of denial.

Instructions

(a) Determine the transaction price of the arrangement for Browning Biotech.

(b) Assuming that regulatory approval was granted on December 23, 2017, and that Browning received the payment from Alpha on January 19, 2018, prepare the journal entries for Browning.

Solution to Exercise 6-1

(a) $15,000

EXPLANATION: Because the arrangement has only two possible outcomes (regulatory approval is achieved or not), Browning should determine the transaction price based on the **most likely** approach. Thus, the best measure for the transaction price is $15,000.

(b)

12/23/17	Accounts receivable	15,000	
	Revenue		15,000
1/19/18	Cash	15,000	
	Accounts receivable		15,000

EXERCISE 6-2

PURPOSE: This exercise illustrates the allocation of the transaction price to separate performance obligations.

Harper Company manufactures equipment. Harper's products range from simple automated machinery to complex systems containing numerous components. Unit selling prices range from $140,000 to $1,200,000 and are quoted inclusive of installation. The installation process does NOT involve changes to the features of the equipment to perform to specifications. Harper has the following relationship with Magnolia Inc.

- Magnolia can purchase equipment from Harper for a price of $250,000 and contracts with Harper to install the equipment. Using market data, Magnolia determines installation service is estimated to have a fair value of $40,000. The cost of the equipment is $128,000.

- Magnolia is obligated to pay Harper the $250,000 upon delivery and installation of the equipment.

    Harper delivers the equipment on July 17, 2017, and completes the installation of the equipment on September 27, 2017. The equipment has a useful life of eight years. Assume the equipment and the installation are two distinct performance obligations that should be accounted for separately.

Instructions

(a) How should the transaction price of $250,000 be allocated among the service obligations?

(b) Prepare the journal entries for Harper for this revenue arrangement for 2017, assuming Harper receives payment when installation is completed.

Solution to Exercise 6-2

(a)

Total revenue	$250,000
Less: Installation	(40,000)
Allocated to equipment (residual)	$210,000

EXPLANATION: Having been provided the market value of the installation, Harper should use the residual approach. This involves starting with the total price for the contract and deducting the observable selling price of individual items being sold.

(b) 7/17/17

Accounts receivable	210,000	
Sales revenue		210,000
Cost of equipment sold	128,000	
Equipment inventory		128,000

9/27/17	Cash	250,000	
	Installation revenue		40,000
	Accounts receivable		210,000

EXERCISE 6-3

PURPOSE: This exercise will demonstrate revenue recognition when a repurchase agreement exists.

Zenith Corp. sells idle machinery to Eden Company on June 1, 2017, for $50,000. Zenith agrees to repurchase this equipment from Eden on May 31, 2018, for a price of $53,500 (an imputed interest rate of 7%).

Instructions

(a) Prepare the journal entry for Zenith for the transfer of the asset to Eden on June 1, 2017.

(b) Prepare any other necessary journal entries for Zenith for 2017.

(c) Prepare the journal entry for Zenith when the machinery is repurchased on May 31, 2018.

Solution to Exercise 6-3

(a) 6/1/17	Cash	50,000	
	Liabilities		50,000

EXPLANATION: In this case, due to the existence of a repurchase agreement, Zenith continues to have control of the asset. Therefore, this transaction is a financing (borrowing) transaction and not a sale. The asset (machinery) is *not* removed from the books of Zenith.

(b) 12/31/17

	Interest expense	2,042	
	Liabilities ($50,000 $\times$ 7% $\times \frac{7}{12}$)		2,042

Interest rate of 7% is imputed from the agreement

(c) 5/31/18

	Interest expense	1,458	
	Liabilities ($50,000 $\times$ 7% $\times \frac{5}{12}$)		1,458

Interest rate of 7% is imputed from the agreement

5/31/18	Liabilities ($50,000 + $2,042 + $1,458)	53,500	
	Cash		53,500

EXERCISE 6-4

PURPOSE: This exercise will review calculations related to consignment sales.

On April 15, 2017, Stayfit Company consigns 70 treadmills, costing $600 each, to Parmar Company. The cost of shipping the treadmills amounts to $800 and is paid by Stayfit Company. On December 31, 2017, an account sales report is received from the consignee, reporting that in 2017, 35 treadmills were sold for $700 each. The consignee remits the amount due after deducting a commission fee of 6%, advertising costs of $200, and total delivery costs of $300 on the treadmills sold.

Instructions

(a) Calculate the inventory value of the unsold units remaining on the consignee's property at December 31, 2017.

(b) Calculate the consignor's profit on the units sold in 2017.

(c) Calculate the amount of cash that was remitted by the consignee at the end of 2017.

Solution to Exercise 6-4

(a) Calculation of consignment inventory at cost, as at December 31, 2017:

70 units shipped at cost of $600 each	$42,000
Add freight on delivery to consignee	800
Consignment inventory at cost, April 15, 2017	$42,800
Consignment inventory at cost, December 31, 2017 (35 units unsold as at that date [$\frac{1}{2} \times \$42,800$])	$21,400

(b) Calculation of consignor's 2017 profit:

Consignment sales revenue (35 × $700)	$24,500
Less cost of units sold ($\frac{1}{2} \times \$42,800$)	(21,400)
Less commission charged by consignee (6% × $24,500)	(1,470)
Less advertising costs	(200)
Less delivery costs to customers	(300)
Profit on consignment sales	$1,130

(c) Calculation of consignee's remittance at the end of 2017:

Consignment sales revenue		$24,500
Less: Commissions	$1,470	
Advertising costs	200	
Delivery costs to customers	300	1,970
Remittance from consignee		$22,530

EXERCISE 6-5

PURPOSE: This exercise will demonstrate accounting for assurance-type and service-type warranties.

On December 31, 2017, Petite Company sells production equipment to Farnham Inc. for $60,000. Petite includes a one-year assurance warranty service with the sale of all its equipment. The customer receives and pays for the equipment on December 31, 2017. Petite estimates the prices to be $57,300 for the equipment and $2,700 for the cost of the warranty.

Instructions

(a) Prepare the journal entry to record this transaction on December 31, 2017.

(b) Repeat the requirements for (a), assuming that, in addition to the assurance warranty, Petite sold an extended warranty (service-type warranty) for an additional two years (2019–2020) for $1,800.

Solution to Exercise 6-5

(a)	12/31/17	Cash ($57,300 + $2,700)	60,000	
		Warranty expense	2,700	
		Warranty liability		2,700
		Sales revenue		60,000

EXPLANATION: Companies often warranty that the product meets agreed-upon specifications in the contract at the time the product is sold. This type of warranty is referred to as an assurance-type warranty and is included in the sales price of the company's product.

(b)	12/31/17	Cash ($57,300 + $2,700 + $1,800)	61,800	
		Warranty expense	2,700	
		Warranty liability		2,700
		Sales revenue		60,000
		Unearned warranty revenue		1,800

EXPLANATION: A warranty that provides an additional service beyond the assurance-type warranty is not included in the sales price and is referred to as a service-type warranty. It is recorded as a separate performance obligation. Petite should record this as unearned revenue in 2017. Subsequently, they should recognize $900 of warranty revenue in each of 2019 and 2020.

ILLUSTRATION 6-2

Journal Entries for Long-Term Construction Contracts

Entry	Percentage-of-Completion Method	Zero-Profit Method[a]	Completed-Contract Method[a]

To record costs of construction (recorded during the year, as incurred)	Construction in Process
	    Materials, Cash, Payables, etc.
		Construction in Process
		    Materials, Cash, Payables, etc.
			Construction in Process
			    Materials, Cash, Payables, etc.

To record progress billings (recorded during the year, as billed)	Accounts Receivable
	    Billings on Construction in Process
		Accounts Receivable
		    Billings on Construction in Process
			Accounts Receivable
			    Billings on Construction in Process

To record collections (recorded during the year, as collected)	Cash
	    Accounts Receivable
		Cash
		    Accounts Receivable
			Cash
			    Accounts Receivable

To recognize current period revenue and gross profit (recorded prior to financial statement preparation)	Construction Expenses[b] (for current period costs)
	Construction in Process[c] (for current period gross profit)
	    Revenue from Long-Term Contracts (for current period revenue)
		Construction Expenses (for current period costs)
		    Revenue from Long-Term Contracts (for current period revenue)[d]
			No Entry

To record completion of the contract (recorded only in the period of contract completion)	Billings on Construction in Process (for total balance to date)
	    Construction in Process (for total balance to date)
		Billings on Construction in Process (for total balance to date)
		    Construction in Process (for total balance to date)
		    Revenue from Long-Term Contracts (for total contract revenue not yet recognized to date)
			Billings on Construction in Process (for total contract revenue)
			    Revenue from Long-Term Contracts (for total contract revenue)
			Construction Expenses (for total costs)
			    Construction in Process (for total costs)

[a] Under IFRS, the zero-profit method is used in contracts where a specific act is much more significant than other acts, or where it is difficult to estimate costs to completion and therefore the percentage complete. Under ASPE, the completed-contract method is used if the outcome of the contract is not determinable.

[b] The Construction Expenses account can be titled Construction Costs or Costs of Construction.

[c] When a loss is estimated, this account (Construction in Process) is credited for the estimated amount of loss.

[d] This entry is recorded for current period costs and revenue, respectively, assuming that the entity is reasonably assured that it will be able to recover its costs incurred in the current period.

Regardless of the revenue recognition method or approach, an estimated loss on an overall unprofitable long-term construction contract is recognized in the period when the loss is determined. Recognizing loss on an unprofitable contract before completion of the contract (even under the zero-profit and completed-contract methods) is required in order for financial statements to be free from bias and consistent with the neutrality principle.

ILLUSTRATION 6-3

The Percentage-of-Completion, Zero-Profit, and Completed-Contract Methods of Revenue Recognition

Revenue Recognition Method	Criteria for Use of Method	Reason(s) for Use of Method
Percentage-of-completion method	At least one of the criteria in IFRS 15.35 is met, and company can reasonably estimate its progress toward satisfaction of the performance obligations	Recognition of revenue over a period of time, rather than at a point in time
Zero-profit method (IFRS)	Contracts where a specific act is much more significant than other acts; contracts where it is difficult to estimate costs to completion and therefore the percentage complete	If there are inherent risks in determining the progress toward contract completion, only recoverable revenues equal to costs incurred should be recognized.
Completed-contract method (ASPE)	Short-term contracts and contracts that do not meet criteria for use of percentage-of-completion method	If there are inherent hazards in the contract beyond normal, recurring business risks, related contract income should not be recognized until contract completion.

EXERCISE 6-6

PURPOSE: This exercise will demonstrate revenue recognition over time under the percentage-of-completion method.

Foster Ltd. contracts to build a high-rise for $4,800,000. Construction begins in 2017 and is expected to be completed in 2020. Data for 2017 and 2018 are:

	2017	2018
Cost incurred	$720,000	$1,360,000
Estimated costs to complete	2,880,000	1,920,000

Instructions

Using the percentage-of-completion method and the cost-to-cost basis,

(a) How much gross profit should be reported in 2017? Show your calculation.
(b) How much gross profit should be reported in 2018? Show your calculation.
(c) Prepare the journal entry to record the revenue and gross profit for 2018.

Solution to Exercise 6-6

(a) Gross profit $= \dfrac{\$720,000}{\$3,600,000} \times (\$4,800,000 - \$3,600,000) = \$240,000$

EXPLANATION: To calculate the percent complete under the cost-to-cost basis, a company compares the costs incurred to date with the most recent estimate of the total costs required to complete the contract. The resulting percentage is multiplied by the estimated total gross profit on the contract. This will provide the gross profit to be recognized to date.

(b) Gross profit $= \dfrac{\$2,080,000}{\$4,000,000} \times (\$4,800,000 - \$4,000,000) = \$416,000$

Less 2017 gross profit	(240,000)
Gross profit in 2018	$176,000

EXPLANATION: In the second year (and subsequent years), after calculating the gross profit to be recognized to date, the company subtracts the total gross profit already recognized in prior years. This provides the gross profit for the current year.

(c) 12/31/18	Construction in Process (gross profit)	176,000	
	Construction Expenses	1,360,000	
	Revenue from Long-term Contracts		1,536,000

ANALYSIS OF MULTIPLE-CHOICE QUESTIONS

Question

1. The process of formally including an item in the financial statements of an entity is:
   a. presentation.
   b. measurement.
   c. realization.
   d. recognition.

EXPLANATION: Write down a brief definition of each term listed. Select the one that matches the description in the question. **Presentation** is the process of determining where and how an item will be presented in the financial statements. **Measurement** refers to the amount recorded for the item in the financial statements. **Realization** is the process of converting non-cash resources and rights into cash (such as sale of assets for cash or claims to cash). **Recognition** is the process of including an item in the financial statements of an entity. (Solution = d.)

Question

2. Dot Point Stores Inc. is a clothing retailer. It signed a consignment agreement to display uniquely designed t-shirts manufactured and delivered to Dot Point by Trendy Clothiers (consignor). As the consignee, Dot Point:

    a. has legal title and ownership of the t-shirts.

    b. records a sale each time a t-shirt is sold.

    c. increases (credits) a "payable to consignor" account each time a t-shirt is sold.

    d. includes the t-shirts in its calculation of inventory.

EXPLANATION: Recall the fundamentals of consignment accounting. In a consignment arrangement, the consignor retains legal title of the consigned goods, and thus, ownership of the inventory. The consignee does not record a sale when a consigned good is sold. Each time a consigned good is sold, the consignee records a debit to cash (or accounts receivable) and a credit to a "payable to consignor" account. (Solution = c.)

Question

3. On December 31, 2017, Mahoney sold a piece of equipment to C. Bailey for $30,000 with the following terms: 2% cash discount if paid within 30 days, 1% discount if paid between 31 and 60 days of purchase, or payable in full within 90 days if not paid within a discount period. Bailey had the right to return this equipment to Mahoney if Bailey could not resell it before the end of the 90-day payment period, in which case Bailey would no longer be obligated to purchase the equipment. Mahoney has no past history of completing a similar transaction. How much should be included in Mahoney's net sales for 2017 due to the sale of this machine?

    a. $30,000

    b. $29,700

    c. $29,400

    d. $0

EXPLANATION: According to terms of the sale/purchase, Bailey has a right to return the equipment to Mahoney if Bailey is not able to resell the equipment before expiration of the 90-day payment period. Therefore, there is significant uncertainty surrounding this transaction. Although legal title and possession of the equipment have transferred to Bailey as at December 31, 2017, it is arguable that the risks and rewards of ownership have not transferred, as Mahoney must provide a refund if Bailey is not able to sell the equipment within the 90-day payment period. Mahoney retains considerable business risk related to the equipment. As well, if a sale were to be recorded, accrual accounting requires an attempt to measure and accrue an amount relating to the uncertainty (as a cost or reduced revenue). However, Mahoney has no history of completing a similar transaction, and estimating an amount related to the uncertainty would be difficult at best. (Solution = d.)

Question

4. The new IFRS standard, IFRS 15 *Revenue from Contracts with Customers*, adopts a(n):
    a. earnings approach to revenue recognition.
    b. asset-liability approach to revenue recognition.
    c. cash-based approach to revenue recognition.
    d. earned and realized approach to revenue recognition.

EXPLANATION: The IASB has determined that this brings more discipline to the measurement of revenue than the "earned and realized" criteria in prior IFRS standards. (Solution = b.)

Question

5. Where there are potentially multiple performance obligations within a single contract, if products or services are interdependent and interrelated, they must be:
    a. accounted for as multiple performance obligations.
    b. combined and reported as a single performance obligation.
    c. sold separately.
    d. combined under a new contract.

EXPLANATION: If the multiple performance obligations are distinct but are interdependent and interrelated, they should be accounted for as one performance obligation. If they are distinct and not interdependent (often can be sold separately), they are treated as separate obligations, and revenue must be recognized separately for each obligation. (Solution = b.)

Question

6. Measurement uncertainty does NOT arise from:
    a. the inability to reasonably estimate related costs of the transaction.
    b. the inability to reasonably estimate the consideration of the transaction.

c. the ability to measure the outcome of the transaction.

d. the inability to allocate costs already recorded to the correct account.

EXPLANATION: The inability to reasonably estimate the consideration of a transaction, for example to deliver something in the future, can increase measurement uncertainty because we do not always know what will happen in the future. Similarly, the right to receive consideration in the future creates measurement uncertainty of the outcome, since there is risk the customer will not pay. Similarly, the inability to estimate related costs of the transaction gives rise to measurement uncertainty. The allocation of costs to the correct account is not a measurement uncertainty issue. (Solution = d.)

Question

7. A product and service are bundled together and sold to customers for $450. The fair values of the product and service are $350 and $150, respectively. Under the relative fair value method, how much would be allocated to the product?

 a. $150.00

 b. $315.00

 c. $350.00

 d. $300.00

EXPLANATION: The total fair value to consider is $350 + $150 = $500.

$$\text{Product} = \frac{\$350}{\$500} \times \$450 = \$315.00$$

$$\text{Service} = \frac{\$150}{\$500} \times \$450 = \$135.00 \text{ (Solution} = \text{b.)}$$

Question

8. Bella Construction Co. uses the percentage-of-completion method. In 2017, Bella began work on a contract for $2.2 million; it was completed in 2018. The following cost data pertain to this contract:

	Year Ended December 31	
	2017	**2018**
Costs incurred during the year	$780,000	$560,000
Estimated costs to complete, as at end of year	520,000	—

The amount of gross profit to be recognized on the statement of income for the year ended December 31, 2017, is:

 a. $0.

 b. $516,000.

 c. $540,000.

 d. $900,000.

EXPLANATION: Write down the formula used to calculate gross profit recognized to date at the end of 2017. Use the data given to calculate the gross profit.

$$\left[\frac{\text{Costs incurred to date}}{\text{Estimate of total costs}} \times \begin{array}{c}\text{Estimated total}\\ \text{gross profit}\end{array}\right] - \begin{array}{c}\text{Total gross}\\ \text{profit recognized}\\ \text{in prior periods}\end{array} = \begin{array}{c}\text{Current period}\\ \text{gross profit}\end{array}$$

$$\left[\frac{\$780,000}{\$520,000 + \$780,000} \times [\$2,200,000 - (\$780,000 + \$520,000)]\right] - \$0$$

$$= \left[\frac{\$780,000}{\$1,300,000} \times (\$2,200,000 - \$1,300,000)\right] - \$0 = [.60 \times \$900,000] - \$0$$

$$= \underline{\$540,000}$$

(Solution = c.)

Question

9. Refer to the facts for Question 8 above. The amount of gross profit to be recognized on the statement of income for the year ended December 31, 2018, is:

   a. $860,000.   c. $344,000.
   b. $360,000.   d. $320,000.

EXPLANATION: Use the formula shown for Question 8 and plug in the data for 2018.

$$\left[\frac{\$780,000 + \$560,000}{\$780,000 + \$560,000 + \$0} \times [\$2,200,000 - (\$780,000 + \$560,000)]\right] - \$540,000]$$

$$= \left[\frac{\$1,340,000}{\$1,340,000} \times (\$2,200,000 - \$1,340,000)\right] - \$540,000$$

$$= \$860,000 - \$540,000 = \$320,000$$

(Solution = d.)

Question

10. Refer to the data for Question 8 above. If the completed-contract method of accounting were used, the amount of gross profit to be reported for years 2017 and 2018 would be:

	2017	2018
a.	$0	$860,000
b.	$0	$900,000
c.	$900,000	$(40,000)
d.	$860,000	$0

EXPLANATION: The completed-contract method calls for deferral of all revenue and costs related to the contract to the period of completion. Thus, the entire gross profit ($2,200,000 total revenue − $1,340,000 total costs = $860,000 total gross profit) would be recognized in the period the contract is completed. (Solution = a.)

Question

11. Ronway Builders Ltd. is using the completed-contract method for a $2,200,000 contract that will take two years to complete. Data at December 31, 2017, the end of the first year, are:

Costs incurred to date	$1,125,000
Estimated costs to complete	$1,100,000
Billings to date	$1,050,000
Collections to date	$950,000

The gross profit or loss that should be recognized for 2017 is:
a. $50,000 gross profit.
b. $75,000 loss.
c. $25,000 loss.
d. $0

EXPLANATION:

Estimated total revenue	$2,200,000
Cost to date (12/31/17)	$1,125,000
Estimated costs to complete	1,100,000
Estimated total costs	$2,225,000
Expected contract loss	$(25,000)

(Solution = c.)

CASE STUDY

Investico Limited

Investico Limited (IL) is a small real estate development company that was started up by two investors. Adam de Groote, one of the investors, runs the company and makes the key decisions, whereas the other investor, Brent Boudreau, contributed half of the initial capital required and is basically a silent partner. The main objective of the company, initially agreed upon by the two investors, is to invest in low-risk real estate properties and sell them for profit once the properties appreciate to a certain point.

The first project that IL invested in was some vacation property. Adam found the property and made the decision to buy it without consulting Brent. Adam planned to subdivide and service the resulting lots and to sell them as vacation properties. Even though the purchase did not quite fit with IL's objectives, Adam figured that he could sell the lots at a better-than-average profit before Brent could have a chance to object.

Adam subdivided the lots and was able to sell all of them on the following terms:

- $2,500 down payment (5% of the sale price).
- IL takes back a note receivable from the purchaser under an agreement of sale. The note is interest-free and title to the land remains with IL until the note is fully paid (five-year term).
- The purchaser takes immediate possession.
- IL services the lot with electricity within a year of the purchase date.

Most of the lots were sold at the beginning of 2017; however, by the end of 2017, about 30% of the purchasers were behind in their note/loan payments. Adam was not anxious to repossess the properties and had worked out an arrangement with the owners allowing him to cut down for resale the wood on the properties. The owners claim that the resale value of the wood should more than cover the overdue payments.

Meanwhile, Brent found out about the property, and that it was all sold, and is considering taking some of his investment out of the company. He has requested financial statements for the year ended December 31, 2017. Adam has hired you, a chartered professional accountant (CPA), to advise him as to how he should prepare the financial statements. He is considering selling the notes receivable connected with the property sales in order to have some cash on hand should Brent want his money back.

Instructions

Assume the role of the CPA and prepare a memo to Adam analyzing the accounting and reporting issues. Your memo should consider the users and constraints and provide recommendations.

Suggested Approach to Case Study

Memo: Re Investico
To: Adam
From: CPA
(Overview: It is very important to set a framework for your analysis, especially when ASPE provides only guidelines, as opposed to strict rules.)
Brent is a key user and needs information to determine (1) whether to divest himself of his interest in the company, (2) whether you are looking after the company (and therefore are exercising the stewardship function), and (3) whether the level of business risk taken on by Investico is consistent with the company's objective of investing in low-risk properties. Therefore, Brent needs realistic and faithfully representative financial statements.

The potential purchasers of the notes receivable need conservative financial statements to determine whether to purchase the notes.

ASPE will be a constraint and is intended to provide unbiased financial statements to the users. Even though Brent and external users may want financial statements that are neutral and free from bias, as the key decision-maker for IL, presenting the company and yourself in the most favourable light would be favourable for you. Due to the intended investment objectives of the company, downplaying business risk would also be favourable for you. Brent would like to know if you are looking after his best interests; as well, encouraging someone to purchase the notes would improve cash flows.

Analysis and Recommendations

The issues are as follows: (*Where possible, issues should be ranked in order of importance. A more important issue is one that will have a major impact on users.*)

1. When to recognize revenues.
2. How to value the notes receivable, given the collectibility problem.
3. How to value the wood.

Revenue Recognition

Recognizing revenue on the vacation property lots as each contract is signed may be possible given that the purchaser takes immediate possession, and it could be argued that the risks and rewards of ownership have transferred. (That is, possession has transferred and a down payment has been received, indicating some certainty that the deal will be completed as planned.) Also, the sale price is measurable (as stated in the sales agreement).

However, at the time of contract signing, legal title has not transferred yet and therefore it could be argued that control of the property has not transferred yet. As well, the earnings process is not substantially complete, as IL will continue servicing the lots after contract signing. (It may also be difficult to estimate servicing costs.) Collectibility is also an issue, as evidenced by the overdue payments.

In summary, recognizing revenue upfront would be aggressive and would support your financial reporting objective, but control and legal title do not transfer upfront and there is significant uncertainty with respect to measuring profit on the sale, as well as collectibility.

Another alternative would be to wait until the end of the earnings process to recognize revenue. At that time, legal title would have transferred, there would be no question regarding collectibility, and all revenues and costs would be measurable.

Recommendation

(*Focus on the objectives of the major user. Never contravene ASPE in order to meet an objective.*)
Even though you may prefer aggressive financial statements, revenue should probably not be recognized until the lots are at least serviced. At that point, uncertainty regarding costs will be settled and IL will be better able to assess collectibility. Recognizing revenue at that point might still be considered aggressive since legal title has not yet transferred; however, the intent is that payments will be made

and that legal title will transfer and, therefore, in substance, a sale has been made. (Other arguments are possible. It is important to integrate the economics of the transaction into the accounting analysis; that is, accounting should reflect the economic reality of the situation.)

Asset Valuation (Notes Receivable)

ASPE requires that an allowance for bad debts be estimated if there are collection problems. In this case, payments are still being made, although the payments are "nonmonetary."

One alternative is to set up an allowance as required under ASPE. This would provide a more realistic value of the notes and satisfy a need of potential purchasers of the notes. As a chartered accountant, knowing that potential purchasers will rely on the values stated in the financial statements, I will want to ensure that the notes are properly valued in order to reflect the economic reality of the situation. Even though the payments are being made (in kind) at the present time, there is uncertainty as to whether the note holders will be able to make future payments (especially since they are currently having problems paying). Another alternative is to make no allowance since payments in kind that are of value are just as good as monetary payments.

Recommendation

It is recommended that an allowance be recorded to properly value the notes receivable. There would be high exposure to legal action if the potential purchasers rely on the value shown in the financial statements and subsequently suffer a loss.

Value of the Wood

(A relatively minor issue on its own—it should be considered with the issue above.)
This issue is tied in with the one above. The wood must be valued to assess whether it covers the overdue payments. How should the value of the wood be determined? The value must be net of any additional costs to sell the wood. The value of the wood would directly affect the amount of any allowance for the notes receivable.

Chapter 7

Cash and Receivables

OVERVIEW

In previous chapters, the basic format of general-purpose financial statements was discussed. In this chapter, we begin an in-depth study of accounting for items appearing on the statement of financial position, including: (1) what is included in an item classification, (2) guidelines for determining the dollar amount to be reported for an item, (3) special accounting procedures that may be required, (4) disclosure requirements, and (5) related internal control procedures. In this chapter specifically, you will learn what items are included in the cash and receivables captions on the statement of financial position, the definition of financial assets, methods of accounting for accounts receivable and notes receivable, and key internal controls for effective safeguarding and control of cash.

STUDY STEPS

Understanding Cash and Accounts Receivable from a Business Perspective

Cash management is a key issue for many companies. For companies without surplus cash, cash is managed to minimize borrowings and facilitate the smooth flow of operations. For companies with surplus cash, "idle" cash may be minimized by putting surplus cash in short-term deposits. Cash must also be safeguarded and controlled carefully to minimize theft and improper use.

Many businesses grant credit to customers. They know that credit sales "on account" expose a business to some credit risk because some accounts may never be collected. However, business managers consider that the cost of these bad debts is usually more than offset by the extra sales made as a result of granting credit to customers. A company's collections department may make many attempts to collect an account before "writing off" an account to bad debt expense. Often, bad debt accounts are not deemed uncollectible until a year or more after the date of the credit sale. The allowance method of accounting for bad debts is used to properly value accounts receivable on the statement of financial position. The allowance method requires that an estimate of bad debt expense be recorded and matched with current period sales revenue on the statement of income (rather than recording the related bad debt expense in a future period when an account is actually written off).

Cash and liquid assets are crucial to any business because a company needs to keep a certain amount of liquid assets on hand in order to pay operating expenses and short-term payables. Therefore, financial statement users often focus on liquid assets and current liabilities to assess a company's liquidity.

Understanding the Definition of Financial Assets

A financial asset is any asset that is

- cash,
- a contractual right to receive cash or another financial asset from another party,
- a contractual right to exchange financial instruments with another party under conditions that are potentially favourable to the entity, or
- an equity instrument of another entity.

Financial assets are covered in various chapters of the textbook. This chapter covers cash, cash equivalents, accounts receivable, and notes and loans receivable. Chapter 9 covers other major categories of financial assets (mainly investments in debt and equity securities of other companies).

Understanding the Basics of Receivables

Receivables are claims held against customers or others for money, goods, or services. When receivables represent contractual rights to receive cash or other financial assets from another party, they are termed "financial assets." Receivables are classified as either current or non-current (depending on expected date of collection), and may be either trade (amounts that result from normal operating transactions) or non-trade receivables.

Unfortunately, when credit is granted, some parties will eventually fail to pay some or the entire amount they owe. Under ASPE receivables are **impaired** if there has been a significant adverse change in the expected timing or amount of future cash flows. Under IFRS 9, for receivables without a significant financing component, a loss allowance should be recorded based on "lifetime expected credit losses."

Recognition and measurement of accounts receivable require an understanding that accounts receivable should be shown on the financial statements at no more than estimated net realizable value. Because accounts receivable are realized (converted to cash) after the statement of financial position date, and actual total sales returns and bad debts related to the accounts receivable are unknown as at that date, special accounting procedures are required in order to show accounts receivable at estimated net realizable value. Specifically, an allowance for sales returns and allowances and an allowance for doubtful accounts are estimated and recorded in contra accounts receivable accounts, which bring net accounts receivable to net realizable value as at the statement of financial position date.

Recognition and measurement of notes and loans receivable require an understanding that, whether the notes and loans receivable are short-term or long-term, if the business will receive payment at some time in the future (beyond normal credit terms), the receivable should be recorded at present value initially, and interest income (including amortization of any discount or premium) should be accrued at each financial statement date.

Understanding Transfer of Receivables to Generate Cash

Sometimes a company will experience a cash shortage because it has a significant amount of working capital tied up in accounts receivable (as a result of growth in credit sales, delayed payment terms, or slow-paying customers). The company may choose to transfer those receivables to generate cash for immediate use. One way of doing this is to pledge or assign the receivables to a lender. Another way of doing this is to sell or dispose of the receivables, for a fee, to a financial intermediary that will then directly collect the amounts owed from customers. This is sometimes called "factoring" or "securitization." It is important to understand this business transaction prior to analyzing the related accounting issues. Generally, in exchange for an immediate receipt of cash, the company pays a fee and gives up rights to a future stream of cash receipts.

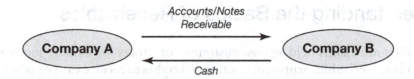

In the transaction shown above, if Company A surrenders control of the accounts/notes receivable, the transaction should be accounted for as a sale by Company A. However, after determining that the transaction should be accounted for as a sale, it must also be determined whether Company A has continuing involvement with the receivables after the transfer. For example, if Company A has no further responsibility to Company B should the receivables prove to be uncollectible in future periods, then the receivables are considered sold without recourse, and the transaction should be recorded by Company A as a normal sale. However, if the arrangement allows Company B to seek compensation from Company A if some of the receivables prove to be uncollectible, then the receivables are considered sold with recourse, and the transaction should be recorded by Company A as a sale using the financial components approach. The financial components approach makes it possible to assign values to components such as recourse rights or servicing rights, for example.

Generally, the amount of cash received by Company A from Company B would be less than the book value of the receivables. This discount would compensate Company B for its collection efforts and for any potential losses from uncollectible amounts. Company B would probably rather purchase the receivables with recourse from Company A for uncollectible amounts, although it may be willing to give up this right for a lower cash payment up front.

- Pledging or assigning receivables is a method of generating cash from receivables immediately, usually resulting in a secured borrowing or loan using the receivables as collateral. The legal right to the cash collected from the receivables is not transferred to the creditor unless the company defaults on the loan.

- Factoring is also a method of generating cash from receivables immediately. However, factoring transfers the legal right to collect the receivables to the other party. Factoring is a type of sale of receivables. Sales of receivables may be with or without recourse, depending on the transfer arrangements.

- "With recourse" means that the risks and rewards of ownership of the receivables may still rest, at least partially, with the company (or transferor).

TIPS ON CHAPTER TOPICS

- Cash is the most liquid asset; it is the standard medium of exchange and the basis for measuring and accounting for most items. It is also very susceptible to theft or improper use. Internal controls are imperative in order to safeguard cash and ensure accuracy of accounting records.

- Restricted cash is classified as either a current or long-term asset, depending on the date of availability or expected disbursement.

- Cash equivalents are short-term, highly liquid investments that are both readily convertible to known amounts of cash and so near to their maturity that risk of change in their value is insignificant. Generally, only investments with maturities of three months or less qualify as cash equivalents.

- Bank overdrafts occur when cheques are written for more than the balance in the related bank account. Bank overdrafts are classified as current liabilities. (This is sometimes done by adding the bank overdraft amount to the amount that is reported for accounts payable.)

- Trade accounts receivable result from normal sales of products or services to customers. Non-trade accounts receivable (amounts that are due from non-trade parties that do not buy goods or services in the normal course of the company's business operations) should be listed separately on the statement of financial position. (That is, they should be shown apart from trade accounts receivable.)

- In the event that a customer's account has a credit balance as at the statement of financial position date, the account should be classified as a current liability; it should not be offset against other accounts receivable that the company expects to collect and ultimately convert to cash.

- Writing down related journal entry(ies), analyzing debits and credits, and using T accounts are helpful ways of analyzing the effects of (1) recording bad debt expense, (2) writing off an account receivable, and/or (3) collecting an account receivable that was previously written off. (See **Illustration 7-1** for examples.)

- The two methods of accounting for bad debts are:

  1. **Direct writeoff method:** No journal entry is made (bad debt expense is not recorded) until a specific customer's account is actually deemed uncollectible. At that time, the journal entry recorded is a credit to Accounts Receivable and a debit to Bad Debt Expense. (This method is used only where the effect of not applying the allowance method is highly immaterial.)

  2. **Allowance method:** Uncollectible trade accounts receivable are estimated based on either (1) percentage-of-receivables or (2) a combination of percentage-of-sales (used during the year) and percentage-of-receivables (used at the end of the fiscal year). The estimate results in an entry that debits Bad Debt Expense and credits Allowance for Doubtful Accounts (a contra accounts receivable account) in the same period in which the related sales are recorded.

- If an entity has a material amount of bad debts or accounts receivable, the direct writeoff method is not an appropriate method of accounting for bad debts. The direct writeoff method fails to properly value accounts receivable at net realizable value, and it fails to match bad debt expense with related sales revenue. (Under the direct writeoff method, bad debt expense is not recorded in the same period in which the related credit sale is recorded.)

- Trade receivables with normal credit terms are generally recorded at face value (less allowances) because the interest implicit in the maturity value is immaterial. In contrast, long-term notes receivable, and short-term notes receivable that extend the collection period beyond normal credit terms, are recorded at the present value of the cash expected to be collected.

(continued)

- A note receivable is considered impaired when it is probable that the issuer will be unable to collect all (principal and interest) amounts due according to contractual terms of the loan. In this case, the present value of expected future cash flows is determined by discounting those flows at the market rate at acquisition. This present value amount is deducted from the carrying amount of the receivable to calculate the loss.

- In general, receivables should be derecognized (removed from the statement of financial position) when **control** over the right to the related cash flows expires and substantially all of the **risks and rewards of ownership** of the receivables have transferred. If a company "sells" its receivables but has some continuing involvement with the receivables after transferring them to a third party, it may be unclear whether the receivables may be recorded as sold (and derecognized). Under **IFRS**, if (1) the company transfers the contractual rights to receive cash flows from the receivables, or (2) the company retains the contractual rights to receive cash flows from the receivables but has a contractual obligation to pay the cash flows to one or more recipients upon receipt (and three additional conditions are met that would support the claim that the receivables have been sold), then the receivables may be recorded as sold (and derecognized, with recording of a resulting gain or loss). Under **ASPE**, if three conditions are satisfied, which demonstrate that the transferor of the receivables has surrendered control, the receivables may be recorded as sold (and derecognized, with recording of a resulting gain or loss).

- In general, if control over receivables is not transferred to a third party, but the receivables are used as collateral in obtaining a loan, the transaction is recorded and disclosed as a **secured borrowing** (a loan secured by the receivables as collateral for the loan).

- The objective of a bank reconciliation is to explain any differences between, and to identify any errors or omissions within, the bank's and the company's records of cash. In a bank reconciliation, the term "per bank" refers to the bank's records of the depositor's (company's) account, and the term "per books" refers to the company's records of the same bank account.

- "Total receipts per bank" for a month include all deposits made by the depositor company during the month, plus any bank credit memos (such as interest credited by the bank or a note receivable collected by the bank on the company's behalf).

- "Total disbursements per bank" for a month include all of the depositor company's cheques that cleared the banking system during the month, plus any bank debit memos (such as bank service charges or a customer's NSF cheque).

- Beginning cash balance per bank

    + total receipts for the month per bank

    − total disbursements for the month per bank

    = ending cash balance per bank.

- Beginning cash balance per books

    + total receipts for the month per books

    − total disbursements for the month per books

    = ending cash balance per books.

EXERCISE 7-1

PURPOSE: This exercise reviews items that are included in the "Cash" caption on a statement of financial position.

In auditing the statement of financial position dated December 31, 2017, for the Show-Me-the-Money Company, you find the following:

1. Coins and currency for change funds
2. Coins and currency from the current day's receipts, which have not yet been deposited in the bank
3. Petty cash
4. General chequing account at First Union Bank
5. General chequing account at Sun Trust Bank
6. Deposit in transit
7. Unused postage stamps
8. Customer's NSF cheque (returned with bank statement)
9. Postdated cheques from customers
10. Certificate of deposit—60-day CD purchased on December 1, 2017
11. Certificate of deposit—five-year CD purchased two years ago
12. 100 shares of a public company (the intention is to sell in one year or less)
13. Cash to be used to retire long-term debt
14. Travel advances made to executives for business purposes

Instructions

Select the items from the list above that should be included in the "Cash" caption on the statement of financial position as at December 31, 2017. For any item not included in "Cash," indicate the proper classification.

Solution to Exercise 7-1

Items to be **included** as "Cash" on the statement of financial position are:

1. Coins and currency for change funds.
2. Coins and currency from the current day's receipts that have not yet been deposited in the bank; these are considered "cash on hand" or could be considered "deposit in transit."
3. Petty cash.
4. General chequing account at First Union Bank: The amount included should be the "adjusted (correct) cash balance" per the bank reconciliation.

5. General chequing account at Sun Trust Bank: The amount included should be the "adjusted (correct) cash balance" per the bank reconciliation.

6. Deposit in transit: This amount is already included in the "balance per books" and the "adjusted (correct) cash balance" per the bank reconciliation.

Items **not included** as "Cash" on the statement of financial position are:

7. Unused stamps: Report as prepaid expense.

8. Customer's NSF cheque: Return to accounts receivable.

9. Postdated cheques from customers: Are accounts receivable.

10. Certificate of deposit: The 60-day original maturity date is three months or less; therefore, this is a cash equivalent. Some entities include cash equivalents with cash; others report them with short-term investments.

11. Certificate of deposit: The original maturity date is not three months or less; therefore, classify as a long-term investment.

12. 100 shares of a public company: These are readily marketable and there is no intention to hold this investment in the long term; therefore, classify as a short-term investment.

13. Cash to be used to retire long-term debt: This is a long-term investment (assuming the related debt is classified as long-term).

14. Travel advances made to executives for business purposes: Are prepaid expense.

ILLUSTRATION 7-1

Entries for the Allowance Method

Journal Entry			Effect on Net Income	Effect on Working Capital	Effect on Allowance Account	Effect on Net Receivables
Entry to record bad debt expense, $1,000						
Bad Debt Expense	1,000		−$1,000	No effect	No effect	No effect
Allowance for Doubtful Accounts		1,000	No effect	−$1,000	+$1,000	−$1,000
Net effect of entry			−$1,000	−$1,000	+$1,000	−$1,000
Entry to write off a customer's account, $200						
Allowance for Doubtful Accounts	200		No effect	+$200	−$200	+$200
Accounts Receivable		200	No effect	−$200	No effect	−$200
Net effect of entry			No effect	No effect	−$200	No effect

Illustration 7-1   195

Journal Entry			Effect on Net Income	Effect on Working Capital	Effect on Allowance Account	Effect on Net Receivables
Entries to record collection of account receivable previously written off, $120						
Accounts Receivable	120		No effect	+$120	No effect	+$120
Allowance for Doubtful Accounts		120	No effect	−$120	+$120	−$120
Cash	120		No effect	+$120	No effect	No effect
Accounts Receivable		120	No effect	−$120	No effect	−$120
Net effect of entries			No effect	No effect	+$120	−$120

- Be careful to distinguish the entry to record bad debt expense from the entry to record the writeoff of a customer account. The entry to adjust accounts receivable to estimated net realizable value and therefore to record bad debt expense for a period involves a debit to Bad Debt Expense and a credit to Allowance for Doubtful Accounts. The entry to write off an individual customer's account (an actual bad debt) involves a debit to Allowance for Doubtful Accounts and a credit to Accounts Receivable.

- Two entries are necessary to record recovery of an account that was previously written off:

  1. An entry to record reinstatement of the account receivable (debit Accounts Receivable and credit Allowance for Doubtful Accounts). This is simply a reverse of the writeoff entry.

  2. An entry to record collection of the account receivable (debit Cash and credit Accounts Receivable).

- Allowance for Doubtful Accounts is often called "Allowance for Uncollectible Accounts." "Reserve for Bad Debts" is a frequently used but objectionable title for the allowance account. ("Reserve for Bad Debts" is an objectionable title for the allowance account because the title "Reserve" is frequently used to describe a "Reserve" asset account of funds set aside for future payments.) Bad Debt Expense is often called "Uncollectible Accounts Expense" or "Doubtful Accounts Expense." The Bad Debt Expense account is also sometimes referred to as "Provision for Bad Debts."

- Notice that the entry to record bad debt expense reduces current assets and reduces net income. The entry to record the actual writeoff of an individual customer's account has **no** net effect on current assets or net income. The entry to record the writeoff of an account only reduces Accounts Receivable and Allowance for Doubtful Accounts (which is a contra item), so the entry has no **net** effect on the net realizable value of accounts receivable. Thus, it is the bad debt expense entry that affects both the statement of income and statement of financial position.

- The normal balance of Allowance for Doubtful Accounts is a credit. Therefore, a debit balance in this account indicates an abnormal balance. It is not

(*continued*)

uncommon to have a debit balance in the allowance account before adjusting entries are prepared. This is because individual customer accounts may be written off at various times during a period and the entry to adjust the allowance account is prepared at the end of the period before financial statements are prepared. After adjustment, the allowance account should have a credit balance. However, significant and consistent debit balances in Allowance for Doubtful Accounts may signal that allowances for doubtful accounts recorded in previous periods were generally not sufficient, and that the company should review its method of and percentages used in estimating uncollectible accounts.

● When using the allowance method of accounting for bad debts, there are two approaches used to determine the adjusting entry amount. Each approach has adaptations.

1. Percentage-of-receivables approach:

   (a) Average percentage relationship between uncollectible accounts receivable and outstanding accounts receivable is determined from experience. This percentage, adjusted for current conditions, is applied to the ending balance in accounts receivable to determine the desired balance of the allowance account at the end of the period, or

   (b) Total uncollectible accounts at the end of an accounting period is determined by the aging method. The balance in the allowance account is adjusted so that it equals the total amount of estimated uncollectible accounts determined by the aging analysis. This aging method is preferable to the method in part 1(a) above because it applies a different percentage probability of uncollectibility to each age category, which is more sensitive to the actual status of the accounts receivable. (The older the receivable, the higher the probability of uncollectibility.)

2. Mix between the percentage-of-sales approach and the percentage-of-receivables approach:

   (a) To prepare financial statements on a monthly basis, a company may use the faster and simpler percentage-of-sales approach to estimate bad debts. In the percentage-of-sales approach, the average percentage relationship between actual bad debt losses and net credit sales is determined from past experience. This percentage, adjusted for current conditions, is then applied to actual net credit sales of the period to determine the amount of bad debt expense for the period. However, at the end of the fiscal year, prior to preparing its financial statements, the company should apply the percentage-of-receivables approach to determine the appropriate balance for the allowance account, in order to properly value net accounts receivable at net realizable value.

   (b) In applying the percentage-of-sales approach, the percentage of bad debts to total sales (including cash sales) is sometimes used. However, the method described in part 2(a) above (using the percentage of bad debts to net credit sales) is strongly preferred because cash sales (included in total sales) do not result in bad debts, and, if the relationship between cash sales and credit sales shifts, the percentage of bad debts to total sales, based on past experience, will be much less relevant. Regardless of the percentage used in the percentage-of-sales approach, the percentage-of-receivables approach should be applied prior to preparing annual financial statements.

● Note that in both methods listed above, the percentage-of-receivables approach is emphasized, as is the importance of valuing the allowance account, and therefore net accounts receivable at net realizable value. The percentage-of-receivables approach only incidentally measures bad debt expense, which may not be directly related to credit sales of the current period. Furthermore, the aging method is the preferred percentage-of-receivables technique as it provides an estimate of allowance for doubtful accounts that is based on more detailed and relevant analysis.

● Under the percentage-of-sales approach, when preparing the adjusting entry for bad debt expense, the balance before adjustment (existing balance) in Allowance for Doubtful Accounts is **not** considered in determining the amount of the adjusting entry. However, under the percentage-of-receivables approach, the balance before adjustment in Allowance for Doubtful Accounts **is** used in determining the amount of the adjusting entry. The application of these two guidelines is illustrated in the **Solution to Exercise 7-2**.

● When applying the percentage-of-sales approach and estimating bad debt expense as a percentage of credit sales for the period, the calculated amount is the amount of bad debt expense recorded for the period; a by-product of this approach is an increase in the allowance account. When applying the percentage-of-receivables approach, the calculated amount is the amount of uncollectible accounts and the new ending balance of the allowance account. The adjusting entry records the amount necessary to increase (or decrease) the allowance account balance to equal the new ending balance; a by-product of this approach is an increase in bad debt expense for the period.

EXERCISE 7-2

PURPOSE: This exercise will require you to record: (1) the adjusting entry to recognize bad debt expense and adjust Allowance for Doubtful Accounts, and (2) the transfer of accounts receivable without recourse.

For Lang Company, sales (all on credit) and sales returns and allowances for the month of November 2017 amount to $52,000 and $900, respectively.

The trial balance before adjustment at December 31, 2017, shows the following balances:

	Dr.	**Cr.**
Accounts receivable	$97,000	
Allowance for doubtful accounts	3,250	
Sales (all on credit)		$520,000
Sales returns and allowances	8,700	

Instructions

Using the data above, give the journal entries required to record each of the following (each situation is **independent**):

(a) For November 30, 2017, the company estimates bad debts to be 1.5% of net credit sales. Recreate the November 30, 2017, journal entry that recorded bad debt expense.

(b) Lang Company performs an aging analysis at December 31, 2017, which indicates an uncollectible accounts estimate of $7,000.

(c) Under the percentage-of-receivables approach as at December 31, 2017, the company wants to maintain Allowance for Doubtful Accounts at 4% of gross accounts receivable.

(d) To obtain additional cash, Lang factors, without recourse, $25,000 of accounts receivable to Fleetwood Finance. The finance charge is 10% of the amount factored.

Solution to Exercise 7-2

(a) Bad Debt Expense [($52,000 − $900) × 1.5%]   767
         Allowance for Doubtful Accounts   767

EXPLANATION: The percentage of net credit sales approach focuses on determining an appropriate bad debt expense figure. The existing balance in the allowance account is **not** relevant in the calculation.

(b) Bad Debt Expense   10,250
         Allowance for Doubtful Accounts ($7,000 + $3,250)   10,250

EXPLANATION: An aging analysis provides the best estimate of what the balance in Allowance for Doubtful Accounts should be. By using aging analysis results to adjust the allowance account, the amount reported for net receivables on the statement of financial position is the net realizable value of accounts receivable. It is important to notice that the balance in the allowance account before adjustment is a determinant in the adjustment required. The following T account reflects the facts used to determine the necessary adjustment:

Allowance for Doubtful Accounts		
Unadjusted balance 3,250	Adjustment needed	10,250
	Desired balance at 12/31/17	7,000

(c) Bad Debt Expense   7,130
         Allowance for Doubtful Accounts   7,130
         [($97,000 × 4%) + $3,250]

Illustration 7-2   199

EXPLANATION: This entry adjusts the allowance account to 4% of gross accounts receivable. A by-product of this entry is the recording of bad debt expense. Because an appropriate balance for the valuation (allowance) account is a percentage of accounts receivable as at the statement of financial position date, the existing balance ($3,250 debit) in the allowance account **must** be considered in calculating the necessary adjustment.

(d) Cash   22,500

   Loss on Sale of Receivables ($25,000 × 10%)   2,500

      Accounts Receivable   25,000

EXPLANATION: The factoring of accounts receivable without recourse is accounted for as a sale of accounts receivable. The related receivables are removed from accounts receivable, cash received is recorded, and a loss is recognized for the excess of the face value of the receivables over the cash proceeds received.

ILLUSTRATION 7-2

Accounting for Transfers of Receivables

Under ASPE, if any one of the three conditions signalling surrender of control does not apply, the transferring company records the transfer as a secured borrowing:

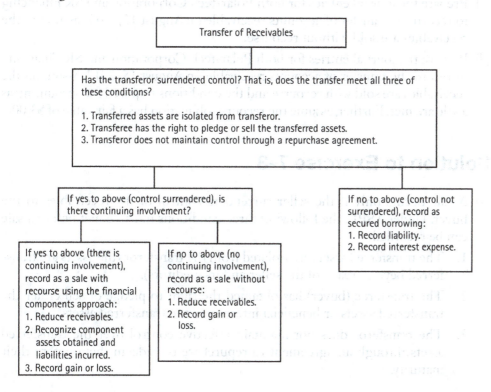

If there is continuing involvement in a sale transaction, the component (individual) assets obtained and liabilities incurred in the transfer must be recorded at fair value.

EXERCISE 7-3

PURPOSE: This exercise will help you to compare two possible ways of selling accounts receivable: (1) without recourse, or (2) with recourse.

Polar-tech Corporation factors $80,000 of accounts receivable to SR Financing Inc. SR Financing will collect the receivables. The receivable records are transferred to SR Financing on August 15, 2017. SR Financing assesses a finance charge of 3% of the accounts receivable amount transferred and retains an amount equal to 7% of accounts receivable to cover probable adjustments. Both Polar-tech Corporation and SR Financing follow ASPE.

Instructions

(a) Explain the conditions that must be met for a transfer of receivables with recourse to be accounted for as a sale.

(b) Explain when the financial components approach is used in accounting for a transfer of accounts receivable.

(c) Prepare the journal entries for both Polar-tech Corporation and SR Financing to record the transfer of accounts receivable on August 15, 2017, assuming the receivables are sold without recourse.

(d) Prepare the journal entries for both Polar-tech Corporation and SR Financing to record the transfer of accounts receivable on August 15, 2017, assuming the receivables are sold with recourse and the conditions required for accounting as a sale are met. Further, assume the recourse obligation has a fair value of $3,000.

Solution to Exercise 7-3

(a) A sale occurs only if the seller surrenders control of the receivables to the buyer. Under ASPE, the following three conditions must be met before a sale can be recorded:

1. The transferred assets are isolated from the transferor (the assets are transferred beyond reach of the seller and its creditors).

2. The transferee (buyer) has obtained the right to pledge or sell either the transferred assets or beneficial interests in the transferred assets.

3. The transferor does not maintain effective control over the transferred assets through an agreement to repurchase or redeem them before their maturity.

Only if all three conditions are met is control assumed to be given up, and the transaction recorded as a sale. Otherwise, the transferor should record the transfer as a secured borrowing. If the transfer is recorded as a sale and if the seller has continuing involvement with the receivables after the transfer, it is necessary to record, at fair value, any assets obtained and liabilities incurred in the transaction.

(b) The **financial components approach** is used to account for a sale of accounts receivable with recourse (see answer [a] above). If receivables are sold (factored) with recourse, the seller guarantees payment to the purchaser in the event the customer fails to pay. Under the financial components approach, each party to the sale recognizes the assets and liabilities that it controls after the sale and removes the assets and liabilities that were sold or extinguished.

(c) Sale of receivables without recourse:

Polar-tech Corp.			**SR Financing**	
Cash	72,000		Accounts Receivable 80,000	
Due from Factor	5,600*		Due to Polar-tech	5,600
Loss on Sale of			Finance Revenue	2,400
Receivables	2,400**		Cash	72,000
Accounts Receivable		80,000		

*$80,000 × 7% = $5,600
**$80,000 × 3% = $2,400

The factor's profit is the difference between the finance revenue of $2,400 and the amount of any uncollectible receivables. The $5,600 due to Polar-tech is an amount withheld to cover probable sales discounts, sales returns, and sales allowances.

(d) Sale of receivables with recourse:

Polar-tech Corp.			**SR Financing**	
Cash	72,000		Accounts Receivable 80,000	
Due from Factor	5,600		Due to Polar-tech	5,600
Loss on Sale of			Finance Revenue	2,400
Receivables	5,400***		Cash	72,000
Accounts Receivable		80,000		
Recourse Liability		3,000		

***Cash received	$72,000
Add amount due from factor	5,600
Subtotal	77,600
Less recourse liability	(3,000)
Net proceeds expected	$74,600
Carrying (book) value	$80,000
Less net proceeds expected	(74,600)
Loss on sale of receivables	$ 5,400

In this case, a liability of $3,000 is recorded by Polar-tech to indicate the estimated payment to SR Financing to cover uncollectible receivables. Ultimately, if SR Financing collects all receivables, Polar-tech would eliminate this recourse liability and increase net income. In this situation, SR Financing's profit is the finance revenue of $2,400, because it will have no bad debts related to these receivables.

EXERCISE 7-4

PURPOSE: This exercise will illustrate the calculations and entries involved in accounting for transfer of receivables treated as a secured borrowing transaction.

Wellington Wines transfers $360,000 of its accounts receivable to Kingston International Financial (KIF) as collateral for a $240,000 note dated September 1, 2017. Wellington will continue to collect the accounts receivable; the customers (account debtors) are not notified of the arrangement. KIF assesses a finance charge of 1% of accounts receivable and interest on the note of 12%. Settlement by Wellington Wines to KIF is made monthly for all cash collected on the receivables.

Instructions

Prepare the journal entries for both Wellington Wines and Kingston International Financial to record the following:

(a) On September 1, 2017, the accounts receivable are transferred and the note is issued.

(b) In September, Wellington collects $240,000 of the transferred accounts receivable, less cash discounts of $3,000. In addition, sales returns of $7,000 related to the transferred accounts receivable are processed.

(c) On October 1, Wellington remits September collections plus accrued interest to KIF.

(d) In October, Wellington collects the balance of the transferred accounts receivable, less $1,000 written off as uncollectible.

(e) On November 1, Wellington remits the $3,000 ($240,000 – $237,000) balance due on the note, plus interest.

Solution to Exercise 7-4

(a)

	Wellington Wines			**Kingston International Financial**		
Cash	236,400			Notes Receivable	240,000	
Finance Expense	3,600*			Finance Revenue		3,600*
Notes Payable		240,000		Cash		236,400

*1% × $360,000 = $3,600

(b)   **Wellington Wines**   **Kingston International Financial**

Cash   237,000   (No Entry)

Sales Discounts   3,000

Sales Returns   7,000

    Accounts Receivable   247,000*

*$240,000 + $7,000 = $247,000

(c)   **Wellington Wines**   **Kingston International Financial**

Interest Expense   2,400*   Cash   239,400

Notes Payable   237,000   Interest Income   2,400*

    Cash   239,400   Notes Receivable   237,000

*$240,000 × 12% × $\frac{1}{12}$ = $2,400

(d)   **Wellington Wines**   **Kingston International Financial**

Cash   119,000   (No Entry)

Allowance for Doubtful

    Accounts   1,000

    Accounts Receivable   120,000*

*$360,000 − $240,000 = $120,000

(e)   **Wellington Wines**   **Kingston International Financial**

Interest Expense   30*   Cash   3,030

Notes Payable   3,000   Interest Income   30*

    Cash   3,030   Notes Receivable   3,000

*$3,000 × 12% × $\frac{1}{12}$ = $30

● Receivables are often used as collateral in a borrowing transaction. The creditor often requires that the debtor designate or pledge receivables as security for the loan. If the loan is not paid when due, the creditor has the right to convert the collateral to cash; that is, to collect the receivables. **Factors** are finance companies or banks that buy receivables from businesses for a fee and then collect remittances directly from the businesses' customers. This exercise (**Exercise 7-4**) illustrates a borrowing transaction, whereas **Exercise 7-3** illustrates a sales transaction.

EXERCISE 7-5

PURPOSE: This exercise will help you review reconciling items on a bank reconciliation and identify those that require adjusting entries on the depositor's books.

A sketch of Ace Electric Company's bank reconciliation at July 31, 2017, and a list of possible reconciling items appear below.

ACE ELECTRIC COMPANY
Bank Reconciliation
July 31, 2017

Balance per bank statement, July 31			$X,XXX
A. Add:		$XXX	
		XXX	XXX
			X,XXX
B. Deduct:		XXX	
		XXX	XXX
Correct cash balance, July 31			$X,XXX
Balance per books, July 31			$X,XXX
C. Add:		$XXX	
		XXX	XXX
			X,XXX
D. Deduct:		XXX	
		XXX	XXX
Correct cash balance, July 31			$X,XXX

_____ 1. July 30 deposits amounting to $1,482 have not reached the bank as at July 31.

_____ 2. The bank returned a customer's NSF cheque amounting to $40 that was deposited on July 20; the NSF return has not been recorded by Ace.

_____ 3. Bank service charge for July amounts to $3.

_____ 4. Included with the bank statement was cheque No. 422 for $702 for payment of an account payable. In comparing the cheque with the cash disbursement records, it was discovered that the cheque was incorrectly entered in the cash disbursements journal for $720.

_____ 5. Outstanding cheques at July 31 amount to $1,927.

_____ 6. The bank improperly charged a $25 cheque of Ace Plumbing Co. to Ace Electric Company's account.

_____ 7. During July, the bank charged $8 for printing cheques.

_____ 8. During July, the bank collected a customer's note receivable on behalf of Ace Electric Company; face amount $1,000 and interest $20. The bank charged a $2 collection fee. This transaction has not been recorded by Ace.

_____ 9. In June, Ace Electric Company wrote a cheque for $180 that cleared the bank in July.

_____ 10. June 30 deposits of $1,200 were recorded by the company on June 30 but were not recorded by the bank until July 2.

Instructions

(a) Indicate where each of the 10 items listed above would appear on the bank reconciliation by placing the proper code letter in the space provided. The applicable code letters appear in the sketch of the bank reconciliation. Use the code "NR" for any item that is not a reconciling item on July 31.

(b) Assume that the July 31 balance per bank statement was $4,332. Complete the bank reconciliation using the items given and answer the questions that follow:

   1. What is the adjusted (correct) cash balance at July 31? $_____

   2. What is the balance per books **before** adjustment at July 31? $_____

   3. What reconciling items require an adjusting entry on Ace Electric Company's books? (Identify by item numbers.) _____

   4. What item(s) require(s) a special entry on the bank's records to correct an error(s)? _____

Solution to Exercise 7-5

(a)

   1. A
   2. D
   3. D
   4. C
   5. B
   6. A
   7. D
   8. C, D
   9. NR
   10. NR

(b)

   1. $3,912 ($4,332 + $1,482 + $25 − $1,927 = $3,912)

   2. $2,927 [(X + $18 + $1,020 − $40 − $3 − $8 − $2 = $3,912 (answer to question 1)); X = $2,927]

   3. 2; 3; 4; 7; 8

   4. 6 (See the completed bank reconciliation below.)

Items 9 and 10 would have been reconciling items on the June 30 (prior month's) bank reconciliation.

APPROACH: You can calculate the correct cash balance by completing the top half of the bank reconciliation (balance per bank to correct cash balance). The correct cash balance can then be entered on the last line of the bottom half of the reconciliation and used along with certain reconciling items to "work backwards" to calculate the $2,927 cash balance per books before adjustment.

ACE ELECTRIC COMPANY
Bank Reconciliation
July 31, 2017

Balance per bank statement, July 31		$4,332
Add: Deposits in transit on July 31	$1,482	
Cheque improperly charged by bank	25	1,507
		5,839
Deduct: Cheques outstanding as of July 31		1,927
Correct cash balance at July 31		$3,912
Balance per books, July 31		$2,927
Add: Error in recording cheque No. 422	$ 18	
Collection of customer's note receivable and interest by bank	1,020	1,038
		3,965
Deduct: Customer's NSF cheque	40	
Bank service charge for July	3	
Cost of printing cheques	8	
Bank collection fee	2	53
Correct cash balance at July 31		$3,912

The required adjusting entries on Ace's books would be:

Cash	18	
Accounts Payable		18
(To correct error in recording cheque No. 422)		
Cash	1,020	
Notes Receivable		1,000
Interest Income		20
(To record collection of note receivable by bank)		
Accounts Receivable	40	
Cash		40
(To record customer's NSF cheque)		
Office Expense	13	
Cash		13
(To record bank service charges: [$3 + $8 + $2 = $13])		

    The above entries can be combined into one compound entry.

- If you have a chequing account, look at the back of your bank statement. Bank statements often include a form to assist in reconciling the bank account. Usually, that form reconciles the cash balance per bank statement and the cash balance per books (your records) to the correct (adjusted) cash balance.

- The "Balance per bank" caption on a bank reconciliation is often replaced with "Balance per bank statement," and "Balance per books" is often titled "Balance per ledger."

- The "Correct cash balance" caption on a bank reconciliation is often replaced with "Adjusted cash balance." The adjusted cash balance as determined by the bank reconciliation is included in the amount reported for cash on the statement of financial position. (The Cash account in the general ledger often includes cash on hand and cash in the bank, although separate ledger accounts and any other unrestricted cash accounts, such as the Petty Cash account, are added together to report cash on the statement of financial position.)

- Some items in a bank reconciliation require adjustments either on the depositor's books or in the bank's records, while the others do not. When reconciliation of the balance per bank to correct cash balance format is used in preparing a single-column bank reconciliation, if the balance per books differs from the correct cash balance, correcting the balance per books to match the correct cash balance will require adjusting entries on the depositor's books. All of the reconciling items appearing in the upper half of the reconciliation, except for deposits in transit and outstanding cheques, will require an adjustment in the bank's records.

- Unless otherwise indicated, an NSF cheque is assumed to be a customer's NSF cheque (originally written by a customer of the depositor, rather than the depositor's NSF cheque).

- A depositor's chequing account is a liability on the bank's books, so a bank debit memo decreases the depositor's cash balance and a bank credit memo increases the depositor's cash balance. On the bank statement, debits appear as a result of cheques that have cleared during the month or bank debit memos for items such as bank service charges (BSC). Credits on the bank statement represent deposits or bank credit memos.

EXERCISE 7-6

PURPOSE: This exercise will illustrate how to determine deposits in transit and outstanding cheques.

Shown below for Molly's Folly are the:

1. bank reconciliation at September 30, 2017.
2. listing of deposits for October per the bank statement.
3. listing of deposits for October per the books.
4. listing of cheques cleared by the bank during October.
5. listing of cheques written by Molly's during October.

MOLLY'S FOLLY
Bank Reconciliation
September 30, 2017

Balance per bank statement		$15,000
Add: Deposits in transit		
September 29	$2,000	
September 30	1,600	3,600
		18,600
Deduct: Outstanding cheques		
No. 514	650	
No. 516	410	
No. 520	560	
No. 521	740	
No. 522	1,000	3,360
Correct cash balance		$15,240
Balance per books		$15,690
Deduct: Customer's NSF cheque	$400	
Bank service charge	50	450
Correct cash balance		$15,240

Bank Statement for October—Deposits

Date	Amount	Date	Amount	Date	Amount
10/1	$2,000	10/11	$1,200	10/25	$ 100
10/2	1,600	10/15	200	10/27	600
10/3	500	10/18	400	10/28	800
10/5	300	10/21	700	10/29	1,300
10/11	1,100	10/22	900	Total	$11,700

Cash Receipts Journal

Date	Amount	Date	Amount	Date	Amount
10/1	$ 500	10/20	$ 700	10/29	$ 1,400
10/4	300	10/21	900	10/30	1,500
10/8	1,100	10/23	100	10/31	550
10/10	1,200	10/25	600	Total	$11,550
10/13	200	10/27	800		
10/16	400	10/28	1,300		

Bank Statement for October—Cheques Paid and Debit Memos (DMs)

Date	Cheque #	Amount	Date	Cheque #	Amount
10/1	514	$ 650	10/13	534	$ 220
10/1	520	560	10/14	535	240
10/4	521	740	10/18	538	380
10/4	522	1,000	10/18	536	250
10/5	525	120	10/18	537	320
10/5	526	140	10/18	539	430
10/6	528	230	10/19	540	510
10/8	529	310	10/23	541	330
10/8	527	210	10/25	542	340
10/8	530	420	10/29	545	540
10/11	532	160	10/29	546	470
10/11	531	130	10/31	DM	30
10/12	533	190	Total		$8,920

Cash Payments Journal—Cheques Issued

Date	Cheque #	Amount	Date	Cheque #	Amount
10/1	525	$120	10/14	538	$ 380
10/1	526	140	10/15	539	430
10/3	527	210	10/17	540	510
10/4	528	230	10/20	541	330
10/5	529	310	10/23	542	340
10/5	530	420	10/25	543	110
10/7	531	130	10/26	544	160
10/7	532	106	10/27	545	540
10/7	533	190	10/28	546	470
10/11	534	220	10/31	547	590
10/11	535	240	10/31	548	640
10/12	536	250	Total		$7,386
10/14	537	320			

Instructions

(a) Prepare a list of deposits in transit at October 31, 2017.

(b) Prepare a list of outstanding cheques at October 31, 2017.

(c) Identify any errors in the books, assuming that the information recorded in the bank's records is correct.

(d) Identify any bank memoranda that will need to be recorded on the books.

Solution to Exercise 7-6

(a) Deposits in transit at October 31, 2017:

October 29	$1,400
October 30	1,500
October 31	550
Total	$3,450

(b) Outstanding cheques at October 31, 2017:

No.	Amount
516	$ 410
543	110
544	160
547	590
548	640
	$1,910

(c) Cheque No. 532 was recorded on the depositor's books for $106 when it should have been recorded for the correct amount of $160.

(d) The debit memo (DM) for $30 on October 31 will need to be recorded on Molly's books. (The DM is likely for bank service charges for October.)

EXPLANATION:

(a) To identify the deposits in transit at October 31:

1. Compare the deposits in transit at September 30 (per the company's bank reconciliation at that date) with the October bank statement. If a September deposit in transit did not get recorded by the bank during October, it is considered a deposit in transit at October 31. (It would be extremely rare for a deposit to be listed as a deposit in transit on **two** successive bank reconciliations, because it would indicate the deposit was lost in the mail or somehow lost in the bank's facilities.)

   For Molly's Folly, the $2,000 and $1,600 items deposited at the end of September (deposits in transit at September 30, 2017) were both recorded by the bank in early October as expected.

2. Compare the deposits made during October per company records (Cash Receipts Journal) with the October deposits per the bank statement. Deposits not recorded by the bank represent **deposits in transit**. As expected, the receipts recorded in the cash receipts journal at the very end of October have not yet been processed by the bank by the end of the day on October 31. These include the deposits made by Molly's Folly on October 29 ($1,400), October 30 ($1,500), and October 31 ($550).

(b) To identify the outstanding cheques at October 31:

1. Compare the cheques outstanding at September 30, 2017 (per the September 30 bank reconciliation) with the cheques that cleared the bank

according to the October bank statement. If a September cheque remains uncleared/unpaid at the end of October, it remains an outstanding cheque at October 31.

For Molly's Folly, cheque numbers 514, 520, 521, and 522 all cleared the bank during October, but cheque number 516 ($410) remains unpaid at October 31, 2017. (The cheque could be lost in the mail or lost in the banking system. More likely, the cheque is still in the hands of the payee, who for some reason has not yet deposited it to their account.)

2. Compare the cheques written by Molly's Folly during October according to the Cash Payments Journal, with the cheques cleared/paid by the bank according to the bank statement. Issued cheques that have not yet been paid by the bank represent **outstanding cheques**.

    For Molly's Folly, October cheque numbers 543 ($110), 544 ($160), 547 ($590), and 548 ($640) were written during October and are still outstanding at October 31.

(c) To identify errors in either the bank's records or the depositor's books, compare all of the items on the October bank statement with the items listed on the depositor's records. If there are any discrepancies, determine which is in error.

For Molly's Folly, cheque number 532 correctly cleared the bank for $160 but was entered in the cash payments journal as $106. (The facts given state that the bank's records are correct.) This transposition-type error caused the depositor's bank balance per ledger to be overstated by $54 ($160 − $106 = $54).

Note that a transposition error (reversing the order of numbers in a figure) will cause a difference that is divisible by 9.

EXERCISE 7-7

Purpose: This exercise will allow you to practise preparing a bank reconciliation. A bank reconciliation should be prepared by the depositor every month.

The cash balance per bank at October 31 is $17,780, and the cash balance per Molly's Folly's books at October 31 is $19,404.

Instructions

(a) Using the data in **Exercise 7-6** and the solution to that exercise, prepare a bank reconciliation for Molly's Folly at October 31, 2017.

(b) Prepare the adjusting entries at October 31 for the depositor's books. Assume cheque No. 532 was issued to the power company for utilities.

Solution to Exercise 7-7

(a)

MOLLY'S FOLLY
Bank Reconciliation
October 31, 2017

Balance per bank statement		$17,780*
Add: Deposits in transit [Answer (a) Exercise 7-6]		3,450
		21,230
Deduct: Outstanding cheques [Answer (b) Exercise 7-6]		1,910
Correct cash balance		$19,320
Balance per books		$19,404**
Deduct: Bank service charge	$30	
Error in recording cheque No. 532	54	84
Correct cash balance		$19,320

*To add to the complexity of this exercise, you could be asked to solve for the $17,780 cash balance per bank statement at October 31, 2017. The calculation would be as follows:

Balance per bank statement at September 30, 2017	$15,000
Add: Deposits recorded during October and credit memoranda	11,700
Deduct: Cheques paid during October and debit memoranda	8,920
Balance per bank statement at October 31, 2017	$17,780

**To add to the complexity of this exercise, you could be asked to solve for the $19,404 cash balance per books at October 31, 2017. The calculation would be as follows:

Balance per books at September 30, 2017, before adjustment	$15,690
Deduct: NSF cheque recorded by an adjusting entry	400
Deduct: Bank service charge for September recorded by an adjusting entry	50
Correct cash balance at September 30	15,240
Add: Deposits made during October	11,550
Deduct: Cheques written (issued) during October	7,386
Balance per books at October 31, 2017	$19,404

An alternative approach to solving for the balance per books before adjustment is illustrated in the **Solution to Exercise 7-5** part (b) 2.

Keep in mind that deposits in transit and outstanding cheques are reconciling items but do not require adjusting entries on either the bank's books or the depositor's books.

(b) Oct. 31 Office Expense   30
          Cash   30
          (To record bank service charges for October)

   Oct. 31 Utilities Expense   54
          Cash   54
          (To correct error in recording cheque no. 532)

EXERCISE 7-8

PURPOSE: This exercise reviews the journal entries involved in establishing and maintaining a petty cash fund.

The Winnipeg Honey Corporation pays for most expenditures by cheque. The following transactions relate to an imprest petty cash fund established by the Winnipeg Honey Corporation to handle small expenditures on an expedient basis.

Transactions

May 4	Wrote a $250 cheque to establish the petty cash fund.
6	Paid taxi $15 to deliver papers to a branch office.
6	Purchased stamps, $13.
8	Paid $20 for advertising posters.
12	Paid $8 for mail received with "postage due."
12	Paid $10 for coffee supplies.
13	Paid $15 for office supplies.
14	Paid bus charges of $18 to ship goods to a customer.
15	Counted the remaining coins and currency in the fund, $141.
15	Wrote a cheque to replenish the fund.

Instructions

(a) Record the transactions in general journal form.

(b) Answer the questions that follow:

   1. How much coin and currency should have been in the petty cash box at the end of the day on May 12?

   2. How much coin and currency should have been in the petty cash box on May 15 before replenishment?

   3. What was the balance in the Petty Cash ledger account on May 12?

   4. What was the balance in the Petty Cash ledger account at the end of the day on May 15?

In order to answer the last two questions, it would be helpful to post the journal entries to a T account for Petty Cash.

Solution to Exercise 7-8

(a) May 4   Petty Cash   250
                 Cash   250
            (To establish the petty cash fund)

     May 15 Miscellaneous Expense ($15 + $10)   25
                 Postage Expense ($13 + $8)   21
                 Advertising Expense   20
                 Office Supplies   15
                 Freight-Out   18
                 Cash Over and Short   10
                 Cash   109
            (To replenish the petty cash fund)

(b) 1. There should have been $184 in coin and currency in the fund at the end of the day on May 12. ($250 − $15 − $13 − $20 − $8 − $10 = $184)

    2. There should have been $151 in coin and currency in the fund on May 15 before replenishment. ($250 − $15 − $13 − $20 − $8 − $10 − $15 − $18 = $151)

    3. $250

    4. $250

● Because only $141 was found in the fund on May 15, there was a shortage of $10, which is recorded by a debit to the Cash Over and Short account.

● The balance of the Petty Cash account changes only when the fund is established or the size of the fund is increased or decreased. The Petty Cash account balance is not affected by expenditures from or replenishments to the fund. No journal entry is made at the time expenditures are paid from the fund. Expenditures paid from the fund are recorded on the date of replenishment.

● Petty cash is not normally reported separately on the statement of financial position. The balance of the Petty Cash account is generally grouped with all other cash items when a statement of financial position is prepared.

EXERCISE 7-9

PURPOSE: This exercise will allow you to practise preparing a bank reconciliation. The following data pertain to the Costain Company for 2017:

1. Per the February bank statement: January 31 balance, $21,000; February receipts, $20,000; February disbursements, $23,000; February 28 balance, $18,000.

2. Per the books: January 31 unadjusted balance, $17,670; February receipts, $19,410; February disbursements, $21,505; February 28 balance, $15,575.

3. Bank service charge of $20 for January is included in disbursements per the books for February.

4. Bank service charge of $35 for February is included on the bank statement for February.

5. The first deposit shown on the February bank statement was $4,000 and was included in January's cash receipts per books.

6. $6,000 of cheques written in February have not cleared the bank by February 28.

7. A cheque written for office supplies in February for $970 was incorrectly recorded in the cash disbursements journal and in the cheque register as $790. This cheque cleared the bank in February for $970. Office supplies are charged to Office Supplies Expense when purchased.

8. In February, the bank credited Costain's account in error for $800 for another firm's deposit.

9. In February, the bank collected a $1,000 note receivable plus $90 interest on behalf of Costain. Costain has not yet recorded this transaction.

10. February 28 cash receipts of $5,000 did not reach the bank until March 2.

11. All $9,000 of cheques outstanding at January 31 cleared the banking system during February.

12. A customer's NSF cheque in the amount of $250 was returned with the February bank statement. This cheque was redeposited in March. As at the end of February, Costain had not yet recorded an entry for the return of this cheque by the bank.

Instructions

(a) Prepare a bank reconciliation for the Costain Company for February.

(b) Prepare any adjusting entry(ies) required in the books.

Solution to Exercise 7-9

(a)

COSTAIN COMPANY
Bank Reconciliation
For February 2017

Balance per bank statement	$18,000*
Add: Outstanding deposit (February 28)	5,000
	23,000

Deduct: Outstanding cheques		$6,000	
	Bank error	800	6,800
Correct cash balance			$16,200
Balance per books			$15,575*
Add: Cash collection on Note			
	(including $90 interest)**	$1,090	1,090
			16,665
Deduct: Bank service charge		35	
	Error in recording cheque (office supplies)	180	
	NSF cheque	250	465
Correct cash balance			$16,200

* The two starting points are the cash ending balances on the bank statement and company books. Only items that the other party does not know about need to be listed as reconciling items. (For example, the January Bank Service Charge recorded in February is already included in the opening balance of the company's books and does not need to be reconciled.)

** The note collected by the bank and related interest can be recorded individually or together; however, the net journal entry(ies) must record interest income separately (see below).

(b)
Office Expense		35	
	Cash		35
Office Supplies Expense		180	
	Cash		180
Cash		1,090	
	Notes Receivable		1,000
	Interest Income		90
Accounts Receivable		250	
	Cash		250

ANALYSIS OF MULTIPLE-CHOICE QUESTIONS

Question

1. Which of the following items should **not** be included in the Cash caption on the statement of financial position?

    a. Coins and currency in the cash register

    b. Cheques, from other parties, presently in the cash register

    c. Amounts on deposit in a chequing account at the bank

    d. Postage stamps on hand

EXPLANATION: Cash on hand, cash in banks, and petty cash are often combined and reported simply as Cash. Undeposited cheques from other parties are included in cash on hand. Postage stamps on hand are classified as a prepaid expense. (Solution = d.)

Question

2. Legally restricted deposits held at a bank as compensating balances against long-term borrowing arrangements should be:

   a. used to reduce the amount reported as long-term debt on the statement of financial position.

   b. reported separately among the "cash and cash equivalent items" in Current Assets on the statement of financial position.

   c. separately classified as non-current assets in either the Investments or Other Assets section of the statement of financial position.

   d. used to reduce the amount reported as short-term debt on the statement of financial position.

EXPLANATION: Restricted deposits held as compensating balances against long-term borrowing arrangements should be separately classified as non-current assets in either the Investments or Other Assets section, using a caption such as "Cash on deposit maintained as compensating balance." To use the asset balance to directly reduce a debt (answer selections "a" and "d") would be offsetting assets against liabilities, which is not appropriate. Only in rare circumstances is it permissible to offset assets against liabilities. (Solution = c.)

Question

3. SC Inc. recorded bad debt expense of $32,000 and wrote off accounts receivable of $23,000 during the year. The net effect of these two transactions on working capital is a decrease of:

   a. $9,000.   c. $32,000.

   b. $23,000.   d. $55,000.

EXPLANATION:

			Effect on Working Capital
Bad Debt Expense	32,000		None
Allowance for Doubtful Accounts		32,000	Decrease 32,000
Allowance for Doubtful Accounts	23,000		Increase 23,000
Accounts Receivable		23,000	Decrease 23,000
Net Effect			Decrease 32,000
			(Solution = c.)

Question

4. Kamloops Corporation performed an aging analysis of its accounts receivable at December 31, 2017, which disclosed the following:

Accounts receivable balance	$112,000
Allowance for doubtful accounts balance	7,000
Estimated uncollectible accounts as of December 31, 2017	13,700

The net realizable value of accounts receivable at December 31 is:

a. $98,300.   c. $105,000.

b. $91,300.   d. $103,300.

EXPLANATION: Write down the definition of net realizable value of accounts receivable—it is the amount of accounts receivable ultimately expected to be converted into cash. Read the details of the question. If the aging analysis determines that $13,700 of the $112,000 accounts receivable are expected to be uncollectible, then the remaining $98,300 is expected to be converted into cash. (Because the balance of the allowance account does not agree with the estimated uncollectible amount per the aging analysis, the allowance for uncollectible accounts balance must be adjusted.) (Solution = a.)

Question

5. The following data are available for January 2017:

Sales Revenue, cash	$200,000
Sales Revenue, credit	500,000
Accounts Receivable, January 1	80,000
Accounts Receivable, January 31	72,000
Allowance for Doubtful Accounts, January 1	4,000
Accounts written off during January 2017	4,600

The company is preparing a set of financial statements for January 2017 and estimates the company's bad debts for the month using the percentage-of-sales method. The journal entry to record bad debt expense for the month and to adjust the allowance account is based on an estimate of 1% of credit sales. The entry to record bad debt expense for January 2017 would include a debit to the Bad Debt Expense account for:

a. $7,200.   c. $4,400.

b. $5,600.   d. $5,000.

EXPLANATION: Under the percentage-of-sales approach, a bad debt expense estimate of 1% of credit sales equals $5,000 ($500,000 × 1%) in this case. The balance of the allowance account before adjustment does not affect this calculation or entry. (Solution = d.)

Question

6. The following data are available for 2017:

Sales Revenue, cash	$175,000
Sales Revenue, credit	600,000
Accounts Receivable, January 1	87,000
Accounts Receivable, December 31	78,000
Allowance for Doubtful Accounts, January 1	5,000
Accounts written off during 2017	5,400

The company uses the percentage-of-receivables aging analysis approach to adjust the allowance account and record bad debt expense. An aging analysis of accounts receivable at December 31, 2017, reveals that $6,100 of existing accounts receivable are estimated to be uncollectible. The entry to record bad debt expense for 2017 will involve a debit to the Bad Debt Expense account for:

a. $6,100.

c. $5,700.

b. $6,500.

d. $5,400.

EXPLANATION: Aging analysis is performed to determine an appropriate balance for the allowance (contra accounts receivable) account, in order to show net accounts receivable at net realizable value on the statement of financial position. In this case, $6,100 is the desired balance for the allowance account at the reporting date. Determine the existing balance in the allowance account and the adjusting entry needed to arrive at the desired ending balance.

Allowance for Doubtful Accounts

Writeoffs, 2017	5,400	Balance, 1/1/17	5,000	
Balance before adjustment	400	Adjustment needed	X	← **Entry Needed**
		Desired balance at 12/31/17	6,100	

Solving for X: X − $400 = $6,100
            X   = $6,100 + $400
            X   = $6,500   (Solution = b.)

Question

7. The following data are available for January 2017:

Allowance for Doubtful Accounts, January 1	$ 41,000
Writeoffs of accounts receivable during January	35,000
Net credit sales in January	1,300,000

The company uses the percentage-of-sales approach to estimate bad debts when preparing monthly financial statements. Bad debts are estimated to be 3% of net credit sales. The balance of the allowance account after adjustment should be:

a. $4,000.

c. $45,000.

b. $39,000.

d. $80,000.

EXPLANATION: Draw a T account. Enter the data given and solve for the required amount.

Allowance for Doubtful Accounts

Writeoffs	35,000	41,000	Beginning Balance
		39,000	Bad Debt Expense = 3% × $1,300,000
		45,000	Ending Balance

(Solution = c.)

Question

8. An adjusting entry debits Sales Returns and Allowances and credits Allowance for Sales Returns and Allowances. This entry:

a. reduces assets and net sales.

b. increases assets and net sales.

c. reduces net sales and liabilities.

d. increases net sales and liabilities.

EXPLANATION: A debit to Sales Returns and Allowances reduces net sales (and shareholders' equity) because it results in an increase in a contra sales account. A credit to Allowance for Sales Returns and Allowances increases a contra accounts receivable account and therefore reduces total assets. This entry is necessary to record sales returns and allowances in the period in which the related sales revenue is recorded. At the end of a period, an estimate of sales returns and allowances is calculated for sales earned during the last few weeks of the period. The sales returns and allowances may arise due to customer refunds granted during the beginning weeks of the subsequent accounting period. (Solution = a.)

Question

9. A company has a large amount of accounts receivable and an immediate need for cash. The company may accelerate the receipt of cash from accounts receivable through:

	Factoring	Assignment
a.	Yes	Yes
b.	Yes	No
c.	No	Yes
d.	No	No

EXPLANATION: The company can transfer accounts receivable to a third party for cash by assignment or factoring (sale) of its accounts receivable. (Solution = a.)

Question

10. The receivables turnover ratio measures the:
    a. number of times the average balance of accounts receivable is collected during the period.
    b. percentage of accounts receivable turned over to a collection agency during the period.
    c. percentage of accounts receivable arising during certain seasons.
    d. number of times the average balance of inventory is sold during the period.

EXPLANATION: Write down the components of the receivables turnover ratio. Think about why it is calculated. The calculation is as follows:

$$\text{Receivables Turnover Ratio} = \frac{\text{Net Sales}}{\text{Average Trade Receivables (net)}}$$

Because cash sales do not affect accounts receivable, technically only net credit sales should be included in the numerator amount; however, the amount of net credit sales is often not available. The receivables turnover ratio measures the number of times, on average, the accounts receivable balance was collected during the period. This ratio is used to assess the liquidity of accounts receivable. The calculated result of this ratio can be divided into 365 days to obtain the average days to collect accounts receivable. (Solution = a.)

Question

11. The term "outstanding cheques" refers to:
    a. cheques that have been lost in the mail or misplaced.
    b. depositor cheques that have been processed by the bank but not yet recorded by the depositor.
    c. customer cheques that have been returned by the bank because the customer's bank would not honour them.
    d. depositor cheques that have not yet cleared the banking system.

EXPLANATION: There is a time lag between the date a cheque is issued and the date the cheque clears the banking system. In the time between these two dates, the cheques are referred to as "outstanding cheques." Cheques written by a company but not mailed until after the statement of financial position date should not be included with outstanding cheques. Rather, they should be added back to the cash balance and reported as accounts payable because payment has not yet been issued. (Solution = d.)

Question

12. The following information pertains to Wheeler Co. at December 31, 2017:

Bank statement balance	$27,500
Chequebook balance	35,350
Deposit in transit	9,800
Outstanding cheques	2,100
Bank service charges for December	150

On Wheeler's statement of financial position at December 31, 2017, the cash balance reported should be:

a. $25,400.   c. $37,300.

b. $27,500.   d. $35,200.

EXPLANATION: When a question relates to information in a bank reconciliation, try sketching the outline of a bank reconciliation, inserting the information given, and solving for the unknown item.

Balance per bank statement	$27,500
Deposit in transit	9,800
Outstanding cheques	(2,100)
Correct cash balance	$35,200
Balance per books	$35,350
Bank service charges	(150)
Correct cash balance	$35,200

In this particular question, completion of either the top half or the bottom half of the reconciliation using the bank-to-correct-balance method would solve for the required answer. (Solution = d.)

Question

13. The following data relate to the bank account of Springfield Cleaners:

Cash balance, September 30, 2017, per bank	$10,000
Cash balance, October 31, 2017, per bank	21,500
Cheques paid during October per bank	5,900
Cheques written during October per books	800
Cash balance, October 31, 2017, per books	22,200
Bank service charges for October, not recorded on books	100
Deposits per books for October	19,000

The amount of deposits recorded by the bank in October is:

    a. $19,000.

    b. $17,500.

    c. $11,500.

    d. $5,700.

EXPLANATION: Think about how the cash balance per bank is affected by deposits and other items. Insert the information given to solve for the unknown.

Balance per bank, September 30	$10,000
Deposits per bank during October	X
Bank credit memoranda	0
Cheques cleared by bank during October	(5,900)
Bank service charge for October and other bank debit memoranda	(100)
Balance per bank, October 31	$21,500

Solving for X:

$$\$10,000 + X - \$5,900 - \$100 = \$21,500$$

$$X = \$21,500 - \$10,000 + \$5,900 + \$100$$

$$X = \underline{\$17,500}$$ (Solution = b.)

Question

14. The following information pertains to Kimbell Corporation at December 31, 2017:

Balance per bank	$10,000
Deposit in transit	3,000
Outstanding cheques	8,000
Bank service charges for December	200
Bank error that charged Kimbell account for $700 cheque written by Franklin Co. As at December 31, the bank had not corrected this error.	700

Kimbell's cash balance per ledger (books) before adjustment at December 31, 2017, is:

    a. $14,100.

    b. $5,900.

    c. $5,500.

    d. $4,100.

EXPLANATION: The balance per books (before adjustment) can be calculated by putting the information into an outline for a bank reconciliation. Either reconciling balance per bank to balance per books, or reconciling balance per bank to correct balance, will result in the cash balance per ledger (books before adjustment). Both approaches are illustrated below.

Balance per bank statement	$10,000
Deposit in transit	3,000
Outstanding cheques	(8,000)
Bank service charges	200
Bank charge for cheque in error	700
Balance per books (ledger)	$ 5,900
Balance per bank statement	$10,000
Deposit in transit	3,000
Outstanding cheques	(8,000)
Bank error in charge for cheque	700
Correct cash balance	$ 5,700
Balance per books (ledger)	$ X
Bank service charge	(200)
Correct cash balance	$ 5,700

$$\underline{X = \$5,900} \quad (\text{Solution} = \text{b.})$$

Question

15. Under IFRS 9, receivables without a significant financing component should record a loss allowance based on lifetime expected credit losses. In order to determine the amount of expected credit losses to be recognized in the financial statements:

    a. An entity should use its historical credit loss experience to establish the loss rates.

    b. An entity should use more forward-looking information to establish the loss rates.

    c. An entity can establish a provision matrix for use in recognizing expected credit losses on trade receivables.

    d. All of the above are true.

EXPLANATION: An entity can setup a provision matrix based on its historical observed default rates, which is adjusted for forward-looking estimates. For example:

0-30 days old Non-past due	0.3% of carrying value
31-60 days old	1.5% of carrying value
61-90 days old	3.6% of carrying value

91-120 days old   6.6% of carrying value

 More than 120 days old   10.6% of carrying value

(Solution = d)

CASE STUDY

Dundee Developments

Dixie Dundee, Vice-President Finance of Dundee Developments (DD), stared at the draft financial statements for the November month end. According to the financial statements, it looked as though the company was facing a liquidity crisis. There were significant current liabilities due to be paid, as well as a large principal repayment coming due on a maturing loan. Unless some drastic changes were to take place in December, the year-end financial statements would look even worse.

Dixie was not worried about getting the funds necessary to pay the liabilities coming due. DD was already negotiating to renew the maturing loan. The bank was nowhere near finalizing the deal and would not be ready to do so before year-end statements were issued. However, unless something very disastrous happened, the loan would probably be approved and DD would get the funds.

Dixie's prime concern was how the market would react to the perceived liquidity problem as presented in the financial statements and whether the reaction would cause DD stock prices to tumble. DD was also in the process of making a new share offering in order to finance expansion of the company into the United States. The expansion would not be feasible unless a certain share price could be obtained.

To address DD's perceived liquidity problem, Dixie considered entering a deal to transfer certain notes receivable to EE Ltd. The notes were long-term and had always provided DD with a much-needed steady stream of cash from interest income. The terms of the transfer were as follows:

- DD would transfer the notes to EE on a without recourse basis for the fair value of the notes less a small discount since the notes were considered fully collectible.

- DD would guarantee a 12% rate of return on the notes to EE. That is, if market rates went down, DD would pay EE the difference between the variable interest rate paid to EE under the note and 12%. Conversely, if market rates went up, EE would pay the difference to DD.

- DD would also retain the right to repurchase the notes at book value plus a small premium.

- The debtor owing the money would make payments directly to EE.

The deal was finalized and signed within a few days, bringing DD a significant cash inflow. At year end, market interest rates declined significantly.

Instructions

Discuss the accounting and reporting issues, and advise Dixie as to how these issues affect the year-end financial statements.

Suggested Approach to Case Study

Dundee Developments Overview

The VP Finance is concerned that the financial statements portray the company in a negative light. This is of particular concern because it could cause stock prices to fall at a time when the company prefers higher stock prices to maximize proceeds from an impending stock issue. Financial statement stakeholders include the bank (especially due to the impending loan renewal) and potential investors. Both sets of stakeholders would want information that is faithfully representative, neutral, and free from bias. IFRS is a constraint since the shares are publicly traded.

Assuming that your role is that of the auditor, since the company plans to use the financial statements for refinancing, the engagement would be considered high-risk. If there are in fact liquidity problems, such information would affect the users and influence their decisions; therefore, financial statements should be faithfully representative, neutral, and free from bias, regardless of what Dixie wants. Full disclosure of complex transactions would also be important.

Analysis and Recommendations

The issues are as follows:

- How to account for transfer of the notes
- How to present the loan that is currently due

Notes Receivable

Should the transfer of the notes be treated as a derecognition of notes receivable or merely a secured borrowing?

The resolution would revolve around whether DD has surrendered control of the notes and whether the risks and rewards of owning the notes have transferred to EE.

First, the financial reporting implications will be discussed. If this is genuinely a transfer, the long-term notes receivable should be removed from the financial statements at a small loss, and replaced with cash. This would greatly enhance DD's perceived liquidity position. The journal entry to record the transfer would be as follows:

Cash

Loss

Notes Receivable

However, if this is a financing arrangement, the transaction would increase liabilities (it is questionable whether the liability would be current or long-term) and cash. The discount would be deferred and amortized. If the liability is recorded as long-term, DD's apparent liquidity position would be improved; if the liability is recorded as current, DD's apparent liquidity position would not change.

Cash

Deferred Discount

Current or Non-current Liability

In order to determine whether this is a sale or a secured borrowing, the IFRS standard for derecognition of a financial asset must be considered. Under IFRS, the receivables may be recorded as sold if:

1. the company transfers the contractual rights to receive cash flows from the receivables, or

2. the company retains the contractual rights to receive cash flows from the receivables, but has a contractual obligation to pay the cash flows to one or more recipients upon receipt (and three additional conditions are met that would support that the receivables have been sold), and substantially all of the risks and rewards of ownership of the receivables have been transferred.

In this case, EE is a separate legal entity, and EE has the contractual right to receive cash flows from the receivables. There is a repurchase agreement in place; that is, DD has the right to repurchase the notes receivable and therefore an ability to cause EE to return the notes receivable. The agreement does not obligate DD to reacquire the notes receivable and therefore it may be argued that DD has transferred the risks of ownership. However, having the right to reacquire the notes means that DD has retained some of the rewards of ownership and therefore retains some control over the notes receivable.

Furthermore, note that DD values the "steady stream of income" from the notes receivable. This might be an inducement for DD to exercise its right to repurchase, although DD will not really need the steady stream of income if the loan and equity financing go through, as they likely will. It should be noted that the transfer of notes receivable appears to have been entered into primarily to cause an improvement in DD's liquidity position as at the year-end date.

DD has guaranteed a certain rate of return to EE and, therefore, is at risk for fluctuations in interest rates.

It might be acceptable to argue that the arrangement is a financing arrangement but that DD's intent is not to repurchase the notes until after the upcoming year. This would support recording of a long-term liability as at the year-end date. However, note that interest rates are declining at year end, which is an inducement to repurchase the notes in the shorter term.

Given the fact that DD retains control over the notes receivable through a repurchase agreement and given the facts of the case, the transaction should be accounted for as a financing arrangement. The liability could be recorded as long-term provided that DD confirms its intent not to repurchase the notes until after the upcoming year. Full disclosure of the arrangement would be required due to the significance of the transaction and the interest guarantee (which will affect cash flows).

Loan Refinancing

The loan will have to be classified as current even though there is an intent to refinance. Under IFRS, unless at the statement of financial position date there is an existing agreement in place to refinance the loan for at least 12 months and the decision is solely at the entity's discretion, the loan must be classified as current. DD can consider disclosing its intent to refinance in the notes to the financial statements since the negotiations are in progress and since refinancing will affect future cash flows.

Chapter 8

Inventory

OVERVIEW

In accounting, the term "inventory" refers to assets held for sale in the ordinary course of business or assets that will be used or consumed in the production of goods to be sold or rendering of services. A number of questions regarding inventory are addressed in this chapter, including: (1) What goods should be included in inventory? (2) What costs should be included in inventory cost? (3) What cost flow assumption should be used to determine which items remain in inventory at the statement of financial position date? (4) How will the selection of a particular cost flow assumption affect the statement of income and statement of financial position? (5) How do inventory errors affect the financial statements?

Sometimes a business is faced with a situation where impairment in the value of inventory is so great that items cannot be sold at a normal profit. In particular, both IFRS and ASPE require that, if an inventory item's net realizable value is below cost, the business should write the value of the inventory down to net realizable value. (Net realizable value is estimated selling price less estimated costs to complete and sell.) Writedowns are recognized in the period when the impairment occurs, rather than in a later period when the inventory is disposed of; thus, inventory is reported at the lower of cost and net realizable value on the statement of financial position. Presentation and disclosure of inventories are also discussed in this chapter.

Finally, there are times when a business may need to estimate the cost of inventory on hand at a certain date. Two methods of inventory estimation—the gross profit method and the retail inventory method—are discussed in this chapter. Although the conventional retail inventory method approximates lower of average cost and market valuation of inventory, it can be revised to approximate FIFO cost or weighted-average cost. Markups and markdowns are also discussed in relation to the retail inventory method in this chapter.

STUDY STEPS

Understanding the Importance of Inventory in Business

Inventory Defined

For accounting purposes, inventories are defined as assets held for sale in the ordinary course of business, in the process of production for such sale, or in the form of materials or supplies to be consumed in the production process or in the rendering of services. Therefore, inventory is composed of goods held for resale (finished goods), materials that will be used to produce goods for sale (raw materials), and partially completed goods that will eventually be sold (work in process). The business objective is that the finished product will be sold, hopefully at a profit. Inventory differs from fixed assets in that fixed assets are held for use in the production of goods and services, whereas inventory is sold in the normal course of business to produce profit. It can be difficult at times to distinguish between inventory and fixed assets; professional judgement may be required. This is discussed further in Chapter 10.

Categories of Inventory

Retailers and wholesalers have inventory that is ready for sale. Manufacturing companies have inventories at various stages of completion, including the following:

1. **Raw materials inventory:** Materials on hand that have not yet entered the production process
2. **Work-in-process inventory:** The cost of the raw material, direct labour, and manufacturing overhead that have been applied to inventory currently in the production process
3. **Finished goods inventory:** Completed units that are still on hand and not yet sold

Management of Inventory

Whether a company purchases goods for resale or manufactures goods for sale, effective management of inventory is essential for business success. Having high levels of inventory is costly, including possible excessive carrying costs related to investment, storage, insurance, taxes, obsolescence, risk of theft, and damage. On the other hand, having low levels of inventory may lead to lost sales and unhappy customers. Effective management of inventory requires careful planning and control.

- Inventory includes items that will eventually be sold for profit and/or to recover costs.

- Inventory is an **essential asset** in many businesses since manufacturing and sale of inventory is often the primary source of income. Not only is inventory sold to generate profit, it may also be used as collateral to secure bank loans.

- Because inventory affects the calculation of the current ratio, and is often used to secure loans, the items included in inventory and its amount reported on the statement of financial position are very important.

Understanding Inventory-Related Transactions

Ownership and Shipping Terms

Sometimes inventory may not be physically sitting in the company's warehouse on the statement of financial position date. For example, goods may be sitting on the loading dock, in a railway car, or even in a truck **in transit**. Should these goods be included in the company's inventory as at the statement of financial position date? Analysis of this issue begins with a review of the second component in the definition of an asset. That is, if the entity has control over the asset (for example, if the **risks and rewards** of ownership have transferred to the company buying the inventory), then the goods should be included in the company's inventory as at that date. Sometimes control may be determined by looking at **shipping terms** according to purchase agreements or invoices.

If goods are sent **f.o.b.** (free on board) **shipping point**, the goods are considered inventory of the buying company from the time the goods are shipped by the selling company. The selling company is responsible for the goods only up until the point of shipment. If terms are **f.o.b. destination**, the goods are considered inventory of the selling company until the goods arrive at the destination specified by the buyer (usually the buyer's warehouse). Under f.o.b. destination terms, the selling company is responsible for insuring the goods until they reach their destination.

F.O.B. Shipping Point

Title Transfer

Seller | Buyer's Goods | Buyer

F.O.B. Destination

Title Transfer

Seller | Seller's Goods | Buyer

Shipping terms are important in identifying whether an item should be recorded on the statement of financial position as an asset, because shipping terms determine the point at which the company has control over the item in question.

Inventory on Consignment

See the discussion of business arrangements under consignment sales in Chapter 6 of the Study Guide.

Sales with Buyback Agreement

Also sometimes referred to as "product financing arrangements" or "parking transactions," sales with buyback arrangements are characterized by a sale of inventory plus an agreement to repurchase the inventory at a future time. Depending on the details of the arrangement, it may be seen as two separate transactions (a sale and then a future purchase) or as one transaction (a financing transaction). Professional judgement should be used to determine whether a genuine sale of inventory has occurred or whether the inventory still, in substance, belongs to the company. This type of transaction was also discussed in Chapter 6 of the Study Guide. It is important to determine whether or not the risks and rewards of ownership and therefore control have been transferred.

Sales Involving Uncertainty

See the discussion of sales involving uncertainty in Chapter 6 of the Study Guide. Inventory is not considered sold when there is major uncertainty regarding collection or when there are high rates of return but the returns are highly unpredictable.

Purchase Commitments

If a company enters into a non-cancellable contract to purchase inventory at a future date, and the amounts are abnormal in relation to the entity's normal business operations or financial position, the contract details should be disclosed in the notes to the company's financial statements. Under IFRS, at the statement of financial position date, if the contracted purchase price of the inventory is lower than the market price of the inventory, and completing the contract is unavoidable, a loss (for the difference between the contracted purchase price and the market price) is recognized. This is known as an onerous contract. ASPE has no similar requirement, although in practice, if the loss is likely and measurable, the loss would also be recognized.

Understanding Recognition and Cost Measurement Issues Surrounding Inventory

The key issues in this area are:

- which items to include in inventory (for example, goods in transit, consignment items), and
- which costs to include (for example, freight, factory overhead, labour).

Valuation of Inventory at Cost: Issues, Relevant Criteria/Definitions, Guidance, Special Considerations

		Issue, Relevant Criteria and Definitions	Guidance	Special Considerations
Recognition	When to recognize or derecognize inventory	• Overall, when control over the inventory transfers (or risks and rewards of ownership transfer) • Consider shipping terms (**f.o.b. shipping point versus f.o.b. destination**) • For complex transactions, consider **economic substance** of the arrangement	• Normally **possession** and **legal title** transfer at the time of receipt or shipment of goods • Is it a genuine sale/purchase or is it a financing-type transaction?	• Professional judgement required if selling terms are complex (for example, if the company has either legal title or possession but not both) • Professional judgement required in complex arrangements; may be difficult to determine who has control over, or risks and rewards of, inventory
Measurement	What to include in inventory cost (partly a classification issue) What cost flow method to use	• Under IFRS and ASPE, inventory cost includes **"all costs of purchase, costs of conversion, and other costs incurred in bringing the inventories to their present location and condition"** • **Specific identification, weighted average cost, or FIFO**	• Include any cost incurred to convert inventory to a saleable condition and to get the inventory to the buyer's place of business • The key is to choose an approach that corresponds as closely as possible to the physical flow of goods, and to report an inventory cost on the statement of financial position that is representative of the inventory's recent cost	• **Standard costs** may be used if not significantly different from actual cost • Professional judgement needed to allocate overhead • Costs from abnormal situations generally not included • The method chosen may have a significant impact on net income and, therefore, potential for management bias exists
Presentation/ Disclosure	Note disclosure	• **Full disclosure**	• Disclose basis of valuation and cost flow method	

Becoming Proficient in Using Inventory Costing Methods

Determining the cost of inventory would be simple if there were only a few high-priced items. However, inventory often consists of many different products of varying values purchased at different times and at different prices. Even identical products that were purchased at different times may have different prices.

If all items were purchased at different prices but are otherwise identical, and only half were sold in the period, which items (and corresponding costs) should be left in inventory as at the statement of financial position date and which items should be considered sold in the period? Should the items purchased first be considered sold first, or should an average cost be calculated? An assumption must be made about inventory flow in order to determine inventory cost. The most common assumption is **FIFO (first-in, first-out)**, under which the first (oldest) items purchased are considered sold first. FIFO probably reflects reality best, since most businesses would sell the oldest inventory first.

The LIFO (last-in, first-out) method is not permitted under IFRS or ASPE.

Keeping Track of Quantities: Periodic versus Perpetual Inventory Methods

The **perpetual method** of inventory involves keeping track of each inventory item continuously throughout the year and recording the effect of individual purchases and sales on inventory when they are made. Perpetual inventory records give details about the balance of inventory in the general ledger (similar to a subledger). The perpetual method requires extra bookkeeping but allows the company to see the exact number of items on hand for each inventory item at any point in time. Also, just as the accounts receivable subledger allows the company to verify the related accounts receivable control account in the control ledger, perpetual inventory records allow the company to verify the related inventory control account in the general ledger.

Under the **periodic method**, no such subledger is kept. The inventory account in the general ledger is verified only when physical inventory counts are performed (usually annually).

Under both methods, physical inventory counts are taken. Under a perpetual system, specific items in inventory are counted (spot-checked) and compared with reported amounts in perpetual inventory records. Under a periodic system, however, full inventory counts are performed. The perpetual system offers more control over inventory, but it may be time-consuming and costly. However, with increasing use of inventory tracking systems on computer, this factor is becoming less of an issue.

The Inventory Equation

Cost of goods sold is often determined by the following equation:

Cost of goods sold = beginning inventory + purchases − ending inventory

Cost of goods sold is a residual figure. Beginning inventory and purchases are known in a periodic system: beginning inventory is the previous period's ending inventory amount, and purchases are recorded throughout the year. Ending inventory is usually determined by physical count. It is important to understand the relationship between these components and realize that an error in one will affect the calculation of cost of goods sold.

Understanding the Rationale for Lower of Cost and Net Realizable Value and How to Apply It

Inventory is recognized and carried at cost; however, if the **net realizable value** (estimated selling price less estimated costs to complete and sell) of the inventory declines below cost, the inventory should be written down to net realizable value. This is done to report inventory at an amount that reflects its ability to generate cash flows for the company. Also, a decline in value below cost should be deducted from (matched with) revenues recorded in the period in which the loss occurs.

Writing inventory down to net realizable value may be done using either the direct or indirect (allowance) method. Under the **direct method**, the difference between cost and net realizable value is debited to Cost of Goods Sold and credited to Inventory (directly). Under the **indirect method**, the same amount is debited to Loss on Inventory Due to Decline in NRV (classified with other expenses and losses on the statement of income) and credited to Allowance to Reduce Inventory to NRV, which is a contra inventory account on the statement of financial position.

Exceptions to the Lower of Cost and Net Realizable Value Model

In limited situations, it is possible to record inventory at its net realizable value even if that amount is above cost. The criteria that must be met to report inventory above cost and for revenue to be recognized *before the point of sale* include:

(1) The sale is assured or there is an active market for the product and minimal risk of failure to sell, and

(2) The costs of disposal can be estimated.

Further, in some industries, accounting for inventories at net realizable value is a well-established industry practice. This includes items such as agricultural produce, forest products, and mineral products.

Another exception is to measure inventories at their fair value less costs to sell. This is an established practice for commodity broker-traders.

Under ASPE, inventories of biological assets and the products of biological assets at the point of harvest are excluded from standard inventory measurement requirements and instead are accounted for in accordance with well-established industry practices. For example, biological assets such as olive trees that produce inventory over a long period of time may be treated as property, plant, and equipment.

IAS 41 Agriculture provides a separate standard for the accounting of biological assets and agricultural produce at the point of harvest. Similar to ASPE, these inventories are measured at net realizable value in accordance with well-established industry practices. Biological assets are measured at fair value less costs to sell. Plants, such as grapevines, that are used to grow produce are called "bearer plants." Since they produce saleable products over a longer period of time, they are treated like property, plant, and equipment and are accounted for using the cost or revaluation method.

Becoming Proficient in Applying the Gross Profit and Retail Inventory Methods

Gross Profit Method

The **gross profit method** of determining ending inventory is used to estimate inventory if perpetual records are not kept and/or if a physical count is not practical.

Inventory must be counted at least annually. However, if the value of inventory is needed more frequently, as it usually is (such as for interim reporting), the gross profit method may be used to estimate the amount. Under the gross profit method, ending inventory is calculated as follows:

Ending inventory = beginning inventory + purchases − cost of goods sold

Ending inventory = beginning inventory + purchases − (sales × [1 − gross profit %])

The **gross profit percentage** is determined by analyzing **prior periods'** or prior budgets' gross profit divided by sales. Many companies use this method to estimate cost of sales and ending inventory for interim reporting.

- The gross profit method is used to estimate cost of goods sold and ending inventory if no inventory count is taken.

- Companies often use a normalized historic gross profit percentage to estimate cost of sales and ending inventory, which tends to smooth seasonal and quarterly fluctuations in gross profit percentage and emphasize past trends rather than existing and future trends.

Retail Inventory Method

Retailers often use the **retail inventory method** to value inventory if inventory is high volume/low unit cost. This method uses the same formula as the gross profit method; however, it uses retail value (sales) instead of cost of goods sold to value ending inventory. Where the gross profit and retail inventory methods are used to estimate cost of goods sold and ending inventory when no inventory count is performed, the retail inventory method is also used to estimate ending inventory even when a count is performed.

Under the retail inventory method, **inventory at retail value** (not cost) is determined, because in a retail setting, taking a physical inventory count at retail prices is generally easier. Ending inventory at retail value is then **converted back to cost** by applying the **cost-to-retail ratio** (total goods available for sale at cost divided by total goods available for sale at retail). Normally the following method is used:

Retail Method

	@ retail	@ cost	
Opening inventory	actual	actual	
plus: purchases	actual	actual	
Goods available for sale	total	total	calculate
Less: sales	actual(*)		ratio of cost to retail
Ending inventory	total	× ratio =	ending inventory at cost

(*) from cash/sales register

● The retail inventory method is a way of tracking cost of inventory using retail or sales prices. Where a company has a more sophisticated and computerized inventory tracking system, the need for the retail inventory method decreases.

● Both the gross profit and retail inventory methods are estimation techniques used in the absence of better information. (This is consistent with the cost versus benefits financial reporting constraint.)

Inventory Analysis

Financial ratios can be used to help management decide how much and what types of inventory to carry and to help investors assess management's performance in terms of controlling inventory to maximize profits. Common ratios that are used to evaluate inventory levels are:

(1) Inventory turnover

$$\text{Inventory turnover} = \frac{\text{Cost of goods sold}}{\text{Average inventory}}$$

Inventory turnover measures the number of times on average that the inventory was sold during the period and helps to measure liquidity. A higher inventory turnover ratio indicates a faster turnover and the faster the company generates cash inflows from this asset.

(2) Average days to sell inventory

$$\text{Average days to sell inventory} = \frac{\text{365 days}}{\text{Inventory turnover}}$$

This ratio is very closely related to inventory turnover. It represents the average age of the inventory on hand, or the number of days it takes to sell inventory after it is purchased. Each industry will have acceptable norms for this ratio. For example, the acceptable age of fresh fruits and vegetables inventory would be significantly different than that of other non-perishable household goods.

TIPS ON CHAPTER TOPICS

● The cost of an item in inventory includes all costs necessary to acquire the item and bring it to the location and condition for its intended use. An inventory item's cost includes the item's purchase price, transportation-in, and any special handling charges. However, transportation-out is not included in the cost of inventory; it is classified as a selling expense on the statement of income in the period in which the expense was incurred and the related revenue was earned (consistent with the matching principle).

(continued)

- Under IFRS, the cost of an inventory item should also include any required **decommissioning or asset retirement costs**, even though those costs may not result in cash outflows until far into the future. Adding such costs to inventory (and creating an offsetting deferred liability) results in proper allocation of costs to the assets (inventory) that they relate to. The decommissioning costs then flow to cost of goods sold on the statement of income (along with the rest of the product cost) in the period when the inventory is sold, resulting in matching of expenses with revenues. ASPE does not require that decommissioning or retirement costs be included in inventory; such costs are generally added to the cost of the related property, plant, and equipment.

- Under IFRS, if inventory is a **qualifying asset** (an asset that requires substantial time to get ready for its intended use or sale), and if it is probable that the inventory will bring future economic benefits to the entity, **borrowing costs** that are directly attributable to the acquisition, construction, or production of the inventory are added to the cost of the inventory (capitalized). If the inventory is produced in large quantities on a repetitive basis, the company is not required to capitalize borrowing **costs**, but may choose to do so. ASPE does not require that borrowing costs be capitalized. However, the company's policy and any amounts capitalized must be disclosed.

- Shipping terms generally determine the point at which legal title transfers to the buyer. F.o.b. shipping point (or seller) means that legal title passes to the buyer when the goods leave the seller's dock. F.o.b. destination (or buyer) means that legal title passes to the buyer when the goods arrive at the buyer's dock. For example, if Palmer Company in Richmond Hill, Ontario, sells to Di Nardo Company in St. Catharines, Ontario, the following terms would apply under either f.o.b. shipping point or f.o.b. destination:

f.o.b. shipping point	**f.o.b. destination**
or f.o.b. seller	or f.o.b. buyer
or f.o.b. Richmond Hill, Ontario	or f.o.b. St. Catharines, Ontario

- FIFO (first-in, first-out) means that the costs of the first items purchased and entered in inventory are used to determine the costs of the first items sold (and expensed to cost of goods sold). Thus, the earliest purchase prices are used to determine cost of goods sold for the period, and the latest (most current) purchase prices are used to determine ending inventory.

- When working on a problem that requires calculation of either ending inventory or cost of goods sold, remember that ending inventory plus cost of goods sold (COGS) should equal total cost of goods available for sale.

- Sales revenue consists of the **selling prices** of goods sold, whereas cost of goods sold expense consists of the **cost** of items sold.

- An understatement in year 1 ending inventory will cause an understatement in year 1 net income (because COGS would be overstated) and an overstatement in year 2 net income (because year 2 beginning inventory would be understated). Thus, an understatement in year 1 ending inventory would cause year 1 retained earnings and working capital to be understated. However, assuming there are no other errors in year 2, as at the end of year 2, net retained earnings and working capital would be correctly stated.

- **Net realizable value of inventory** is generally the net amount of cash to be received from sale of inventory. Specifically, net realizable value of inventory is its estimated selling price in the ordinary course of business, less estimated costs to complete and sell.

- The lower of cost and net realizable value standard is a departure from the historical cost principle, which applies when the inventory's future utility (revenue-producing ability) is no longer greater than its original (historical) cost.

- To apply the lower of cost and net realizable value standard, follow these steps.

  1. Determine the cost of inventory using an acceptable cost flow method (specific identification, weighted average cost, or FIFO).

  2. Determine the net realizable value of inventory.

  3. Compare cost with net realizable value.

  4. Use the lower value to value inventory for the statement of financial position.

  The standard specifies that the above steps be applied on an item-by-item basis to arrive at a total value for inventory. Only in certain circumstances is it appropriate to apply the above steps to groups of similar or related items.

- If an inventory item's utility (ability to generate cash flows) declines below cost prior to the period of sale (disposal), a writedown to net realizable value would be required, causing the loss in utility to be recognized in the period of decline rather than in the period of disposal. Thus, if an inventory item becomes obsolete, the amount of writedown to net realizable value would be recognized as a loss in the period the item becomes obsolete, not in the period the item is disposed of.

- Gross profit percentage (expressed as a percentage of selling price) and cost of goods sold percentage (also expressed as a percentage of selling price) are complements; that is, their sum is 100%. When the gross profit method of inventory estimation is used and gross profit is expressed in terms of cost, gross profit must be expressed in terms of selling price before proceeding with the calculations. One way of converting is to use the following formula:

- Percent gross profit on selling price $= \dfrac{\text{Percentage markup on cost}}{100\% + \text{Percentage markup on cost}}$

Another approach to deriving this formula is shown below. It starts with the familiar formula:

Sales (S) − Cost of Goods Sold (COGS) = Gross Profit (GP).

Example: If the markup on cost is 25%, then GP is 25% of COGS.

Putting this information into our formula above: S = 125% × COGS.

Therefore COGS = S ÷ 125%.

Expressing GP in terms of S we get: GP = 20% × S.

Thus, gross profit = 20% of sales.

EXERCISE 8-1

PURPOSE: This exercise will help you practise identifying the effects of inventory errors on financial statements.

The net income per books of Luminus Light Bulb Company was determined without knowledge of the errors shown below:

Year	Net Income Per Books	Error in Ending Inventory	
2017	$145,000	Overstated	$ 8,000
2018	162,000	Overstated	23,000
2019	167,000	Understated	34,000
2020	173,000	No error	

Instructions

Taking into account the inventory errors, calculate the correct net income figure for each year.

Solution to Exercise 8-1

Year	Net Income Per Books	Add Overstatement Jan. 1	Deduct Understatement Jan. 1	Deduct Overstatement Dec. 31	Add Understatement Dec. 31	Corrected Net Income
2017	$145,000			$ 8,000		$137,000
2018	162,000	$ 8,000		23,000		147,000
2019	167,000	23,000			$34,000	224,000
2020	173,000		$34,000			139,000

EXPLANATION: When more than one error affects a given year (such as in 2018), each error should be analyzed separately and then combined to determine the net impact of the errors. Beginning inventory for 2018 (ending inventory for 2017) was overstated by $8,000. Therefore, 2018 cost of goods sold was overstated by $8,000, and 2018 net income was understated by $8,000. Ending inventory for 2018 was overstated by $23,000. Therefore, 2018 cost of goods sold was understated and 2018 net income was overstated by $23,000. Understatement in net income of $8,000 and overstatement in net income of $23,000 in 2018 led to a net 2018 net income overstatement of $15,000. This overstatement of $15,000, combined with the $162,000 amount reported, results in a corrected net income figure of $147,000 for 2018.

Another way of analyzing the effects of an individual error is illustrated below, using the $23,000 overstatement of inventory at the end of 2018.

	Effect on 2018	**Effect on 2019**
Beginning inventory		Overstated $23,000
+ Cost of goods purchased		
= Cost of goods available for sale		Overstated $23,000
− Ending inventory	Overstated $23,000	
= Cost of goods sold	Understated $23,000	Overstated $23,000
Sales		
− Cost of goods sold	Understated $23,000	Overstated $23,000
= Gross profit	Overstated $23,000	Understated $23,000
− Operating expenses		
= Net income	Overstated $23,000	Understated $23,000

Thus, the previously calculated net income figure for 2018 must be reduced by $23,000 to correct for this error. Also, the net income figure for 2019 must be increased by $23,000 to correct for the same error.

Ending inventory for year 1 is beginning inventory for year 2. Thus, an overstatement in year 1 ending inventory will cause an overstatement in year 1 net income and an understatement in year 2 net income (by the same amount). This error will cause retained earnings at the end of year 1 to be overstated because year 1 net income (which is overstated) is closed to retained earnings. The balance of retained earnings at the end of year 2 will be unaffected by this error because year 2 net income (which is understated by the same amount as the overstatement in retained earnings at the end of year 1) is closed to retained earnings. At this point, the error counterbalances. Working capital at the end of year 1 would be overstated (because inventory is a current asset), but working capital at the end of year 2 would be unaffected because the inventory figure at the end of year 2 is determined by a physical inventory count and the cost flow method is reapplied.

EXERCISE 8-2

PURPOSE: This exercise reviews the characteristics and effects of using various cost formulas to determine inventory costs.

Instructions

Answer each of the following questions by inserting the appropriate abbreviation in the space provided.

SI	(specific identification)
FIFO	(first-in, first-out)
WA	(weighted average)

_____ (a) Which inventory cost method is the approach that generally approximates the actual physical flow of goods?

_____ (b) Which method results in the most exact ending inventory valuation when inventory items of the same type are not homogeneous?

_____ (c) Which method is based on the assumption that inventory flow is "mixed" and therefore "mixes" all purchase prices?

_____ (d) Between FIFO and WA, during a period of **rising prices,** which method yields the lowest cost of goods sold figure?

Between FIFO and WA, during a period of **declining prices,** which method yields the:

_____ (e) lowest net income figure?

_____ (f) lowest amount for inventory on the statement of financial position?

_____ (g) lowest shareholders' equity figure?

Solution to Exercise 8-2

(a) FIFO

(b) SI

(c) WA

(d) FIFO

(e) FIFO

(f) FIFO

(g) FIFO

APPROACH: Write down a description of the specific identification, weighted average, and FIFO cost flow formulas. Note the relative effects of these methods on the statement of income and on the statement of financial position in a period of rising prices and in a period of declining prices.

● **FIFO (first-in, first-out)** means the costs of the first items purchased and entered into inventory are used to determine the costs of items sold and expensed to cost of goods sold. Thus, the earliest purchase costs are used to determine cost of goods sold for the period, and the latest (most current) purchase costs are used to determine ending inventory.

● Comparing FIFO and WA in a period of rising prices:

Method	COGS	Net Income	Ending Inventory
FIFO	Lower	Higher	Higher
WA	Higher	Lower	Lower

Illustration 8-1   2 4 3

ILLUSTRATION 8-1

Perpetual versus Periodic Inventory Systems

Features of a Perpetual System	**Features of a Periodic System**
1. Purchases of merchandise for resale are debited to Inventory rather than to Purchases.	1. Purchases of merchandise for resale are debited to Purchases.
2. Freight-in, purchase returns and allowances, and purchase discounts are recorded in Inventory rather than in separate accounts.	2. Freight-in, Purchase Returns and Allowances, and Purchase Discounts are recorded in separate accounts used to track information about inventory purchases during the accounting period.
3. Cost of goods sold is recognized by debiting the Cost of Goods Sold account and crediting Inventory after each sale.	3. Cost of goods sold is recognized only at the end of the accounting period when:
	(a) the ending inventory amount (determined by physical count and application of a cost formula) is recorded in the Inventory account;
	(b) the Purchases, Freight-in, Purchase Returns and Allowances, and Purchase Discounts account balances are closed to the Cost of Goods Sold account; and
	(c) the beginning inventory amount is transferred from the Inventory account to the Cost of Goods Sold account.
4. Inventory is a control account that is supported by a subsidiary ledger of inventory records by individual item. The subsidiary ledger shows the quantity and cost of each inventory item on hand. At any point during the accounting period (assuming all postings are up to date), the balance of the Inventory account reflects the cost of the items that should be on hand at that point in time.	4. There is no subsidiary ledger for inventory. During the accounting period, the Inventory account reflects the cost of the inventory items on hand at the beginning of the period (beginning inventory). The Inventory account is not updated for purchases or sales of inventory during the period; it is updated only at the end of the period to reflect the cost of the items on hand at the statement of financial position date.

Comparing Entries under Perpetual versus Periodic Inventory Systems

Example	
Perpetual System	**Periodic System**
1. There are 8 units in beginning inventory at a cost of $2,000 each.	
The Inventory account shows $16,000 of inventory on hand.	The Inventory account shows $16,000 of inventory on hand.
2. Purchase 12 items on account at $2,000 each.	

Inventory   24,000
   Accounts Payable   24,000
	Purchases 24,000
	   Accounts Payable 24,000

3. Return one defective item for $2,000 credit.	

Accounts Payable   2,000
   Inventory   2,000
	Accounts Payable 2,000
	   Purchase Returns and
	   Allowances 2,000

4. Sell 15 items on account for $3,000 each.	

Accounts Receivable 45,000
   Sales Revenue   45,000
Cost of Goods Sold 30,000
   Inventory   30,000
	Accounts Receivable 45,000
	   Sales Revenue 45,000

5. End-of-period entries for inventory-related accounts (4 units on hand at $2,000 each).	

No entries are necessary:
The Inventory account shows an ending balance of $8,000 ($16,000 + $24,000 − $2,000 − $30,000)
	Inventory (ending, determined by physical count) 8,000
	Purchase Returns and Allowances 2,000
	Cost of Goods Sold 30,000
	   Purchases 24,000
	   Inventory (beginning) 16,000

EXERCISE 8-3

PURPOSE: This exercise will help you practise performing calculations to determine inventory cost under two costing formulas, using both the periodic and the perpetual systems.

The Halifax Toy Company is a multi-product firm. Presented below is information for one of its products, Infusion-47:

Date	Transaction	Quantity	Cost
1/1	Beginning inventory	1,200	$13
2/4	Purchase	1,900	18
2/20	Sale	2,400	
4/2	Purchase	3,000	20
11/4	Sale	2,200	

Instructions

Calculate the cost of ending inventory, assuming Halifax Toy uses:

(a) Periodic system, FIFO cost formula.
(b) Perpetual system, FIFO cost formula.
(c) Periodic system, weighted average cost formula.
(d) Perpetual system, moving-average cost formula.

Solution to Exercise 8-3

(a) **Periodic—FIFO:**

	Units
Beginning inventory	1,200
Purchases (1,900 + 3,000)	4,900
Units available for sale	6,100
Sold (2,400 + 2,200)	4,600
Units on hand (assumed)	1,500

1,500 units × $20 = $30,000

(b) **Perpetual—FIFO:** Same as periodic: $30,000

> Using FIFO with a perpetual system always yields the same results as using FIFO with a periodic system.

(c) **Periodic—weighted average:**

1,200 × $13 = $ 15,600
1,900 × $18 = 34,200
3,000 × $20 =   60,000
6,100 $109,800 ÷ 6,100 = $18 weighted average cost per unit
1,500 units on hand × $18 weighted average cost per unit = $27,000

(d) **Perpetual—moving-average:**

Date	Purchased	Sold	Balance
1/1			$1,200 \times \$13 = \$15,600$
2/4	$1,900 \times \$18 = \$34,200$		$3,100 \times \$16.065^a = \$49,800$
2/20		$2,400 \times \$16.065 = \$38,556$	$700 \times \$16.065 = \$11,244$
4/2	$3,000 \times \$20 = \$60,000$		$3,700 \times \$19.255^b = \$71,244$
11/4		$2,200 \times \$19.255 = \$42,361$	$1,500 \times \$19.255 = \$28,883$

[a] $1,200 \times \$13 = \$15,600$

$\underline{1,900 \times \$18 = \quad 34,200}$

$3,100 \qquad \underline{\underline{\$49,800}}$

$\$49,800 \div 3,100 = \$16.065$

[b] $700 \times \$16.065 = \$11,244$

$\underline{3,000 \times \$20 \quad = \quad 60,000}$

$3,700 \qquad\qquad \underline{\underline{\$71,245}}$

$\$71,245 \div 3,700 = \$19.255$

When using the weighted average cost formula in a perpetual system, a new average unit cost is calculated only after each new purchase; sales do **not** affect average unit cost. Because a new average unit cost is calculated after each purchase, the weighted average cost formula in a perpetual system is called the **moving-average cost formula**.

EXERCISE 8-4

PURPOSE: This exercise will help you practise accounting for goods in transit and other items necessary for proper inventory valuation.

Jennifer Laudermilch Company, a supplier of artworks, provided the following information from its account records for the year ended December 31, 2017:

Inventory at December 31, 2017 (at cost, based on a physical count of goods in Laudermilch's warehouse on 12/31/17)	$ 820,000
Accounts payable at December 31, 2017	460,000
Net sales (sales less sales returns)	7,000,000

Additional information is as follows:

1. Laudermilch received goods costing $32,000 on January 2, 2018. The goods were shipped f.o.b. shipping point on December 27, 2017, by Geoffrey Harrill Company.
2. Laudermilch received goods costing $41,000 on January 4, 2018. The goods were shipped f.o.b. destination on December 28, 2017, by Nanula Company.

3. Laudermilch sold goods costing $18,000 to O'Toole Company on December 29, 2017. The goods were picked up by the company's common carrier on that same date and shipped f.o.b. shipping point. The goods were expected to arrive at O'Toole's dock as early as January 3, 2018. An invoice for $29,000 was recorded and mailed on December 29.

4. Laudermilch sold goods costing $30,000 to Matheson Company on December 31, 2017. The goods were picked up by the company's common carrier on that same date and shipped f.o.b. destination. The goods were expected to arrive at Matheson's store as early as January 2, 2018. The goods were billed to Matheson for $45,000 on December 31 and were not included in the physical count at December 31.

5. Laudermilch is the consignor of a collection of prints. The prints are hanging in the showroom of The Dizzy Decorator. They cost Laudermilch $62,000 and are priced to sell at $95,000. They were not included in the physical count at December 31.

6. Laudermilch is the consignee of some goods from Asian Collectibles. They cost the consignor $50,000 and are priced to sell for $76,000. The agreement entitles Laudermilch to a 10% commission on sales. The goods were included in Laudermilch's December 31 ending inventory at selling price.

7. Included in the December 31 physical count were goods billed to a customer f.o.b. shipping point on December 31. These items originally cost $24,000 and were invoiced for $38,000. The shipment was on Laudermilch's loading dock on December 31 waiting to be picked up by the company's common carrier. The goods were included in the physical count at December 31.

8. Goods received from a vendor on December 26, 2017, were included in the physical count. However, the related $44,000 vendor invoice was not included in accounts payable at December 31, 2017, because the accounts payable copy of the receiving report was lost. These goods are marked to sell for $65,000.

Instructions

Using the format shown below, prepare a schedule of required adjustments as at December 31, 2017, the company's year end and physical inventory count date. Show separately the effect, if any, of each of the eight transactions on the unadjusted December 31, 2017, account balances below. If the transactions would have no effect on the unadjusted balances shown, state NONE.

Adjustments increase (decrease)	Inventory	Accounts Payable	Net Sales
Unadjusted balances	$820,000	$460,000	$7,000,000
1.			
2.			
3.			
4.			

Adjustments increase (decrease)	Inventory	Accounts Payable	Net Sales
Unadjusted balances	$820,000	$460,000	$7,000,000
5.			
6.			
7.			
8.			
Total adjustments			
Adjusted amounts	$_____	$_____	$_____

Solution to Exercise 8-4

Adjustments increase (decrease)	Inventory	Accounts Payable	Net Sales
Unadjusted balances	$820,000	$460,000	$7,000,000
1.	32,000	32,000	None
2.	None	None	None
3.	None	None	None
4.	30,000	None	(45,000)
5.	62,000	None	None
6.	(76,000)	None	None
7.	None	None	(38,000)
8.	None	44,000	None
Total adjustments	48,000	76,000	(83,000)
Adjusted amounts	$868,000	$536,000	$6,917,000

EXPLANATION:

1. When the terms of the purchase are f.o.b. shipping point, ownership of the goods transfers to the buyer when the carrier accepts the goods from the seller. Therefore, legal title transferred to Laudermilch on December 27, 2017, even though the goods were not physically present to be included in the physical count at December 31, 2017.

2. These goods would not have been included in the physical count at December 31, 2017, and are not to be included in inventory at that date. Legal title did not transfer to Laudermilch until the goods were received on January 4, 2018.

3. With f.o.b. shipping point terms, legal title transferred to the customer (O'Toole) when the goods were picked up by the common carrier on December 29, 2017. Therefore, the goods were properly excluded from ending inventory, and the sale was properly recorded in 2017.

4. With f.o.b. destination terms, legal title did not pass to Matheson (the buyer) until the goods were received by it, which was sometime in 2018. Therefore, the sale was improperly recorded in 2017. The goods were not on Laudermilch's premises late on December 31, 2017, and were excluded from the physical count. However, their cost should be included in ending inventory reported on the statement of financial position.

5. Under a consignment arrangement, the holder of the goods (the **consignee**) does not own the goods. Ownership remains with the shipper of the goods (the **consignor**) until the goods are sold to a customer. Laudermilch, the consignor, should include in its inventory consignment inventory held by the consignee. The prints were not in Laudermilch's warehouse when the physical count was taken; however, they should be included as part of Laudermilch's inventory balance at December 31, 2017.

6. As the consignee, Laudermilch does not own the goods in this consignment arrangement. Therefore, these goods should be excluded from Laudermilch's inventory; they should be included in the inventory of Asian Collectibles.

7. The $24,000 of goods on the loading dock were properly included in the physical count because they had not been released to the common carrier by the end of December 31, 2017. However, the sale was improperly recorded; an adjustment is needed to reduce sales by the billing price of $38,000.

8. The $44,000 of goods received on December 26, 2017, were properly included in the physical count of inventory; however, $44,000 must be added to accounts payable since the invoice was not included in the December 31, 2017, accounts payable balance.

EXERCISE 8-5

PURPOSE: The following exercise will help you determine what costs are inventoriable costs.

Hamilton Corporation manufactures a single product. Assume the following data for the 2017 year:

Variable cost per unit:

Administrative	$4
Production	$6

Fixed cost in total:

Administrative	$18,000
Production	$36,000

During the period, 9,000 units were produced and 8,200 units were sold (assume beginning inventory is zero). Normal capacity is 9,000 units.

Instructions

(a) Determine the inventoriable cost per unit.

(b) Determine the cost of ending inventory.

(c) Determine the cost of goods sold.

Solution to Exercise 8-5

(a) Cost per unit

Variable production cost	$6
Fixed production cost	$4 ($36,000 ÷ 9,000 units)
Total inventoriable cost	$10

Manufacturing overhead is allocated based on normal production levels. Administrative costs are not inventoriable costs. They would be expensed in the period incurred.

(b) Ending inventory

800 units × $10 inventory cost = $8,000

Ending inventory consists of 800 units (0 beginning + 9,000 produced − 8,200 units sold).

(c) Cost of goods sold

Beginning inventory	$ 0
Add: current production (9,000 × $10)	90,000
Cost of goods available for sale	90,000
Less: Ending inventory (from b)	8,000
Cost of goods sold	$82,000
Proof: COGS = 8,200 units sold × $10 =	$82,000

EXERCISE 8-6

PURPOSE: This exercise reviews the steps involved in applying the lower of cost and net realizable value standard for inventory.

The Richard G. Long Company has 10 different items in inventory.

Instructions

In the chart below, apply the lower of cost and net realizable value standard to each item and complete the blanks to determine the total value to be reported for inventory.

Item	No. of Units on Hand	Cost	Replacement Cost	Expected Selling Price	Expected Cost to Sell	NRV	LC & NRV	Item Total
1	100	$ 7.00	$ 7.50	$10.00	$1.00			
2	10	6.00	6.25	10.00	1.00			
3	50	5.75	9.25	10.00	1.00			
4	70	10.00	9.25	10.00	1.00			
5	20	5.00	6.25	10.00	1.00			
6	100	8.00	7.25	10.00	1.00			
7	50	16.50	11.50	16.00	1.00			
8	10	10.00	15.50	16.00	1.00			
9	20	14.00	11.00	20.00	2.00			
10	10	12.00	16.00	20.00	2.00			
					Grand Total			

Solution to Exercise 8-6

Item	Per Unit NRV	Per Unit LC & NRV	# of Units	Item Total
1	$ 9.00	$ 7.00	100	$ 700.00
2	9.00	6.00	10	60.00
3	9.00	5.75	50	287.50
4	9.00	9.00	70	630.00
5	9.00	5.00	20	100.00
6	9.00	8.00	100	800.00
7	15.00	15.00	50	750.00
8	15.00	10.00	10	100.00
9	18.00	14.00	20	280.00
10	18.00	12.00	10	120.00
	Grand Total			$3,827.50

EXPLANATION: Write down the steps involved in determining lower of cost and net realizable value and perform the steps in order for each item:

Step 1: Determine net realizable value.

	Item 1	Item 2	Item 3	Item 4
Estimated selling price	$10.00	$10.00	$10.00	$10.00
Less cost to complete and sell	1.00	1.00	1.00	1.00
= Net realizable value	$ 9.00	$ 9.00	$ 9.00	$ 9.00

In applying the lower of cost and net realizable value standard, both IFRS and ASPE require the use of net realizable value, defined as estimated selling price less estimated costs to complete and sell. Using replacement cost instead of net realizable value is not permitted.

Step 2: Compare cost with net realizable value and use the lower value to calculate inventory.

	Item 1	Item 2	Item 3	Item 4
Cost	$7.00	$6.00	$5.75	$10.00
NRV (from Step 1)	9.00	9.00	9.00	9.00
Lower of cost and NRV	7.00	6.00	5.75	9.00

EXERCISE 8-7

PURPOSE: This exercise explores the accounting for inventories that may be valued at amounts other than the lower of cost and net realizable value under both ASPE and IFRS.

True North Trees Inc. grows pine, fir, and spruce trees. The farm cuts and sells trees during the Christmas season and exports most of the trees to the United States. The remaining trees are sold to local tree-lot operators in Ontario and Quebec. It normally takes 14 years for a tree to grow to a suitable size, and the average selling price of a tree is $28. The biggest costs to the business are pest control, fertilizer, and pruning trees over the 14-year period. These costs average $21 per tree (assume these are incurred evenly over the 14-year growing cycle).

Instructions

(a) How should this inventory be recorded under ASPE?

(b) How should the costs of pest control, fertilizer, and pruning be recognized under IFRS?

(c) Assume that the fair value of each tree at the end of 2017 is $12 and the opening value was $9. Prepare the journal entries if the costs are *capitalized* each year.

(d) Assume that the fair value of each tree at the end of 2017 is $12 and the opening value was $9. Prepare the journal entries if the costs are *expensed* each year.

Solution to Exercise 8-7

(a) Accounting for inventories of biological assets and agricultural produce at the point of harvest is excluded from the measurement requirements of Section 3031 if net realizable value is used according to well-established industry practice, but are included in the expense recognition and disclosure requirements.

So, under ASPE there is no specific guidance on how this inventory should be measured. Research indicates that most companies use the lower of cost and net realizable value.

(b) Under IFRS, accounting for biological assets is covered by *IAS 41 Agriculture*. Generally, such assets are measured at fair value less selling costs. Where fair value is used, the assets are remeasured at each reporting date and any gains or losses are recognized in income. Fair value is reasonable for these assets since biological assets tend to increase in value as they grow or mature, and the time lapse between growth and harvesting can be quite long.

Many costs go into the biological transformation process (planting, weeding, etc.). IFRS does not prescribe the treatment of these costs. They may be capitalized or expensed.

(c) Journal entries—capitalized

Biological Assets	1.50	
Cash		1.50

(assume cost of $21 ÷ 14 = $1.50/year)

Biological Assets	1.50	
Unrealized Gain		1.50

EXPLANATION: Record the change in fair value from the beginning of the year to the end of the year, less the $1.50 capitalized during the year:

*supporting calculations

Carrying value, at beginning of year	$9.00
Capitalized during the year	1.50
Carrying value, before adjustment	10.50
Fair value, at end of year	12.00
Change in fair value (income)	$1.50

Financial presentation

Gain on biological asset	$1.50
Expenses	0
Income	$1.50

(d) Journal entries—expensed

Expenses	1.50	
Cash		1.50

(assume cost of $21 ÷ 14 = $1.50/year)

Biological Assets	3.00	
Unrealized Gain		3.00

EXPLANATION: If the actual costs are expensed during the year, then the full change in the fair value must be adjusted at the reporting date.

*supporting calculations

Carrying value, at beginning of year	$9.00
Fair value, at end of year	12.00
Change in fair value (income)	$3.00

Financial presentation

Gain on biological asset	$3.00
Expenses	1.50
Income	$1.50

EXERCISE 8-8

PURPOSE: This exercise illustrates the use of the gross profit method of inventory estimation when: (1) gross profit is expressed as a markup on cost and (2) gross profit is expressed as a percentage of selling price.

Bill Goneau requires an estimate of the cost of goods lost in a fire on April 2. Merchandise on hand on January 1 was $52,000. Since January 1, purchases were $48,000; freight-in, $4,500; and purchase returns and allowances, $2,500. Sales totalled $98,000 to April 2. Goods costing $8,700 were left undamaged by the fire; all other goods were destroyed.

Instructions

(a) Calculate the cost of goods destroyed, assuming that markup on cost is 25%.

(b) Calculate the cost of goods destroyed, assuming that gross profit is 30% of sales.

Solution to Exercise 8-8

(a) Merchandise on hand, January 1		$ 52,000
Purchases	$48,000	
Purchase returns and allowances	(2,500)	
Net purchases	45,500	
Freight-in	4,500	50,000
Total merchandise available for sale		102,000
Estimated cost of goods sold*		(78,400)
Estimated ending inventory on April 2		23,600
Undamaged goods		(8,700)
Estimated fire loss		$ 14,900

*Gross profit on selling price = 25% ÷ (100% + 25%) = 20%. Therefore, cost of goods sold = 80% of sales. If sales totalled $98,000, cost of goods sold = $78,400.

(b) If gross profit is 30% of sales, cost of goods sold = 70% of sales. If sales totalled $98,000, cost of goods sold = $68,600.

Total merchandise available for sale (as calculated above)	$102,000
Estimated cost of goods sold	(68,600)
Estimated ending inventory on April 2	33,400
Undamaged goods	(8,700)
Estimated fire loss	$ 24,700

It is important to understand that inventory is accounted for in terms of the cost of goods purchased, and that sales reflects the **selling prices** of goods that have been sold during the period. Therefore, the profit element must be removed from the sales amount to arrive at cost of the goods sold.

APPROACH: Use these steps to perform the calculations:

1. **Calculate cost of goods available for sale** for the period January 1 to April 2. This is done by adding the cost of inventory on hand at the beginning of the year (January 1) to the net cost of purchases during the period (net purchases plus freight-in).

2. **Determine estimated cost of goods sold** during the period. This is done by multiplying sales for the period by the cost of goods sold percentage. The cost of goods sold percentage is 100% minus the gross profit percentage, where the gross profit percentage is stated in terms of selling price. In part (b) of this exercise, gross profit is given in terms of selling price. In part (a), however, the "25% markup on cost" must be converted to gross profit on selling price of 20% before the cost of goods sold percentage of 80% can be applied to the sales amount.

3. **Calculate estimated inventory on hand at the end of the period** (on April 2, date of fire) by subtracting estimated cost of goods sold (Step 2) from cost of goods available for sale (Step 1).

4. **Determine the estimated fire loss** by deducting the cost of undamaged goods from the estimated cost of inventory on hand at April 2 (Step 3).

EXERCISE 8-9

PURPOSE: This exercise illustrates the use of the conventional retail inventory method to value inventory.

The records of Nancy Klintworth's Baubles report the following data for the month of May.

Sales	$79,000
Sales returns	1,000
Markups	10,000
Markup cancellations	1,500
Markdowns	9,300
Markdown cancellations	2,800
Freight on purchases	2,400
Purchases (at cost)	48,000
Purchases (at sales price)	88,000
Purchase returns (at cost)	2,000
Purchase returns (at sales price)	3,000
Beginning inventory (at cost)	30,000
Beginning inventory (at sales price)	46,500

Instructions

Calculate ending inventory using the conventional retail inventory method.

Solution to Exercise 8-9

	Cost	Retail
Beginning inventory	$30,000	$46,500
Purchases	48,000	88,000
Purchase returns	(2,000)	(3,000)
Freight-in	2,400	
Goods available for sale	78,400	131,500
Net markups:		
Markups	$10,000	
Markup cancellations	(1,500)	8,500
	78,400	140,000
Net markdowns:		
Markdowns	9,300	
Markdown cancellations	(2,800)	(6,500)
	78,400	133,500
Net sales ($79,000 − $1,000)		(78,000)
Ending inventory, at retail		55,500

Cost-to-retail ratio = $78,400 ÷ $140,000 = 56%

Ending inventory, at cost = Ending inventory at retail × cost-to-retail ratio

Ending inventory, at cost = $55,500 × 56% = $31,080

EXPLANATION:

Step 1: Calculate ending inventory at retail. This is done by determining the retail value of goods available for sale, adjusting that figure for net markups and net markdowns, and deducting the retail value of goods no longer on hand (sold or estimated theft, and so on).

Step 2: Calculate the cost-to-retail ratio. The conventional retail inventory method uses the cost-to-retail ratio, which includes net markups but excludes net markdowns.

Step 3: Calculate ending inventory at cost. Apply the appropriate cost-to-retail ratio (Step 2) to total ending inventory at retail (Step 1).

ANALYSIS OF MULTIPLE-CHOICE QUESTIONS

Question

1. At December 31, 2017, a physical count of inventory belonging to Rhoda Corp. showed that inventory costing $1 million was on hand. The $1 million amount does not include these items:

   - $80,000 of goods shipped f.o.b. shipping point to Rhoda on December 30, 2017; the goods were received on January 3, 2018.
   - $72,000 of goods shipped f.o.b. destination to Rhoda on December 30, 2017; the goods were received on January 3, 2018.
   - $95,000 of goods shipped f.o.b. destination by Rhoda to a customer on December 28, 2017. The customer received the goods on January 4, 2018.

   The correct amount to report for inventory on Rhoda's statement of financial position at December 31, 2017, is:
   a. $1,080,000.
   b. $1,095,000.
   c. $1,175,000.
   d. $1,247,000.

EXPLANATION:

1. The $80,000 of goods should be added to the $1 million of inventory because f.o.b. shipping point means that legal title transferred to Rhoda when the goods left the seller's dock on December 30, 2017.

2. The $72,000 of goods is properly excluded from ending inventory because legal title did not pass to Rhoda until Rhoda received the goods on January 3, 2018.

3. The $95,000 of goods should be added to the $1 million of inventory because the goods belonged to Rhoda until they were received by the customer (in 2018).

$ 1,000,000

+   80,000

+   95,000

$ 1,175,000   Amount to report for ending inventory at December 31, 2017.

(Solution = c.)

Question

2. The following amounts relate to the current year for West Regina Company:

Beginning inventory	$ 46,000
Ending inventory	62,200
Purchases	347,000
Purchase returns	11,300
Freight-out	14,000

Cost of goods sold for the period totals:
a. $319,500.
b. $333,500.
c. $342,100.
d. $356,100.

EXPLANATION: Write down the formula for cost of goods sold. Enter the amounts given and solve for the unknown.

	$ 46,000		Beginning inventory
+	347,000	+	Purchases
−	11,300	−	Purchase returns and allowances
	0	−	Purchase discounts
	0	+	Freight-in
	381,700	=	Cost of goods available for sale
−	62,200	−	Ending inventory
	$319,500	=	Cost of goods sold

(Solution = a.)

Freight-out is classified as a selling expense, not a component of cost of goods sold. Freight-out is not a cost necessary to get the inventory item to the intended location and condition for sale; it is a cost incurred in the selling of the inventory.

Question

3. An accountant is preparing financial statements for the year ended December 31, 2017, for Orion Sales Company. Orion uses the periodic inventory system. The January 1, 2017, inventory balance will appear:

   a. only as an asset on the statement of financial position.

   b. only in the cost of goods sold section of the statement of income.

   c. as a deduction in the cost of goods sold section of the statement of income and as a current asset on the statement of financial position.

   d. as an addition in the cost of goods sold section of the statement of income and as a current asset on the statement of financial position.

EXPLANATION: The January 1, 2017, inventory amount is the beginning inventory figure. Beginning inventory is a component of cost of goods available for sale for the period, which is a component of cost of goods sold. (Solution = b.)

Question

4. If 2016 beginning inventory is overstated, the effects of this error on 2016 cost of goods sold, 2016 net income, and assets at December 31, 2017, respectively, are:

   a. overstatement, understatement, overstatement.

   b. overstatement, understatement, no effect.

   c. understatement, overstatement, overstatement.

   d. understatement, overstatement, no effect.

EXPLANATION: For questions concerning inventory errors, assume a periodic system is used unless otherwise indicated. Write down the cost of goods sold formula and analyze the effects of the error(s) on net income.

		2016	2017
	Beginning inventory	Overstated	No effect
+	Cost of goods purchased		
=	Cost of goods available for sale	Overstated	
−	Ending inventory		
=	Cost of goods sold	Overstated	
	Net income	Understated	

Assuming that there are no other errors in this process, inventory at the end of 2016 and inventory at the end of 2017 are both free of error because inventory cost at a statement of financial position date is determined by physical count and application of cost formulas. (Solution = b.)

- The fact that inventory at the beginning of 2016 was in error indicates that inventory at the end of 2015 was in error, because the ending inventory of one period is the beginning inventory of the next period.

- When analyzing this type of question, it is often helpful to create an example with numbers.

Question

5. If beginning inventory is understated by $8,000 and ending inventory is over-stated by $5,000, net income for the period will be:
    a.   overstated by $13,000.
    b.   overstated by $3,000.
    c.   understated by $3,000.
    d.   understated by $13,000.

EXPLANATION: Each error's effect on net income should be determined separately. The effect on net income is dependent on the effect on cost of goods sold (which is an expense affecting net income). Then the effects should be combined to determine the total effect on net income for the period.

	First Error	Second Error	Total Effect
Beginning inventory	Understated $8,000		Understated $8,000
+ Purchases			
= Cost of goods available for sale	Understated $8,000		Understated $8,000
− Ending inventory		Overstated $5,000	Overstated $5,000
= Cost of goods sold	Understated $8,000	Understated $5,000	Understated $13,000
Net income	Overstated $8,000	Overstated $5,000	Overstated $13,000

(Solution = a.)

Question

6. The Woodstock Salt Company purchased goods with a list price of $75,000, subject to trade discounts of 15% and 10%, with a 3% cash discount allowed if payment is made within 15 days of receipt. Woodstock uses the gross method of recording purchases. Woodstock should record the cost of this merchandise as:
    a. $75,000.
    b. $55,654.
    c. $54,000.
    d. $57,375.
    e.   none of the above.

EXPLANATION: Trade discounts are not recorded separately in the accounts; they are used to calculate a sales (purchase) price. Using the gross method of recording purchases, the cash discount allowed does not affect the amount recorded in the Purchases account; the cash discount allowed will be recorded (only if it is taken) as a credit to Purchase Discounts.

CALCULATIONS:

List price	$75,000
First trade discount ($75,000 × 15%)	(11,250)
Subtotal	63,750
Second trade discount ($63,750 × 10%)	(6,375)
Purchase price	$57,375

(Solution = d.)

A chain discount occurs when a list price is subject to several trade discounts. When a chain discount is offered, the amount of each trade discount is determined by multiplying (1) the list price of the merchandise **less** the amount of prior trade discounts by (2) the trade discount percentage.

Question

7. In 2017, Grennan Retail Company incurred the following costs related to inventory:

   Freight-in on purchases

   Interest on loan to acquire inventory

   Selling costs

   Under IFRS, should the above items be included or excluded in determining the cost of Grennan's inventory?

	Freight-in	Interest	Selling Costs
a.	Include	Include	Include
b.	Include	Include	Exclude
c.	Include	Exclude	Exclude
d.	Exclude	Exclude	Exclude

EXPLANATION: Freight-in is a product cost. The cost of inventory should include all costs necessary to get the inventory to the intended location and condition for sale. Freight-in is necessary to get the inventory to the location for sale. Interest costs should not be capitalized for inventory that is acquired by a merchandiser, because the goods do not require a period of time to get ready for intended use or sale. In this case, interest costs are considered a period cost. Selling costs are also treated as a period cost. (Solution = c.)

Question

8. The following facts pertain to one product carried in the inventory of the Herara Store:

Inventory on hand, January 1	200 units @ $20 = $4,000
Purchase, March 18	600 units @ $24 = $14,400
Purchase, July 20	800 units @ $26 = $20,800
Purchase, October 31	400 units @ $30 = $12,000

A physical count of inventory on December 31 reveals that 500 units are on hand. If the FIFO cost formula is used with a periodic inventory system, inventory should be reported on the statement of financial position at:

   a. $40,000.
   b. $36,600.
   c. $14,600.
   d. $11,200.
   e. none of the above.

EXPLANATION: Think about what FIFO stands for: the first costs in are the first out to cost of goods sold. Therefore, ending inventory should be valued using the most recent costs.

400 units @ $30 =	$12,000	
100 units @ $26 =	2,600	
Ending inventory at FIFO	$14,600	(Solution = c.)

Question

9. Refer to the facts in question 8 above. If the weighted average cost formula is used, cost of goods sold for the year amounts to:
   a. $38,400.
   b. $37,500.
   c. $12,800.
   d. $12,500.

EXPLANATION: Read the question carefully. Notice it asks for cost of goods sold and not for ending inventory.

Total cost of goods available for sale:

Beginning inventory	$ 4,000
Purchases ($14,400 + $20,800 + $12,000)	47,200
Cost of goods available for sale	$51,200

$ 51,200   Cost of goods available for sale

÷ 2,000*   Units available for sale

$ 25.60 Weighted average cost per unit

$25.60 weighted average cost per unit × 500 units = $12,800 ending inventory

$25.60 weighted average cost per unit × 1,500** units = $38,400 cost of goods sold

*200 + 600 + 800 + 400 = 2,000 units available for sale.

**2,000 units available for sale − 500 units in ending inventory = 1,500 units sold.

(Solution = a.)

Question

10. Which of the following items would not likely be classified as inventory?
    a. Cleaning supplies held by a janitorial firm
    b. Tracts of land held by a land developer
    c. Laying hens held by a farmer
    d. Work-in-process held by an equipment manufacturer

EXPLANATION: Laying hens would be considered a biological asset. Laying hens may seem to have some characteristics of both inventory (possibly held for resale) and fixed assets (held to produce inventory). However, biological assets are not classified as inventory or fixed assets on the statement of financial position; they are classified separately. (Solution = c.)

Question

11. In applying the lower of cost and net realizable value standard to inventory as at December 31, 2017, Xavier Corporation is writing inventory down from $500,000 to $420,000. Under the indirect (or allowance) method, this write-down may be reported:
    a. as a prior period adjustment.
    b. as a decrease in sales.
    c. as an increase in selling expense.
    d. under "other expenses and losses."

EXPLANATION: Under the indirect method, the $80,000 loss may be shown separately from cost of goods sold on the statement of income. (Solution = d.)

Question

12. In 2017, Lucas Manufacturing signed a contract with a supplier to purchase raw materials in 2018 for $700,000. Before the December 31, 2017, statement

of financial position date, the market price for these materials dropped to $510,000. Under IFRS, this should be recorded on the 2017 financial statements as follows:

a. As a valuation account to Inventory on the statement of financial position

b. As a current liability

c. As an appropriation of retained earnings

d. In the notes to financial statements only

EXPLANATION: Normally, purchase commitments are only disclosed in notes to financial statements because they are executory contracts (meaning that neither party has performed or fulfilled their part of the contract). However, IAS 37 states that, if the contracted amount is higher than the market price of the contracted goods or services at the financial statement date, and if the unavoidable costs of completing the contract are higher than the benefits expected from receiving the contracted goods or services, a loss provision should be recognized. Because Lucas is obligated to purchase the raw materials in 2018, the loss provision would be classified as a current liability on the statement of financial position. (Solution = b.)

Question

13. The following information pertains to the Godfrey Company for the six months ended June 30:

Inventory, January 1	$ 700,000
Purchases	5,000,000
Freight-in	400,000
Sales	6,000,000

Gross profit is normally 25% of sales. What is the estimated amount of inventory on hand at June 30?

a. $100,000

b. $1,600,000

c. $2,100,000

d. $4,600,000

EXPLANATION: Apply the following steps to solve a gross profit method inventory question:

Step 1: Calculate cost of goods available for sale:

Beginning inventory	$ 700,000
Purchases	5,000,000
Freight-in	400,000
Cost of goods available for sale	$6,100,000

Step 2: Determine estimated cost of goods sold:

Sales	$6,000,000
Cost of goods sold percentage (100% – 25%)	× 75%
Estimated cost of goods sold	$4,500,000

The above calculation was simple because the gross profit percentage given in the problem is stated in terms of sales. When the gross profit percentage is expressed in terms of cost, the percentage must be converted to a percentage in terms of selling price before other calculations can be performed.

Step 3: Calculate estimated inventory on hand at the end of the period:

Cost of goods available for sale	$6,100,000
Estimated cost of goods sold	(4,500,000)
Estimated ending inventory (at cost)	$1,600,000

(Solution = b.)

Question

14. Cost of goods available for sale for 2017 for Missakila Corporation was $2.7 million. The gross profit rate was 20% of sales. Sales for the year amounted to $2.4 million. The ending inventory is estimated to be:

 a. $0.

 b. $480,000.

 c. $540,000.

 d. $780,000.

EXPLANATION:

Step 1: Calculate cost of goods available for sale.

Cost of goods available is given:	$2,700,000

Step 2: Determine estimated cost of goods sold:

Sales	$2,400,000
Cost of goods sold percentage (100% – 20%)	× 80%
Estimated cost of goods sold	$1,920,000

Step 3: Calculate estimated inventory on hand at the end of the period:

Cost of goods available for sale	$2,700,000
Estimated cost of goods sold	(1,920,000)
Estimated ending inventory (at cost)	$ 780,000

(Solution = d.)

Question

15. If gross profit is 25% of cost, then gross profit as a percentage of sales equals:
    a. 80%.
    b. 75%.
    c. 33.66%.
    d. 20%.

EXPLANATION:

Sales (S) − Cost of goods sold (COGS) = Gross profit (GP)

If GP = 25% of cost, then S = 25% × COGS + COGS, and

S = 125% × COGS.

S = 125% × (S − GP).

Expressing gross profit (GP) in terms of sales (S), we get:

GP = 20% × S.

Thus, gross profit = 20% of sales.

(Solution = d.)

Question

16. A company uses the retail inventory method to estimate ending inventory for interim reporting purposes. If the retail inventory method is used to approximate a lower of average cost and market valuation, which one of the following alternatives describes the proper treatment of net markups and net markdowns in the cost-to-retail ratio calculation?

	Net Markups	Net Markdowns
a.	Include	Include
b.	Include	Exclude
c.	Exclude	Include
d.	Exclude	Exclude

EXPLANATION: First note that the lower of average cost and market approach to the retail inventory method is often referred to as the "conventional retail inventory method." Recall that the retail inventory method involves multiplying ending inventory at retail by a cost-to-retail ratio. The lower the ratio, the lower the calculated ending inventory cost. Including net markups (increases in retail prices) but excluding net markdowns (decreases in retail prices) gives the highest denominator possible for the cost-to-retail ratio calculation, which yields the lowest ratio possible. (*Note:* Net markups are often called "net additional markups.") (Solution = b.)

Question

17. The following information relates to the inventory of Orono Company:

Beginning inventory at cost	$15,500
Beginning inventory at selling price	21,500
Purchases at cost	33,120
Purchases at selling price	50,000

What is the cost-to-retail ratio for Orono Company?

a. 147%

b. 76%

c. 68%

d. 74%

EXPLANATION:

Ratio = Cost ÷ Retail

Ratio = ($15,500 + $33,120) ÷ ($21,500 + $50,000)

Ratio = $48,620 ÷ $71,500

Ratio = 68%

(Solution = c.)

Question

18. The Ruffier Department Store uses the retail inventory method. The following information is available at December 31, 2017:

	Cost	Retail
Beginning inventory	$ 37,800	$ 60,000
Purchases	200,000	290,000
Freight-in	7,200	
Sales		275,000

What is the estimated cost of ending inventory?

a. $47,250

b. $52,500

c. $53,586

d. $192,500

CALCULATION:

	Cost	Retail
Beginning inventory	$ 37,800	$ 60,000
Purchases	200,000	290,000
Freight-in	7,200	
Cost of goods available for sale	$245,000	350,000
Sales		(275,000)
Ending inventory at retail		$ 75,000

Step 1: Calculate ending inventory at retail.

Step 2: Calculate cost-to-retail ratio = $245,000 ÷ $350,000 = 70%

Step 3: Calculate estimated cost of ending inventory = $75,000 × 70% = $52,500

EXPLANATION: Think about how the retail inventory method of inventory estimation works. An estimate of ending inventory at retail is made by deducting sales from the retail value of goods available for sale, and ending inventory at retail is converted to cost by applying an appropriate cost-to-retail ratio, which is an expression of the relationship between inventory cost and retail value. Apply the following steps to calculate the amount required:

Step 1: Calculate ending inventory at retail. Deduct net sales from the retail price of all goods available for sale during the period. Arrive at $75,000.

Step 2: Calculate cost-to-retail ratio. Divide the cost of goods available for sale ($245,000) by the retail value of those same goods ($350,000). Arrive at 70%.

Step 3: Determine estimated cost of ending inventory. Apply the cost-to-retail ratio (70%) to ending inventory at retail ($75,000). Arrive at $52,500. (Solution = b.)

Question

19. The Billy Dial Department Store uses the conventional retail inventory method. The following information is available at December 31, 2017:

	Cost	Retail
Beginning inventory	$ 37,200	$ 60,000
Purchases	200,000	290,000
Freight-in	4,000	
Net markups		30,000
Net markdowns		20,000
Sales		285,000

What is ending inventory at cost (round to the nearest dollar)?

a. $46,763

b. $47,400

c. $47,603

d. $50,250

CALCULATION:

	Cost	Retail
Beginning inventory	$ 37,200	$ 60,000
Purchases	200,000	290,000
Freight-in	4,000	
Goods available for sale	241,200	350,000
Net markups		30,000
	$241,200	380,000
Net markdowns		(20,000)
		360,000
Sales		(285,000)
Ending inventory at retail		$ 75,000

$$\text{Cost-to-retail ratio} = \frac{\$241,200}{\$380,000} = 63.47\%$$

Ending inventory at cost = 63.47% × $75,000 = $47,603

EXPLANATION: Think about how the conventional retail inventory method of estimating inventory cost works. An estimate of ending inventory at retail is calculated by deducting sales from the retail value of goods available for sale. Then, ending inventory at retail is converted to cost by applying an appropriate cost-to-retail ratio (which is the relationship between inventory cost and retail value). Apply the following steps to calculate the amount required:

Step 1: Calculate ending inventory at retail. Arrive at $75,000.

Step 2: Calculate cost-to-retail ratio. The ratio for the conventional retail inventory method should include net markups but not net markdowns.

Step 3: Determine ending inventory at cost. Multiply the cost-to-retail ratio by ending inventory at retail (including markdowns) = $47,603. (Solution = c.)

Question

20. The inventory turnover ratio is a measure of inventory liquidity. This ratio is calculated by dividing:
    a. cost of goods sold by 365 days.
    b. cost of goods sold by the average amount of inventory on hand.
    c. net credit sales by the average amount of inventory on hand.
    d. 365 days by cost of goods sold.

EXPLANATION: Write down the formula to calculate inventory turnover. Consider each of its components. The formula is as follows:

$$\text{Inventory turnover ratio} = \frac{\text{Cost of goods sold}}{\text{Average inventory}}$$

The cost of an inventory item is included in Inventory until the item is sold, at which time the cost is transferred to Cost of Goods Sold. The inventory turnover ratio measures the number of times on average that the inventory was sold during the period. A closely related ratio is the **average days to sell inventory** ratio. (Solution = b.)

Question

21. Average days to sell inventory is calculated by dividing:
    a. 365 days by the inventory turnover ratio.
    b. the inventory turnover ratio by 365 days.
    c. net sales by the inventory turnover ratio.
    d. 365 days by cost of goods sold.

EXPLANATION: Average days to sell inventory is closely related to the inventory turnover ratio. It is calculated by dividing 365 days by the inventory turnover ratio. It measures the average number of days it takes to sell inventory after it is purchased. (Solution = a.)

Question

22. The gross profit method is often used to estimate inventory and cost of goods sold. Under which of the following scenarios would it not be acceptable?
    a. Where ending inventory numbers are not available due to fire
    b. For interim reporting purposes
    c. For year-end reporting purposes
    d. For projection purposes

EXPLANATION: The gross profit method is an estimation technique only, and should not be used to prepare official, audited financial statements at year end. Having said this, the method may be used if the relevant numbers are not otherwise available (due to theft, fire, and so forth) or if an estimate is acceptable (for internal decision-making or interim financial reporting purposes). (Solution = c.)

Question

23. Standard costs may be used for year-end financial statement purposes, under the following circumstances:
    a. Where standard costs do not differ materially from actual cost
    b. Where actual cost is not available
    c. Where management uses it for internal decision-making
    d. Where the company is a manufacturing company and needs the information in order to track variances

EXPLANATION: Standard costing systems are used by management to control operations and to monitor costs. While these functions are critical to a manufacturing company, the most relevant information for financial statement users is actual cost, and therefore, both should be tracked. (Solution = a.)

Question

24. Dino Corporation agreed to buy 10 tonnes of raw materials from a supplier at a fixed price over the next year. The amount is material and the contract is non-cancellable. Which of the following statements is true?

   a. The transaction should be recorded on the statement of financial position as it represents a liability to the company.
   b. The transaction should be recorded since it is material.
   c. The transaction should not be recorded on the statement of financial position since it is an executory contract.
   d. The transaction should be recorded since it is non-cancellable.

EXPLANATION: The contract would generally not be recorded as it represents a promise by both parties to do something in the future (an executory contract); however, it would be disclosed in the notes to the financial statements. (Solution = c.)

Question

25. Which of the following criteria does NOT have to be met in order to be able to value inventory above cost?

   a. The cost of disposal can be estimated.
   b. The sale is assured.
   c. There is an active market for the product.
   d. The sale must already have occurred.

EXPLANATION: The criteria that must be met to value inventory above cost are (1) the sale is assured or there is an active market for the product, and (2) the costs of disposal can be estimated. (Solution = d.)

CASE STUDY # 1

Acme Limited

Acme Limited (AL) is a manufacturing company that produces various synthetic construction materials. Its shares trade on the local stock exchange. In 2017, the company was able to negotiate an extremely low price for raw materials. As part of the deal, AL agreed to buy more raw material than was needed. However, because AL had excess cash, and because the production manager, Owen, was able to assure the purchasing manager, Tatjana, that all of the raw material would be used in production within the next year, the deal was signed.

Unfortunately, the following year, demand for AL's products fell dramatically because new housing starts were down significantly. As a result, cash was short and AL was seeking financing from the bank.

After preliminary discussions with the bank, Warren, the V.P. Finance, learned that AL was considered a high-risk company. The bank was reluctant to lend funds to AL and would do so only at a significant premium. Warren felt that the interest rate was excessive and started considering alternative means of financing. He called a meeting with his managers to discuss the problem.

Warren: We are short of cash and we need some operating capital. Demand is down and our customers are taking longer to pay than usual due to the state of the housing market. Any suggestions?

Hiroko (controller): I guess we've tried the usual sources, like the bank?

Warren: Of course! But the bank is not willing to lend us funds unless we pay them some exorbitant interest rate. Owen, what are we doing with all this raw material? Can't we sell it off? That would generate the cash that we need. Or do we need the inventory for production?

Owen: Well, we don't really need it in the short run since demand has fallen off. However, I'm not sure that we can find a buyer. Besides, I don't really want to let too much of it go because demand should pick up again within the next few months. Prices have already started to go up.

Warren: Well, it seems to me that we have too much working capital tied up in that darn inventory. Whose decision was it to buy that much?

Tatjana: It was mine. At the time, we felt that the price was too good to pass up, but we had to buy a large quantity to get the price. But I think that I might have a solution to our problem. Recently, I had lunch with the controller of Warehouses Unlimited. He was dismayed over the fact that they had excess warehouse space they couldn't "give away." I know that they have excess cash as well. Perhaps we can work something out with them.

Warren: I have another meeting to run to now. Tatjana, will you please follow up on your idea and report back to me as soon as possible?

Tatjana contacted Warehouses Unlimited (WU) and was able to strike the following deal.
WU agreed to:

- Buy the excess raw material from AL for $700,000 cash. AL's cost was $600,000.
- Store the inventory and insure it.
- Sell it back to AL over the next year on an as-needed basis, provided that all of the raw material is repurchased within the year.

AL agreed to:

- Buy back the inventory over the year at a total cost of $800,000 (to cover inventory costs including carrying costs) and provide a reasonable return on WU's money.

Tatjana called Warren immediately to tell him about the deal.

Tatjana: Warren, I think that I've solved our problem. I've negotiated a deal that will get us $700,000 cash, ensure a steady supply of raw materials at not much more than market rates, and boost our net income before tax by $100,000!

Instructions

Assume the role of an independent advisor to the company and comment on how the proposed transaction should be accounted for.

Suggested Approach to Case Study # 1

Acme Limited Overview

Since AL is a public company, IFRS is a constraint. Financial statement stakeholders include WU (which may use the statements to determine AL's solvency) and shareholders (who will want to assess management stewardship and the value of their investment).

AL management (Tatjana and Owen) will want the financial statements to show that they are making good business decisions (and performing with effective management stewardship). Since the first inventory transaction turned out to be less than ideal, they will want the second transaction to show good management ability.

As an independent advisor, however, you must ensure that the financial statements are not misleading and that the needs of the users are met.

Analysis and Recommendations

The issue is how to account for the deal that Tatjana has set up.

1. Either the transaction may be treated as a sale, in which case the inventory would be removed from the statement of financial position with (perhaps) recognition of a profit since the sale price is greater than book value; or
2. The arrangement may be treated as a financing transaction, with the inventory treated as collateral for a $700,000 loan.

Sale of the Inventory

The journal entry to record this transaction as a sale would be as follows:

Cash	700,000	
Sales Revenue		700,000
Cost of Goods Sold	600,000	
Inventory		600,000

This would result in a profit of $100,000 being recorded, and no liability on AL's statement of financial position. Note that if AL had borrowed money from the bank, it would have had to record a liability. Possession and legal title of the inventory is with WU. This would seem to imply that the inventory should be removed from AL's books.

Financing Arrangement

The underlying substance of this transaction must be reviewed. This could be viewed as a form of off–balance sheet financing. Has a sale really taken place? It could be argued that the risks and rewards of ownership still rest with AL. The inventory is still theirs since they have agreed to buy it all back. They are also effectively covering the costs of carrying the inventory, albeit indirectly. (They will pay more for the inventory when they buy it back, to compensate WU for storage, insurance, and interest costs.) The return to WU is ($800,000 − $700,000) ÷ $700,000 = 14.3%. Because the risks and rewards of ownership have not been transferred, the inventory should remain on AL's books.

Recommendation

Since the substance of the transaction is that the risks and rewards of ownership have not really transferred to WU, the transaction should be treated as a financing arrangement, with the inventory remaining on AL's books and the $700,000 being recorded as a loan. The transaction should also be adequately disclosed in notes to the financial statements since legal title to the inventory will temporarily rest with WU.

This case is a good example of how the motivations of managers to achieve a desired accounting result (which was not successful in this case) may lead them to make poor economic decisions.

CASE STUDY # 2

Sheung Steel Limited

Sheung Steel Limited (SSL), a Canadian private entity, manufactures steel. The market for its raw material is fairly volatile and prices are a function of supply and demand. In the past, SSL has often purchased more raw material than necessary in order to get a good price. In mid-December of 2017, Chuck Chung, the general manager, was reviewing current raw material prices and inventory levels in order to determine how much he should buy. Samantha Tse, a recently hired employee, stopped by his office.

Samantha: Free for lunch today, Chuck?

Chuck: Maybe a bit later, Samantha. I have to make a decision today on how much raw material to purchase. The price is at an all-time low and I'm not sure that it will get any better. The problem is that we don't really need all this inventory now, not to mention the fact that the boss is worried about cash flows.

Samantha: You know that there are other costs involved besides the purchase price. Have you considered the storage costs and the cost of tying up cash in inventory that is not in use?

Chuck: I guess not. I always make my decision based on the purchase price alone. I guess that I should factor in those other costs as well. But the purchase price is so low that it's probably still a good deal.

Samantha: Why don't you see if you can lock the price in now but not take delivery of the product until we need it? That way, we wouldn't incur storage costs and we wouldn't have to pay until we take delivery. You might have to lock in at a higher price but, considering the other benefits, it might be worth it.

Chuck: Sounds good. I'll call the supplier right away. We've got a pretty good working relationship. Maybe he'll join us for lunch. I have to get this finalized today so that I can work on the year-end financial statements. It's already mid-December and before you know it, year end and the auditors will descend on us. I'll have to think about how this would be accounted for.

Chuck negotiated a deal with the supplier to purchase the raw materials at a very good price, and the deal was signed on December 15, 2017. By signing the non-cancellable contract, SSL agreed to take delivery of a fixed amount of raw materials within the next six months, and to pay a fixed total price even if SSL does not take delivery of the full amount.

On December 31, 2017, the price of the raw material dropped even further. Chuck was annoyed since he could have saved SSL $200,000 had he waited. Prices have since begun to move (slowly) upward, however.

It is now January 15, 2018, and SSL has not yet taken delivery of the first shipment.

Instructions

Assume the role of an independent advisor to the company and consider how the raw material deal should be presented in the financial statements.

Suggested Approach to Case Study # 2

Sheung Steel Limited Overview

Favourable presentation of the deal will be important to Chuck. He might not be very keen on showing the fact that, had he delayed the signing of the deal, he could have saved the company $200,000. ASPE is a constraint since it is mentioned that the auditors will be coming in soon. Financial statement stakeholders will want faithfully representative information in order to assess their investment in the company.

Analysis and Recommendations

The issue is how the raw material purchase commitment should be accounted for. The arrangement for the undelivered material is an executory contract since both parties have agreed to do something but neither has fulfilled their part of the deal. SSL has agreed to take delivery of the material and to pay the supplier for the goods, and the supplier has agreed to sell the goods to SSL at an agreed-upon price. There is no liability for the goods as yet; that is, until they are delivered.

The commitment should be disclosed in the notes to the financial statements since it will help users predict the company's cash flows. Furthermore, it must be decided whether Chuck should accrue the difference between the contract price and the market price of the raw material at year end.

Accrue the Loss

Since the market price is below the committed purchase price at the financial statement date, and the contract is non-cancellable, the loss should be accrued. Otherwise, when the inventory is delivered and recorded on the books, the inventory would be overvalued. Since inventory must be carried at the lower of cost and net realizable value, the inventory would be written down to net realizable value anyway. However, since the decline in value of the inventory occurred in the current year, it would make sense for the loss to be booked in 2017. The resulting loss on inventory due to decline in NRV would be included in net income under "Other expenses and losses."

Therefore, accrual of the loss would reduce net income and highlight the fact that the company could have saved money had it waited.

Should the loss be presented as part of cost of goods sold? Since it relates to inventory, this would make sense. If booked to cost of goods sold, gross profit and gross profit percentage would decline.

Do Not Accrue the Loss

If the market price increases after year end and before the financial statements are issued, it is hard to argue that a loss will be incurred. In fact, if the price remains high prior to each delivery date, there will be no loss. In this case, prices have already begun to move upward (albeit slowly).

It might also be argued that since the price is volatile, it is not easy to estimate the potential loss, if any.

Recommendation

Because the price is volatile and rising, no loss should be accrued in the financial statements. The notes to the financial statements should describe the deal but not necessarily mention that market value is below cost. It is not likely that a loss will occur.

Chapter 9

Investments

companies have the amortized cost model implies ... investee main ... in the major and longer-term ... and financing the ... Under ASPE, if the ... the accounted for ... in further ... amortized cost model, except for equity instruments the ... quoted in an active market ... reporting ... Under IFRS, debt investments that are managed on a contractual basis where the entity ... separate ... report fixed payment fund the investments ... by an ... covered by under the amortization model. Under the cost ... value ... model, the investment ...

OVERVIEW

This chapter covers accounting for basic financial assets, including investments in debt and equity securities, and begins with a discussion of investments that give the investor little or no influence over the investee. There are three major models for accounting for such investments: (1) cost/amortized cost model; (2) fair value through net income model (FV-NI); and (3) fair value through other comprehensive income model (FV-OCI). The IFRS standards are in transition. The mandatory implementation date for IFRS 9, a new standard dealing with accounting for investments, has been pushed back to 2018. Until that time, accounting in accordance with IAS 39 is still permitted. Under ASPE, equity investments quoted in an active market are accounted for under the FV-NI model (although entities can choose the FV-NI model for any financial instrument), and other investments are accounted for under the cost/amortized cost model. To disclose investment values on the statement of financial position that are relevant and neutral, investments are also reviewed for possible impairment as at each financial statement date. Impairment of investments under the incurred loss model, expected loss model, and fair value loss model is discussed in this chapter.

This chapter also discusses investments that give the investor significant influence or control over the investee. Significant influence investments, also called investments in associates, are accounted for under the equity method under IFRS. Under ASPE, investments in associates are accounted for under the equity method or cost method; however, if the shares are quoted in an active market, FV-NI may be used but the cost method cannot be used. Investments that give the investor control over the investee are also called investments in subsidiaries. Under IFRS, an investor with subsidiaries must consolidate its financial statements with the financial statements of the subsidiaries under its control. Under ASPE, consolidation is permitted but not required.

STUDY STEPS

Understanding the Differences between the Accounting Models for No Significant Influence Investments

No significant influence investments are investments that give the investor little or no influence over (or less than 20% ownership in) the investee. The three major models of accounting for no significant influence investments are:

1. cost/amortized cost model,
2. fair value through net income model (FV-NI), and
3. fair value through other comprehensive income model (FV-OCI).

Each of these models has different rules for measurement of investments at acquisition, treatment of unrealized holding gains and losses (if applicable), and treatment of realized gains and losses.

The **cost model** applies to investments in equity instruments (shares) of other companies, whereas the **amortized cost model** applies to investments in debt instruments and long-term notes and loans receivable. Under **ASPE**, all investments are accounted for under the cost/amortized cost model, except for equity instruments that are quoted in an active market or derivatives. Under **IFRS**, debt investments that are managed on a contractual yield basis where the entity's business model requires that the entity hold the investments to maturity are accounted for under the amortized cost model. Under the cost/amortized cost model, the investment is recorded at acquisition cost (usually equal to fair value of the investment as at the acquisition date plus transaction costs), and subsequent changes in fair value are not recorded. Unless the investment becomes impaired, the investment is reported at cost/amortized cost. Only realized gains and losses are recorded and therefore affect net income. Throughout the life of the investment, dividend revenue and/or interest income are accrued, which also affect net income.

Under **ASPE**, investments accounted for under the **FV-NI model** are generally equity investments that trade in an active market or derivatives, although entities can choose the FV-NI model for any financial instrument. Under **IFRS**, investments under the FV-NI model are generally equity instruments that are not accounted for under the FV-OCI model, debt instruments that are not accounted for using the amortized cost model, or derivatives. Entities can also choose the FV-NI model for certain investments. Because FV-NI investments are recorded at fair value at the acquisition date (with transaction costs expensed in the period) and remeasured to fair value at each reporting date, net income is affected by unrealized holding gains and losses and dividend revenue and/or interest income earned throughout the life of the investment, as well as any gain or loss recorded at the date of disposal. ASPE requires that interest income be reported separately from net gains or losses recognized on debt instruments. Under IFRS, dividend revenue and/or interest income may be combined and reported together with the net gains or losses recognized on the FV-NI investments, especially if the FV-NI investments are held for trading purposes. Use of one investment income account would eliminate the need for amortization of discounts and premiums on debt instruments. (Note that ASPE allows a choice of either the straight-line or effective interest method of amortization where applicable, whereas IFRS requires the effective interest method of amortization where interest income is reported separately.) If an entity reports interest income separately from net gains or losses recognized on debt instruments, discounts and premiums on those debt instruments are amortized before calculating and recording changes in fair value. Thus, for entities that report interest income separately under the FV-NI model, unrealized holding gains or losses on debt instruments equal fair value less amortized cost at each financial statement date.

The **FV-OCI model** does not apply under ASPE. Under **IFRS**, investments accounted for under the **FV-OCI model** are generally longer-term equity investments that do not give the investor significant influence or control and are not held for trading purposes. They also include debt instruments where the business model is to hold the investment to maturity OR sell them.

Investments accounted for under the FV-OCI model are reported at fair value, with unrealized holding gains or losses recorded in other comprehensive income (OCI). Unrealized holding gains or losses recorded in OCI are closed to Accumulated Other Comprehensive Income (AOCI; a shareholders' equity account) at the end of each reporting period. All dividend revenue is recorded in net income except for dividend revenue that is a return of investment, which is recognized as OCI. Under the **FV-OCI with recycling model** (IAS 39 and IFRS 9 for debt instruments), at the date of disposal of the investment, the previously unrealized holding gains or losses accumulated in AOCI are transferred or "recycled" into net income, and subsequently closed to retained earnings in the year of disposal. Under IFRS 9, equity investments using FV-OCI are accounted for **without recycling**, which requires that at the date of disposal of the investment the previously unrealized holding gains or losses accumulated in AOCI are transferred directly to retained earnings. However, debt investments accounted for under IFRS 9 using FV-OCI are accounted for **with recycling**, as described above.

Understanding the Differences between the Impairment Models for No Significant Influence Investments

The three major models for accounting for impairment of no significant influence investments are:

1. incurred loss model,
2. expected loss model, and
3. fair value loss model.

Under **ASPE**, the incurred loss model is applied to investments under the cost/amortized cost model. ASPE's use of the incurred loss model calculates impairment loss as the carrying amount of the investment, less the higher of discounted cash flow of the investment (discounted at the market interest rate) and net realizable value of the investment.

Under IAS 39, the incurred loss model is applied to investments under the cost/amortized cost model, and investments under the FV-OCI model where a loss/trigger event has occurred. The incurred loss model under IAS 39 calculates impairment loss for investments under the cost/amortized cost model as the carrying amount of the investment, less the discounted cash flow of the investment (discounted using the historic interest rate for debt instruments and the current market interest rate for equity instruments measured at cost). The incurred loss model under IAS 39 calculates impairment loss for investments under the FV-OCI model as the carrying amount of the investment, less the fair value of the investment, with the impairment loss recognized in net income. Under IFRS 9, the incurred loss model is not permitted.

Under IFRS 9, the **expected loss model** is applied to investments under the cost/amortized cost model as well as debt investments carried at FV-OCI. The expected loss model first determines whether the credit risk of the investment has significantly increased. If it has not, a 12-month time frame is used for assessing defaults. If it has, the risk of default over the life of the investment must be considered. The impairment loss is the difference between the investment's gross carrying amount and the present value of the expected cash flows discounted at the same effective interest rate used when the investment was first acquired. Unbiased probabilities must be factored in. The following decision tree summarizes the approach followed by the expected loss model for impairment under IFRS 9:

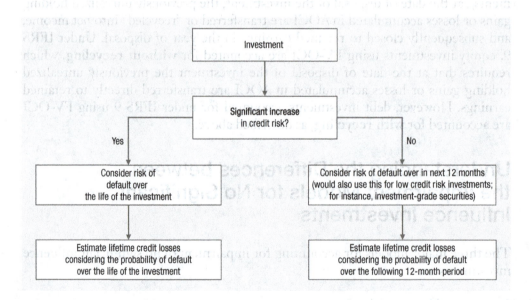

Both ASPE and IFRS (IAS 39 and IFRS 9) agree that the fair value loss model should be applied to investments under the FV-NI model. IFRS 9 also requires use of the fair value loss model for equity investments accounted for at FV-OCI. The fair value loss model does not require a separate impairment test since the assets are continually revalued to fair value, with gains and losses booked to net income. Investments under the FV-NI model are adjusted to fair value at each statement of financial position date and fair value should reflect any impairment as at that date.

Becoming Proficient in Accounting for Strategic Investments

In general, for strategic purposes, an entity may purchase investments resulting in no significant influence, significant influence, or control over an investee. However, in the context of this chapter, the term "strategic investments" includes investments in associates over which the investor has significant influence and investments in subsidiaries over which the investor has control.

Significant Influence

Determining whether an investor has significant influence over an investee may require professional judgement. Significant influence is defined by the IASB as "the power to participate in the financial and operating policy decisions" of an entity but not control over those policies. In practice, if the investor has less than 20% shareholdings (or ownership) in the investee, it is assumed (in the absence of any other information) that the investor does not have significant influence over the investee. However, the definition of significant influence requires that other factors be considered, including:

- the investor's representation on the investee's board of directors.
- the investor's level of participation in the investee's policy-making processes.
- material intercompany transactions between the investor and investee.
- interchange of managerial personnel.
- provision of technical information.

Therefore, percentage of share ownership alone may not determine whether an investor has significant influence over the investee. For example, consider an investor with greater than 20% share ownership in the investee. If, after considering the factors above, it is determined that the investor still does not have significant influence over the investee, the investor would account for the no significant influence investment under either the cost/amortized cost model, FV-NI model, or FV-OCI model.

> In determining whether significant influence exists, be careful in applying the 20% rule. It may be that an investment resulting in 25% ownership of the investee does not represent significant influence, whereas in a different situation, an investment resulting in 10% ownership of the investee does represent significant influence.

Under **ASPE**, if an investor entity has significant influence over an investee entity, the investor entity uses either the equity method or cost method to account for the investment (and the investor entity must use the selected method for all other significant influence investments). An exception to this standard is if the equity investment consists of shares quoted in an active market, in which case the cost method cannot be used, and the FV-NI model can be used.

Under **IFRS**, if an investor entity has significant influence over an investee entity, the investor entity uses the equity method to account for the investment.

The **equity method** recognizes that the investor has influence over the investee's dividend decisions and, therefore, does not record income when the investee declares or pays a dividend. Instead, because the investor has significant influence over the investee, the investor's investment income or loss is its share of the investee's net income or loss. Theoretically, the investor could recognize its share of revenue as the investee earns each dollar of revenue; however, practically speaking, the investor records its share of the investee's net income or loss on a monthly or perhaps annual basis (with a debit to the Investment in Associate account and a credit to the Investment Income account). If the investor owns 25% of the investee's shares, then the investor would record 25% of the investee's profits or losses as its investment income or loss.

Receipt of dividends is recorded as a debit to Cash and a credit to Investment in Associate. Income is not recognized because the investor already recorded investment income in a previous period when the investor recognized its share of the investee's net income.

Therefore, under the equity method, pro rata income is accrued by the investor and treated as increases in the Investment in Associate account, and pro rata dividends are treated as decreases in the Investment in Associate account. Although the investment is recorded at cost originally, its value on the statement of financial position increases as earnings are accrued and decreases as dividends are received. This makes intuitive sense because the equity in the investee company (and therefore the value of the investment) increases as the investee earns profits and decreases as the investee pays dividends.

In addition, both IFRS and ASPE require that the investment be assessed at each statement of financial position date to determine if there are any indicators of non-temporary decline in value or **impairment**. An impairment loss equal to carrying amount less recoverable amount is recorded and included in net income if (1) there are indicators of impairment, and (2) the carrying amount of the investment is higher than its recoverable amount. (The recoverable amount is the higher of its value-in-use and fair value less costs to sell, where value-in-use refers to the present value of cash flows discounted at an appropriate current market interest rate.)

Each time the investor records investment income, the investor must also adjust investment income for amortization of part or all of the difference between what the investor paid for the share investment, and the investor's share of the book value of the investment. If part of the payment in excess of the share of book value was due to an amount paid in excess of the investor's share of the book value of depreciable assets or inventory on the investee's books, the payment in excess of the share of book value related to these items is amortized over time.

For instance, assume that Beakman Limited pays $4 million for 25% of World Limited, and the following information is available for World Limited at the time of the purchase:

- Net book value (NBV) of World Limited = $12 million.
- Fair value of underlying net assets of World Limited = $15 million.

The payment in excess of the share of book value is calculated as follows:

Cost of 25% investment in World Limited shares	$4,000,000
Less 25% of book value of World Limited ($12,000,000 × 25%)	3,000,000
Payment in excess of share of book value	$1,000,000

Why would Beakman pay $1 million more than 25% of World Limited's recorded NBV? One reason may be that the recorded values (NBV) of assets do not reflect the fair value of the underlying assets due to the use of cost models and application of the historical cost principle. Another reason may be that companies often have unrecorded, internally generated goodwill. **Goodwill** is the extra value attributable to a going concern company as a result of, for example, the reputation of the company; the company having steady, loyal customers; and/or the company having established suppliers. Goodwill is not recorded on the statement of financial position of a company unless it is purchased.

- Purchase price discrepancies (PPDs) arise due to perceived excess of fair value over NBV inherent in a company purchased. PPDs arise either because underlying tangible assets are seen to have greater value than their recorded NBV or because there is unrecorded, internally generated goodwill.

- In most cases, at least some amount of the PPD is attributable to the perceived excess of fair value over NBV of tangible assets since the use of cost models and application of the historical cost principle often result in recorded asset values that are below fair value.

In this example, Beakman could have paid more than 25% of World Limited's book value for 25% share ownership in World Limited because some or all of World Limited's assets have fair value greater than NBV, or because of goodwill, or both.

Therefore, each time investment income is recorded, Beakman must also adjust investment income for (current year) amortization of differences between fair value over NBV of tangible assets (that existed at the time of purchase of the investment). These differences are amortized over the remaining life of the underlying assets. For example, if $750,000 of the $1,000,000 PPD is due to payment in excess of Beakman's share of NBV for a building with 15 years of life remaining, annual amortization of this excess would be $50,000 ($750,000 ÷ 15). Beakman would record this $50,000 amount each year as a debit to Investment Income and a credit to Investment in Associate. The remaining amount of PPD ($1,000,000 − $750,000 = $250,000) would be attributable to goodwill and included in the Investment in Associate account, which is subject to impairment testing each year. The amount attributed to goodwill is not amortized.

Control

Control over an investee is generally assumed when the investor owns 50% or more of the voting shares of another company. According to **ASPE**, control is the continuing power to determine the strategic operating, financing, and investing policies of another entity without the co-operation of others. According to **IFRS**, an investor controls another entity if it has the power to direct the activities of the other entity to generate returns, either positive or negative, for the investor. If control over an investee is evident, the investor accounts for the investment using the **consolidation method**. This involves adding all assets, liabilities, revenues, and expenses of the subsidiary to the investor's (parent's) financial statements. Care must be taken to eliminate any intercompany transactions.

TIPS ON CHAPTER TOPICS

- An investment is classified as current if management expects to sell or realize (convert to cash) the investment within the entity's normal operating cycle or within 12 months from the statement of financial position date, or if the investment is held primarily for trading purposes, or if the investment is a cash equivalent. Note that **classification between current or long-term** does not depend on the accounting model used; investments accounted for under the cost/amortized cost model and FV-NI model may be current or long-term. Because FV-OCI investments are held for longer-term strategic purposes by definition, however, they are usually long-term assets.

- **Amortized cost** is acquisition cost, reduced by principal payments received, adjusted for amortization of any discount or premium, less any impairment writedowns.

- Under IFRS, **amortization of discount or premium** must be done using the effective interest method (unless the amount is immaterial, in which case the straight-line method would be permitted). Under ASPE, either the straight-line or effective interest method may be used.

- Investments accounted for under the **FV-OCI model** are reported at fair value, with unrealized holding gains and losses included in other comprehensive income (OCI). At the end of each reporting period, OCI is closed to accumulated other comprehensive income (AOCI), which is a separate component of shareholders' equity. Unrealized holding gains and losses remain in AOCI until the investment is disposed of. At the time of disposition, accumulated unrealized holding gains and losses are **recycled** through (recognized in) net income if the entity is following IAS 39 (or debt investments under IFRS 9), or **not recycled** through net income (and therefore transferred directly to retained earnings) for equity investments under IFRS 9.

- Investments that are **held for trading** are usually marketable securities quoted in an active market and accounted for under the FV-NI model.

- **Fair value** is the amount that would be received to sell an asset or paid to transfer a liability in an orderly, arm's-length transaction between market participants at the measurement date.

- Under **ASPE**, equity investments quoted in an active market are accounted for under the FV-NI model (although, under the fair value option, entities can choose the FV-NI model for any financial instrument). Other investments are accounted for under the cost/amortized cost model. Under **IFRS**, longer-term equity investments not held for trading purposes may be accounted for under the FV-OCI model, and debt investments where the entity's business model requires holding to maturity are accounted for under the amortized cost model. All other investments are accounted for under the FV-NI model.

- At the time of investment acquisition, **adoption of the appropriate accounting model** is important as it determines the impact of various items (including transaction costs and future unrealized holding gains and losses) on net income. Under **ASPE**, if the FV-NI model is selected under the fair value option, the decision is irrevocable; that is, the entity cannot switch to the cost/amortized cost model at a later date. Under **IAS 39**, reclassification is permitted only in

Illustration 9-2   287

certain limited circumstances (for example, if the investment is no longer held for trading or if the entity no longer intends to or is unable to hold the debt investment to maturity). Under **IFRS 9**, adoption of any of the accounting models for a particular investment is irrevocable except on the rare occasion that there is a change in the entity's business model.

ILLUSTRATION 9-1

Summary of No Significant Influence Investments in Debt and Equity Securities

The major accounting models for no significant influence investments in debt and equity securities are summarized below.

Category	Valuation	Unrealized Holding Gains or Losses
ASPE		
Cost/amortized cost	Cost/amortized cost	Not recognized
FV-NI	Fair value	Recognized in net income
IFRS		
Amortized cost	Amortized cost	Not recognized
FV-NI	Fair value	Recognized in net income
FV-OCI with recycling (IAS 39 and IFRS 9 debt investments)	Fair value	Recognized in other comprehensive income (OCI), and transferred to accumulated other comprehensive income (AOCI) at the end of each reporting period
FV-OCI without recycling (IFRS 9 equity investments)	Fair value	Recognized in other comprehensive income (OCI), and transferred to accumulated other comprehensive income (AOCI) at the end of each reporting period

ILLUSTRATION 9-2

Classification of No Significant Influence Investments under IFRS 9

The following summarizes the process used to determine the classification and measurement of no significant influence financial assets under IFRS 9:

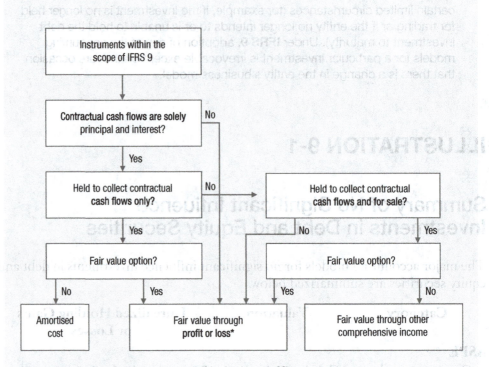

* Presentation option for equity investments to present fair value changes in OCI

EXERCISE 9-1

PURPOSE: This exercise will review the required year-end adjustment to the Investment account for equity securities that are accounted for under the FV-NI model.

Inland Transport has a portfolio of marketable equity securities and accounts for the investments under the FV-NI model. All securities in the portfolio were purchased in 2017 for an aggregate cost of $168,000. Total fair value of the portfolio at five successive statement of financial position dates is as follows:

Date	Fair value
12/31/17	$162,000
12/31/18	$171,000
12/31/19	$179,000
12/31/20	$212,000
12/31/21	$203,000

Instructions

At each statement of financial position date, determine the unrealized holding gain or loss to be recorded. Ignore tax effects.

Solution to Exercise 9-1

Date	Unrealized holding gain (loss) to be recorded
12/31/17	$(6,000)
12/31/18	$9,000
12/31/19	$8,000
12/31/20	$33,000
12/31/21	$(9,000)

The total unrealized holding gain at the end of 2021 is $35,000. This is confirmed by comparing the initial cost of $168,000 with fair value at the end of 2021 of $203,000.

EXPLANATION: Investments under the FV-NI model are initially recorded at cost, but subsequently reported at fair value. Since there is more than one security in the portfolio, determination of the adjustment to fair value (and unrealized holding gain [loss]) can be done on a portfolio basis. The total carrying amount of the portfolio is compared with fair value at each statement of financial position date and the adjustment amount is calculated as the increase or decrease in carrying amount required to bring the portfolio to fair value as at the statement of financial position date. The adjustment amounts are called unrealized holding gains (losses) and included in each respective period's net income.

- In the above example, it was assumed that the same securities were held in the portfolio between 2017 and 2021. This is a simplifying assumption to show the impact of the unrealized holding gains and losses on net income. In practice, if a security in the portfolio is sold, a realized gain or loss equal to the difference between the security's sale proceeds and carrying amount would be recorded in net income. If a security is purchased and added to the portfolio, the carrying amount of the portfolio would increase by the new security's cost, and the fair value of the new security would be included in the fair value of the portfolio as at the next statement of financial position date.

- In the above exercise, it would also be acceptable to use an allowance account to track unrealized holding gains and losses.

EXERCISE 9-2

PURPOSE: This exercise will review accounting for equity investments under the FV-OCI model.

As at December 31, 2016, Northumberland Corporation had no investments. On November 15, 2017, Northumberland purchases an equity investment for $243,700; commission costs on the purchase amount to $2,300. At December 31, 2017, Northumberland's statement of financial position date, the fair value of the investment is $225,000. At December 31, 2018, the investment's fair value is $235,000.

On January 15, 2019, the investment is sold for $300,000. Northumberland Corporation prepares financial statements in accordance with IFRS.

Instructions

(a) Assume that Northumberland Corporation accounts for the investment as an FV-OCI investment under IFRS 9. Prepare all relevant journal entries to record the acquisition, subsequent measurement, and disposition of the investment. Ignore tax effects.

(b) Discuss how the answer to part (a) would be different if Northumberland Corporation accounted for the investment as an FV-OCI investment under IAS 39.

Solution to Exercise 9-2

(a) FV-OCI without recycling

November 15, 2017

FV-OCI Investments	246,000	
Cash		246,000

December 31, 2017

Unrealized Holding Gain or Loss—OCI	21,000	
FV-OCI Investments		21,000

The unrealized holding loss is included in other comprehensive income (OCI) and transferred to accumulated other comprehensive income (AOCI) at the end of the 2017 reporting period. AOCI is a separate component of shareholders' equity.

December 31, 2018

FV-OCI Investments	10,000	
Unrealized Holding Gain or Loss—OCI		10,000

The unrealized holding gain is included in OCI and transferred to AOCI at the end of the 2018 reporting period. Note that the AOCI amount is cumulative and reflects total unrealized holding gains and losses to date, while the entry to OCI represents the unrealized holding gain or loss for the year.

January 15, 2019

Entry #1

FV-OCI Investments	65,000	
Unrealized Holding Gain or Loss—OCI		65,000

This entry adjusts the Fair Value-OCI Investments to fair value as at the date of disposal, and records the adjustment in OCI.

Entry #2

Cash	300,000	
FV-OCI Investments		300,000

This entry removes the carrying amount of the asset and records the sale proceeds.

Entry #3

Unrealized Holding Gain or Loss—OCI	54,000	
Retained Earnings		54,000

This entry is a reclassification adjustment that removes the now-realized holding gain from AOCI and transfers it to retained earnings, consistent with the accounting treatment of FV-OCI equity investments under IFRS 9, which requires no recycling of total realized gains/losses through net income. Essentially, the cumulative net unrealized holding gain that was "stored" in the AOCI account is transferred to retained earnings upon being realized at the time of disposition.

(b) If Northumberland Corporation accounted for the investment as an FV-OCI investment under IAS 39, the previously unrealized holding gains or losses accumulated in AOCI would be transferred or "recycled" into net income at the time of disposition, and subsequently closed to retained earnings in the year of disposal. The journal entries on November 15, 2017; December 31, 2017; December 31, 2018; and entry #1 and entry #2 on January 15, 2019, would be the same as in part (a). However, entry #3 on January 15, 2019, would require a credit to Gain on Sale of Investments (to net income) instead of a credit to Retained Earnings.

EXERCISE 9-3

PURPOSE: This exercise will review accounting for a debt investment under the amortized cost model.

A five-year $100,000 bond with a 7% stated interest rate and a 5% yield rate is purchased on December 31, 2017, for $108,660. The bond matures on December 31, 2022. Interest is due at the end of each year. The following amortization schedule reflects interest to be received, interest income, amortization of bond premium, and amortized cost of the bond investment at each year end. The investment is accounted for under the amortized cost model.

Date	Cash Received	Interest Income	Premium Amortization	Carrying Amount
12/31/17				$108,660
12/31/18	$ 7,000	$ 5,433	$1,567	107,093
12/31/19	7,000	5,354	1,646	105,447
12/31/20	7,000	5,272	1,728	103,719

Date	Cash Received	Interest Income	Premium Amortization	Carrying Amount
12/31/21	7,000	5,186	1,814	101,905
12/31/22	7,000	5,095	1,905	100,000
Total	$35,000	$26,340	$8,660	

The following chart shows amortized cost and fair value of the bond at each year end:

Date	Amortized Cost	Fair Value	Difference
12/31/17	$108,660	$108,660	$ 0
12/31/18	107,093	106,000	(1,093)
12/31/19	105,447	107,500	2,053
12/31/20	103,719	105,500	1,781
12/31/21	101,905	103,000	1,095
12/31/22	100,000	100,000	0

Instructions

(a) Record the required journal entries at December 31, 2017; December 31, 2018; and December 31, 2019.

(b) Describe what will be reflected on the income statement and statement of financial position prepared at December 31, 2018, and December 31, 2019, with respect to this investment.

(c) Prepare the journal entry to record the sale of the investment if it is sold on January 2, 2020, for $107,250.

Solution to Exercise 9-3

(a)

December 31, 2017

Bond Investment at Amortized Cost	108,660	
Cash		108,660

The bond premium is included in the Bond Investment at Amortized Cost account.

December 31, 2018

Cash	7,000	
Interest Income		5,433
Bond Investment at Amortized Cost		1,567

December 31, 2019

Cash	7,000	
Interest Income		5,354
Bond Investment at Amortized Cost		1,646

(b) The Bond Investment at Amortized Cost would be reported in the long-term investments section of the statement of financial position at an amortized cost of $107,093 at December 31, 2018, and $105,447 at December 31, 2019. Interest income of $5,433 would be reported on the income statement for the year ended December 31, 2018, and interest income of $5,354 would be reported on the income statement for the year ended December 31, 2019. Interest income is classified under "Other revenues and gains" on a multiple-step income statement.

(c)

January 2, 2020

Cash	107,250	
Bond Investment at Amortized Cost		105,447[a]
Gain on Sale of Investments		1,803

[a]$108,660 − ($1,567 + $1,646) = $105,447 balance

EXERCISE 9-4

PURPOSE: This exercise will illustrate (1) the calculations and journal entries for a bond investment purchased at a discount and accounted for under the amortized cost model, (2) the accounting treatment required when the bond investment is sold prior to the bond's maturity date, and (3) the journal entries for a bond investment purchased at a discount and accounted for under the FV-NI model under ASPE or IFRS.

Hitt Company purchased bonds to be accounted for under the amortized cost model. The following details pertain:

Face value	$100,000.00
Coupon interest rate	7%
Yield rate	10%
Maturity date	January 1, 2020
Date of purchase	January 1, 2017
Interest receipts due	Annually on January 1
Method of amortization	Effective interest
Purchase price	$92,539.95
Fair value on December 31, 2017	$96,000.00

Instructions

(a) Calculate the amount of purchase premium or discount.

(b) Prepare the journal entry to record the purchase of the bonds.

(c) Prepare the bond amortization schedule.

(d) Prepare all journal entries related to these bonds (subsequent to the purchase date) for 2017 and 2018. Assume the accounting period coincides with the calendar year. Assume reversing entries are not used.

(e) Prepare the journal entry to record the sale of the bonds on January 1, 2019, for $102,000. Assume the sale occurs immediately after the annual interest receipt.

(f) Assume that Hitt Company follows ASPE and accounts for the bonds under the FV-NI model. Prepare the journal entries related to this bond for 2017.

(g) Assume that Hitt Company follows IFRS and accounts for the bonds under the FV-NI model. Prepare the journal entries related to this bond for 2017.

Solution to Exercise 9-4

(a)

Face value	$100,000.00
Less purchase price	92,539.95
Discount on bond investment	$ 7,460.05

(b)

January 1, 2017

Bond Investment at Amortized Cost	92,539.95	
Cash		92,539.95

The discount of $7,460.05 is included in the Bond Investment at Amortized Cost account.

(c)

Date	7% Cash Received	10% Interest Income	Discount Amortization	Carrying Amount
1/1/17				$ 92,539.95
1/1/18	$ 7,000.00	$ 9,254.00	$2,254.00	94,793.95
1/1/19	7,000.00	9,479.40	2,479.40	97,273.35
1/1/20	7,000.00	9,726.65[a]	2,726.65	100,000.00
	$21,000.00	$28,460.05	$7,460.05	

[a]Includes rounding effect of $0.69.

EXPLANATION: Cash received is determined by multiplying the par (face) value ($100,000) by the coupon rate of interest (7%). Interest income is calculated by multiplying the carrying amount at the beginning of each interest period by the yield (effective interest) rate (10%). Discount amortization is the excess of interest income over coupon interest (cash) received. Revised carrying amount is the carrying amount at the beginning of the interest period plus discount amortization for the interest period.

- Interest income of $9,479.40 appearing on the "1/1/19" line is the amount of interest income for the interest period ending on that date. Thus, in this case, $9,479.40 is the interest income for the 12 months preceding the date 1/1/19, which would be the calendar year 2018.

- Any rounding effect should be plugged to (included in) the last period's interest income amount. Otherwise, there would be a small balance left in the Investment in Bonds account after the bonds are settled.

- Notice that total interest income ($28,460.05) over the three-year period equals total cash interest received ($21,000.00) plus total purchase discount ($7,460.05). Thus, the purchase discount represents an additional amount of interest to be recognized over the period the bonds are held.

(d)

12/31/17	Bond Investment at Amortized Cost	2,254.00	
	Interest Receivable	7,000.00	
	Interest Income		9,254.00

EXPLANATION: This entry records (1) accrual of interest for the preceding 12 months, and (2) discount amortization for the first 12 months the bonds are held. This compound entry could be replaced with two single entries. The first entry would be a debit to Interest Receivable and a credit to Interest Income for $7,000.00. The second entry would be a debit to Bond Investment at Amortized Cost and a credit to Interest Income for $2,254.00. The two-entry approach is sometimes preferred when reversing entries are used because the first of the two single entries can be reversed, but the second of the two single entries (the one that records discount or premium amortization) should **never** be reversed.

1/1/18	Cash	7,000.00	
	Interest Receivable		7,000.00
12/31/18	Bond Investment at Amortized Cost	2,479.40	
	Interest Receivable	7,000.00	
	Interest Income		9,479.40

(e)

1/1/19	Cash	7,000.00	
	Interest Receivable		7,000.00
	Cash	102,000.00	
	Bond Investment at Amortized Cost		97,273.35[a]
	Gain on Sale of Investments		4,726.65[b]

[a]$92,539.95 + $2,254.00 + $2,479.40 = $97,273.35 carrying amount
[b]$102,000.00 − $97,273.35 = $4,726.65 gain

Gains or losses on sales of investments are classified in the "other revenues, gains, expenses, and losses" section of a multiple-step income statement.

(f) Under ASPE, for a bond investment accounted for under the FV-NI model, there is a requirement to report interest income separately.

1/1/17	FV-NI Investments	92,539.95	
	Cash		92,539.95

12/31/17	FV-NI Investments	2,254.00	
	Interest Receivable	7,000.00	
	Interest Income		9,254.00

12/31/17	FV-NI Investments	1,206.05[c]	
	Unrealized Gain or Loss		1,206.05

[c]$96,000.00 − ($92,539.95 + $2,254.00)

(g) Under IFRS, for a bond investment accounted for under the FV-NI model, there is no requirement to report interest income separately.

1/1/17	FV-NI Investments	92,539.95	
	Cash		92,539.95

12/31/17	Interest Receivable	7,000.00	
	Investment Income or Loss		7,000.00

12/31/17	FV-NI Investments	3,460.05[c]	
	Investment Income or Loss		3,460.05

[c]$96,000.00 − $92,539.95

EXERCISE 9-5

PURPOSE: This exercise will illustrate the calculations and journal entries for an investment that is impaired (1) under ASPE, and (2) under IFRS 9.

Milton Corporation owns corporate bonds at December 31, 2017, accounted for using the amortized cost model. These bonds have a par value of $900,000 and an amortized cost of $856,000. After an impairment review was triggered, Milton determined that the discounted impaired cash flows are $792,500 using the current market rate of interest, but are $788,000 using the market rate when the bonds were first acquired. The company follows a policy of directly reducing the carrying amount of any impaired assets. Assume that no impairment loss had been recorded earlier.

Instructions

(a) Assuming Milton is a private enterprise using ASPE, prepare any necessary journal entry(ies) related to (1) the impairment at December 31, 2017, and (2) a December 31, 2018, fair value of $802,000 and an adjusted carrying value of $792,000.

(b) Assuming Milton applies IFRS 9 and that there has been a significant increase in credit risk, prepare any necessary journal entry(ies) related to (1) the impairment at December 31, 2017, and (2) a December 31, 2018, fair value of $802,000 and an adjusted carrying value of $792,000. Assume that the discounted cash flow numbers provided reflect the lifetime expected risk of default.

Solution to Exercise 9-5

(a) 12/31/17	Loss on Impairment	63,500[a]	
	Bond Investment at Amortized Cost		63,500
	[a]$856,000 − $792,500		
12/31/18	Bond Investment at Amortized Cost	10,000[b]	
	Recovery of Loss from Impairment		10,000
	[b]$802,000 − $792,000		

EXPLANATION: Under ASPE, the carrying amount is reduced to the higher of the discounted cash flow using a current rate or the bond's net realizable value. This latter amount is not provided in this situation. Impairment losses may be subsequently reversed.

(b) 12/31/17	Loss on Impairment	68,000[c]	
	Bond Investment at Amortized Cost		68,000
	[c]$856,000 − $788,000		
12/31/18	Bond Investment at Amortized Cost	10,000[d]	
	Recovery of Loss from Impairment		10,000
	[d]$802,000 − $792,000		

EXPLANATION: Under IFRS 9, the carrying amount is reduced to the discounted remaining estimated cash flows using the historic discount rate. Impairment losses may be subsequently reversed.

EXERCISE 9-6

PURPOSE: This exercise will allow you to compare the results of using the FV-NI model and equity method of accounting for an investment in shares.

On January 1, 2017, Big Rock Corporation acquired 150,000 of the 500,000 out-standing common shares of Small Valley Corporation as a long-term investment at a cost of $45 per share. The fair value and net book value of the investee's net assets were both $22.5 million at January 1, 2017. Small Valley Corporation paid a cash dividend of $3.00 per common share on September 5, 2017, and reported net income of $1.8 million for the year ended December 31, 2017. The fair value of Small Valley shares was $40 per share at December 31, 2017.

Instructions

(a) Assuming Big Rock does **not** exercise significant influence over the investee, and that the investment is accounted for under the FV-NI model, determine the following:

1. Total investment income or loss for the year ended December 31, 2017.

2. Amount to report as the carrying amount of the FV-NI investment at December 31, 2017.

(b) Assuming Big Rock **does** exercise significant influence over the investee, and that the investment is accounted for under the equity method, determine the following:

1. Total investment income or loss for the year ended December 31, 2017.

2. Amount to report as the carrying amount of the Investment in Associate at December 31, 2017.

Solution to Exercise 9-6

(a) 1. $450,000ª − $750,000ᵇ = $300,000 total investment loss

   ª150,000 shares × $3 per share dividend revenue

   ᵇ150,000 shares × $5 ($45 carrying amount − $40 fair value) per share unrealized loss

2. $6,000,000

EXPLANATION: Under the FV-NI model, the investor must report the investment at fair value. At December 31, 2017, the fair value is ($40 × 150,000 shares = $6,000,000); therefore, the FV-NI Investments account would decrease by $750,000.

(b) 1. $540,000

   2. $6,840,000

Investment in Associate					Investment Income or Loss	
1/1/17	6,750,000	9/5/17	450,000ª		12/31/17	540,000ᵇ
12/31/17	540,000ᵇ					
12/31/17 Bal.	6,840,000				12/31/17 Bal.	540,000

ª150,000 shares × $3 = $450,000

ᵇ150,000 ÷ 500,000 = 30% ownership; 30% × $1,800,000 = $540,000

EXPLANATION: The equity method is used when the investment allows the investor to exercise significant influence over the investee. The investor recognizes its proportionate share of the investee's income by a debit to the Investment in Associate account and a credit to Investment Income or Loss. When the investee distributes income via dividends, the investor records an increase in Cash and a decrease in the carrying amount of the Investment in Associate. Because the cost of this investment was equal to the investor's share of the carrying amount of the investee's underlying net assets, there was no purchase price discrepancy (PPD), and therefore amortization of PPD need not be considered. (Amortization of PPD would decrease net investment income and the Investment in Associate account balance.) Fair value of the shares at the statement of financial position date is not relevant under the equity method.

> Under the **equity method**, the investment is originally recorded at cost and subsequently adjusted by the investor's **proportionate share** of the investee's net income and dividend payments. Income earned by the investee results in the recording of investment income and an increase in the Investment in Associate account on the books of the investor. Net loss incurred by the investee, as well as dividend payments, reduce the Investment in Associate account on the books of the investor. If the investor acquires the shares at a price greater than its share of the book value of the investee's underlying net assets, the investor must amortize any portion of the difference related to fair value in excess of book value of the investee's tangible assets as at the date of acquisition. This amortization decreases investment income as well as the Investment in Associate account balance.

EXERCISE 9-7

PURPOSE: This exercise will illustrate the equity method of accounting.

Delight Corporation acquired 30% of the 1 million outstanding shares of Touch Corporation on January 1, 2017, for $3,240,000 when the book value of Touch's net assets totalled $9,600,000. At January 1, 2017, Touch's plant assets, with a remaining life of 10 years, had a fair value in excess of book value by $700,000.

Touch Corporation reported net income of $1.6 million for 2017 and $2 million for 2018. Touch paid dividends of $400,000 on December 6, 2017, and $500,000 on December 5, 2018.

Instructions

(a) Prepare all journal entries related to this investment for 2017 and 2018.

(b) Indicate the amount that should appear as investment income on Delight's income statement for the years ended (1) December 31, 2017, and (2) December 31, 2018.

(c) Indicate the amount that should appear as the balance of Delight's investment on the statement of financial position at (1) December 31, 2017, and (2) December 31, 2018.

Solution to Exercise 9-7

(a)

1/1/17	Investment in Associate	3,240,000	
	Cash		3,240,000

12/6/17	Cash	120,000	
	Investment in Associate		120,000
	(30% × $400,000 = $120,000)		

12/31/17	Investment in Associate	480,000	
	Investment Income or Loss		480,000
	(30% × $1,600,000 = $480,000)		

	Investment Income or Loss	21,000	
	Investment in Associate		21,000
	(30% × $700,000 = $210,000*;		
	$210,000 / 10 years = $21,000)		
	(To amortize difference, plant assets)		

*Calculations to support amortization of fair value difference, plant assets:

Total book value of net assets of investee at 1/1/17	$9,600,000
Investor's percentage	30%
Book value of investor's share of investee's net assets	2,880,000
Cost of investment	3,240,000
Excess of investment cost over book value of underlying net assets	360,000
Portion attributable to excess of fair value over book value of plant assets ($700,000 × 30% = $210,000)	(210,000)
Excess assumed to be goodwill—not amortized	150,000

12/5/18	Cash	150,000	
	Investment in Associate		150,000
	(30% × $500,000 = $150,000)		

12/31/18	Investment in Associate	600,000	
	Investment Income or Loss		600,000
	(30% × $2,000,000 = $600,000)		

	Investment Income or Loss	21,000	
	Investment in Associate		21,000

$$(30\% \times \$700,000 = \$210,000;$$
$$\$210,000 / 10 \text{ years} = \$21,000)$$

EXPLANATION: The equity method is an accrual method of accounting for an investment in shares. The investor's share of the investee's earnings is recorded as income by the investor in the same time period the investee earns it. Dividends received are recorded as a recovery of investment, not as income. (To record dividends as income would "double count" income already recorded as investment income.)

The excess of the investor's investment cost over its share of the carrying amount of the underlying net assets on the investee's books must be determined and amortized. In this exercise, a portion ($210,000) of that excess is due to the fact that the investee has identifiable plant assets with fair values in excess of carrying amounts as at the purchase date. Therefore, the $210,000 portion should be amortized by the investor over the remaining life of the underlying assets (10 years in this case). The remaining excess of cost over book value ($150,000) is attributed to goodwill internally generated by the investee. The investor does not amortize or record this amount separately. It is considered included in the overall carrying amount of the Investment in Associate.

(b) 1. $459,000 for the year ended December 31, 2017.
   2. $579,000 for the year ended December 31, 2018.

APPROACH: Post the amounts from the entries in part (a) to a T account to solve.

Investment Income or Loss

12/31/17	21,000	12/31/17	480,000
		12/31/17 Balance	459,000 (closed to income summary)
12/31/18	21,000	12/31/18	600,000
		12/31/18 Balance	579,000 (closed to income summary)

(c) 1. $3,579,000 at December 31, 2017.
   2. $4,008,000 at December 31, 2018.

APPROACH: Post the amounts from the entries in part (a) to a T account to solve.

Investment in Associate

1/1/17	3,240,000	12/6/17	120,000
12/31/17	480,000	12/31/17	21,000
12/31/17 Balance	3,579,000		
12/31/18	600,000	12/5/18	150,000
		12/31/18	21,000
12/31/18 Balance	4,008,000		

ANALYSIS OF MULTIPLE-CHOICE QUESTIONS

Question

1. An investor purchased bonds with a face amount of $110,000. The investor purchased the bonds for $106,000, paid transaction costs of $1,000, and paid for three months of accrued interest amounting to $2,750. The investor accounts for the investment under the amortized cost model. At acquisition, this investment should be recorded at:

   a. $106,000.
   b. $107,000.
   c. $109,750.
   d. $110,000.

EXPLANATION: Acquisition cost is determined as follows:

Purchase price	$106,000
Transaction costs to acquire	1,000
Total acquisition cost of investment	$107,000

Under the amortized cost model, at acquisition, an investment should be recorded at cost, which includes purchase price and all incidental costs of acquisition (such as brokerage commissions, fees, and taxes). Any accrued interest is recorded by a debit to Interest Receivable or by a debit to Interest Income; accrued interest is **not** included in the investment's cost. (Solution = b.)

Question

2. Refer to the facts in question 1 above. The amount of cash outlay required to acquire the investment is:

   a. $106,000.
   b. $107,000.
   c. $109,750.
   d. $110,000.

EXPLANATION: Accrued interest does not increase the investment's cost, but it does increase the cash outlay to acquire the investment. The amount of cash required to acquire the investment is determined as follows:

Purchase price	$106,000
Transaction costs to acquire	1,000
Total acquisition cost of investment	107,000
Accrued interest for three months	2,750
Total cash required to acquire investment	$109,750

(Solution = c.)

Question

3. When an investor's accounting period ends on a date that does not coincide with an interest receipt date for bonds held as an investment, the investor must:

   a. make an adjusting entry to debit Interest Receivable and to credit Interest Income for the amount of interest accrued since the last interest receipt date.

   b. notify the issuer and request that a special payment be made for the appropriate portion of the interest period.

   c. make an adjusting entry to debit Interest Receivable and to credit Interest Income for the total amount of interest to be received at the next interest receipt date.

   d. do nothing and ignore the fact that the accounting period does not coincide with the bond's interest receipt date.

EXPLANATION: Think of the requirements of accrual accounting: revenues are to be recognized (recorded and reported) when earned and expenses are to be recognized when incurred. Interest is earned with the passage of time and is usually collected after the time period in which it was earned. Thus, to comply with the revenue recognition and realization principle, an adjusting entry is necessary to record accrued interest income (income earned but not yet received). (Solution = a.)

Question

4. At the statement of financial position date, fair value of Security A exceeds its cost, and fair value of Security B is less than its cost. Both securities are accounted for under the FV-NI model. How should each of these assets be reported on the statement of financial position?

	Security A	**Security B**
a.	Fair value	Fair value
b.	Cost	Cost
c.	Cost	Fair value
d.	Fair value	Cost

EXPLANATION: Review the accounting requirements under the FV-NI model. Securities under this model are required to be reported (measured) at fair value, with unrealized holding gains or losses included in net income. (Solution = a.)

Question

5. ABC Entertainment holds four equity securities at December 31, 2017. They are all accounted for under the FV-NI model. All securities were purchased in 2017. The portfolio of securities appears as follows at December 31, 2017:

	Cost	Fair Value	Difference
McKinnet Corp.	$100,000	$ 80,000	$(20,000)
Hip Corp.	220,000	230,000	10,000
Big Sea Corp.	210,000	150,000	(60,000)
Adams Corp.	140,000	145,000	5,000
Total	$670,000	$605,000	$(65,000)

What is the amount of unrealized holding gain (loss) to be recognized in 2017?
a. $(80,000)
b. $(65,000)
c. $0
d. $15,000

EXPLANATION: A security accounted for under the FV-NI model is remeasured to fair value at the end of each reporting period. Both unrealized holding gains and losses are included in net income under this model; therefore, the value of the total portfolio is considered in calculating the amount. (Solution = b.)

Question

6. During 2017, Cambridge Company purchased 2,000 Windsor Corp. common shares for $67,000 and accounted for the investment under the FV-NI model. Fair value of these shares was $61,000 at December 31, 2017. Cambridge sold all of the Windsor shares for $35 per share on December 3, 2018, incurring $2,500 in brokerage commissions. On December 3, 2018, Cambridge Company should record a gain on sale of investments of:
a. $500.   c. $6,500.
b. $3,000.   d. $9,000.

EXPLANATION: The gain is calculated as follows:

Selling price ($35 × 2,000 shares)	$70,000
Cost of sale—commissions	(2,500)
Net proceeds (or net selling price)	67,500
Fair value at Dec. 31/17	61,000
Gain on sale of investments	$ 6,500

(Solution = c.)

The FV-NI investment would have been adjusted to $61,000 on December 31, 2017.

Question

7. Before preparing its December 31, 2017, statement of financial position, Rahim
    Company appropriately recorded a $4,000 debit to its FV-NI Investments account.
    There was no change in the composition of Rahim's portfolio of FV-NI equity
    securities during 2018. The following information pertains to that portfolio:

Security	Cost	Fair value at	
		12/31/17	12/31/18
A	$ 50,000	$ 58,000	$ 65,000
B	40,000	39,000	38,000
C	70,000	67,000	50,000
	$160,000	$164,000	$153,000

    What is the adjustment required to FV-NI Investments at the end of 2018?

    a. $0
    b. $7,000 (credit)
    c. $11,000 (credit)
    d. $18,000 (credit)

    EXPLANATION: At the end of 2017, the FV-NI Investments account showed a bal-
    ance of $164,000. At the end of 2018, the fair value of the portfolio dropped
    by $11,000 to $153,000. Therefore, the FV-NI Investments account must be
    reduced by $11,000. (Solution = c.)

Question

8. An investor has long-term investments in shares. Regular cash dividends
    received by the investor are recorded as:

No significant influence	Significant influence—equity method
a. Income	Income
b. A reduction of the Investment in Associate account	A reduction of the Investment in Associate account
c. Income	A reduction of the Investment in Associate account
d. A reduction of the Investment in Associate account	Income

    EXPLANATION: If an equity investment does not give the investor significant influence
    over the investee, it is accounted for under the cost model, FV-NI model, or FV-OCI
    model. Under all three models, normal dividend revenue is recorded and included in
    net income. If the investor has significant influence over the investee, and the equity
    method is used, the investor would record its share of the investee's income (or loss)
    each reporting period. Dividends received would be recorded as a reduction of the
    Investment in Associate account. (Solution = c.)

Note that net income would also be affected by unrealized holding gains and losses for securities accounted for under the FV-NI model.

Question

9. Halton Corporation purchased 5,000 common shares of Bayside Corporation for $30 per share on January 2, 2017. Bayside Corporation had 50,000 common shares outstanding during 2017, paid cash dividends of $25,000 during 2017, and reported net income of $100,000 for 2017. Bayside Corporation's shares are not quoted in an active market. Halton prepares financial statements in accordance with ASPE. Halton Corporation should report investment income for 2017 in the amount of:

   a. $2,500.

   b. $7,500.

   c. $10,000.

   d. $12,500.

EXPLANATION: Because Halton Corporation owns only 10% of the outstanding common shares of Bayside Corporation, it is assumed that Halton cannot exercise significant influence over the financing and operating policies of Bayside. Therefore, under ASPE, the investment would be accounted for under the cost model or FV-NI model. Assuming there is no change in the shares' fair value since the purchase date, regardless of which model is used, Halton would report investment income equal to the amount of cash dividends received during the period ($25,000 × 10% = $2,500). (Solution = a.)

For an investment accounted for under the FV-NI model, net income would be affected by the change in fair value of the security from one period to the next, in addition to dividend revenue.

Question

10. When the equity method is used to account for an investment in common shares of another corporation, the journal entry on the investor's books to record receipt of cash dividends from the investee will:

   a. include a debit to Cash and a credit to Dividend Revenue.

   b. reduce the carrying amount of the Investment in Associate.

   c. increase the carrying amount of the Investment in Associate.

   d. be the same journal entry that would be recorded if the cost model were used to account for the investment.

EXPLANATION: The journal entry would be a debit to Cash and a credit to Investment in Associate. The credit portion of this entry would reduce the balance of the Investment in Associate account and, therefore, reduce its carrying amount. (Solution = b.)

Question

11. To which of the following investments would the equity method be appropriately applied?

    a. A 30% investment in preferred shares of a company

    b. A 20% investment in common shares of a company where the investor has no significant influence

    c. A 25% investment in subordinated non-voting shares of a company

    d. A 15% investment in the common shares of a company where the investor has significant influence

EXPLANATION: The existence of significant influence is the key factor here, regardless of percentage ownership. Note also that the investor's shares must be voting shares in order for the investor to have significant influence. (Solution = d.)

Question

12. On January 1, A Company Limited purchased 30% of the common shares of B Company Limited for $3.6 million. B's shares trade on a public stock exchange. At the time, the book value of B was $10 million. The excess paid was due to the excess of fair value over book value of identifiable intangible assets, which will be amortized over 15 years. During the year, B Company Limited had profits of $300,000, and dividends of $400,000 were paid. Fair value of the shares at year end was $3 million. Assume significant influence. What is the amount that should be recorded as investment income for the year?

    a. $90,000

    b. $120,000

    c. $50,000

    d. $0

EXPLANATION:

• Paid	=	$3,600,000
30% × 10,000,000	=	3,000,000
		600,000
		÷ 15 years
• Amortization	=	40,000
• Income	=	300,000
		× 30%
		90,000
• 90,000 − 40,000	=	50,000

(Solution = c.)

Question

13. Assuming the same information as in question 12 above, what would investment income be, assuming no significant influence and use of the cost model?

   a. No change
   b. $120,000
   c. $80,000
   d. $0

EXPLANATION: Assuming no significant influence and use of the cost model, investment income would be based on dividend revenue calculated as follows: $400,000 × 30% = $120,000. For no significant influence investments, any purchase price discrepancy is ignored, as are the earnings of the investee. (Solution = b.)

If accounted for under the FV-NI model or FV-OCI model, the investment would also be adjusted by the drop in fair value. Under FV-NI, the adjustment or unrealized holding loss would be recorded as an investment loss. Under FV-OCI, the adjustment or unrealized holding loss would be recorded in other comprehensive income.

Question

14. Assume that Guelph Inc. invests in a bond for $60,000. The bond is purchased at par and is accounted for using amortized cost. At year end, management has determined that there is no significant increase in credit risk, but that there is a 1% chance that the company will not collect 15% of the face value of the bond (which also represents the present value of the bond) in the next 12 months. The expected loss model is used. What is the amount of loss on impairment that will be reported?

   a. $90
   b. $600
   c. $900
   d. $0

EXPLANATION: If the company determines there is no significant increase in risk, the risk of default is considered for the next 12 months. The expected impairment loss is calculated as $60,000 × 1% × 15% = $90. (Solution = a.)

Chapter 10

Property, Plant, and Equipment: Accounting Model Basics

OVERVIEW

Assets that have physical existence and that are expected to be used in revenue-generating operations for more than one year or operating cycle, whichever is longer, are classified as long-term tangible assets, and more specifically as property, plant, and equipment. Some issues may arise in determining the acquisition cost of a fixed asset. For example, the initial acquisition may be the result of several expenditures, one fixed asset may be exchanged for another fixed asset, a fixed asset may be purchased on a deferred payment plan, or a fixed asset may be constructed internally by the company. After acquisition, a company using ASPE must measure property, plant, and equipment under the cost model. However, a company using IFRS may choose to apply the cost model or a different model in measuring property, plant, and equipment. After acquisition, the company may also incur expenditures related to existing fixed assets. Analysis of the nature of each expenditure is required in order to determine the proper accounting method. These and other issues, and their related accounting procedures, are examined in this chapter.

STUDY STEPS

Understanding Property, Plant, and Equipment within a Business Context

Property, plant, and equipment (PP&E) assets are **tangible assets** that are **used to generate income**. This income generation is what differentiates PP&E from inventory, which is **held for resale in the ordinary course of business**. Generally, PP&E is used up or wears out over time and must be replaced, except for land, which presumably retains its value over time.

PP&E is used to generate income while inventory is held for resale in the ordinary course of business. This is a key distinction, because PP&E is depreciated, while inventory is not.

From time to time, money must be spent on maintaining the revenue-generating capacity of the assets, and they must be safeguarded to reduce the risk of loss from fire, theft, and so on. Even though a certain asset may last a specific period of time (its **physical life**), the company might choose to use the asset for a shorter period (its **useful life**). At the end of the asset's useful life, there may be a **residual value**. The residual value is the estimated amount a company would receive today if it disposed of the asset, less any related disposal costs, if the asset were at the same age and condition expected at the end of its useful life.

- An asset's life may be defined as either useful or physical. **Physical life** is the asset's productive life, which may extend well beyond its useful life to a particular organization. **Useful life** represents the period over which the company intends to use the asset.

- **Residual value** is the estimated amount a company would receive today if it disposed of the asset, less any related disposal costs, if the asset were at the same age and condition expected at the end of its useful life. **Salvage value** is the estimate of the asset's net realizable value at the end of its physical life.

PP&E assets are considered to be nonmonetary assets since their value is not fixed in terms of dollars; that is, their value will change over time. A **barter transaction** occurs if a company trades another nonmonetary asset for PP&E, in which case the company faces the challenge of determining the new asset's cost. In general, the cost of the new asset acquired is determined by the fair value of the asset(s) given up (unless the fair value of the new asset received can be more reliably measured), and any gains or losses that result are recognized in income. This **fair value standard** applies to nonmonetary exchanges unless the transaction lacks commercial substance or fair values are not reliably measurable. If the nonmonetary exchange lacks commercial substance or fair values are not reliably measurable, the new asset's cost is determined by the carrying amount of the asset(s) given up, and no gain is recognized. However, a loss is recognized if the fair value of the new asset is less than the carrying amount of the asset(s) given up.

Becoming Proficient with Calculations and Accounting Methods Relating to PP&E

There are some complex calculations and accounting methods specific to this topic. For example, calculating the amount of borrowing costs to capitalize on self-constructed qualifying assets is a multi-step process, which will be discussed in this chapter. Under ASPE, a company can choose either to capitalize borrowing costs on self-constructed qualifying assets or to expense them as incurred.

Understanding the Effects of the Cost Model, Revaluation Model, and Fair Value Model

After acquisition, under IFRS, a company may maintain measurement of all PP&E, including investment property, under the cost model. However, under IFRS, the alternative measurement model for investment property is the fair value model, and the alternative measurement model for all other PP&E is the revaluation model.

Using the revaluation model and fair value model generally results in more current PP&E asset values on the statement of financial position. However, the effects of both models should be carefully considered. Changes in asset fair values may affect reported income and financial ratios (such as return on assets). However, changes in asset fair values do not necessarily reflect the company's performance, and do not usually affect the company's ability to yield returns from those fixed assets used in revenue-generating operations (as a change in return on assets would imply). Users should be aware of the financial statement effects of each model.

TIPS ON CHAPTER TOPICS

- **Tangible capital assets** are also referred to as **property, plant, and equipment, fixed assets**, or **plant assets**. Included in this section should be long-lived tangible assets that are currently being used in operations to generate goods and services for customers. Two exceptions to this guideline are (1) construction of plant in process, and (2) deposits on machinery. In each of these cases, the asset is not yet being used in operations but the related expenditures should be classified in the property, plant, and equipment section of the statement of financial position. Idle fixed assets are to be classified as other assets. Plant assets no longer used and held for sale are presented separately as held for sale on the balance sheet (if material). Under ASPE, assets held for sale retain their original classification as either current or non-current. Under IFRS, assets held for sale are generally classified as current assets.

(continued)

- In the context of accounting for PP&E, the term **capitalize** means to record as an asset by debiting the appropriate PP&E statement of financial position account. An expenditure can be capitalized only if it meets the definition of an asset. (For example, it would meet this definition if it is probable that the expenditure will bring some future economic benefit to the entity, and if the entity has control over that benefit.)

- In the context of tangible capital assets, **carrying amount** equals the balance in the asset account less the balance in the related accumulated depreciation account. Other terms for "carrying amount" are **book value**, **carrying value**, net asset value, and unamortized value. Under the cost model, book value may be very different from fair value. ASPE terminology may refer to fair value as fair market value or market value. The calculation of book value is **not** affected by estimated residual value or salvage value.

- IFRS terminology refers to amortization of property, plant, and equipment as **depreciation** of property, plant, and equipment.

- The same basic guideline that is used for determining inventory cost is also used for determining the acquisition cost of a plant asset. Specifically, the acquisition cost of a plant asset (initial carrying amount) includes all costs necessary to acquire the item, bring it to its intended location, and ready it for its intended use.

- In determining the cost of a plant asset, it is useful to refer to the definition of cost according to IAS 16. **Cost** is measured by the amount of cash paid or the fair value of the noncash consideration given to acquire the asset. **Fair value** is the price that would be received to sell the asset in an orderly transaction between market participants at the measurement date. When cash is given to acquire an asset, it is a relatively simple matter to determine the asset's cost. However, when a noncash asset is given in exchange, or when a deferred payment plan is involved, it is more challenging to determine the asset's cost.

- At acquisition, if the asset consists of component parts that are significant relative to the total cost of the asset, and the component parts have different useful lives or different patterns of use, the component parts should be capitalized separately. For example, consider an aircraft with a useful life of 15 years, containing an engine with a useful life based on flight hours and requiring replacement earlier than the body of the aircraft. Assuming that the cost of the engine relative to the cost of the aircraft is significant, under **component accounting**, the acquisition would be recorded as a debit to Aircraft—Engine (a PP&E asset account) for the cost of the engine, and a debit to Aircraft (also a PP&E asset account) for the balance of the aircraft cost. Component accounting allows significant components and components with different useful lives, different patterns of use, and/or different expected overhaul/replacement schedules compared with the whole asset, to be recorded and depreciated separately. The concept of component accounting exists under both IFRS and ASPE, but in practice, component accounting is more rigidly applied under IFRS.

- Under component accounting, components may be physical (tangible) or non-physical such as a **major overhaul or inspection**. If scheduled major overhauls or inspections will be required as a condition of operating the asset, an amount of the acquisition cost of the asset may be allocated to the cost of one overhaul, capitalized separately, and depreciated over the period until the first scheduled overhaul. The cost of the overhaul is estimated using the current cost of an overhaul at the time of acquisition of the asset. At the time of the first scheduled overhaul, the initially recorded overhaul is removed. This is done by debiting its accumulated depreciation account, debiting a loss on overhaul (if the asset was overhauled before the overhaul was fully depreciated), and crediting its PP&E asset account. The new overhaul is capitalized at cost and amortized over the period until the next overhaul.

● If a company constructs an asset, only **costs that are directly attributable** to the construction of the asset are capitalized. Borrowing costs that could have been avoided if the project to build the qualifying asset was not undertaken are considered directly attributable to the construction of the asset. Under IFRS, these **avoidable borrowing costs** must be capitalized and included in the cost of the asset.

● In general, **borrowing costs to capitalize** equals:

[(Lesser of asset-specific debt and weighted-average accumulated expenditures) × borrowing rate on asset-specific debt]

Less

Investment income on temporary investment of any asset-specific debt required to construct the asset

Plus, if asset-specific debt < weighted-average accumulated expenditures,

[(Weighted-average accumulated expenditures − asset-specific debt) × weighted-average borrowing costs on all other debt]

where **borrowing costs to be capitalized in a year cannot exceed total actual interest cost in the same year**, and **asset-specific debt** is amounts borrowed specifically for construction of the asset.

● When a **deferred payment plan** is involved in the acquisition of a noncash asset, pay careful attention to whether a fair interest rate is stated in the agreement. When an unreasonably low stated interest rate is in the agreement, interest must be imputed so that the effective amount of interest reported reflects the market rate of interest.

● There are several areas in accounting that use the formula to allocate a single sum between two or more items based on the **relative fair values** of the items involved. That formula is as follows:

$$\frac{\text{Fair value of one item in group}}{\text{Total fair value of ALL items in group}} \times \frac{\text{Amount to be}}{\text{allocated}} = \frac{\text{Amount assigned}}{\text{to item designated}}_{\text{in the numerator}}$$

● The above formula is used in Chapter 10 to allocate one lump-sum amount of cost to the individual assets acquired in a **lump-sum purchase** (often called a **basket purchase**). The formula is also used to allocate:

1. the proceeds from the issuance of several classes of securities,

2. the proceeds from the issuance of bonds with detachable warrants,

(continued)

3. the cost of certain inventory items to units based on their relative sales values, and

4. the cost of an investment.

● Under both IFRS and ASPE, when **one noncash asset is exchanged for another noncash asset**, the acquired asset is recorded at the total **fair value of the cash asset(s) and noncash asset(s) given up**, unless the fair value of the asset received is measured more reliably. The acquired asset is recorded at the carrying amount of the asset(s) given up only if: (1) the transaction lacks commercial substance or (2) fair values are not reliably measurable.

● In **recording an asset exchange**, whether the newly acquired asset is recorded at fair value or carrying amount of the asset(s) given up, the asset(s) given up are removed at their carrying amount. Removing a noncash PP&E asset given up typically requires a debit to accumulated depreciation to remove the asset's accumulated depreciation to date, and a credit to the PP&E asset account to remove the asset itself.

● Under IFRS, if a company exchanges some of its shares for a noncash asset, the fair value standard is applied differently. The acquired asset is recorded at the acquired asset's fair value, rather than the fair value of what is given up (in this case the shares). Fair value of the shares should be used only if fair value of the acquired asset cannot be reliably measured. ASPE requires only that the more reliably measured fair value be used.

● **Contributed assets** from non-owners and **government grants** are recognized under the income approach, which takes the benefit of the contribution into income over the life of the related asset, consistent with accrual basis accounting. Under the **cost reduction method** of the income approach, lower initial cost results in lower depreciation over the life of the asset. Under the **deferral method** of the income approach, the contribution or grant is recorded as a deferred revenue (a liability), which is amortized to revenue over the life of the asset on the same basis that is used to depreciate the related asset.

● Under the **revaluation model**, if the asset value is increased (resulting in a debit in the asset account), the corresponding credit is to **Revaluation Surplus (OCI)**, unless a loss due to revaluation **of the same asset** was previously recognized in income. In that event, the credit is recognized as a **Revaluation Gain** (included in income) to the extent that losses due to revaluation *of the same asset* were previously recorded in income. Any remaining credit balance is recorded in Revaluation Surplus (OCI). If the asset value is decreased (resulting in a credit in the asset account), the loss in value is recorded as a debit to the same Revaluation Surplus (OCI) account. However, the Revaluation Surplus (OCI) account can only be debited to the extent of the credit balance existing in the Revaluation Surplus (OCI) account *in respect of the same asset*. Any remaining debit balance is recorded as a **Revaluation Loss** (included in income). In all, over the life of an asset, net increase in value results in a net increase in accumulated other comprehensive income, and a net decrease in value is recognized through income.

● When revaluing an asset to fair value under the revaluation model, there are two acceptable methods of accounting for the change. (1) Under the **asset adjustment (or elimination) method**, the accumulated depreciation account to date is eliminated against the related asset account, and then the asset account is adjusted to the new fair value of the asset. (2) Under the **proportionate method**, both the asset account and the related accumulated depreciation account are adjusted proportionately (by the new fair value of the asset, divided by the current carrying amount of the asset), so that the net balance of both accounts amounts to the new fair value of the asset.

- Under the asset adjustment (or elimination) method and the proportionate method, the adjustment(s) to Revaluation Surplus (OCI) and/or Revaluation Gain/Loss (to income) are the same.

- Under the **revaluation model**, increases and/or decreases in asset value often affect income indirectly because depreciation is taken on the new revalued amount.

- Under the **fair value model**, all increases and decreases in fair value of the investment property are recorded as gains and losses, respectively, and recognized directly in income, and no depreciation is recorded for the remainder of the life of the investment property.

- After acquisition of an asset, **additions, replacements, major overhauls, and inspections** that add to the asset's future service potential are capitalized. These **capital expenditures** that increase the potential future economic benefit of the asset are expected to benefit the company for more than the current accounting period and should be capitalized in order to properly match expenses with revenues over successive accounting periods. **Replacements, major overhauls, and inspections** are usually related to parts of the asset that were included in the cost of the whole asset or initially capitalized as separate components under component accounting. When replacements, major overhauls, and inspections occur, the related costs or components are removed from the related PP&E account (by debiting accumulated depreciation for the related depreciation to date, and crediting the PP&E asset account). The new replacement, major overhaul, or inspection is then capitalized separately under PP&E.

- **Revenue expenditures** are expenditures that are made to yield the normal service potential from an asset and to maintain plant assets in good operating condition. Revenue expenditures do not increase an asset's future economic benefit or service potential and therefore should be expensed in the period incurred.

- There are two main methods of accounting for the cost of oil and gas (natural resource) properties. ASPE Accounting Guideline 16 (AcG 16 *Oil and Gas Accounting—Full Cost*) describes the **full cost method**. Under this method, companies capitalize all exploration costs, even those representing "dry holes." When assessing impairment, it is suggested that recoverability be assessed by cost centre (limit of one cost centre per country) rather than by individual property. Another common approach is the **successful efforts method.** Under this method, the costs of exploration are written off as expenses once it is proven that no reserves exist in a particular property. IFRS 6 does not specifically address either method.

CASE 10-1

PURPOSE: This case will review the costs to be capitalized for property, plant, and equipment.

Kelso Corporation is a newly formed private corporation that incurred expenditures related to land, buildings, and equipment.

Instructions

(a) Explain the distinction between a revenue expenditure and a capital expenditure. Explain why the distinction is important.

(b) Identify at least six costs that should be capitalized as the cost of land. Assume that land with an existing building is acquired for cash and that the existing building is to be removed immediately in order to provide space for a new building on that site.

(c) Identify at least five costs that should be capitalized as the cost of a building.

(d) Identify at least six costs that should be capitalized when equipment is acquired for cash.

Solution to Case 10-1

(a) A **capital expenditure** is expected to increase the future economic benefit or service potential of an asset. Property, plant, and equipment capital expenditures are capitalized (that is, recorded as assets) and, if related to assets of limited life, depreciated over their useful lives. A **revenue expenditure** is an expenditure that maintains the normal productive capacity of an asset and does not increase an asset's future economic benefit or service potential. Revenue expenditures are ordinary expenditures related to maintenance or repairs to maintain the asset's existing condition, and therefore are recorded as expense in the period incurred.

The distinction between capital and revenue expenditures is of significance because it involves the timing of the recognition of expense and, consequently, the determination of periodic earnings. This distinction also affects the net costs reflected in the asset accounts, which will be recovered from future periods' revenues.

If a revenue expenditure is improperly capitalized, net income of the current period is overstated, assets are overstated, and net income will be understated in all the future periods in which the improperly capitalized cost will be depreciated. If the cost is not depreciated, net income in the future periods will not be affected, but assets and retained earnings will continue to be overstated for as long as the asset remains on the books. If a non-depreciable capital expenditure is improperly expensed, net income of the current period is understated, assets are understated, and assets and retained earnings will be understated in all the future periods in which the asset would have remained on the books. If a depreciable capital expenditure is improperly expensed, net income of the current period is understated, assets and retained earnings are understated, and net income will be overstated in all the future periods in which the asset would have been depreciated.

(b) The cost of land may include:

1. purchase price,
2. title search fees,
3. delinquent property taxes assumed by buyer,
4. legal fees,

5. recording fee,

6. unpaid interest assumed by buyer,

7. cost of clearing, grading, and landscaping,

8. cost of removing old building (less salvage value)

9. special assessments such as lighting or sewers if they are permanent in nature,

10. landscaping if it is permanent in nature, and

11. any other cost necessary to acquire the land and bring it to its condition to operate as management intended.

(c) The cost of a building may include:

1. purchase price or construction costs (including an allocation of directly attributable overhead costs if self-constructed),

2. excavation fees,

3. architectural fees,

4. building permit fee,

5. avoidable borrowing costs incurred during construction (under ASPE, avoidable borrowing costs incurred during construction may be capitalized if that is the accounting policy used by the entity), and

6. any other cost necessary to acquire the building and bring it to its condition to operate as management intended.

> Typically, the cost of land includes the cost of activities that occur prior to excavation for a new building. Costs related to the foundation for a new building are elements of building cost.

(d) The cost of equipment may include:

1. purchase price (less discounts allowed),

2. non-recoverable sales tax,

3. installation charges,

4. freight charges during transit,

5. insurance during transit,

6. cost of labour and materials for test runs,

7. cost of special foundations, and

8. any other cost necessary to acquire the equipment and bring it to its required location and condition to operate as management intended.

EXERCISE 10-1

Purpose: This exercise will help you identify which expenditures related to property, plant, and equipment should be capitalized as capital expenditures and which should be expensed as revenue expenditures.

Instructions

Assume all amounts are material. For each of the following independent items, indicate by use of the appropriate letter if it should be:

C = Capitalized   or   E = Expensed

_____ (a) Invoice price of drill press.

_____ (b) Non-recoverable sales tax on computer.

_____ (c) Costs of permanent partitions constructed in an existing office building.

_____ (d) Installation charges for new conveyor system.

_____ (e) Costs of trees and shrubs planted in front of an office building.

_____ (f) Costs of surveying a new land site.

_____ (g) Costs of major overhaul of a delivery truck.

_____ (h) Costs of building new counters in a showroom.

_____ (i) Costs of powders, soaps, and wax for office floors.

_____ (j) Cost of janitorial services for an office and showroom.

_____ (k) Costs of carpets in a new office building.

_____ (l) Costs of annual termite inspection of a warehouse.

_____ (m) Insurance charged for new equipment while in transit.

_____ (n) Property taxes on land used for a parking lot.

_____ (o) Cost of a fan installed to help cool an old factory machine.

_____ (p) Cost of exterminator's services.

_____ (q) Costs of major redecorating of executives' offices.

_____ (r) Cost of fertilizers for shrubs and trees.

_____ (s) Cost of labour services for a self-constructed machine.

_____ (t) Costs of materials used and labour services expended during trial runs of a new machine.

Solution to Exercise 10-1

(a) C	(f) C	(k) C	(p) E
(b) C	(g) C	(l) E	(q) C
(c) C	(h) C	(m) C	(r) E*
(d) C	(i) E*	(n) E	(s) C
(e) C	(j) E	(o) C	(t) C

*This answer assumes the products were consumed during the current period. Material amounts of unused supplies on hand at the statement of financial position date should be reported as a prepaid expense (supplies).

EXERCISE 10-2

Purpose: This exercise will give you practice in identifying capital versus revenue expenditures.

Hughes Supply Company, a newly formed corporation, incurred the following expenditures related to Land, to Buildings, and to Machinery.

Cash paid for land and dilapidated building thereon		$ 350,000
Removal of old building	$55,000	
Less salvage	17,000	38,000
Surveying before construction to determine best position for building		1,400
Interest on short-term loans during construction		19,800
Excavation for basement before construction		60,000
Fee for title search charged by abstract company		1,800
Architect's fees		8,700
Machinery purchased (subject to 2% cash discount, which was not taken)		170,000
Freight on machinery purchased		4,120

Storage charges on machinery, necessitated by
   non-completion of building when machinery was
   delivered on schedule
		6,370

New building constructed (building construction
   took eight months from date of purchase of land
   and old building)
		1,750,000

Assessment by city for sewers (a one-time assessment)		4,900
Transportation charges for delivery of machinery from storage to new building		2,020
Installation of machinery		6,300
Trees, shrubs, and other landscaping after completion of building (permanent in nature)		16,900

Instructions

(a) Identify the amounts that should be debited to Land.
(b) Identify the amounts that should be debited to Buildings.
(c) Identify the amounts that should be debited to Machinery.
(d) Indicate how the costs above **not** debited to Land, Buildings, or Machinery
    should be recorded.

Solution to Exercise 10-2

	(a) Land	(b) Buildings	(c) Machinery	(d) Other
Cash paid for land and old building	$350,000			
Removal of old building ($55,000 − $17,000)	38,000			
Surveying before construction		$ 1,400		
Interest on loans during construction		19,800		
Excavation before construction		60,000		
Abstract fees for title search	1,800			
Architect's fees		8,700		
Machinery purchased			$166,600	$ 3,400 Interest Expense
Freight on machinery			4,120	
Storage charges caused by non-completion of building				6,370 Miscellaneous Expense (Loss)
New building construction		1,750,000		
Assessment by city	4,900			
Transportation charges—machinery				2,020 Miscellaneous Expense (Loss)
Installation—machinery			6,300	
Landscaping	16,900			
Totals	$411,600	$1,839,900	$177,020	$11,790

The purchase price of the machine is the **cash equivalent price** at the date of acquisition, which is the $170,000 reduced by the 2% cash discount allowed ($3,400), whether or not the discount is taken. The additional outlay of $3,400 is due to extending the time for payment, which is equivalent to interest (time value of money). The cost of the machine does **not** include the $6,370 storage charges and $2,020 transportation charges out of storage because these costs were not planned costs necessary to get the equipment to the location and condition to operate as management intended; rather, they were caused by construction delays (hence, a loss or miscellaneous expense).

CASE 10-2

PURPOSE: This case will review the rules for determining a plant asset's cost when the asset is acquired on a deferred payment plan or in a nonmonetary exchange.

Darko Limited, a public corporation, recently acquired two plant assets. One plant asset was acquired on a deferred payment plan, and one plant asset was acquired in an exchange for another nonmonetary asset.

Instructions

(a) Explain how to determine a plant asset's cost if it is acquired on a deferred payment plan.

(b) Explain how to determine a plant asset's cost if it is acquired in exchange for another nonmonetary asset.

Solution to Case 10-2

(a) A plant asset acquired on a deferred payment plan should be recorded at an equivalent cash price excluding interest. If a fair rate of interest is not stated in the sales contract, an imputed interest rate should be determined. The asset should then be recorded at the contract's present value, which is calculated by discounting the payments at an appropriate or imputed interest rate. The objective is to approximate the interest rate that the buyer and seller would negotiate in a similar arm's-length borrowing transaction. Factors such as the borrower's credit rating, the note's amount and maturity date, and prevailing interest rates would be considered in determining an appropriate interest rate. The interest portion of the contract price should be charged to interest expense over the life of the contract. Under IFRS, interest expense is recorded using the effective interest method.

(b) A plant asset acquired in exchange for another nonmonetary asset should be recorded at the fair value (cash equivalent value) of the consideration given up unless the fair value of the nonmonetary asset received can be more reliably measured. Any gain or loss on the exchange should be recognized in income because the earnings process is considered complete on the old asset and the earnings process is starting on the new asset.

The general measurement rule for nonmonetary transactions is fair value, unless:

● the transaction lacks commercial substance or

● fair values are not reliably measurable.

EXERCISE 10-3

PURPOSE: This exercise will provide an example of the capitalization of borrowing costs incurred during construction.

Noreno Company hired Newton Company to construct a special-purpose machine to be used in its factory. The following data pertain:

1. The contract was signed by Noreno on August 30, 2017. Construction began immediately and was completed on December 1, 2017.

2. To help finance this construction, Noreno borrowed $500,000 from the Bank of Saskatoon on August 30, 2017, by signing a $500,000 note due in three years. The note bears an interest rate of 10% and interest is payable each August 30.

3. Noreno paid Newton $300,000 on August 30, 2017, and invested the remainder of the note's proceeds ($200,000) in 5% government securities until December 1.

4. On December 1, Noreno made the final $200,000 payment to Newton.

5. Aside from the note payable to the Bank of Saskatoon, Noreno's only outstanding liability at December 31, 2017, is a $50,000, 9%, five-year note payable dated January 1, 2016, on which interest is payable each December 31.

Instructions

(a) Calculate the weighted-average accumulated expenditures, interest income, avoidable borrowing costs, total actual borrowing costs incurred, and borrowing costs to capitalize during 2017. Round all calculations to the nearest dollar.

(b) Prepare the journal entries needed on the books of Noreno Company at each of the following dates: August 30, 2017; December 1, 2017; and December 31, 2017.

Solution to Exercise 10-3

(a) Calculation of weighted-average accumulated expenditures:

Expenditures			Capitalization		Weighted-Average
Date	Amount	×	Period	=	Accumulated Expenditures
August 30	$300,000		$^{3}/_{12}$		$75,000
December 1	200,000		0		0
					$75,000

$$\text{Interest income: } \$200,000 \times 5\% \times \frac{3}{12} = \underline{\$2,500}$$

Avoidable borrowing costs:

Weighted-Average
Accumulated Expenditures $\times$ Interest Rate = Avoidable Borrowing Costs
$75,000   10% $7,500

Total actual borrowing costs incurred:

$500,000 \times 10\% \times \dfrac{4}{12}$ = $16,667 (on asset-specific debt)

$50,000 \times 9\%$ = $\underline{4,500}$ (on non-asset-specific debt)

$\underline{\$21,167}$

Borrowing costs to capitalize in 2017: $7,500 (lesser of avoidable borrowing costs and total actual borrowing costs incurred)

(b)

8/30	Cash	500,000	
	Notes Payable		500,000
	Machinery	300,000	
	Other Investments	200,000	
	Cash		500,000
12/1	Cash	202,500	
	Interest Income		
	($200,000 \times 5\% \times \frac{3}{12}$)		2,500
	Other Investments		200,000
	Machinery	200,000	
	Cash		200,000
12/31	Machinery [avoidable borrowing costs		
	from part (a)]	7,500	
	Interest Expense		
	($21,167 − $7,500)	13,667	
	Cash ($50,000 × 9%)		4,500
	Interest Payable		
	($500,000 \times 10\% \times \frac{4}{12}$)		16,667

EXPLANATION:

Assets that qualify for borrowing cost capitalization are qualifying assets that require substantial time to get ready for their intended use or sale. **Qualifying assets** can be: (1) assets that an enterprise constructs for its own use (such as facilities), or (2) assets intended for sale or lease that are constructed as discrete projects (such as ships or real estate projects). Borrowing costs cannot be capitalized for inventory that is routinely manufactured or otherwise produced in large quantities on a repetitive basis. Noreno's machine requires substantial time to construct for its intended use. Therefore it is a qualifying asset for capitalization of borrowing costs.

The amount of borrowing costs to be capitalized is the portion of the borrowing costs incurred during the asset's acquisition period that theoretically could have been avoided (for example, by avoiding additional borrowings or by using the funds expended for the asset to repay existing borrowings) if expenditures to construct the asset had not been made.

Avoidable borrowing costs are determined by applying an appropriate interest rate(s) to the weighted-average amount of accumulated expenditures for the asset during the period. The **avoidable borrowing costs on the asset-specific debt** would be reduced by the investment income on any temporary investment of the funds. The **avoidable borrowing costs on the non-asset-specific debt** is the total weighted-average amount of accumulated expenditures reduced by the weighted-average expenditures financed by asset-specific debt, multiplied by the weighted-average capitalization rate on the general-purpose debt.

The weighted-average amount of accumulated expenditures for the asset represents the average investment tied up in constructing the qualifying asset during the period. For Noreno, a $300,000 balance in Machinery for the three-month capitalization period (date of expenditure to the date the asset is ready for use) means an equivalent (average) investment of $75,000 on an annual basis. Noreno uses only the 10% asset-specific borrowing rate to calculate avoidable interest because asset-specific borrowing ($500,000) exceeds weighted-average accumulated expenditures.

The amount of borrowing costs to be capitalized is not to exceed the actual borrowing costs incurred. Thus, Noreno compares avoidable borrowing costs of $7,500 with total actual borrowing costs incurred of $21,167 and chooses the lower amount to capitalize. Any interest amounts earned on funds borrowed that are temporarily in excess of the company's needs are to be reported as interest income rather than used to offset the amount of borrowing costs to be capitalized. Thus, Noreno will report $2,500 as interest income, which will not affect the amount of borrowing costs to be capitalized.

In all, $7,500 of borrowing costs is capitalized with the cost of the machine, representing only the borrowing costs incurred on the $300,000 payment during the period of machine construction. The $200,000 remainder of the $500,000 note payable was not paid to Newton Company until construction was complete on December 1. The borrowing costs related to the $200,000 amount were not required to get the asset ready for its intended use, and therefore were not included in the calculation of borrowing costs to be capitalized.

EXERCISE 10-4

PURPOSE: This exercise will give you practice in accounting for the acquisition of a plant asset on a deferred payment plan.

St. John's Fishing Inc. purchased a computer network on December 31, 2016, for $200,000, paying $50,000 upfront and agreeing to pay the balance in five equal instalments of $30,000 payable each December 31 beginning in 2017. An assumed interest rate of 10% is implicit in the purchase price.

Instructions

Round amounts to the nearest cent.

(a) Prepare the journal entry(ies) at the date of purchase.

(b) Prepare an amortization schedule for the instalment agreement.

(c) Prepare the journal entry(ies) at December 31, 2017, to record the cash payment and the applicable interest expense (assume the effective interest method is used).

(d) Prepare the journal entry(ies) at December 31, 2018, to record the cash payment and the applicable interest expense (assume the effective interest method is used).

Solution to Exercise 10-4

(a) Time diagram:

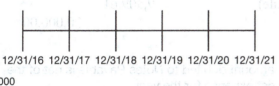

| | 12/31/16 | 12/31/17 | 12/31/18 | 12/31/19 | 12/31/20 | 12/31/21 |

$50,000
PV

$30,000 $30,000 $30,000 $30,000 $30,000

?
PV

Entry:

Equipment	163,723.70*	
Cash		50,000.00
Notes Payable ($30,000 × 3.79079)		113,723.70

*PV of a $30,000 ordinary annuity @ 10% for 5 years ($30,000 × 3.79079)	$113,723.70
Down payment	50,000.00
Capitalized value of equipment	$163,723.70

(b)

Date	Cash Payment	10% Interest Expense	Reduction of Principal	Liability Balance
12/31/16				$113,723.70
12/31/17	$ 30,000.00	$11,372.37	$ 18,627.63	95,096.07
12/31/18	30,000.00	9,509.61	20,490.39	74,605.68
12/31/19	30,000.00	7,460.57	22,539.43	52,066.25
12/31/20	30,000.00	5,206.63	24,793.37	27,272.88
12/31/21	30,000.00	2,727.12*	27,272.88	-0-
Totals	$150,000.00	$36,276.30	$113,723.70	

*This is the difference between $30,000.00 and $27,272.88, and includes a rounding effect of $0.17.

(c)

December 31, 2017

Notes Payable	18,627.63	
Interest Expense (see schedule)	11,372.37	
Cash		30,000.00

(d)

December 31, 2018

Notes Payable	20,490.39	
Interest Expense (see schedule)	9,509.61	
Cash		30,000.00

For each entry in (c) and (d), the amount debited to Notes Payable is net of the $30,000 cash payment and interest expense for the year.

EXERCISE 10-5

PURPOSE: This exercise reviews the calculations involved in a lump-sum purchase of plant assets.

Ellerton Company paid $800,000 cash for a package of plant assets. The package consisted of the following:

	Seller's Book Value	Fair Value
Land	$ 70,000	$ 360,000
Building	130,000	480,000
Equipment	230,000	300,000
Tools	110,000	60,000
Total	$540,000	$1,200,000

Instructions

(a) Prepare the journal entry for Ellerton to record the acquisition of these assets on the company's books.

(b) Why must you allocate the total cost to separate accounts for the individual assets? Why is it not appropriate to simply use "Plant Assets" as an account and record the total cost to that account? Explain.

Solution to Exercise 10-5

(a)

Land	240,000	
Buildings	320,000	
Equipment	200,000	
Tools	40,000	
Cash		800,000

EXPLANATION:

The total cost ($800,000) is allocated to the individual assets based on the relative fair values of the assets. The formula that can be used to accomplish this objective is as follows:

$$\frac{\text{Fair value of one item in group}}{\text{Total fair value of ALL items in group}} \times \frac{\text{Amount to}}{\text{be allocated}} = \frac{\text{Amount assigned to item}}{\text{designated in numerator}}$$

Land: ($360,000 ÷ $1,200,000) × $800,000 = $240,000

Building: ($480,000 ÷ $1,200,000) × $800,000 = $320,000

Equipment: ($300,000 ÷ $1,200,000) × $800,000 = $200,000

Tools: ($60,000 ÷ $1,200,000) × $800,000 = $ 40,000

$800,000

The sum of the four answers obtained by using the formula should total the amount you set out to allocate ($800,000, in this case).

(b) The total cost must be allocated to the individual assets because land is not subject to depreciation, and annual depreciation for the depreciable assets (with different useful lives and different patterns of use) may be calculated differently.

ILLUSTRATION 10-1

Accounting for Asset Exchanges

Type of Exchange	Accounting Guidance	Rationale
Monetary asset exchanged for monetary asset	Asset received recorded at total fair value of asset(s) given up (unless fair value of asset received can be more reliably measured) Recognize gains and losses immediately	Company's economic situation has changed, and earnings process related to exchanged (old) asset is substantially complete
Nonmonetary asset exchanged for monetary asset (or significant monetary asset plus nonmonetary asset) OR Monetary asset (or significant monetary asset plus nonmonetary asset) exchanged for nonmonetary asset	Asset received recorded at total fair value of asset(s) given up (unless fair value of asset(s) received can be more reliably measured) Recognize gains and losses immediately	Company's economic situation has changed, and earnings process related to exchanged (old) asset is substantially complete
Nonmonetary asset exchanged for nonmonetary asset	Asset received recorded at total fair value of asset(s) given up (unless fair value of asset(s) received can be more reliably measured) Recognize gains and losses immediately	Company's economic situation has changed, and earnings process related to exchanged (old) asset is substantially complete
Nonmonetary assets exchanged, where exchange lacks commercial substance, or where fair value of either asset in the exchange cannot be reliably measured	Asset received recorded at carrying amount (book value) of asset given up No gains recognized; losses recognized immediately	Company's economic situation has not changed; amount, timing, or risk of future cash flows has not changed; or earnings process related to exchanged (old) asset is not substantially complete

EXERCISE 10-6

PURPOSE: This exercise will allow you to practise recording an exchange of assets.

Sigmund Company exchanged equipment used in its manufacturing operations for equipment used in the operations of Pung Go Company. The following information pertains to the exchange:

	Sigmund Co.	Pung Go Co.
Equipment (cost)	$94,000	$94,000
Accumulated depreciation	60,000	34,000
Fair value of equipment	42,000	50,000
Cash given up	3,000	

Instructions

Prepare the journal entries to record the exchange on the books of both companies.

Solution to Exercise 10-6

Sigmund Company:

Equipment (New)	45,000	
Accumulated Depreciation	60,000	
Equipment (Old)		94,000
Cash		3,000
Gain on Disposal of Equipment		8,000

Fair value of assets given up:

Fair value of equipment	$42,000
Cash	3,000
	$45,000

Pung Go Company:

Cash	3,000	
Equipment (New)	50,000	
Accumulated Depreciation	34,000	
Loss on Disposal of Equipment	7,000	
Equipment (Old)		94,000

EXPLANATION:

Refer to **Illustration 10-1**, which summarizes the rules for asset exchanges. The fair value of what is given up is used to value the new equipment, unless certain circumstances apply, in which case the carrying amount of the old equipment is used. There is no indication that this exchange lacks commercial substance or that the fair value of the equipment exchanged is not reliably measurable. Therefore, Sigmund Company will record its new equipment at the fair value of the equipment it gave up plus $3,000 cash paid (resulting in a gain), and Pung Go Company will record its new equipment at the fair value of the equipment it gave up (resulting in a loss).

- It is important to note that Pung Go had an asset that was carried in excess of its fair value. Had this transaction not occurred (and a loss been recognized), it would be subject to impairment testing.

- Further, Pung Go's new equipment may be subject to an impairment test, since it has a fair value estimated at $42,000 but has been recorded at $50,000 (fair value of the asset given up). Care must be taken when recording fair values on nonmonetary exchanges to ensure that the new asset is not overvalued.

ILLUSTRATION 10-2

Expenditures Subsequent to Acquisition

A plant asset often requires expenditures subsequent to acquisition. Generally, four major types of expenditures may be incurred relating to existing plant assets:

- **Additions:** Increase or extension of existing assets
- **Replacements, major overhauls, and inspections:** Substitution of a new part or component for an existing asset, and performing significant overhauls or inspections of assets whether or not physical parts are replaced
- **Rearrangement and reinstallation:** Movement of assets from one location to another
- **Repairs:** Servicing expenditures that maintain assets in good operating condition

Costs that are incurred subsequent to acquisition are to be capitalized if they are material, nonrecurring in nature, and beneficial to future periods in that they do one or more of the following:

1. They extend the useful life of a plant asset.
2. They enhance the quality of a plant asset's services.
3. They add new plant asset services.
4. They reduce future operating costs of existing plant assets.
5. They are required to meet governmental regulations (such as environmental regulations).
6. They increase the number of units produced by a plant asset.

The accounting treatment appropriate for various costs incurred subsequent to the acquisition of capitalized assets is summarized as follows:

Type of expenditure	Normal accounting treatment
Additions	Capitalize cost of addition to asset account.
Replacements, major overhauls, and inspections	(a) **Carrying amount of old asset known or initially capitalized as a separate component:** Remove cost and accumulated depreciation on old asset, and recognize the difference as a loss (if any). Capitalize cost of replacement, major overhaul, and/or inspection (separately, if the cost is significant relative to the cost of the whole asset, and if component accounting is being applied*). (b) **Carrying amount of old asset unknown and not initially capitalized as a separate component:** Estimate cost and accumulated depreciation on old asset, and recognize the difference as a loss (if any). Capitalize cost of replacement, major overhaul, and/or inspection (separately, if the cost is significant relative to the cost of the whole asset, and if component accounting is being applied*). *Note that, in practice, component accounting is more rigidly applied under IFRS, and not as strictly applied under ASPE.
Rearrangement and reinstallation	(a) **If original installation cost and accumulated depreciation to date are known,** account for cost of rearrangement and/or reinstallation as a replacement. (b) **If original installation cost is unknown,** account for cost of rearrangement and/or reinstallation as an expense of the current period. Under ASPE, if the rearrangement and/or reinstallation cost is material in amount, if the cost of original installation was included in the original cost of the whole asset and likely depreciated to a significant extent, and if the rearrangement and/or reinstallation will increase the future economic benefit of the asset, the cost of rearrangement/reinstallation may be capitalized.
Repairs	(a) **Ordinary:** Expense cost of repairs in period incurred. (b) **Major:** As appropriate, treat as a replacement, major overhaul, or inspection.

CASE 10-3

PURPOSE: This case will provide a few examples of accounting for costs subsequent to the acquisition of fixed assets.

Hardent Resources Group has been in its plant facility for 20 years. Although the plant is quite functional, numerous repair costs are incurred to maintain it in sound working order. The company's plant asset book value is currently $750,000, as indicated below:

Original cost	$1,350,000
Accumulated depreciation	600,000
Book value	$ 750,000

During the current year, the following expenditures were made involving the plant facility:

1. The entire plant was repainted at a cost of $26,000.
2. The roof was an asbestos cement slate one; for safety purposes, it was removed and replaced with a new and better-quality roof at a cost of $62,000. Book value of the old roof was $31,000.
3. Because of increased demand for its product, the company increased its plant capacity by building a new addition at a cost of $315,000.
4. The plumbing system was completely updated at a cost of $53,000. The cost of the old plumbing system was not known. It is estimated that the useful life of the building will not change as a result of this updating.
5. A series of major repairs were made at a cost of $50,000, because parts of the wood structure were rotting. The cost of the old wood structure was not known. These extensive repairs are estimated to increase the useful life of the building.

Instructions

Indicate how each of these transactions would be recorded in the accounting records.

Solution to Case 10-3

1. Expenditures that do not increase the future economic benefit or service potential of the asset are expensed. Painting costs are considered ordinary repairs because they maintain the existing condition of the asset or restore it to normal operating efficiency.
2. It is assumed that the expenditure increases the future economic benefit of the asset. The book value of the old roof (cost and accumulated depreciation to date) should be removed, with the difference recognized as a loss (if any). The $62,000 cost of the new roof should be capitalized (separately, if the cost of the new roof is significant relative to the cost of the building, and/or if Hardent is applying component accounting).
3. This addition increases the future economic benefit and service potential of the plant. Any addition to plant assets is capitalized because a new asset has been created.

4. Assuming that the $53,000 update to the plumbing system is not a normal, recurring repair, the new plumbing system should be accounted for as a replacement and capitalized (separately, if the cost of the updated plumbing system is significant relative to the cost of the building, and/or if Hardent is applying component accounting). Even though the carrying amount of the old plumbing system is not known, it should be estimated and removed from plant assets. The original cost of the old plumbing system may be estimated based on current cost of a plumbing system similar to the old one, adjusted for normal price increases since the original purchase date, for example. Once the original cost is estimated, accumulated depreciation to date should be calculated and removed from accumulated depreciation of plant assets. The difference between the original cost and accumulated depreciation to date removed is recorded as a loss (if any).

5. See the discussion in item (4) above. These major repairs increase the useful life of the building and should be accounted for as replacements.

EXERCISE 10-7

Purpose: This exercise will (1) illustrate several different ways in which you may dispose of property, and (2) discuss the appropriate accounting procedures for each.

Presented below is a schedule of property dispositions for Friedlander Co.

Schedule of Property Dispositions

	Cost	Accumulated Depreciation	Cash Proceeds	Fair Value	Nature of Disposition
Land	$ 80,000	—	$ 64,000	$ 64,000	Condemnation
Building	30,000	—	7,200	—	Demolition
Warehouse	130,000	$22,000	148,000	148,000	Destruction by fire
Machine	16,000	6,400	3,600	14,400	Trade-in
Furniture	20,000	15,700	—	5,600	Contribution
Automobile	16,000	6,920	5,920	5,920	Sale

Additional information:

- **Land.** On January 7, Friedlander received a condemnation award from the government as compensation for unimproved land the company held primarily as an investment. (A condemnation comes about from a government unit exercising its right of eminent domain. Eminent domain is defined as "expropriation of assets by a government.") On April 7, the company purchased another parcel of unimproved land to be held as an investment at a cost of $70,000.

- **Building.** On May 4, land and building were purchased at a total cost of $150,000, of which 20% was allocated to the building on the corporate books. The real estate was acquired with the intention of demolishing the building, and this was done during August. Cash proceeds received in August represent the net proceeds from demolition of the building.
- **Warehouse.** On January 2, the warehouse was destroyed by fire. The warehouse had been depreciated by $22,000. On June 15, part of the insurance proceeds was used to purchase a replacement warehouse at a cost of $130,000.
- **Machine.** On October 31, the machine was exchanged for another similar machine having a fair value of $10,800, plus cash received of $3,600.
- **Furniture.** On July 2, furniture was contributed to a qualified charitable organization. No other contributions were made or pledged during the year.
- **Automobile.** On December 31, the automobile was sold to Dee Dee Burgess, a shareholder.

Instructions

Indicate how these items would be reported on the income statement of Fried-lander Co.

Solution to Exercise 10-7

The following accounting treatment appears appropriate for these items:

- **Land.** The loss on the condemnation of the land of $16,000 ($80,000 − $64,000) should be reported in the "other expenses and losses" section of the income statement. The $70,000 land purchase has no income statement effect.
- **Building.** There is no recognized gain or loss on the demolition of the building. The entire purchase cost ($30,000), decreased by the demolition proceeds ($7,200), is allocated to land.
- **Warehouse.** The gain on the destruction of the warehouse is calculated as follows:

Insurance proceeds		$148,000
Less: carrying amount of destroyed warehouse		
Cost	$130,000	
Accumulated depreciation	(22,000)	(108,000)
Realized gain		$40,000

The gain would be reported in the "other revenues and gains" section of the income statement.

- **Machine.** There is no indication that the exchange lacks commercial substance or that the fair value of the machines exchanged is not reliably measurable. Referring to the rules for asset exchanges, Friedlander Co. should record its new machine at the fair value of the machine it gave up, resulting in a gain calculated as follows:

Cost of new machine (fair value of machine given up)		$14,400
Plus: cash received		3,600
Less: carrying amount of old machine given up		
Machine	$16,000	
Accumulated depreciation	(6,400)	(9,600)
Realized gain		$8,400

The gain would be reported in the "other revenues and gains" section of the income statement. The cost of the new machine would be capitalized at $14,400.

- **Furniture.** The contribution of the furniture to a charitable organization would be reported as a contribution expense of $5,600 (the donated asset's fair value), resulting in a gain calculated as follows:

Contribution expense (fair value of donated asset)		$5,600
Less: carrying amount of furniture given up		
Furniture	$20,000	
Accumulated depreciation	(15,700)	(4,300)
Realized gain		$1,300

The contribution expense and the related gain may be netted, if desired, for reporting purposes.

- **Automobile.** The loss on sale of the automobile is calculated as follows:

Cash proceeds		$5,920
Less: carrying amount of automobile given up		
Automobile	$16,000	
Accumulated depreciation	(6,920)	(9,080)
Realized loss		$3,160

The loss would be reported in the "other expenses and losses" section of the income statement. This is a related party transaction; such transactions require special disclosure.

- The receipt of the condemnation award (January 7) represents an **involuntary conversion of nonmonetary assets to monetary assets**. Any gain or loss related to the transaction shall be recognized even though the enterprise reinvests or is obligated to reinvest the monetary assets in replacement of nonmonetary assets. The receipt of insurance proceeds due to the destruction of the warehouse is also an involuntary conversion of nonmonetary assets to monetary assets.

- When a plant asset is disposed of, accumulated depreciation must be updated before the gain or loss can be calculated. The discussions above assume that that updating has taken place.

- The sale of property, plant, and equipment for cash should be accounted for as follows:

   1. The carrying amount at the date of the sale (cost of the property, plant, and equipment less the accumulated depreciation) should be removed from the accounts.

   2. The excess of cash from the sale over the carrying amount removed is accounted for as a gain on the sale, whereas the excess of the carrying amount removed over cash from the sale is accounted for as a loss on the sale.

EXERCISE 10-8

PURPOSE: This exercise is designed to give you additional practice in analyzing changes in property, plant, and equipment accounts during a period. Problems of this type frequently appear on professional exams.

At December 31, 2016, certain accounts included in the property, plant, and equipment section of Busch Company's statement of financial position had the following balances:

Land	$100,000
Buildings	800,000
Leasehold improvements	500,000
Machinery and equipment	700,000

During 2017, the following transactions occurred:

- Land site number 52 was acquired for $1 million. Additionally, to acquire the land, Busch paid a $60,000 commission to a real estate agent. Costs of $15,000 were incurred to clear the land. During the course of clearing the land, timber and gravel were recovered and sold for $5,000.

- A second tract of land (site number 53) with a building was acquired for $300,000. The closing statement indicated that the land value was $200,000 and the building value was $100,000. Shortly after acquisition, the building was demolished at a cost of $30,000. A new building was constructed for $150,000 plus the following costs:

Excavation fees	$11,000
Architectural design fees	8,000
Building permit fee	1,000
Imputed interest on equity funds used during construction	6,000
(The company had no debt outstanding and no actual interest cost incurred.)	

The building was completed and occupied on September 30, 2017.

- A third tract of land (site number 54) was acquired for $600,000 and was put on the market for resale.
- Extensive work was done to a building occupied by Busch under a lease agreement that expires on December 31, 2023. The total cost of the work was $125,000, which consisted of the following:

Painting of ceilings	$ 10,000	estimated useful life is 1 year
Electrical work	35,000	estimated useful life is 10 years
Construction of extension to current working area	80,000	estimated useful life is 30 years
	$125,000	

The lessor paid one half of the costs incurred in connection with the extension to the current working area.

- During December 2017, costs of $65,000 were incurred to update fixtures and flooring in leased office space. The related lease will terminate on December 31, 2019, and is not expected to be renewed.
- A group of new machines were purchased under a royalty agreement that provides for payment of royalties based on units of production for the machines. The invoice price of the machines was $75,000, freight costs were $2,000, unloading charges were $1,500, and royalty payments for 2017 were $13,000.

Instructions

(a) Prepare a detailed analysis of the changes in each of the following statement of financial position accounts for 2017:

Land	Leasehold Improvements
Buildings	Machinery

Disregard the related accumulated depreciation accounts.

(b) List the items in the situation that were not used to determine the answer to part (a) above, and indicate where, or if, these items should be included in Busch's financial statements.

Solution to Exercise 10-8

(a)

BUSCH COMPANY
Analysis of Land Account
for 2017

Balance at January 1, 2017		$ 100,000
Land site number 52		
Acquisition cost	$1,000,000	
Commission to real estate agent	60,000	
Clearing costs	$15,000	
Less amounts recovered	5,000	10,000
Total land site number 52		1,070,000
Land site number 53		
Land value		200,000
Building value		100,000
Demolition cost		30,000
Total land site number 53		330,000
Balance at December 31, 2017		$1,500,000

BUSCH COMPANY
Analysis of Buildings Account
for 2017

Balance at January 1, 2017		$800,000
Cost of new building constructed on land site number 53		
Construction costs	$150,000	
Excavation fees	11,000	
Architectural design fees	8,000	
Building permit fee	1,000	170,000
Balance at December 31, 2017		$970,000

BUSCH COMPANY
Analysis of Leasehold Improvements Account
for 2017

Balance at January 1, 2017	$500,000
Electrical work	35,000
Construction of extension to current work area ($80,000 × $\frac{1}{2}$)	40,000
Office space improvements	65,000
Balance at December 31, 2017	$640,000

BUSCH COMPANY
Analysis of Machinery Account
for 2017

Balance at January 1, 2017		$700,000
Cost of new machines acquired		
Invoice price	$75,000	
Freight costs	2,000	
Unloading charges	1,500	78,500
Balance at December 31, 2017		$778,500

(b) Items in the situation that were not used to determine the answer to part (a) above are:

- Imputed interest of $6,000 on equity funds used during construction should not be included anywhere in Busch's financial statements. Only borrowing costs actually incurred during construction should be capitalized.

- Land site number 54, which was acquired for $600,000 and held for resale, should be included in Busch's statement of financial position in the investment classification.

- Painting of ceilings for $10,000 should be included as a normal operating expense in Busch's income statement.

- Royalty payments of $13,000 should be included as a normal operating expense in Busch's income statement.

EXERCISE 10-9

PURPOSE: This exercise will give you additional practice in accounting for assets with significant components.

Sailaway Corporation, a cruise vacation company, paid cash to acquire a new cruise ship on December 1, 2017. The total cost of the new cruise ship is $600 million, which is composed of:

	Cost	Useful Life
Engine	$180 million	12 years
Ship frame	225 million	15 years
Other components	195 million	10 years
	$600 million	

Sailaway Corporation uses straight-line depreciation, and all asset components are expected to have zero residual value. According to regulations, the cruise ship must be dry-docked every five years for mandatory inspection and overhaul. The first dry dock is scheduled for December 1, 2022, and should take one month

to complete. The current market price for a similar inspection and overhaul is $4 million, although the price is projected to increase to $5 million by 2022. Sailaway Corporation has a December 31 year end and prepares financial statements in accordance with IFRS.

Instructions

(a) Prepare the journal entry to record the acquisition on December 1, 2017.

(b) Prepare the journal entry to record 2018 depreciation on December 31, 2018.

(c) Prepare the journal entries to record the first dry dock completed on December 31, 2022, for an actual cost of $4.6 million, paid in cash. Assume that 2022 depreciation journal entries have already been recorded.

Solution to Exercise 10-9

(a) The journal entry to record the acquisition on December 1, 2017, is:

Ship—Engine	178,800,000	
Ship—Frame	223,500,000	
Ship—Other Components	193,700,000	
Ship—Major Inspection and Overhaul	4,000,000	
Cash		600,000,000

IFRS mandates the use of component accounting, which requires that significant components with differing useful lives and/or differing patterns of use be capitalized separately. Under component accounting, components may also include non-physical components such as major inspections and overhauls. Major inspections and overhauls are considered non-physical components because they may not necessarily result in physical replacement of an asset component. To apply component accounting, a portion of the $600-million total acquisition cost should be allocated to major inspection and overhaul.

It is assumed that the mandatory inspection and overhaul will be conducted on the entire ship. Based on the information given, a reasonable allocation method would be to deduct a proportionate share of the $4-million major inspection and overhaul cost from each physical component category. Given more information, a different allocation method may also be reasonable. Deducting the cost of the major inspection and overhaul based on the percentage cost of each component category relative to the total cost of the ship, the cost of Ship—Engine would be capitalized at $178.8 million ($180 million less [$180 million ÷ $600 million × $4 million]).

Note that only the first major inspection and overhaul is capitalized, and that it is capitalized at the current market price at the time of acquisition (not the price that is expected when the inspection and overhaul will be performed).

(b) The journal entry to record depreciation on December 31, 2018, is:

Depreciation Expense	49,970,000	
Accumulated Depreciation—Ship—Engine		14,900,000
Accumulated Depreciation—Ship—Frame		14,900,000
Accumulated Depreciation—Ship—Other Components		19,370,000
Accumulated Depreciation—Ship—Major Inspection and Overhaul		800,000

Depreciation on each component is calculated based on the company's straight-line depreciation policy and each component's useful life. For example, Accumulated Depreciation—Ship—Engine equals $14.9 million (cost of $178.8 million divided by a useful life of 12 years). The $4-million major inspection and overhaul is depreciated over the period until the next major inspection and overhaul is expected, which is five years.

(c) The journal entries to record the first dry dock completed on December 31, 2022, for an actual cost of $4.6 million, paid in cash, are:

Accumulated Depreciation—Ship—Major Inspection and Overhaul	4,000,000	
Ship—Major Inspection and Overhaul		4,000,000
Ship—Major Inspection and Overhaul	4,600,000	
Cash		4,600,000

By December 31, 2022, the first major inspection and overhaul is fully depreciated and should be removed from the books. The actual cost of the first inspection and overhaul is capitalized and depreciated over the period until the next major inspection and overhaul is expected (five years). Note that the first major inspection and overhaul was depreciated over the ship's first five years of operations, thus matching the expense of the inspection and overhaul to the revenues and periods that gave rise to the need for inspection and overhaul.

If dry docking had taken place before December 31, 2022 (or before the first scheduled inspection and overhaul), Accumulated Depreciation would have been debited (for accumulated depreciation to date), and Ship—Major Inspection and Overhaul would have been credited for $4 million. However, the debit to Accumulated Depreciation would be less than $4 million (since it would not have been fully depreciated yet), requiring a balancing debit to be recorded as a "Loss on Inspection and Overhaul" (included in "other expenses and losses" on the income statement).

EXERCISE 10-10

PURPOSE: This exercise will give you additional practice in applying the cost model, revaluation model, and fair value model.

Duncan Property Management Corporation accounts for its property, plant, and equipment as follows:

Class	Model
Land	Revaluation model
Buildings	Cost model
Investment property	Fair value model

Duncan is approaching its financial year end and has gathered the following information for its property, plant, and equipment, as at December 31, 2017:

Asset	Carrying amount	Fair value	Cumulative (income/(loss)) effect of past adjustments to fair value, on net income	Cumulative effect of past adjustments to fair value, on revaluation surplus (OCI)
Land—King St.	$ 525,000	$ 455,000	-	CR $53,500
Land—Queen St.	420,000	492,000	-	CR 33,700
Land—Front St.	345,000	400,000	$ (25,800)	-
Land—Total	$ 1,290,000	$ 1,347,000	$ (25,800)	CR $87,200
Building—King St.	$ 337,895	$ 295,000	-	-
Building—Queen St.	410,550	350,000	-	-
Building—Front St.	294,555	316,000	-	-
Buildings—Total	$ 1,043,000	$ 961,000		
Investment property—Condo A	$ 3,345,000	$ 3,150,000	$ 426,500	-
Investment property—Condo B	4,115,000	4,250,000	157,000	-
Investment property—Condo C	4,867,000	5,000,000	(75,000)	-
Investment property—Total	$ 12,327,000	$12,400,000	$ 508,500	

Additional information:

- Under the revaluation model, a revaluation is not required every year, although it has been three years since Duncan last revalued land. Duncan would like to revalue land this year since the fair value has become materially different from the carrying amount.
- The carrying amount of each building is net of accumulated depreciation updated to December 31, 2016.

Instructions

(a) Prepare any year-end journal entries required under Duncan's measurement models for property, plant, and equipment (excluding depreciation entries).

(b) Which property, plant, and equipment assets require 2017 depreciation journal entries, if any? Explain.

Solution to Exercise 10-10

(a) Revaluation model journal entries are:

Revaluation Surplus (OCI)	53,500	
Revaluation Loss (to income)	16,500	
Land—King St.		70,000
Land—Queen St.	72,000	
Revaluation Surplus (OCI)		72,000
Land—Front St.	55,000	
Revaluation Gain (to income)		25,800
Revaluation Surplus (OCI)		29,200

Fair value model journal entry:

Investment Property—Condo B	135,000	
Investment Property—Condo C	133,000	
Investment Property—Condo A		195,000
Gain on Investment Property		73,000

Note that under the revaluation model, a decrease in an asset's carrying amount is recorded as a debit to Revaluation Surplus (OCI), only to the extent of the credit balance in Revaluation Surplus (OCI) associated with that asset. For Land—King St., the remaining loss of $16,500 is included in income for the period. The $16,500 Revaluation Loss would be included in "other expenses and losses" on the income statement. Under the revaluation model, an increase in an asset's carrying amount is recorded as a Revaluation Gain (and included in income) only to the extent of a prior revaluation loss included in income, in respect of that asset. Any excess increase is recorded as Revaluation Surplus (OCI). For Land—Front St., the remaining gain of $29,200 is included in Revaluation Surplus (OCI) for the period.

Buildings are not revalued to fair value in this example, because assets under the cost model are not revalued to fair value. However, Building—King St. and Building—Queen St. have carrying amounts in excess of fair value and would be subject to impairment testing.

Under the fair value model, changes in value are reported directly in income in the period of the change. The gain in value of investment property would be included in "other revenues and gains" on the income statement, as would the $25,800 revaluation gain on Land—Front St.

(b) Only the buildings require depreciation entries. Under the revaluation model, depreciation is normally calculated based on the assets' revalued amounts. However, in this example, land is the asset accounted for under the revaluation model and depreciation is not usually recorded for land. Under the fair value model, no depreciation is recorded over the life of the investment property.

ANALYSIS OF MULTIPLE-CHOICE QUESTIONS

Question

1. Buena Vista Hotel purchases the Embassy Hotel with the intention of demolishing the Embassy Hotel and building a new high-rise hotel on the site. The cost of the Embassy Hotel should be:

   a. capitalized as part of the cost of the land.

   b. capitalized as part of the cost of the new hotel.

   c. written off as a loss when it is torn down.

   d. depreciated over the life of the new hotel structure.

   EXPLANATION: The cost of the land should include all costs necessary to acquire it and prepare it for its intended use by the buyer—which is to provide a site for a new building. (Solution = a.)

Question

2. A manufacturing company decides to build its own factory equipment. The cost of self-constructed plant assets may include which of the following:

	Materials	Labour	Manufacturing Overhead
a.	Yes	Yes	Yes
b.	Yes	Yes	No
c.	Yes	No	No
d.	No	Yes	No

Explanation: In addition to the materials and labour used to build a plant asset, the manufacturer should include a pro rata portion of the manufacturing overhead in the asset's cost. However, the asset should not be recorded for more than its fair value (the total amount that would be charged by an outside independent producer). (Solution = a.)

Question

3. J.-R. Mousseau Inc. has a fiscal year ending October 31. On November 1, 2016, J.-R. Mousseau borrowed $15 million at 12% to finance construction of a new plant. Repayments of the loan are to start the month following completion of the plant. During the year ended October 31, 2017, expenditures for the partially completed structure totalled $9 million. These expenditures were incurred evenly through the year. Interest earned on the unexpended portion of the loan amounted to $400,000 for the year. What amount of borrowing costs should be capitalized as at October 31, 2017?

   a. $140,000
   b. $540,000
   c. $1,400,000
   d. $1,800,000

Explanation: The new plant is a qualifying asset; therefore, under IFRS, avoidable borrowing costs incurred during the period of construction should be capitalized with the cost of the asset. The following steps show calculation of the borrowing costs to capitalize.

1. **Find the weighted-average accumulated expenditures for the period.**

Total expenditures at beginning of the period	$ 0
Total expenditures at end of the period	9,000,000
Sum	$9,000,000

   $9,000,000 ÷ 2 = average of $4,500,000

2. **Determine the avoidable borrowing costs on asset-specific debt.** Because the amount of asset-specific debt ($15 million) exceeds weighted-average accumulated expenditures ($4.5 million), avoidable borrowing costs on asset-specific debt equal $540,000 ($4.5 million multiplied by the 12% interest rate on asset-specific debt).

3. **Determine the avoidable borrowing costs on non-asset-specific debt.** Because asset-specific debt exceeds weighted-average accumulated expenditures, there are zero avoidable borrowing costs on non-asset-specific debt.

4. **Determine the borrowing costs to capitalize.** Borrowing costs to capitalize equal avoidable borrowing costs on asset-specific debt from step 2 ($540,000), plus avoidable borrowing costs on non-asset-specific debt from

step 3 ($0), where borrowing costs to capitalize cannot exceed actual borrowing costs incurred in the year (12% × $15,000,000 = $1,800,000). Therefore, borrowing costs to capitalize equals $540,000. (Solution = b.)

The interest earned ($400,000) is to be reported as interest income on the income statement and should not be used to offset the borrowing costs to capitalize.

Question

4. A local entrepreneur donated a building to Kihara Corporation to allow the company to expand and provide new jobs in the community. The building should be recorded on Kihara's books at:

    a. the cost of the lawyer's fees involved in handling the transaction.

    b. the value assigned by Kihara's board of directors.

    c. the building's fair value.

    d. no more than $1 because the building was obtained for no cost.

EXPLANATION: A donation (contribution) is a nonreciprocal transfer. (That is, the value goes in only one direction rather than in both directions as happens in an exchange transaction.) A nonreciprocal transfer is to be recorded at the fair value of the property, goods, or services involved. (Solution = c.)

The credit side to the above transaction would be recorded using the income approach, which reflects the contribution in net income over the period when the building is used. For example, under the deferral method of the income approach, the credit would be recorded as a deferred credit (a liability) and amortized to revenue over the useful life of the building.

Question

5. Holstrum Corporation intends to acquire some plant assets from Danyluk Corporation by issuing common shares in exchange. The cost of the assets should be measured by:

    a. the fair value of the shares.

    b. the fair value of the plant assets acquired.

    c. the book value of the shares.

    d. Danyluk's carrying amount of the assets.

EXPLANATION: In a share-based payment, IFRS requires that cost be measured by the fair value of the plant assets acquired. If the fair value of the assets acquired cannot be determined reliably, cost is measured by the fair value of the shares given in exchange. ASPE is more flexible, in that cost can be determined either by the fair value of the assets or the fair value of the shares, whichever is more reliably measured. (Solution = b.)

Question

6. Two home builders, Bolton Corporation and Pringle Homes Inc., agree to exchange tracts of land that each holds for purposes of development. An appraiser was hired and the following information is available:

	Bolton	Pringle
Book value of land given up	$ 60,000	$ 85,000
Fair value of land given up	100,000	115,000
Cash paid	8,000	

Under IFRS, in recording this exchange, should Bolton, Pringle, or both parties recognize a gain?

	Bolton	Pringle
a.	No	No
b.	Yes	No
c.	No	Yes
d.	Yes	Yes

EXPLANATION: In general, asset(s) received in nonmonetary transactions should be recorded at the fair value of the asset(s) given up (unless the fair value of the asset(s) received can be more reliably measured). Carrying amount is used only if the transaction lacks commercial substance or if fair values are not determinable. There is no indication of these conditions; therefore, fair value is appropriate. (Solution = d.)

Question

7. Refer to the facts of question 6. The amount to be recorded by Bolton for the acquisition cost of the new tract of land is:
   a. $68,000.
   b. $108,000.
   c. $92,000.
   d. $100,000.

EXPLANATION: The cost of the new asset is based on the fair value of what was given up, unless the fair value of what was received is more clearly evident. The fair value of what was given up equals $100,000 plus $8,000 in cash: $108,000. (Solution = b.)

Question

8. Under ASPE, which of the following measurement model applications would be permitted?

    a. Accounting for investment property under the fair value model

    b. Accounting for motor vehicles under the revaluation model

    c. Accounting for investment property under the cost model

    d. Accounting for investment property under the revaluation model

EXPLANATION: Under ASPE, the cost model is the only measurement model permitted. Note that choices (a) and (b) are permitted under IFRS, but that choice (d) is not permitted under either IFRS or ASPE. Under IFRS, investment property must be measured under either the cost model or the fair value model. (Solution = c.)

Question

9. Landsdowne Corporation acquires a gold mine at a cost of $700,000. Development costs that were incurred total $150,000, including $13,500 of depreciation on movable equipment to construct mine shafts. Based on construction to date, the legal obligation to restore the property after the mine is exhausted has a present value of $80,000. Landsdowne has publicly pledged an additional $15,000 (present value) for improved reclamation of the area surrounding the mine. The recorded acquisition cost of the mine on Landsdowne's books should be:

    a. $700,000.

    b. $850,000.

    c. $836,500.

    d. $945,000.

EXPLANATION: Assuming that this mine is not a "dry hole," the cost is the same under either the full cost or successful efforts method. All costs pertaining to acquisition, exploration, development, and site restoration are capitalized. (Solution = d.)

Question

10. Village Assets Inc., a publicly listed company, has a building with an initial cost of $500,000. At December 31, 2017, the date of revaluation, accumulated depreciation amounted to $100,000. The fair value of the building, by comparing it with transactions involving similar assets, is assessed to be $425,000. If Village follows the proportionate method for revaluing plant assets, the debit to Buildings on December 31, 2017, will be:

    a. $31,250.

    b. $25,000.

    c. $75,000.

    d. $0.

EXPLANATION: Revaluation would be based on the percentage change in the fair value when compared to the current carrying value of the building. The cost in the Building account as a result of revaluation is $500,000 × ($425,000 ÷ $400,000) = $531,250. The debit required to increase the Building account to this value is $531,250 − $500,000 = $31,250. (Solution = a.)

CASE STUDY

Laidle Disposal Limited (Part 1)

(Part 2 is in Chapter 11.)

Laidle Disposal Limited (LDL) is a small company that collects household garbage and disposes of it in a manner that is acceptable to the communities it services. The company has a fleet of trucks that pick up the garbage weekly. The garbage is then trucked to a local disposal site where it is dumped and then covered with topsoil. LDL is usually the owner of the disposal site, having purchased the site after required permits for zoning were obtained from government authorities.

This is the first year that LDL will be up and running and Leonard Laidle, the president of the company, is deliberating how he should account for the landfill sites (either as inventory or as fixed assets). The sites are purchased, filled with garbage, and ultimately sold as industrial land. The resale will be accompanied by a guarantee that no toxic materials were buried in the landfill.

Financial statements are presented to prospective client communities to obtain new contracts and to existing client communities to maintain existing contracts. Obtaining new contracts and maintaining existing contracts depends on competitive bidding, profile in the community, past work performance, financial stability, and adherence to strict environmental standards.

Instructions

As an independent consultant to Leonard Laidle, discuss the financial reporting issues and provide recommendations.

Suggested Approach to Case Study

Overview

The financial statements will be presented to prospective and existing client communities, which will focus on financial stability and adherence to environmental standards. Management will want the financial statements to show the company in the most favourable light (that is, maximize profits and assets and minimize negative disclosures). The statements will likely be constrained by ASPE since the users will want reliable statements.

Analysis

Issue: Are the landfill sites inventory (in which case they do not have to be depreciated) or are they fixed assets (in which case they must be depreciated)?

To the extent that the land is purchased and always resold, likely at a profit, it could be deemed inventory. On the other hand, land resale is incidental to the real reason for buying the land, which is to fill it up with waste. The process of filling it up with waste is LDL's primary revenue-producing activity; land resale is secondary. Many fixed assets are resold once their usefulness has ended.

Recommendation

It would, therefore, seem reasonable to treat the landfill sites as fixed assets.

The inventory versus fixed assets issue can be very difficult at times. Consider an organization that has returnable containers (such as a brewery or a water cooler company). Are these containers inventory or fixed assets? It is likely they are fixed assets, but consider the impact the decision can have on the financials—current versus long-term, non-depreciable versus depreciable, and lower of cost and net realizable value versus recoverable amount. It is important to consider the impact decisions like this have on the external financial statements.

Chapter 11

Depreciation, Impairment, and Disposition

OVERVIEW

Expenses arise from the cost of goods or services that are consumed in the process of generating revenue. When a long-term tangible asset is acquired, it represents a bundle of services to be consumed in generating future revenue. The total depreciable cost of these services equals the acquisition cost of the asset **minus** the asset's expected (estimated) residual value. In a process called **depreciation**, this total cost is allocated or charged to expense over the accounting periods during which the asset is used or available for use. **Depletion** is the process of allocating the cost of natural resource assets to inventory (and later to cost of goods sold). Over the life of a long-term tangible asset, it may become apparent that the asset's carrying amount may not be recoverable, in which case the asset is subject to **impairment** testing and possibly written down to a lower carrying amount. Accounting for long-lived assets held for sale and **disposal** of long-lived assets is also covered in this chapter.

STUDY STEPS

Understanding the Concept of Depreciation within a Business Context

Depreciation is a systematic and rational **allocation of costs** over the useful life of a long-lived tangible asset. While judgements and estimates are involved in its calculation, depreciable components and amounts, as well as depreciation periods and patterns selected, should result in cost allocation that reasonably reflects the asset's economic benefits consumed by the entity each period. For entities that have depreciable assets that represent a significant portion of total assets reported on the statement of financial position, depreciation expense can have a material impact on net income. Net income is a key number for financial statement users and management in their decision-making.

Choice of depreciable components and amounts, as well as depreciation periods and patterns, can impact net income significantly and, hence, impact users' decisions significantly.

Depreciation has no cash flow impact, and depreciation is not a reserve of funds intended for asset replacement, although allocating the cost of the asset to the product that it is used to produce, or to the periods in which the product will be produced or sold, is very important from a business perspective. It helps management determine the **full cost** to produce a product or to run the business.

Even though depreciation has no cash flow impact, it provides important information for product pricing as well as strategic decisions (such as deciding whether or not to stay in business).

Capital cost allowance (CCA) is the depreciation method for tax purposes according to the Income Tax Act. CCA is the amount that may be deducted for tax purposes in arriving at taxable income. The Income Tax Act specifically prescribes how CCA should be calculated, unlike IFRS and ASPE, which require judgements and estimates in the calculation of depreciation. Depreciation under IFRS and ASPE results in reasonable matching of costs with revenues each period, whereas the Income Tax Act has different objectives and may, for example, encourage spending on certain types of assets in order to promote job creation. For instance, the Income Tax Act might allow certain assets to be charged to taxable income over a shorter period of time, thereby giving the company a tax break earlier in the life of the asset.

Depreciation under IFRS and ASPE results in reasonable matching of costs with revenues each period, whereas CCA (depreciation for tax purposes) may provide incentives for businesses to invest in certain types of assets.

Becoming Proficient in Calculating Depreciation under the Various Generally Accepted Methods

Any long-term asset that has a limited life should be depreciated in order to reasonably **match** the cost of the asset with the revenue that it helps generate. The three most widely used depreciation methods are straight-line, decreasing charge, and activity method.

In deciding which depreciation method to apply, note that the method used should reflect the pattern in which the entity is expected to consume the benefits of the asset. Also, consider the effect that depreciation expense plus expected repairs and maintenance expense would have on net income at the beginning of the asset's useful life and toward the end of its useful life. What is the pattern over time, and would the depreciation method chosen result in reasonable overall allocation of costs to revenues earned?

Understanding the Accounting Issues related to Asset Impairment

Impairment is a condition that exists when the carrying amount of a long-lived asset exceeds its **recoverable amount**. Impairment may be caused by **external factors** (such as a significant decrease in the asset's market value), or **internal factors** (such as a significant change in the extent or manner in which the asset is used by the company). If any factors or indicators of impairment arise, the recoverable amount of the asset is calculated in order to apply impairment testing. IFRS requires that assets be assessed on an annual basis for indicators of impairment. Calculation of the recoverable amount, measurement of an impairment loss, and rules for subsequent recovery of impairment losses are each different under IFRS and ASPE.

Understanding the Accounting Issues related to Disposition of Long-Lived Assets

If a long-lived asset is to be disposed of by sale, then it is reclassified as **held for sale** and remeasured to the lower of the carrying amount and fair value less costs to sell. There are strict criteria for classifying an asset as held for sale, which were discussed in Chapter 4 under discontinued operations.

If a long-lived asset is to be disposed of other than by sale, it is not reclassified. It will, however, be subject to impairment testing as discussed above.

TIPS ON CHAPTER TOPICS

- **Depreciation** refers to amortization of tangible assets, and **depletion** refers to amortization of wasting assets such as oil and gas or forestry industries. **Amortization** refers to cost allocation of intangible assets.

- **Four basic questions in the depreciation process** are:

  1. What asset components (or component groups consisting of minor assets categorized together) should be depreciated separately?

  2. What is the depreciable amount of each asset component or component group of assets?

  3. Over what period should each be depreciated?

  4. What pattern and method of depreciation would best reflect how the economic benefits of each component or component group would be consumed?

  Separation of asset costs into asset components, and therefore depreciation of assets by component, is more strictly applied under IFRS than under ASPE (as discussed in Chapter 10).

- For most depreciation methods, the **depreciable amount** is cost less expected net residual value. The exception to this rule is the declining-balance method, under which the residual value is not deducted from the cost to arrive at the depreciable amount. Instead, the declining-balance rate is multiplied by the asset's carrying amount at the beginning of each period to arrive at depreciation for the period. Depreciation is recorded this way until the asset's carrying amount reaches its residual value, at which time the asset is no longer depreciated going forward.

- **Residual value** is the estimated amount the company would receive today if it disposed of the asset, less any related disposal costs, if the asset were at the same age and condition expected at the end of its useful life. Therefore, residual value is related to an asset's useful life to the company. **Salvage value** (or scrap value) is the asset's net realizable value at the end of its total service life (which is equal to or greater than its useful life to the company), and is usually not a factor in calculating depreciation.

- Depreciation begins when the asset is **available for use** (when it is in place and in the condition necessary for it to be able to operate as management intends), not when the asset is put into use. For example, consider a building that is constructed for use by a company that does not move into the building for a period of time. Depreciation is calculated from the date that construction is complete and the building is ready for use, not the date that the company begins operating out of the building.

- The **declining-balance depreciation** method applies a constant depreciation rate to a declining book value to calculate depreciation. If the rate used is twice the straight-line rate, the method is referred to as the **200% declining-balance method** or the **double-declining-balance method**.

- The **activity method** is often called the **variable charge** approach, or the **unit of production method**. This is most useful when use of the asset in producing revenue streams differs from one period to another. A limitation of this method is that it is often difficult to arrive at a reliable measure of total units of output to be received over the useful life of the asset.

● Under IFRS, estimates of an asset's residual value, its useful life, and the pattern of consumption of the asset's benefits should be reviewed at least annually. Changes in these estimates (which would affect depreciation expense) are accounted for **prospectively**, meaning remaining book value of the asset is depreciated using the revised estimates in the current year and going forward.

● The **book value** of a plant asset is determined by deducting the balance of accumulated depreciation and accumulated impairment losses from the balance of the related plant asset account. Under the cost model, the balance in the related asset account is the asset's original cost. Under the revaluation model asset adjustment (or elimination) method, the balance in the related asset account is the asset's fair value. Thus, estimated residual value does not directly affect the calculation of book value. Book value is often called **carrying value**, **carrying amount**, or **net asset value**.

● It is not uncommon for companies to have two different "sets of books" because financial reporting to shareholders can use any acceptable depreciation method under IFRS or ASPE, while tax reporting requires companies to use the capital cost allowance (CCA) depreciation method required by the Canada Revenue Agency.

● **Existence of external or internal indicators** of asset impairment would require a company to conduct **impairment testing** on the asset. Asset impairment occurs if carrying amount exceeds recoverable amount. Recoverable amount under IFRS equals the higher of the *discounted* future cash flows (value in use) of the asset or current fair value less costs to sell, whereas recoverable amount under ASPE equals the *undiscounted* future cash flows of the asset. Recoverable amounts under IFRS and ASPE may be especially different if the long-term asset is forecast to have cash flows lasting many years! Therefore, it is quite possible that an asset may be impaired under IFRS, but not impaired under ASPE.

● **If carrying amount exceeds recoverable amount, an impairment loss should be recorded**. Under IFRS, an impairment loss equals carrying amount less recoverable amount, and the asset's carrying amount is decreased to its recoverable amount. Under ASPE, an impairment loss equals carrying amount less fair value, and the asset's carrying amount is decreased to its fair value. Fair value may involve a calculation of the asset's net cash flows on a discounted basis. Under both IFRS and ASPE, impairment losses are recognized in profit or loss in the year of impairment, except for impairment losses for assets under the revaluation model (which are recognized as revaluation decreases).

● In the years after recognition of an impairment loss, the asset is monitored for indicators of further impairment, and possibly a further asset writedown. Under IFRS, the asset is also monitored for indicators of impairment reversal and a possible **recovery of impairment losses** previously recognized. In recognizing the recovery of impairment losses for assets under the IFRS cost model, the asset's carrying amount cannot exceed what it would have

(continued)

been (net of depreciation) if the original impairment loss had never been recognized. For recovery of impairment losses for assets under the revaluation model, if the recoverable amount exceeds the carrying amount, the full amount of impairment losses previously recognized may be recorded as a revaluation increase. Recovery of impairment losses is not permitted under ASPE.

- If a **cash generating unit (CGU)** of assets is impaired, an asset writedown is allocated to each asset in the group, based on relative carrying amounts. Note that a CGU is not the same as a group of minor assets grouped and capitalized into one component under component accounting. A CGU is a level of impairment testing, or a set of individually capitalized assets whose collective carrying amount is compared with their collective recoverable amount for impairment testing. Therefore, if a CGU is impaired and gives rise to an impairment loss, that loss would affect the carrying amount of each asset in the CGU (each of which has its own carrying amount). Under ASPE, no individual asset in the group can be reduced to below its fair value, if known. Under IFRS, no individual asset in the group can be reduced to below the highest of its fair value less costs to sell, its value in use, or zero.

- Under the IFRS **revaluation model**, an impairment loss is accounted for on the same basis as a revaluation decrease, as explained in Chapter 10. The impairment loss is charged first through other comprehensive income to the extent that any revaluation surplus exists for that asset, and only the excess impairment loss is recognized in income.

- Under the IFRS **fair value model**, impairment of investment property is reflected and accounted for as a decrease in the fair value of the investment property.

EXERCISE 11-1

PURPOSE: This exercise will give you practice in calculating depreciation for three successive periods with two commonly used methods.

Lower Lakes Company purchased equipment on January 1, Year 1, at a cost of $720,000. The asset is expected to have a useful life of 10 years and a residual value of $40,000.

Instructions

(a) Calculate the amount of depreciation for each of years 1 through 3 using the straight-line depreciation method.

(b) Calculate the amount of depreciation for each of years 1 through 3 using the double-declining-balance method.

Solution to Exercise 11-1

(a) $\dfrac{\$720,000 - \$40,000}{10} = \underline{\$68,000}$ Depreciation for each of years 1 through 3

(b) Double-declining-balance depreciation $= \dfrac{100\%}{10} \times 2 = 20\%$

$$\$720,000 \times 20\% = \underline{\$144,000} \quad \text{Depreciation Year 1}$$

$$(\$720,000 - \$144,000) \times 20\% = \underline{\$115,200} \quad \text{Depreciation Year 2}$$

$$(\$720,000 - \$144,000 - \$115,200) \times 20\% = \underline{\$92,160} \quad \text{Depreciation Year 3}$$

EXERCISE 11-2

PURPOSE: This exercise is designed to test your ability to solve for missing data by applying your knowledge regarding depreciation calculations.

Athabasca Company acquired a plant asset at the beginning of year 1. The asset has an estimated useful life of six years. An employee has prepared depreciation schedules for this asset using three different methods to compare the results of using one method with the results of using other methods. You are to assume that the following schedules have been correctly prepared for this asset using the (1) straight-line (SL) method, (2) activity method (AM), and (3) double-declining-balance (DDB) method (switching to the straight-line method after the mid-point of the asset's useful life).

Year	Straight-Line	Activity	Double-Declining-Balance
1	$ 6,500	$12,000	$15,000
2	6,500	10,000	10,000
3	6,500	6,000	6,667
4	6,500	5,000	2,444
5	6,500	4,000	2,444
6	6,500	2,000	2,445
Total	$39,000	$39,000	$39,000

Instructions

Answer the following questions.

(a) What is the cost of the asset being depreciated?

(b) What amount, if any, was used in the depreciation calculations for the residual value of this asset?

(c) Which method will produce the highest charge to income in year 1?

(d) Which method will produce the highest charge to income in year 4?

(e) Which method will produce the highest book value for the asset at the end of year 3?

(f) If the asset were sold at the end of year 3, which method would yield the highest gain (or lowest loss) on disposal of the asset?

Solution to Exercise 11-2

(a) If there is any residual value and the amount is unknown (as is the case here), the cost of the asset can be determined by looking at data for the double-declining-balance method in year 1.

100% ÷ 6 = 16.67%; 16.67% × 2 = 33.3%

Cost × 33.3% = $15,000; $15,000 ÷ 0.33 = $45,000 cost of the asset

(b) $45,000 cost (answer a) − $39,000 total depreciation = $6,000 residual value

EXPLANATION: Write down the formula for each of the depreciation methods mentioned. Fill in the data given for year 1. Analyze what remains to be solved.

(Cost − Residual Value) ÷ Estimated Useful Life = SL depreciation

(Cost − Residual Value) ÷ 6 = $6,000

$$\frac{(\text{Cost} - \text{Residual Value})}{\text{Total Estimated Units}} = \text{AM depreciation rate}$$

AM depreciation rate × Number of units in year 1 = AM depreciation year 1

AM depreciation rate × Number of units in year 1 = $10,000

DDB depreciation rate × Cost = DDB depreciation

33.3% × Cost = $15,000

Cost and residual value cannot be determined using the formulas for SL and AM above. However, cost can be determined using the formula for DDB, as it was in part (a). Residual value can be solved, knowing the cost is $45,000.

(c) The highest charge to income for year 1 will be yielded by the double-declining-balance method.

EXPLANATION: Examine the depreciation schedules. Notice the method that results in the highest depreciation amount for year 1.

(d) The highest charge to income for year 4 will be yielded by the straight-line method.

EXPLANATION: Examine the depreciation schedules given. Notice the method that results in the highest depreciation amount for year 4.

(e) The method to yield the highest book value at the end of year 3 would be the method that yields the lowest accumulated depreciation at the end of year 3, which is the straight-line method.

EXPLANATION: Write down the formula to calculate book value: Cost − Accumulated Depreciation = Book Value. For a high book value, accumulated depreciation should be low. Examine the depreciation schedules to determine the method that would yield the lowest total depreciation for the first three years.

Calculations:

SL = $45,000 − ($6,500 + $6,500 + $6,500)
   = $25,500 book value at the end of year 3.

AM = $45,000 − ($12,000 + $10,000 + $6,000)
   = $17,000 book value at the end of year 3.

DDB = $45,000 − ($15,000 + $10,000 + $6,667)
   = $13,333 book value at the end of year 3.

(f) The method to yield the highest gain (or lowest loss) if the asset is sold at the end of year 3 would be the method that yields the lowest book value at the end of year 3. In this case, it is the double-declining-balance method.

EXPLANATION: Write down the formula to calculate gain or loss on disposal: Selling Price − Book Value = Gain (Loss). For a high gain, book value should be low. Examine the formula for book value. For a low book value, accumulated depreciation should be high. Use the depreciation schedules to determine the method that would yield the highest accumulated depreciation balance at the end of three years.

EXERCISE 11-3

PURPOSE: This exercise will allow you to practise using various depreciation methods and it will also give you the opportunity to compare the results of using one method with the results of using another method.

On January 1, 2017, Inkwell Company, a machine-tool manufacturer, acquires a piece of new industrial equipment for $1.3 million. The new equipment has a useful life of six years and a residual value of $100,000. Inkwell estimates that the new equipment can produce a total of 75,000 units and is expected to produce 15,000 units in its first year. Production is estimated to decline by 1,000 units per year over the remaining useful life of the equipment.

The following depreciation methods may be used:

- Straight-line
- Double-declining-balance
- Unit of production

Instructions

(a) Identify which depreciation method would result in maximization of profits for the **three**-year period ending December 31, 2019. Prepare a schedule showing the amount of accumulated depreciation at December 31, 2019, under the method selected (show supporting calculations in good form). Ignore present value and income tax considerations in your answer.

(b) Identify which depreciation method would result in minimization of profits for the **three**-year period ending December 31, 2019. Prepare a schedule showing the amount of accumulated depreciation at December 31, 2019, under the method selected (show supporting calculations in good form). Ignore present value and income tax considerations in your answer.

Solution to Exercise 11-3

(a) The straight-line method of depreciation would result in maximization of profits for financial statement reporting for the three-year period ending December 31, 2019.

INKWELL COMPANY
Accumulated Depreciation Using
Straight-Line Method
December 31, 2019

(Cost − Residual Value) ÷ Estimated Useful Life

($1,300,000 − $100,000) ÷ 6 years = $200,000

Year	Depreciation Expense	Accumulated Depreciation
2017	$200,000	$200,000
2018	200,000	400,000
2019	200,000	600,000
	$600,000	

(b) The double-declining-balance method of depreciation would result in minimization of profits for the three-year period ending December 31, 2019.

INKWELL COMPANY
Accumulated Depreciation Using
Double-Declining-Balance Method
December 31, 2019

Straight-line rate is six years, or 16.67%. Double-declining-balance rate is 33.3% (16.67% × 2). Ignore residual value.

Year	Book Value at Beginning of Year	Depreciation Expense	Accumulated Depreciation
2017	$1,300,000	$433,333	$433,333
2018	866,667	288,889	722,222
2019	577,778	192,593	914,815
		$914,815	

Other supporting calculations:

INKWELL COMPANY
Accumulated Depreciation Using
Unit of Production Method
December 31, 2019

(Cost – Residual Value) ÷ Total Units of Output = ($1,300,000 − $100,000) ÷ 75,000 = $16.00 depreciation expense per unit produced

15,000 × $16.00 = $240,000
14,000 × $16.00 = $224,000
13,000 × $16.00 = $208,000

Year	Depreciation Expense	Accumulated Depreciation
2017	$240,000	$240,000
2018	224,000	464,000
2019	208,000	672,000
	$672,000	

EXERCISE 11-4

PURPOSE: This exercise will give you practice in calculating depletion.

During 2017, Raising Spirits Corporation acquired a mineral mine for $3.6 million, of which $400,000 is attributable to the land value after the mineral has been removed. Engineers estimate that 16 million units of mineral can be recovered from this mine. During 2017, 1.5 million units were extracted and 900,000 units were sold.

Instructions

Calculate depletion for 2017.

Solution to Exercise 11-4

($3,600,000 − $400,000) ÷ 16,000,000 = $0.20
$0.20 × 1,500,000 = $300,000 depletion for 2017

EXPLANATION: Write down the formulas to calculate depletion, enter the data given, and solve.

$$\frac{\text{Acquisition Cost + Costs to Explore and Develop}}{\text{Number of Units to be Extracted}} = \frac{\text{Depletion Cost Per}}{\text{Recoverable Unit}}$$

$$\begin{array}{ccc} \text{Depletion Cost} & \text{Units Extracted} & \text{Depletion} \\ \text{per Recoverable} \times & \text{During} & = \text{for the} \\ \text{Unit} & \text{Period} & \text{Period} \end{array}$$

> The $300,000 depletion charge for the period is debited to (mineral) Inventory and credited to Accumulated Depletion (contra account to mineral mine asset). The depletion charge is based on the units extracted from the earth during the period. Of the $300,000, $180,000 (900,000 units sold in 2017 multiplied by $0.20 depletion cost per unit) is removed from inventory in 2017 and included in cost of goods sold on the period's income statement.

EXERCISE 11-5

PURPOSE: This exercise will illustrate the calculations for depreciation in partial periods.

Koehn Company purchased a new plant asset on April 1, 2017, at a cost of $345,000. It was estimated to have a useful life of 20 years and a residual value of $30,000. Koehn's accounting period is the calendar year.

Instructions

Round all final answers to the nearest dollar.

(a) Calculate the amount of depreciation for this asset for 2017 and 2018 using the straight-line method.

(b) Calculate the amount of depreciation for this asset for 2017 and 2018 using the double-declining-balance method.

Solution to Exercise 11-5

(a)
$$\frac{\$345,000 - \$30,000}{20 \text{ years}} \times \frac{9}{12} = \$11,813 \text{ depreciation for 2017}$$

$$\frac{\$345,000 - \$30,000}{20 \text{ years}} = \$15,750 \text{ depreciation for 2018}$$

EXPLANATION: Write down and apply the formula for straight-line depreciation. Multiply the annual depreciation amount by the portion of the asset's first year of service that falls in the given accounting period.

$$\frac{\text{Cost} - \text{Residual Value}}{\text{Estimated Useful Life}} \times \frac{\text{\# months available for use}}{12 \text{ months}} = \text{Depreciation charge for the year}$$

(b) Straight-line rate $= \frac{100\%}{20} = 5\%$; Double-declining-balance depreciation rate $= 5\% \times 2 = 10\%$

10% $\times$ \$345,000 = \$34,500 depreciation for asset's first full year (April 1, 2017, to March 31, 2018)

10% $\times$ (\$345,000 $-$ \$34,500) = \$31,050 depreciation for asset's second full year (April 1, 2018, to March 31, 2019)

Depreciation charge for 2017:

$\frac{9}{12} \times$ \$34,500 = \$25,875 (April 1, 2017, to December 31, 2017)

Depreciation charge for 2018:

$\frac{3}{12} \times$ \$34,500 = \$8,625 (January 1, 2018, to March 31, 2018) + $\frac{9}{12} \times$ \$31,050 = \$23,288 (April 1, 2018, to December 31, 2018) = \$31,913

EXPLANATION: Write down and apply the formula for the double-declining-balance method. Apportion a full year's depreciation for the specific asset between the two accounting periods involved.

$$\text{Double-declining-balance depreciation rate} \times \begin{array}{c}\text{Book value at} \\ \text{beginning of} \\ \text{asset's full year}\end{array} = \begin{array}{c}\text{Full year of depreciation} \\ \text{for the asset}\end{array}$$

An alternative approach is as follows:

After the first partial year, calculate depreciation for a full **accounting year** by multiplying the double-declining-balance depreciation rate by the book value of the asset at the beginning of the accounting period. Thus, the calculation for 2018 would be as follows: 10% $\times$ (\$345,000 $-$ \$25,875) = \$31,913.

- Companies can use various methods to deal with partial year depreciation as long as a method is applied consistently; for example, charging a full year's depreciation in the year of purchase and no depreciation in the year of disposal, or charging a half-year's depreciation in the year of acquisition and a half-year's depreciation in the year of disposal.

- CCA requires use of the half-year rule, which states that in the year of acquisition, an asset's CCA is limited to one half of the first full year of CCA (CCA rate multiplied by the net addition). In effect, this deems that all asset purchases are made at the mid-point in the fiscal year of purchase, regardless of the actual date of purchase.

EXERCISE 11-6

PURPOSE: This exercise will illustrate how to account for a change in the estimated useful life and residual value of a plant asset due to an expenditure subsequent to acquisition.

Roland Company purchased a machine on January 1, 2007, for $145,000. The machine was being depreciated using the straight-line method over an estimated useful life of 20 years, with a $20,000 residual value. At the beginning of 2017, when the machine had been in use for 10 years, the company paid $25,000 to overhaul the machine. As a result of this overhaul, the company estimated that the machine's useful life would be extended by five years and the residual value would be reduced to $20,000.

Instructions

Calculate the depreciation charge for 2017.

Solution to Exercise 11-6

Cost	$145,000
Accumulated depreciation at 1/1/2017	60,000[a]
Book value at 1/1/2017	85,000
Additional expenditure capitalized	25,000
Revised book value	110,000
Current estimate of residual value	20,000
Remaining depreciable cost at 1/1/2017	90,000
Remaining years of useful life at 1/1/2017	÷ 15[b]
Depreciation expense for 2017	$ 6,000

[a]Cost	$145,000
Original estimate of residual value	25,000
Original depreciable cost	120,000
Original useful life in years	÷ 20
Original depreciation per year	6,000
Number of years used	× 10
Accumulated depreciation at 1/1/2017	$ 60,000
[b]Original estimate of useful life in years	20
Number of years used	(10)
Additional useful life due to overhaul	5
Remaining years of useful life at 1/1/2017	15

● A change in the estimated useful life and/or residual value of an existing depreciable asset is accounted for prospectively (in current and/or future periods). Therefore, the book value at the beginning of the period of change in estimate, less the new estimate of residual value, is allocated over the remaining useful life, using the appropriate depreciation method.

● The $25,000 cost of the overhaul is capitalized because the cost benefits future periods by extending the useful life of the machine. The $25,000 cost of the overhaul was added to the cost of the entire machine because the overhaul was not recorded as a separate component under component accounting at the time of acquisition. If the overhaul was planned since the date of acquisition and required to continue operating the machine, the cost of the overhaul may have been capitalized as a separate non-physical component under component accounting. In 2017, at the time of the overhaul, the original overhaul component would be removed, and the new overhaul would be capitalized as a component and depreciated over the period until the next major overhaul. The only effect on the machine asset itself would have been a change in useful life from 20 years to 25 years, which would have been accounted for prospectively.

EXERCISE 11-7

PURPOSE: This exercise will give you practice in calculating CCA.

Eastcoast Fishing purchased equipment for its boat (class 8—20%); the equipment was valued at $80,000 in March 2017. The undepreciated capital cost in class 8 at the beginning of 2017 was $220,000. In 2018, the company sold a boat for $30,000 for which it had originally paid $46,000. In 2019, the company sold another boat for $170,000, which had originally cost $300,000. This was the last asset in the class.

Instructions

Calculate CCA for each of years 2017, 2018, and 2019. Determine if there was any recapture, terminal losses, or capital gains for the company.

Solution to Exercise 11-7

Draw up a chart to calculate CCA and undepreciated capital cost (UCC) for the year. Remember the half-year rule is in effect for equipment purchases. Since there is an opening balance in UCC, two separate calculations will need to be done to calculate CCA in 2017.

Class 8—20%		CCA	UCC
December 31, 2016			$220,000
Additions less disposals, 2017			
Equipment ($80,000)			80,000
			300,000
CCA, 2017			
$220,000 \times 20\% =$	$44,000		
$80,000 \times \frac{1}{2} \times 20\% =$	8,000	$52,000	(52,000)
December 31, 2017			$248,000

Additions less disposals, 2018

Equipment (lesser of original cost $46,000
and proceeds of disposal $30,000)   (30,000)
                                                                                        218,000

CCA, 2018

$218,000 × 20% $43,600   (43,600)
December 31, 2018   174,400

Additions less disposals, 2019

Equipment (lesser of original cost $300,000
and proceeds of disposal $170,000)   (170,000)
                                                                                          4,400

Terminal loss, 2019 $4,400   (4,400)
                                                                                        $ 0

The company experienced a terminal loss in 2019 because the boat sold in 2019 was the last asset in the class. After disposition, there was a positive $4,400 balance left in UCC, which is deducted from taxable income in 2019. In essence, in reconciling the class after disposition of the last asset, and considering the timing of the disposals and proceeds received, the company did not "claim enough" CCA over the life of the asset class.

If the UCC balance at the end of 2019 had been negative (instead of positive), there would have been a recapture of CCA, which would have been added to taxable income in 2019.

There were no capital gains on either boat because in each case, proceeds on disposition did not exceed original cost.

ILLUSTRATION 11-1

Accounting for Impairment

	ASPE	IFRS	
Accounting model	Cost model	Cost model	Revaluation model
Impairment model	Cost recovery model	Rational entity impairment model	Rational entity impairment model
Frequency of impairment test	Impairment test is required if events or changes in circumstances indicate that an asset's carrying amount may not be recoverable.	Assets must be assessed for indicators of impairment at the end of each reporting period; if indicators of impairment exist, impairment test must be conducted.	Assets must be assessed for indicators of impairment at the end of each reporting period; if indicators of impairment exist, impairment test must be conducted.

Illustration 11-1   3 6 7

	ASPE	IFRS	
Impairment test	If carrying amount of the asset (or asset group) > undiscounted future cash flows of the asset (or asset group), the asset (or asset group) is impaired.	If carrying amount of the asset (or CGU) > recoverable amount of the asset (or CGU), the asset (or CGU) is impaired. Recoverable amount is the higher of value in use (discounted future cash flows of the asset or CGU) and current fair value less costs to sell.	If carrying amount of the asset (or CGU) > recoverable amount of the asset (or CGU), the asset (or CGU) is impaired. Recoverable amount is the higher of value in use (discounted future cash flows of the asset or CGU) and current fair value less costs to sell.
Calculation of impairment loss	Impairment loss = carrying amount of the asset (or asset group) − fair value of the asset (or asset group)	Impairment loss = carrying amount of the asset (or CGU) − recoverable amount of the asset (or CGU)	Impairment loss = carrying amount of the asset (or CGU) − recoverable amount of the asset (or CGU)
Recording of impairment loss for an individual asset	DR Loss on Impairment (to income), CR Accumulated Impairment Losses	DR Loss on Impairment (to income), CR Accumulated Impairment Losses	DR Revaluation Surplus (OCI) (up to the asset's past net revaluation surplus, with remaining balance of loss, DR to Loss on Impairment [to income]), CR Accumulated Impairment Losses
Recording of impairment loss for an asset group or CGU	DR Loss on Impairment (to income), CR is allocated to Accumulated Impairment Losses accounts for each asset in the asset group. Allocation is based on relative carrying amounts, with no individual asset reduced to a carrying amount below its fair value, if known.	DR Loss on Impairment (to income), CR allocated to Accumulated Impairment Losses accounts for each asset in the CGU. Allocation is based on relative carrying amounts, with no individual asset reduced to a carrying amount below the highest of its value in use, fair value less costs to sell, or zero.	DR Revaluation Surplus (OCI) (for each asset, up to past net revaluation surplus, with remaining balance of each asset's loss, DR to Loss on Impairment [to income]), CR allocated to Accumulated Impairment Losses accounts for each asset in the CGU. Allocation is based on relative carrying amounts, with no individual asset reduced to a carrying amount below the highest of its value in use, fair value less costs to sell, or zero.
Subsequent recovery of impairment loss, if indicators of recovery exist	Not permitted	Permitted, up to lesser of revised recoverable amount and what the asset's carrying amount would have been, net of depreciation, if the original impairment loss had never been recognized	Permitted and accounted for as a revaluation increase

- Note that under the IFRS fair value model of accounting for investment property, impairment of investment property is reflected and accounted for as a decrease in fair value of the investment property.

- The above chart applies to assets that are held for use and assets to be disposed of other than by sale. Held-for-sale assets are carried at fair value less costs to sell, and any decrease in fair value due to impairment would be theoretically included in the writedown to fair value less costs to sell. To be classified as held for sale, the asset must meet the strict criteria for classifying a long-lived asset as held for sale (discussed in Chapter 4).

ANALYSIS OF MULTIPLE-CHOICE QUESTIONS

Question

1. Under the cost model, the term "depreciable cost" refers to:
    a. the total amount to be charged (debited) to expense over an asset's useful life.
    b. cost of the asset less the related depreciation recorded to date.
    c. the estimated fair value of the asset at the end of its useful life.
    d. the acquisition cost of the asset.

    EXPLANATION: Depreciable cost or **depreciable base** is the total amount of asset cost that can be expensed over the useful life of the asset; thus, it is original cost less estimated residual value. Answer selection "b" describes the term "book value." Answer selection "c" describes residual value. Selection "d" represents the total original cost of the asset. (Solution = a.)

Question

2. A machine is purchased by Dundee Company for $27,000. Dundee pays $7,000 in cash and gives a note payable for $20,000 that is payable in instalments over a four-year period. Dundee estimates that the machine could physically last for 12 years, even though Dundee expects to use it in its business for only 10 years. The period of time to be used by Dundee for depreciation purposes is:
    a. 4 years.
    b. 5 years.
    c. 10 years.
    d. 12 years.

    EXPLANATION: Consider the objective of depreciation: to allocate an asset's cost to the periods the entity will benefit from using it. The asset should be depreciated over its useful life, which is the length of time the asset will be of service to the entity using it. (Solution = c.)

Question

3. A machine with an estimated useful life of eight years and an expected residual value of $6,000 was purchased on January 1, 2017, for $64,000. The amount to be recorded for depreciation expense for the years 2017, 2018, and 2019, respectively, using the 200% declining-balance method will be:
   a. $8,000; $7,000; $6,125.
   b. $14,500; $10,875; $8,156.
   c. $21,333; $14,222; $18,963.
   d. $16,000; $12,000; $9,000.

EXPLANATION: Write down the formula for the double-declining-balance method. Enter the data given and solve.

Book value at beginning of year × Double-declining-balance depreciation rate = Depreciation expense

Double-declining-balance depreciation rate = 2 × (100% ÷ Useful life) = 2 × (100% ÷ 8) = 25%

$$2017: \$64,000 \times 25\% = \underline{\$16,000}$$
$$2018: (\$64,000 - \$16,000) \times 25\% = \underline{\$12,000}$$
$$2019: (\$64,000 - \$16,000 - \$12,000) \times 25\% = \underline{\$\ 9,000}$$

(Solution = d.)

Question

4. A machine was purchased for $8 million on January 1, 2017. It has an estimated useful life of eight years and a residual value of $800,000. Depreciation is being calculated using the double-declining-balance method. What amount should be shown for this machine, net of accumulated depreciation, in the company's December 31, 2018, statement of financial position?
   a. $4,000,000
   b. $4,500,000
   c. $6,000,000
   d. $6,125,000

EXPLANATION: Write down the formula to calculate book value and the formula to calculate depreciation using the double-declining-balance method. Fill in the case facts and solve.

Cost − Accumulated Depreciation = Book Value

Double-declining-balance depreciation rate × Book value at beginning of the year = Depreciation expense

Double-declining-balance depreciation rate = 100% ÷ 8 × 2 = 25%

Year	Book Value (Beginning)	Rate	Depreciation Expense	Balance of Accumulated Depreciation	Book Value (End of year)
1	$8,000,000	25%	$2,000,000	$2,000,000	$6,000,000
2	$6,000,000	25%	$1,500,000	$3,500,000	$4,500,000

(Solution = b.)

Question

5. Sammy Corporation purchased a machine on July 1, 2017, for $800,000. The machine has an estimated useful life of eight years and a residual value of $90,000. The machine is being depreciated by the double-declining-balance method. What amount of depreciation expense should be recorded for the year ended December 31, 2018?

   a. $155,313
   b. $175,000
   c. $133,125
   d. $150,000

EXPLANATION: Write down the formula for the 200% declining-balance approach. (Notice the facts indicate there is a partial period for the first year, 2017, and the question asks for depreciation for the 2018 reporting period.) Calculate the rate that is 200% of the straight-line (that is, $1/8 \times 2 = 25\%$). Apply the formula to the facts given. Remember that residual value is not used in this method of calculating depreciation.

   200% declining-balance depreciation rate × Book value at beginning of the year = Depreciation expense

   25% × $800,000 = $200,000 depreciation expense in first full year of asset's life

   25% × (800,000 − $200,000) = $150,000 depreciation expense in second full year of asset's life

   2017 depreciation expense = $\frac{1}{2}$ × $200,000 = $100,000 (for the first 6 months of asset's life)

   2018 depreciation expense = ($\frac{1}{2}$ × $200,000) + ($\frac{1}{2}$ × $150,000) = $175,000

   OR

   2018 depreciation expense = 25% × ($800,000 − $100,000) = $175,000

(Solution = b.)

Question

6. Schoen Company purchased a piece of equipment at the beginning of 2007 for $90,000. The equipment was being depreciated using the straight-line method over an estimated useful life of 15 years, with no residual value. At the beginning of 2017, when the equipment had been in use for 10 years, the company paid $10,000 to overhaul the equipment. As a result of the overhaul, the company estimates that the useful life of the equipment will be extended by three years with no residual value. What should depreciation expense be for this equipment in 2017?

    a. $8,333

    b. $5,000

    c. $3,333

    d. $1,667

EXPLANATION: Write down the model or format to calculate depreciation whenever there has been a change in the estimated useful life and/or residual value. Fill in the case facts and solve.

Cost	$90,000
Accumulated depreciation at 1/1/2017	60,000[a]
Book value (before overhaul) at 1/1/2017	30,000
Additional expenditure capitalized	10,000
Revised book value (after overhaul)	40,000
Current estimate of residual value	0
Remaining depreciable cost at 1/1/2017	40,000
Remaining years of useful life at 1/1/2017	÷ 8[b]
Depreciation expense for 2017	$5,000

(Solution = b.)

[a]Cost	$90,000
Original estimate of residual value	0
Original depreciable cost	90,000
Original useful life in years	÷ 15
Original depreciation per year	6,000
Number of years used	× 10
Accumulated depreciation at 1/1/2017	$60,000
[b]Original estimate of useful life in years	15
Number of years used	(10)
Additional years	3
Remaining years of useful life at 1/1/2017	8

Question

7. Annual assessment for indicators of impairment reveals that market demand has significantly decreased for the product manufactured by a particular cash generating unit (CGU) in Timberlake Company's factory. As a result, Timberlake Company is conducting an impairment test on the CGU. Timberlake estimates that it will receive net discounted future cash flows of $900,000 from using and subsequently disposing of the assets in the CGU. At December 31, 2017, the CGU's fair value less costs to sell is estimated to be $775,000. The equipment was acquired two years ago at a total cost of $1.5 million and has been depreciated using the straight-line method and a 10-year useful life with no residual value. Timberlake Company prepares financial statements in accordance with IFRS. The impairment loss to be reported at the end of 2017 is:

   a. $0.

   b. $125,000.

   c. $300,000.

   d. $425,000.

EXPLANATION: The carrying amount of the CGU at the end of 2017 is $1,200,000 ($1,500,000 cost less $300,000 [2 years × $1,500,000 × 10%]), but the recoverable amount is only $900,000 (higher of $900,000 value in use and $775,000 fair value less costs to sell). Because the carrying amount of the CGU is greater than the recoverable amount of the CGU, the CGU is impaired. Under IFRS, the impairment loss equals carrying amount ($1,200,000) less recoverable amount ($900,000), or $300,000. (Solution = c.)

Question

8. Assume the same information as in question 7, including the impairment loss amount that was calculated. Timberlake provides the following information about the equipment in the CGU, as at December 31, 2017:

	Carrying amount	Fair value less costs to sell	Value in use
Equipment A	$1,105,000	$775,000	$900,000
Equipment B	95,000	(Not determinable)	(Not determinable)
	$1,200,000	$775,000	$900,000

How would the impairment loss calculated in question 7 be allocated between the equipment in the CGU; specifically, what would the journal entry credit amount be to each of Accumulated Impairment Losses—Equipment A, and Accumulated Impairment Losses—Equipment B, respectively?

   a. $205,000; $95,000

   b. $276,250; $23,750

   c. $300,000; $0

   d. None of the above

EXPLANATION: Impairment loss is allocated to the individual assets in the CGU based on relative carrying amount; however, no individual asset in the group can be reduced to below the highest of its value in use, fair value less costs to sell, or zero. The carrying amount of Equipment A, for example, cannot be reduced below its $900,000 value in use (the highest of $900,000, $775,000, or zero). Allocation of the $300,000 impairment loss based only on relative carrying amount would allocate $276,250 ($1,105,000/$1,200,000 × $300,000) of impairment loss to Equipment A, which would result in an Equipment A carrying amount of $828,750 ($1,105,000 − $276,250), which would be below its $900,000 value in use. Therefore, the maximum allocation of impairment loss, and credit journal entry to Accumulated Impairment Losses—Equipment A, is $205,000 ($1,105,000 − $900,000). The $95,000 ($300,000 − $205,000) balance is allocated, or credited, to Accumulated Impairment Losses—Equipment B. (Solution = a.)

Question

9. Assume that at December 31, 2017, Timberlake recorded the impairment loss calculated in question 7, with the credits to Accumulated Impairment Losses—Equipment A and Accumulated Impairment Losses—Equipment B calculated in question 8. At the end of 2019, after assessing the same CGU for indicators of impairment, Timberlake concluded that market demand for the product manufactured by the CGU has increased significantly due to extensive quality problems with the major competing product on the market. Sales of the CGU's product have increased to the levels originally expected, and the growth in sales is expected to continue. Timberlake uses the cost model under IFRS to account for assets in this CGU. In 2019, is Timberlake permitted to reverse the impairment loss recorded in 2017?

   a. No; recovery of previously recorded impairment losses is not permitted.

   b. Yes; recovery of previously recorded impairment losses is permitted.

   c. Yes; recovery of previously recorded impairment losses is permitted up to the lesser of the revised recoverable amount and what the asset's carrying amount would have been, net of depreciation, if the original impairment loss had never been recognized.

   d. None of the above.

EXPLANATION: Under ASPE, reversal or recovery of previously recorded impairment losses is not permitted. Under the revaluation model under IFRS, recovery of previously recorded impairment losses is permitted (up to the extent that the carrying amount does not exceed the revised recoverable amount), and would be accounted for as a revaluation increase. Under the cost model under IFRS, recovery of previously recorded impairment losses is permitted up to the lesser of the revised recoverable amount and what the asset's carrying amount would have been, net of depreciation, if the original impairment loss had never been recognized. (Solution = c.)

Question

10. At December 31, 2017, Northgate Company has decided to discontinue use of a plant asset, intending to dispose of it in the coming year through sale to a competitor. The plant asset's carrying amount is $400,000, its fair value is $225,000, and its expected disposal cost is $20,000. The impairment loss to be reported at the end of 2017 is:

    a. $195,000.
    b. $175,000.
    c. $380,000.
    d. $0.

EXPLANATION: Assuming the plant asset meets the criteria for classification as held for sale, the asset would be reclassified as held for sale and written down to fair value less costs to sell. Therefore, the $20,000 disposal cost would be subtracted from the $225,000 fair value to arrive at $205,000 fair value less costs to sell. Northgate would record an impairment loss of $195,000 ($400,000 − $205,000) and decrease the carrying amount of the plant asset to $205,000, based on fair value less costs to sell. Depreciation would no longer be recorded for the plant asset. (Solution = a.)

Question

11. A plant asset with a five-year estimated useful life and no residual value is sold during the second year of the asset's life. How would use of the straight-line instead of the declining-balance method of depreciation affect the amount of gain or loss on sale of the plant asset?

	Gain	Loss
a.	Increase	Decrease
b.	Decrease	Increase
c.	No effect	Increase
d.	No effect	No effect

EXPLANATION: Declining-balance would result in more accumulated depreciation earlier in the asset's life and, therefore, a lower book value. In contrast, the straight-line method would result in less accumulated depreciation earlier in the asset's life and a higher book value. This means a lower gain or a higher loss would result if a straight-line depreciated asset is sold, compared with a declining-balance depreciated asset. This can be shown by creating a set of case facts (cost, useful life, selling price) and comparing the gain or loss if the asset were depreciated under the declining-balance method with the gain or loss if the asset were depreciated under the straight-line method. (Solution = b.)

Question

12. Antonio Inc. has just sold the last asset in CCA class 8 for $25,000. The original cost of the asset was $22,000. UCC prior to the disposal was valued at $30,000. Antonio would report:

    a. recapture of $5,000.
    b. capital gain of $5,000.
    c. terminal loss of $8,000.
    d. terminal loss of $3,000.

EXPLANATION: Think about the definitions of the terms listed. Recapture occurs when the last asset of a class is disposed of and, after the disposal, the asset class has a negative balance. The balance would be added to taxable income. The capital gain in this case is $3,000 ($25,000 − $22,000). A terminal loss occurs when the last asset of a class is disposed of and, after the disposal, the asset class has a positive balance, as is the case here. (Solution = c.)

CASE STUDY

Laidle Disposal Limited (Part 2)

(See case in Chapter 10.)

If LDL's sites are accounted for as fixed assets, there is an additional issue: which depreciation method to use. Leonard Laidle, the president, has done some research and noted that the following methods are used by a sample of companies in the same industry:

> WasteCo Inc. uses the straight-line method on its property, plant, and equipment.

> Disposal Corp. uses the declining-balance method on its property, plant, and equipment.

Mr. Laidle estimates that the sites will take, on average, 10 years to fill up and that as LDL picks up more contracts, the amount dumped will increase, at least initially. In year 1, it is expected to increase by 3% of total capacity; in year 2, by 5% of total capacity; and in year 3, by 10% of total capacity. On the other hand, most contracts are annual and the possibility exists that LDL may also lose some. The cost of most sites averages $1 million per site and financing has been obtained from various sources at an average rate of 10%. Residual values are not known at this time, although land usually holds its value. Mr. Laidle is not sure about the differences between depreciation methods or what impact they might have on the financial statements. Mr. Laidle is concerned that large amounts of depreciation might make the financial statements look weak. The choice of depreciation method is somewhat subjective and involves judgement.

Instructions

As an independent consultant to Leonard Laidle, discuss the issues and provide recommendations.

Suggested Approach to Case Study

Overview

The financial statements will be provided to potential new clients, and users will focus on the company's financial stability and adherence to environmental standards. Management will prefer the financial statements to show LDL in the most favourable light (that is, with maximized profits and assets). The financial statements will likely be constrained by ASPE since users will want reliable statements.

Analysis and recommendations

Issues: Are the landfill sites inventory (in which case they do not have to be depreciated) or are they fixed assets? If they are fixed assets, which depreciation method is appropriate?

Inventory versus fixed assets

See the discussion in Part 1 to the case in Chapter 10.

Depreciation method

If LDL's sites are accounted for as fixed assets and will be generating income through use, they would be depreciated by allocating their cost to the periods in which LDL is expected to benefit from its use. The question arises as to which depreciation method to use. The straight-line method would result in equal amounts being booked to expense each year and will therefore impact net income consistently. The declining-balance method would provide for decreasing amounts of expense and is best suited for situations where the asset contributes less to revenues over time (that is, as they wear out).

Choice of depreciation method involves professional judgement. In general, the resulting depreciation should reflect the pattern in which the entity expects to consume asset benefits. So far in this case, less revenue is expected to be generated in the earlier years (year 1, 3%; year 2, 5%; and so on). However, usage will not always increase, as contracts are annual and may be lost, resulting in less capacity used. Based on this, the most appropriate choice may not be one of the methods presented, but rather one based on activity or units of production, resulting in depreciation charges based on actual usage in the period. Since each site has a total capacity, which is an estimate of total units of usage over each site's physical life, the activity method would be a reasonable choice in this case.

As a final note, because residual value is not known, the amount depreciated should exclude residual value, although, perhaps because land usually retains its value, there may be nothing to depreciate. However, in this case, the land may not hold its value given that it is being used as a garbage dump and is likely not located in a prime location.

Therefore, assuming that the residual value is not estimable, it would make sense to depreciate based on the amount of the assets used up each year (using an activity method such as unit of production). This will result in more favourable income statements in the earlier years since the site will be used less initially.

Chapter 12

Intangible Assets and Goodwill

OVERVIEW

The intangible assets classification on the statement of financial position is used to report identifiable assets that lack physical existence and are not financial instruments. For instance, bank deposits and accounts receivable are both intangible but are properly classified as financial assets for accounting purposes. Also, an investment in shares is intangible in nature but should be classified as either a current asset or a long-term investment for accounting purposes. Assets such as patents, trademarks, copyrights, and franchises are identifiable, intangible, and nonmonetary in nature and properly classified in the intangible assets section of a statement of financial position. Intangible assets derive their value from the rights and privileges that are granted to the company using the assets. Goodwill is intangible in nature, but usually classified separately as it is not an identifiable asset. Impairment testing of intangible assets and goodwill under ASPE and IFRS is also discussed in this chapter.

STUDY STEPS

Understanding the Nature of Intangible Assets and Goodwill

Intangible Assets

There are many different types of intangible assets, including:

- Marketing-related intangible assets
- Customer-related intangible assets
- Artistic-related intangible assets
- Contract-based intangible assets
- Technology-based intangible assets

Intangible assets with similar characteristics (such as similar risk level and stability) are typically grouped together.

- Intangible assets that are purchased are capitalized at cost, where cost includes acquisition cost and all direct costs necessary to ready the intangible asset for its intended use.

- Identifiable intangible assets that are purchased as part of a business combination are recorded at fair value and included in the same journal entry that records fair value of identifiable net assets acquired in the purchase transaction. Intangibles acquired that are not identifiable assets are considered part of goodwill acquired in the purchase transaction.

- Intangibles that are internally generated must be identifiable, be nonmonetary, and meet all six development phase conditions in order for certain costs to be capitalized. Only direct costs incurred after all six development phase conditions have been met may be capitalized if future economic benefits are reasonably certain. Direct costs may include legal fees, government registration fees, and direct costs necessary to ready the intangible asset for its intended use. Note that expenditures incurred in order to determine or establish the future economic benefit of the intangible (that is, research and early development phase costs) do not meet the definition of an asset and should be expensed as incurred.

- The six development phase conditions that must *all* be demonstrated in order to capitalize certain direct costs are:

  1. Technical feasibility of completing the intangible asset
  2. Intention to complete the intangible asset for use or sale
  3. Ability to use or sell the intangible asset
  4. Availability of technical, financial, and other resources needed to complete and use or sell the intangible asset
  5. Probable future economic benefits of the intangible asset
  6. Ability to reliably measure the development costs related to the intangible asset

The six development phase conditions are very specific conditions stemming from the general definition of an asset. Under IFRS, costs that meet all six development phase conditions and have reasonable certainty of future economic benefit should be capitalized. Under ASPE, costs that meet all six development phase conditions and have reasonable certainty of future economic benefit may be capitalized or expensed.

An intangible asset with a finite or limited life is amortized by systematic charges to expense, over the lesser of legal life (if applicable) and useful life. Ideally, amortization expense should reflect the pattern in which the asset's economic benefits are used up. IAS 38.92 supports an underlying assumption that it is inappropriate to use amortization methods based on revenue generated by an activity. An intangible asset with an indefinite life is not amortized because there appears to be no foreseeable limit to the asset's ability to generate positive cash flows for the company. Both limited-life and indefinite-life intangible assets are subject to impairment testing under IFRS and ASPE.

Goodwill

Goodwill represents the amount paid for a company in excess of the company's fair value of identifiable net assets as at the purchase date. In a transaction where one company purchases another, the acquirer may pay more than the fair value of the acquiree's identifiable net assets if the acquiree is a successful company with established customers, suppliers, trained employees, and a good management team. The amount paid over and above the fair value of the acquiree's identifiable net assets represents goodwill.

- Goodwill is recorded only as a result of purchasing another company and is equal to the excess of the amount paid to acquire the business over the fair value of that business's identifiable net assets. Goodwill that is internally generated as a result of business growth or maturity is not recorded due to the difficulty and subjectivity of measuring a company's own goodwill.

- Goodwill is a fair value–based measure, calculated as purchase price (presumably based on fair value), less fair value of identifiable net assets.

Goodwill is not amortized. However, it is subject to impairment testing under IFRS and ASPE.

Goodwill is calculated as the transaction purchase price, less fair value of identifiable net assets (assets less liabilities) of the purchased company as at the purchase date.

The equation looks at what was paid and what the company received in return.

Amount paid to buy the company	$xxxx
Less: fair value of identifiable net assets purchased	(xxx)
Equals goodwill	$xxxx

Goodwill is relatively straightforward to calculate in situations where a company is being purchased, as long as the fair value of the identifiable assets and liabilities can be determined.

Understanding the Accounting Issues Related to Impairment of Intangible Assets and Goodwill

To provide fair and reliable information to financial statement readers, intangible assets must also be tested to ensure that the carrying amount does not exceed the future economic benefits expected from the assets.

IFRS and ASPE both recognize three categories of intangible assets for impairment testing: (1) limited-life, (2) indefinite-life (other than goodwill), and (3) goodwill. However, for each category, impairment testing, calculation of impairment loss, and recording of impairment loss are different under IFRS and ASPE.

TIPS ON CHAPTER TOPICS

- Under IFRS, the revaluation model is permitted for intangible assets, but only for intangible assets that can be bought and sold and regularly traded in active markets. Because active markets rarely exist for intangible assets, they are usually accounted for under the cost model.

- It can be difficult not only to identify certain types of intangibles, but also to assign a fair value to them in a business combination. As a result, only **identifiable** intangible assets with a fair value that can be reliably measured are recorded separately in a purchase transaction. Other intangibles that do not meet these two criteria are considered part of goodwill acquired in the purchase transaction.

- An asset is **identifiable** if it has at least one of the following characteristics: (1) it results from contractual or other legal rights, or (2) it is separable from the entity (and can be sold, transferred, licensed, rented, or exchanged, either by itself or in combination with another contract, identifiable asset, or liability).

- **Development phase costs** that are incurred to apply proven research findings to a new or improved product or process, prior to commercial production or use, may be capitalized. The distinction between what is research expense, what is development expense, and what may be capitalized as a development cost may not be obvious and may require professional judgement. Only development costs that satisfy all six development phase conditions for capitalization, as listed above, may be capitalized.

- Under **IFRS**, development phase costs that meet the six development phase conditions for capitalization are capitalized.

- Under **ASPE**, development phase costs that meet the six development phase conditions for capitalization may be capitalized or expensed, depending on the entity's accounting policy.

- Whether an intangible asset is purchased separately, purchased as part of a business combination, or internally generated, most expenditures incurred after the asset is ready for its intended use are expensed.

- The cost of successfully defending an intangible asset, and therefore protecting its useful life, is a specific expenditure that may be capitalized after acquisition of the intangible asset.

- When an intangible asset is amortized, the charge (debit) should be reported as Amortization Expense and the credit should be made to the appropriate intangible asset's Accumulated Amortization account.

- Due to uncertainty surrounding a limited-life intangible asset's value at the end of its useful life, its **residual value** is usually assumed to be zero. However, this may not be the case if a third party commits to purchase the intangible asset at the end of its useful life to the entity, or if there is an observable market for the intangible asset, which is still expected to exist at the end of its useful life to the entity.

- Patents have a legal life of 20 years from the date of application. If the average time from application to date of first commercial use is 3 years, useful life is generally a maximum of 17 years.

- **Goodwill** equals purchase price to acquire the business, less the total fair value of identifiable net assets, which is why goodwill is sometimes referred to as a "master valuation" account. Goodwill is the residual: the excess of purchase price over fair value of the identifiable net assets acquired.

- The true value of goodwill may take years to "prove." One approach to estimating the value of goodwill is called the excess-earnings approach (discussed in Appendix 12A), which calculates the difference between what the specific company is projected to earn in the future and what an average company in the industry is expected to earn in the future. The difference, or excess, is due to the company's ability to generate higher income as a result of unidentifiable assets such as key management personnel, corporate strategy, or efficient operations. Other methods used to estimate the amount of goodwill in a business are the total-earnings approach, the number of years method, and the discounted free cash flow method.

- **Negative goodwill** occurs when the fair value of identifiable net assets acquired is higher than the purchase price paid in the business combination transaction. In the past, one approach was to allocate the excess credit (negative goodwill) among the other non-financial assets in the transaction (thereby recording an amount lower than the determined fair value for each of those assets). However, the current standard requires that the fair values of the identifiable net assets in the transaction be reassessed and verified. If, after re-examination, the transaction still appears to be a situation of negative goodwill, the credit should be accounted for as a gain and taken into income in the period of the transaction.

- Goodwill is recorded as an asset and reduced only if it is determined to be impaired or if associated assets are sold or disposed of (for example, if assets in the same cash generating unit are sold or disposed of).

- **Loss on Impairment—Goodwill** is recognized in income separately from other impairment losses. The journal entry credit is to **Accumulated**

(continued)

Impairment Losses—Goodwill, thus decreasing the carrying amount of the goodwill.

● For **limited-life intangible assets**, both IFRS and ASPE follow their respective impairment testing models outlined for property, plant, and equipment.

● For **indefinite-life intangible assets (other than goodwill) and for goodwill**, impairment testing is more rigorous than impairment testing for limited-life intangible assets. Because indefinite-life intangibles and goodwill are not amortized, they are subjected to stricter impairment testing and rules, under both IFRS and ASPE.

● Under IFRS, property, plant, and equipment and limited-life intangibles are assessed for indicators of impairment at the end of each reporting period. IFRS requires a stricter standard for indefinite-life intangibles. Instead of assessing for indicators of impairment at the end of each reporting period, carrying amount and recoverable amount must be compared at the end of each reporting period, whether or not there are any indicators of impairment. This is a more rigorous test for these assets that are not amortized, and therefore do not result in expense charges to income on a regular basis.

● Under ASPE, the impairment test for indefinite-life intangibles (other than goodwill) is a fair value test, which is a discounted cash flow concept. The fair value test is significantly different than the impairment test for property, plant, and equipment and limited-life intangibles under ASPE, which compares carrying amount with undiscounted future cash flows.

EXERCISE 12-1

PURPOSE: This exercise will give you practice in identifying and classifying costs that are associated with various intangibles.

The Hatchling Fish Corporation incurred the following costs during January 2017:

1. Lawyers' fees in connection with the organization of the corporation
2. Meetings of incorporators, filing fees, and other organization costs
3. Improvements to leased offices prior to occupancy
4. Costs to design and construct a prototype
5. Testing of prototype
6. Troubleshooting breakdowns during commercial production
7. Fees paid to engineers and lawyers to prepare patent application; patent granted January 22, 2017
8. Payment of six months' rent on leased facilities
9. Common share issue costs
10. Payment for a copyright
11. Materials purchased for future research and development projects; materials have alternative future use
12. Costs to advertise new business

Instructions

(a) For each item above, identify what account should be debited to record the expenditure.

(b) Indicate the financial statement classification of the related account.

Solution to Exercise 12-1

	(a) Account Debited	(b) Classification
1.	Operating Expenses	Operating Expenses
2.	Operating Expenses	Operating Expenses
3.	Leasehold Improvements	Property, Plant, and Equipment
4.	Research and Development Expense	Operating Expenses
5.	Research and Development Expense	Operating Expenses
6.	Work-in-Process Inventory—Overhead	Current Assets (allocated to Inventory)
7.	Intangible Assets—Patents	Intangible Assets
8.	Prepaid Rent	Current Assets
9.	Common Shares	Shareholders' Equity
10.	Intangible Assets—Copyrights	Intangible Assets
11.	Raw Materials	Current Assets (allocated to Inventory)
12.	Advertising Expense	Operating Expenses

> Expensing organization costs is consistent with the objective of having a statement of financial position that includes "true" assets, not assets created merely to satisfy the matching principle.

EXERCISE 12-2

PURPOSE: This exercise will review the accounting guidelines related to three types of intangible assets—patent, franchise, and trademark.

Information concerning Lester Hendel Corporation's intangible assets is as follows:

1. Hendel incurred $95,000 of experimental research costs in its laboratory to develop a patent that was granted on January 2, 2017. Legal fees and other costs associated with registration of the patent totalled $15,000. Hendel estimates that the useful life of the patent will be 10 years.

2. On January 1, 2017, Hendel signed an agreement to operate as a franchisee of Royal Burger Inc. for an initial franchise fee of $200,000. Of this amount, $40,000 was paid when the agreement was signed and the balance is payable in four annual payments of $40,000 each, beginning January 1, 2018. The agreement provides that the down payment is not refundable and no future services are required of the franchisor. The present value at January 1, 2017, of the four annual payments discounted at 12% (the implicit rate for a loan of this type) is $121,500. The agreement also provides that 5% of the revenue from the franchise must be paid to the franchisor annually. Hendel's revenue from the franchise for 2017 was $1.9 million. Hendel estimates the useful life of the franchise to be 10 years.

3. A trademark was purchased from Waterdown Company for $72,000 on July 1, 2014. Expenditures for successful litigation in defence of the trademark totalling $20,000 were paid on July 1, 2017. Hendel estimates that the useful life of the trademark will be 20 years from the date of acquisition.

Instructions

(a) Prepare a schedule showing the intangible assets section of Hendel's statement of financial position at December 31, 2017. Show supporting calculations in good form.

(b) Prepare a schedule showing all expenses resulting from the transactions that would appear on Hendel's income statement for the year ended December 31, 2017. Show supporting calculations in good form.

Solution to Exercise 12-2

(a)

LESTER HENDEL CORPORATION
Intangible Assets
December 31, 2017

Patent, net of accumulated amortization of $1,500 (Schedule 1)	$ 13,500
Franchise, net of accumulated amortization of $16,150 (Schedule 2)	145,350
Trademark, net of accumulated amortization of $13,188 (Schedule 3)	78,812
Total intangible assets	$237,662

Schedule 1: Patent

Cost of securing patent on 1/2/2017	$15,000
2017 amortization ($15,000 $\times \frac{1}{10}$)	(1,500)
Cost of patent, net of amortization	$13,500

Schedule 2: Franchise

Cost of franchise on 1/1/2017 ($40,000 + $121,500)	$161,500
2017 amortization ($161,500 $\times \frac{1}{10}$)	(16,150)
Cost of franchise, net of amortization	$145,350

Schedule 3: Trademark

Cost of trademark on 7/1/2014	$72,000
Amortization, 7/1/2014 to 1/1/2017 ($72,000 $\times \frac{1}{20} \times$ 2.5)	(9,000)
Book value on 1/1/2017	63,000
Cost of successful legal defence on 7/1/2017	20,000
Book value after legal defence	83,000
Amortization, 1/1/2017 to 12/31/2017 (Schedule 4)	(4,188)
Cost of trademark, net of amortization	$78,812

Schedule 4: Trademark Amortization

Amortization of original cost ($72,000 $\times \frac{1}{20}$)	$3,600
Amortization of legal fees ($20,000 $\times \frac{1}{17} \times \frac{6}{12}$)	588
Total trademark amortization	$4,188

(b)

LESTER HENDEL CORPORATION
Expenses Resulting from Selected Intangibles
Transactions
For the Year Ended December 31, 2017

Interest expense ($121,500 $\times$ 12%)	$ 14,580
Patent amortization (Schedule 1)	1,500
Franchise amortization (Schedule 2)	16,150
Franchise fee ($1,900,000 $\times$ 5%)	95,000
Trademark amortization (Schedule 4)	4,188
Total expenses	$131,418

APPROACH: One approach would be to prepare the journal entries associated with the facts given and post them to T accounts to determine the balances to be reported on the income statement for the year ended December 31, 2017, and on the statement of financial position at December 31, 2017. Under some circumstances (such as exam conditions), time may not permit these additional steps. You should at least think about and visualize the flow of the information through the accounts. This will greatly help you successfully complete the schedules required within the time permitted.

EXPLANATION:

1. Research costs are expensed in the period incurred. Thus, the $95,000 of experimental research costs incurred in developing the patent would have been expensed prior to 2017. Legal fees and other costs associated with obtaining the patent should be matched with each of the eight years estimated to benefit from the patent; therefore, the $15,000 of legal fees and registration costs should be capitalized and amortized.

2. The franchise rights will benefit future periods. Therefore, the initial franchise fee associated with obtaining those rights should be capitalized and amortized over the future periods that will benefit from the franchise. The acquisition cost is determined by the cash given (down payment of $40,000) and the cash equivalent of the related payable (present value of the four annual payments at 12%—$121,500). The fact that "the down payment is not refundable and no future services are required of the franchisor" has no impact on how the franchisee accounts for the franchise. The provision in the agreement that calls for the franchisee to pay 5% of the annual revenue from the franchise to the franchisor does not initially require any accounting treatment; it gives rise to an expense that accrues as revenues are earned from use of the franchise. The capitalized franchise fee is amortized over the useful period of 10 years. The interest expense resulting from deferred payment is recognized annually by applying the implicit interest rate of 12% to the outstanding payable balance.

3. The purchase price of the trademark ($72,000) was capitalized in mid-2014 when the trademark was acquired. That cost is being amortized over the 20-year useful life. (Note that only one half year of amortization was recorded in 2014.) Expenditures of $20,000 for successful litigation in defence of the trademark rights are charged to the Trademark account because defending the trademark establishes the legal rights of the holder of the trademark (which benefits future periods). Because the litigation was settled in the middle of 2017, only one half year of amortization of these legal costs is recorded for 2017. The $20,000 is amortized over the remaining useful life of the trademark (17 years in this case).

EXERCISE 12-3

PURPOSE: This exercise will give you practice in accounting for research and development (R&D) costs.

Listed below are three independent situations involving R&D costs to be accounted for under IFRS.

1. During 2017, Bardon Co. incurred the following costs:

Consulting fees for research study performed by Williams Co. for Bardon	$400,000
Testing for evaluation of new products	250,000
Development costs to adapt an existing product to an unproven market	350,000
R&D services performed by Bardon for Eagle Co.	250,000

How much should Bardon report as R&D expense for the year ended December 31, 2017?

2. Harper Corp. incurred the following costs during the year ended December 31, 2017:

Design, construction, and testing of pre-production prototypes and models	$250,000
Routine, ongoing efforts to increase production efficiency for an existing product	240,000
Routine design of tools, jigs, moulds, and dies	70,000
Quality control during commercial production including routine testing of products	280,000
Laboratory research aimed at discovery of new knowledge	350,000
Conceptual formulation and design of possible product alternatives	150,000

How much should Harper report as R&D expense for the year ended December 31, 2017?

3. Packer Company incurred costs in 2017 as follows:

Equipment acquired for use in various research projects (current and future)	$875,000
Depreciation on the equipment above	125,000
Materials used in research activities	325,000
Salaries of development staff designing a prototype for a product that Packer may abandon due to insufficient financing	140,000
Consulting fees paid to advance a newly developed product to full commercial production	170,000
Indirect costs appropriately allocated to research activities	250,000

How much should Packer report as R&D expense for the year ended December 31, 2017?

Instructions

Provide the correct answer to each of the three situations.

Solution to Exercise 12-3

1.

Consulting fees for research study performed by Williams Co. for Bardon	$ 400,000
Testing for evaluation of new products	250,000
Development costs to adapt an existing product to an unproven market	350,000
Total R&D expense	$1,000,000

● Development costs to adapt an existing product to an unproven market are **expensed** in the period incurred, because the existence of a market for the adapted product has not been established yet. Specifically, of the six conditions listed below that must *all* be demonstrated in order for a development stage cost to be capitalized, condition number 5 is not met if existence of a market for the adapted product has not been established yet:

1. Technical feasibility of completing the intangible asset

2. Intention to complete the intangible asset for use or sale

3. Ability to use or sell the intangible asset

4. Availability of technical, financial, and other resources needed to complete and use or sell the intangible asset

5. Probable future economic benefits of the intangible asset

6. Ability to reliably measure the development costs related to the intangible asset

● R&D costs related to R&D activities conducted for other entities are classified as a receivable (because of the impending reimbursement).

● Sometimes one entity conducts R&D activities for other entities under a contractual arrangement. In this case, the contract usually specifies that all direct costs, and certain specific indirect costs, plus a profit element, should be reimbursed to the entity performing the R&D work. Because reimbursement is expected, the entity records such R&D costs as a receivable. It is the entity for whom the work has been performed that reports these costs as R&D expense or deferred development costs as incurred.

2.

Design, construction, and testing of pre-production prototypes and models	$250,000
Laboratory research aimed at discovery of new knowledge	350,000
Conceptual formulation and design of possible product alternatives	150,000
Total R&D expense	$750,000

Routine, ongoing efforts to increase production efficiency for an existing product, routine design costs, and quality control costs are regular operating expenses of production and not considered R&D.

3.

Depreciation on the equipment acquired for use in various research projects	$125,000
Materials used in research activities	325,000
Salaries of development staff designing a prototype for a product that Packer may abandon due to insufficient financing	140,000
Indirect costs appropriately allocated to research activities	250,000
Total R&D expense	$840,000

- Equipment, facilities, and purchased intangibles that have **alternative future uses** (in other R&D projects or otherwise) are **capitalized as property, plant, and equipment assets**; the **related depreciation is classified as research and development expense**.

- Even though the staff salary incurred is a development stage cost, it cannot be capitalized as an intangible asset if the company does not have sufficient financial resources available to complete development of the product or process. As a result, the staff salary is included in research and development expense in the period incurred.

- Consulting fees paid to advance a newly developed product to full commercial production are a development stage cost that may be capitalized if all six development stage criteria for capitalization are met.

APPROACH: Read the requirement of each situation before you begin detailed work on the first one. Notice that all three items deal with R&D expense. Therefore, review in your mind the definitions of the words "research" and "development," and review the six development stage conditions to be met for capitalization of a development cost. Recall what you can from the list of activities considered to be R&D and from the list of sample expenditures and their accounting treatment.

To minimize confusion, organize your thoughts and recall what you know about the subject before you begin to process the data at hand.

EXPLANATION: To differentiate R&D costs from other similar costs, recall the definitions of "research" and "development."

Research is the planned investigation undertaken with the hope of gaining new scientific or technical knowledge and understanding. Such investigation may or may not be directed toward a specific practical aim or application.

Development is the translation of research findings or other knowledge into a plan or design for new or substantially improved materials, devices, products, processes, systems, or services before starting commercial production or use.

Many costs have characteristics similar to those of R&D costs; for instance, costs of relocation and rearrangement of facilities, start-up costs for a new plant or new retail outlet, marketing research costs, promotion costs for a new product or service, and costs of training new personnel. To distinguish between R&D and those other similar costs, the following schedule provides examples of activities that would typically be considered R&D and those that would not.

1. **R&D activities**
   (a) Laboratory research aimed at discovery of new knowledge
   (b) Searching for applications of new research findings
   (c) Conceptual formulation and design of possible product or process alternatives
   (d) Testing in search of or evaluation of product or process alternatives
   (e) Modification of the design of a product or process
   (f) Design, construction, and testing of pre-production prototypes and models
   (g) Design of tools, jigs, moulds, and dies involving new technology
   (h) Design, construction, and operation of a pilot plant not useful for commercial production
   (i) Engineering activity required to advance the design of a product to the manufacturing stage

2. **Activities not considered R&D**
   (a) Engineering follow-through in an early phase of commercial production
   (b) Quality control during commercial production, including routine testing
   (c) Troubleshooting breakdowns during commercial production
   (d) Routine, ongoing efforts to refine, enrich, or improve the qualities of an existing product
   (e) Adaptation of an existing capability to a particular requirement or customer's need
   (f) Periodic design changes to existing products
   (g) Routine design of tools, jigs, moulds, and dies

(h) Activity, including design and construction engineering, related to the construction, relocation, rearrangement, or start-up of facilities or equipment

(i) Legal work on patent applications, sale, licensing, or litigation

- Research activities are expensed as incurred. Development activities that meet all six development stage capitalization conditions are capitalized under IFRS and may be capitalized or expensed under ASPE; any other development activities are expensed in the period incurred.

- Disclosure should be made in the financial statements (generally in the notes) of the total research and development costs charged to expense in each period for which an income statement is presented.

EXERCISE 12-4

PURPOSE: This exercise will give you practice in accounting for goodwill and impairment losses.

On January 1, 2016, Vancouver Enterprises Limited purchased the net assets of Surrey Company for $615,000 cash. At January 1, 2016, net asset information of Surrey Company was as follows:

	Book value	Fair value
Cash	$ 57,000	$ 57,000
Accounts receivable	132,000	132,000
Inventory	154,000	177,000
Land	85,000	112,000
Buildings (net)	168,000	220,000
Total	$596,000	$698,000
Accounts payable	$144,000	$144,000

No impairment losses were recorded by Vancouver in 2016.

Instructions

(a) Prepare the January 1, 2016, journal entry for Vancouver to record the purchase. Show supporting calculations in good form.

(b) Assume that Vancouver is a private entity and is testing its goodwill for impairment as at December 31, 2017, under ASPE. Management determines the following information for the reporting unit containing goodwill:

Carrying amount	$600,000
Fair value	$550,000

Calculate the impairment loss and prepare the December 31, 2017, journal entry required, if any. If no journal entry is required, state why.

(c) Assume that Vancouver is a public entity and is testing its goodwill for impairment as at December 31, 2017, under IFRS. Carrying amounts of the assets in the cash generating unit (CGU) containing goodwill are as follows:

Land	$112,000
Buildings (net)	198,000
Equipment (net)	129,000
Goodwill	61,000
	$500,000

In addition, management determines the following information for the CGU:

Value in use	$390,000
Fair value	$410,000
Disposal costs	$25,000

Calculate the impairment loss and prepare the December 31, 2017, journal entry required, if any. If no journal entry is required, state why.

Solution to Exercise 12-4

(a) Calculation of goodwill:

Purchase price		$615,000
Less: fair value of identifiable net assets		
Fair value of identifiable assets	$698,000	
Less fair value of liabilities	144,000	554,000
Goodwill		$ 61,000

Vancouver's journal entry to record the purchase is as follows:

Cash	57,000	
Accounts Receivable	132,000	
Inventory	177,000	
Land	112,000	
Buildings	220,000	
Goodwill	61,000	
Accounts Payable		144,000
Cash		615,000

In a business combination purchase transaction, the acquirer records the identifiable assets and liabilities acquired at their fair value. Therefore, goodwill is a fair value residual measure as it is the difference between the transaction purchase price (usually based on the fair value of the business acquired) and the fair value of the identifiable assets and liabilities of the business acquired.

(b) To test for impairment of goodwill under ASPE, the carrying amount of the reporting unit containing goodwill is compared with the fair value of the reporting unit containing goodwill. In this case, the carrying amount of the reporting unit containing goodwill ($600,000) is greater than the fair value of the reporting unit containing goodwill ($550,000). The difference is equal to a goodwill impairment loss at December 31, 2017:

Carrying amount of reporting unit	$600,000
Less: fair value of reporting unit	(550,000)
Goodwill impairment loss	$ 50,000

The goodwill impairment loss is recorded as follows:

Loss on Impairment—Goodwill	50,000	
Accumulated Impairment Losses—Goodwill		50,000

EXPLANATION: Because goodwill is not separable from a business and has value only as part of a unit within a business, under ASPE, testing for impairment of goodwill takes place at the reporting unit level. The reporting unit also contains other assets that are tested separately for impairment, prior to the testing of goodwill for impairment. (Any impairment losses related to the other assets in the reporting unit would be recorded prior to testing goodwill for impairment at the reporting unit level.) Therefore, any impairment loss calculated at the reporting unit level is attributable to goodwill only.

(c) To test for impairment of goodwill under IFRS, the carrying amount of the CGU containing goodwill is compared with the recoverable amount of the CGU containing goodwill.

The recoverable amount of the CGU containing goodwill is the higher of value in use ($390,000) and fair value less disposal costs ($410,000 − $25,000 = $385,000). Therefore, the recoverable amount is $390,000.

The CGU impairment loss at December 31, 2017, is calculated as follows:

Carrying amount	$500,000
Less: recoverable amount	(390,000)
CGU impairment loss	$110,000

The impairment loss is recorded as follows:

Loss on Impairment—Goodwill	61,000	
Loss on Impairment	49,000	
Accumulated Impairment Losses—Goodwill		61,000
Accumulated Impairment Losses—Land		12,501[a]
Accumulated Impairment Losses—Buildings		22,100[b]
Accumulated Impairment Losses—Equipment		14,399[c]

[a]Calculated as $49,000 \times (\$112,000 \div [\$112,000 + \$198,000 + \$129,000])$
[b]Calculated as $49,000 \times (\$198,000 \div [\$112,000 + \$198,000 + \$129,000])$
[c]Calculated as $49,000 \times (\$129,000 \div [\$112,000 + \$198,000 + \$129,000])$

EXPLANATION: Under IFRS, goodwill is considered part of a CGU, and the CGU is tested for impairment. Any resulting impairment loss ($110,000 in this case) is attributable to the entire CGU and must be allocated among the assets in the CGU. The CGU's impairment loss is allocated to goodwill first, then to the remaining assets in the CGU based on relative carrying amounts.

ILLUSTRATION 12-1

Determination of Goodwill and Purchase Price (Excess-Earnings Approach)

This illustration relates to material covered in Appendix 12A.

Step 1: **Calculate the average annual "normalized" earnings that the company is expected to earn in the future.** This is usually done by revising the unadjusted average annual net earnings of the company in the past (usually three to six years) to an amount that the company would be expected to earn annually in the future. Unadjusted average annual net earnings is adjusted for annualized differences in accounting policies between the purchaser and acquiree company, differences in depreciation and amortization due to recording of assets at fair value by the purchaser, and the effect of nonrecurring items such as gains or losses on discontinued operations.

Step 2: **Calculate the annual average earnings that the company would generate if it earned the same return as the average firm in the same industry.** This would be calculated as the fair value of the acquiree's identifiable net assets multiplied by the industry average rate of return on net assets.

Step 3: **Calculate the company's excess annual earnings.** This equals average annual "normalized" earnings from Step 1 less the amount from Step 2.

Step 4: **Estimate the value of goodwill based on the excess earnings.** This can be done using an appropriate discount rate and estimating the number of periods for which the excess earnings will be maintained. The estimate could be calculated as a perpetuity by dividing excess earnings calculated in Step 3 by an appropriate capitalization rate. Alternatively, the number of years method could be used.

EXERCISE 12-5

PURPOSE: This exercise illustrates the steps in estimating the value of goodwill using the excess-earnings approach (discussed in Appendix 12A).

Larry Bronston is contemplating the sale of his business, Classic Autos. The following data are available:

Book value of tangible and identifiable intangible assets less liabilities	$200,000
Fair value of tangible and identifiable intangible assets less liabilities	220,000
Estimated average annual normalized earnings expected in future	33,000
Normal rate of return on net assets for the industry	12%

Instructions

(a) Calculate the estimated value of goodwill if excess income is capitalized at a 12% rate.

(b) Calculate the estimated value of goodwill if excess income is capitalized at a 20% rate.

Solution to Exercise 12-5

(a) $220,000 × 12% = $26,400 annual average earnings that Classic Autos would generate if it earned the same return as the average firm in the same industry.

$33,000 − $26,400 = $6,600 excess earnings
$6,600 ÷ 12% = $55,000 goodwill

EXPLANATION: Perform the applicable steps described in **Illustration 12-1.**

Step 1: Calculate the average annual "normalized" earnings that Classic Autos is expected to earn in the future. This calculation is given in the exercise—$33,000.

Step 2: Calculate the annual average earnings that Classic Autos would generate if it earned the same return as the average firm in the same industry. Multiply the fair value of the identifiable net assets ($220,000) by the industry average rate of return on net assets (12%) = $26,400.

Step 3: Calculate Classic Autos' excess annual earnings. This is the amount from Step 1 less the amount from Step 2 ($33,000 − $26,400 = $6,600). Excess annual earnings = $6,600.

Step 4: Estimate the value of the goodwill based on the excess earnings. For a perpetuity, this is calculated as the amount from Step 3, divided by the capitalization rate. $6,600 ÷ 12% = $55,000 goodwill.

(b) $220,000 × 12% = $26,400 annual average earnings that Classic Autos would generate if it earned the same return as the average firm in the same industry.

$33,000 − $26,400 = $6,600 excess earnings
$6,600 ÷ 20% = $33,000 goodwill

- The higher the capitalization rate, the lower the resulting value for goodwill.

- Excess earnings are often referred to as "superior earnings."

- Net identifiable assets is determined by deducting total liabilities from total identifiable (tangible and intangible) assets.

- "Fair value," "market value," and "fair market value" are terms that are often used interchangeably.

- Because goodwill is the excess of purchase price over fair value of identifiable net assets, it is interesting to note that negotiating skills and certain terms of the purchase agreement will influence the value of initially recorded goodwill. However, on an ongoing basis, the carrying amount of goodwill may decrease after impairment testing, if impairment losses are recorded for goodwill.

EXERCISE 12-6

PURPOSE: This exercise will provide an example of how to use the present value method to estimate the value of goodwill (as discussed in Appendix 12A).

As president of Winnie Audio Corp., you are considering purchasing Mehta Video Corp., whose statement of financial position is summarized as follows:

Current assets	$ 400,000	Current liabilities	$ 400,000
Fixed assets (net of amortization)	800,000	Long-term liabilities	500,000
		Common shares	300,000
Other assets	200,000	Retained earnings	200,000
Total	$1,400,000	Total	$1,400,000

The fair value of current assets is $700,000. The carrying amounts of all other assets and liabilities equal their fair values. The normal rate of return on net assets for the industry is 15%. The estimated average annual normalized earnings projected for Mehta Video Corp. is $160,000.

Instructions

Assuming that the excess earnings continue for five years, determine the value of goodwill using the present value method.

Solution to Exercise 12-6

APPROACH: Apply the steps listed in **Illustration 12-1**.

Step 1: Calculate the average annual "normalized" earnings that $160,000
the company is expected to earn in the future (data given).

Step 2: Calculate the annual average earnings that the company
would generate if it earned the same return as the average
firm in the same industry.

Fair value of identifiable net assets	$800,000[a]
Multiplied by industry average rate of return	15%
	$120,000

Step 3: Calculate the company's excess annual earnings

Mehta's average annual "normalized" earnings	$160,000
Less average annual earnings based on industry rate of return	(120,000)
Excess earnings	$ 40,000

Step 4: Excess earnings

Excess earnings	$ 40,000
Present value of an annuity of $1 factor, 5 years @ 15%	3.35216
Estimated goodwill	$134,086

[a]Book value of total assets	$1,400,000
Excess of fair value over book value of current assets	300,000[b]
Fair value of total assets	1,700,000
Less total liabilities ($400,000 + $500,000)	(900,000)
Fair value of net identifiable assets of Mehta	$ 800,000
[b]Fair value of current assets	$ 700,000
Less book value of current assets	(400,000)
Excess of fair value over book value of current assets	$ 300,000

- You should also be able to calculate the purchase price that would result if both parties agree with the estimated goodwill figure calculated above. The fair value of the net identifiable assets ($800,000) plus the present value of the unidentifiable asset (goodwill of $134,086) equals a total fair value of $934,086 for Mehta Video Corp.

- You should also be able to record the purchase of Mehta Video Corp. if Winnie Audio Corp. pays $934,086 to purchase it. The identifiable assets would be recorded at their fair values ($1,700,000), goodwill would be debited for $134,086, the liabilities would be recorded at their fair values ($900,000), and cash would be credited for $934,086.

ANALYSIS OF MULTIPLE-CHOICE QUESTIONS

Question

1. Innoventions Inc. acquired a patent from Whizkid Inc. on January 1, 2017, in exchange for $10,000 cash and an investment security that had been acquired in 2013. The following facts pertain:

Original cost of investment	$15,000
Carrying amount of patent on books of Whizkid Inc.	4,800
Fair value of the investment security on January 1, 2017	24,000

The cost of the patent to be recorded by Innoventions Inc. is:
   a. $10,000.
   b. $14,800.
   c. $25,000.
   d. $34,000.

EXPLANATION: Recall the guideline for determining the cost of any intangible asset. The cost of an intangible asset includes all direct costs incurred to acquire the asset. Cost is measured by the fair value (the cash equivalent value) of the consideration given up or by the fair value of the asset received (if the fair value of the asset received is more reliably measurable). Innoventions Inc. gave $10,000 cash plus the investment security with a fair value of $24,000 at the date of the exchange. The cost of the patent is, therefore, $34,000. (Solution = d.)

Question

2. The adjusted trial balance of Laventhal Corporation as of December 31, 2017, includes the following accounts:

Trademark	$36,000
Research costs	42,000
Organization costs	11,000
Advertising costs (to promote goodwill)	18,000

What should be reported as total intangible assets on Laventhal's December 31, 2017, statement of financial position?

a. $36,000

b. $47,000

c. $65,000

d. $107,000

EXPLANATION: Identify the classification of each item listed. Only the trademark is an intangible asset. Research costs, organization costs, and advertising costs are expensed as incurred, even if they were expenditures related to intangible assets or goodwill. (Solution = a.)

Question

3. A patent with a remaining legal life of 12 years and an estimated useful life of 8 years was acquired for $288,000 by Bradley Corporation on January 2, 2013. In January 2017, Bradley paid $18,000 in legal fees in a successful defence of the patent. What should Bradley record as patent amortization for 2017?

a. $24,000

b. $36,000

c. $38,250

d. $40,500

EXPLANATION: Analyze the Patent account. Use the data given to calculate the amounts reflected therein and the resulting amortization for 2017.

Cost at beginning of 2013	$288,000
Amortization for 2013–2016	(144,000)*
Book value at beginning of 2017	144,000
Legal fees capitalized	18,000
Revised book value, beginning of 2017	162,000
Remaining years of life	÷ 4
Amortization for 2017	$ 40,500 (Solution = d.)

*Beginning of 2013, patent cost	$288,000
Divided by lesser of legal life and estimated useful life	÷ 8
Annual amortization for 2013–2016	36,000
Number of years used (2013–2016)	4
Total amortization 2013–2016	$144,000

Question

4. On January 1, 2017, Teeple Corporation acquired a patent for $45,000. Due to the quickly changing technology associated with the patent, Teeple is amortizing the cost of the patent over five years. What portion of the patent cost will Teeple amortize in years subsequent to 2017?

   a. $0
   b. $9,000
   c. $36,000
   d. $45,000

EXPLANATION: $45,000 ÷ 5 years = $9,000 amortization per year. The amount to be amortized in the future is represented by the unamortized cost of the patent at the end of 2017, calculated as follows:

Total patent cost	$45,000
Amount amortized in 2017	(9,000)
Unamortized cost	$36,000

(Solution = c.)

Question

5. The legal life of a patent is:
   a. 17 years.
   b. 20 years.
   c. 40 years.
   d. the life of the patent plus 50 years.

EXPLANATION: A patent offers its holder an exclusive right to use, manufacture, and sell a product or process over a period of 20 years without interference or infringement by others. It is not subject to renewal. (Solution = b.)

Patents should be amortized over their useful life, which in many cases will be far less than their legal life.

Question

6. If the costs of permits and licences are material to an entity, the costs of these items should be:
   a. expensed in the period acquired.
   b. capitalized and amortized over the useful life of the items.

c. charged against contributed capital.

d. capitalized but not amortized.

EXPLANATION: Licences and permits offer the holder certain rights and privileges. Like all other intangible assets, if material, the cost of these items should be capitalized and amortized over the periods benefited. Permits and licences are often valid for a limited period and should be amortized over a period not exceeding their useful life. (Solution = b.)

Permits and licences may have an indefinite life. If material, they would be capitalized and not amortized, but subject to annual impairment testing.

Question

7. In order for the costs of internally generated intangibles to be capitalized, which of the following conditions must be met?

   a. Technical feasibility of completing the intangible asset must be demonstrated.

   b. The entity must have the intention to complete the intangible asset for use or sale.

   c. The technical, financial, and other resources necessary to complete and to use or sell the intangible asset must be available to the entity.

   d. All of the above.

EXPLANATION: Refer to the six development stage conditions that must be met in order for costs of internally developed intangibles to be capitalized. Choices a, b, and c are conditions 1, 2, and 4 of that list. Intangibles that are purchased from an inventor or an owner are capitalized at cost. However, if a company develops (internally generates) an intangible itself, research and most development costs related to the product or process should be expensed. Only development costs that meet all six specific development stage criteria may be capitalized. Under IFRS, development costs that meet the six development phase conditions for capitalization are capitalized. Under ASPE, development costs that meet the six development phase conditions for capitalization may be capitalized or expensed, depending on the entity's accounting policy. Direct costs incurred in connection with securing the intangible, including lawyers' fees and other unrecovered costs of a successful legal defence, can be capitalized as a part of the cost—subject to recoverability of course! (Solution = d.)

Question

8. The costs of organizing a corporation include legal fees, fees paid for incorporation, and fees paid to underwriters. These costs are said to benefit the corporation for the entity's entire life. These costs should be:

    a. capitalized and never amortized.

    b. capitalized and amortized over 40 years.

    c. capitalized and amortized over 5 years.

    d. expensed as incurred.

EXPLANATION: Organization costs must be expensed as incurred. (Solution = d.)

Question

9. Millennium Corporation purchased the following items at the beginning of 2017:

Materials to be used in research activities; these materials have alternative future uses and they remain unused at the end of 2017.	$ 75,000
Materials to be used in research activities; these materials do not have alternative future uses and $15,000 of them remain unused at the end of 2017.	48,000
Equipment to be used in research activities; this equipment was used in one research project during 2017 and is expected to be used in other research to be undertaken over the following four-year period. It has no residual value. Millennium normally uses the straight-line method of depreciation for equipment.	120,000
Total	$243,000

Based on the above information, Millennium should report research expense for 2017 of:

    a. $48,000.   c. $147,000.

    b. $72,000.   d. $243,000.

EXPLANATION: The cost of materials acquired for use in research activities should be expensed in the period acquired unless the items have alternative future uses (in research projects or otherwise). If they have alternative future uses, they should be carried as inventory and allocated to research expense as used. The cost of equipment and facilities acquired for use in research activities should be expensed in the period acquired unless the items have alternative future uses (in research projects or otherwise). If they have alternative future uses, they should be capitalized and depreciated as used (the resulting depreciation should be classified as research expense). Thus, Millennium would have the following research expense for 2017:

Materials acquired, no alternative future use	$48,000
Depreciation on equipment used in research activities ($120,000 ÷ 5 years)	24,000
Total research expense for 2017	$72,000

                                                       (Solution = b.)

Question

10. The total amount of patent cost amortized to date is usually:

    a. shown in a separate Accumulated Amortization—Patent account, which is shown contra to the Patent account.

    b. shown in the current income statement.

    c. reflected as credits in the Patent account.

    d. reflected as a contra property, plant, and equipment item.

EXPLANATION: In accounting for intangible assets, the amortization of an asset is usually credited directly to the asset's Accumulated Amortization contra asset account. (Solution = a.)

Question

11. Gates Inc., a public entity, develops computer software to be sold to the general public. The costs incurred in creating a new piece of software should be:

    a. charged to Research and Development Expense.

    b. capitalized and amortized.

    c. charged to Research and Development Expense as incurred until all six development stage criteria for capitalization of development costs are met; costs incurred after this point are capitalized.

    d. charged to Cost of Goods Sold.

EXPLANATION: Under IFRS, costs incurred in creating computer software to be sold to external parties should be charged to Research and Development Expense as incurred until all six development stage criteria for the capitalization of development costs are met. Costs incurred subsequent to this point are capitalized and amortized. Note that under ASPE, development costs that meet the six development phase conditions for capitalization may be capitalized or expensed, depending on the entity's accounting policy. (Solution = c.)

Question

12. The owners of Tellmart Shoe Store are contemplating selling the business. The cumulative earnings for the past five years amounted to $750,000, including a gain on discontinued operation of $25,000. The annual earnings based on an average rate of return on investment for this industry would have been $115,000. If excess earnings are to be capitalized at 15%, then implied goodwill should be:

    a. $175,000.

    b. $233,334.

    c. $200,000.

    d. $725,000.

EXPLANATION: Follow the steps in **Illustration 12-1.**

Step 1: Average annual "normalized" earnings	
Cumulative earnings over the past five years	$750,000
Deduct gain on discontinued operation included above	(25,000)
Total earnings excluding discontinued operation	725,000
Divided by number of years included above	÷ 5
Average annual "normalized" earnings	$145,000
Step 2: Average annual earnings based on industry rate of return	$115,000
Step 3: Excess earnings	
Average annual "normalized" earnings	$145,000
Less average annual earnings based on industry rate of return	115,000
Excess earnings	$ 30,000
Step 4: Estimate value of goodwill	
Divide excess earnings by capitalization rate	÷ 15%
Estimated value of goodwill	$200,000

(Solution = c.)

Question

13. Which of the following would not be considered a research and development cost?

    a. Routine or periodic alterations to existing products, production lines, manufacturing processes, and other ongoing operations

    b. Depreciation of equipment being temporarily used for research and development

    c. Laboratory research aimed at the discovery of new knowledge

    d. Testing in search of, or evaluation of, product or process alternatives

EXPLANATION: Routine or periodic alterations would not be included since the expenditures are adjustments or alterations to existing operations. Basically, research and development are focused on new technology or alternatives to existing technology. (Solution = a.)

Question

14. Purchased goodwill should be:

    a. amortized over its useful life.

    b. written off immediately due to uncertainty as to future value and to treat purchased goodwill consistently with internally generated goodwill, which is expensed.

c. charged to shareholders' equity on the basis that, unlike other assets, goodwill is not separable from the business and cannot be sold separately.

d. capitalized and not amortized.

EXPLANATION: Goodwill should be capitalized as an asset and not amortized. It should be tested for impairment annually. (Solution = d.)

Question

15. Under IFRS, the impairment test for goodwill is as follows:
    a. If the carrying amount of the reporting unit containing goodwill is greater than the fair value of the reporting unit containing goodwill, then goodwill is impaired.
    b. If the carrying amount of goodwill is greater than the undiscounted future cash flows from goodwill, then goodwill is impaired.
    c. If the carrying amount of goodwill is greater than the discounted future cash flows from goodwill, then goodwill is impaired.
    d. If the carrying amount of the CGU containing goodwill is greater than the recoverable amount of the CGU containing goodwill, then goodwill is impaired.

EXPLANATION: Because goodwill is not an identifiable asset, impairment of goodwill is assessed as part of a unit within the entity (at the reporting unit level under ASPE and at the CGU level under IFRS). Choice a is the impairment test for goodwill under ASPE. (Solution = d.)

Question

16. Reversal of goodwill impairment losses:
    a. is permitted under ASPE, but not permitted under IFRS.
    b. is permitted under IFRS, but not permitted under ASPE.
    c. is permitted under both IFRS and ASPE.
    d. is not permitted under either IFRS or ASPE.

EXPLANATION: Any subsequent recovery of goodwill impairment losses is treated as internally generated goodwill. Reversal of goodwill impairment losses is not permitted under either IFRS or ASPE. (Solution = d.)